The Influence of Rhetoric in the Shaping of Great Britain

Books by Robert T. Oliver

Training for Effective Speech (1939)
The Psychology of Persuasive Speech (1942)
Four Who Spoke Out: Burke, Fox, Sheridan and Pitt (1946)
Why War Came in Korea (1950)
Verdict in Korea (1952)
Syngman Rhee: The Man Behind the Myth (1954)
Effective Speech for Democratic Living (1959)
Culture and Communication (1962)
Becoming an Informed Citizen (1964)
History of Public Speaking in America (1965)
Communication and Culture in Ancient India and China (1971)
Syngman Rhee and American Involvement in Korea, 1942–1960 (1978)

The Influence of Rhetoric in the Shaping of Great Britain

From the Roman Invasion to the Early Nineteenth Century

Robert T. Oliver

Newark: University of Delaware Press
London and Toronto: Associated University Presses

© 1986 by Robert T. Oliver

Associated University Presses
440 Forsgate Drive
Cranbury, NJ 08512

Associated University Presses
25 Sicilian Avenue
London WC1A 2QH, England

Associated University Presses
2133 Royal Windsor Drive
Unit 1
Mississauga, Ontario
Canada L5J 1K5

The paper used in this publication meets the requirements of the American National Standard for Permanence of Paper for Printed Library Materials Z39.48-1984.

Library of Congress Cataloging-in-Publication Data

Oliver, Robert Tarbell, 1909–
   The influence of rhetoric in the shaping of Great Britain.

   Bibliography: p.
   Includes index.
   1. Oratory—Great Britain—History. 2. Speeches, addresses, etc., English—History and criticism.
3. Great Britain—Civilization. I. Title.
PN4055.G704   1986   808.5'1'0941   85-40519
ISBN 0-87413-289-4 (alk. paper)

Printed in the United States of America

Contents

Preface		9
Introduction: Rhetoric and History—Functions of Persuasion		11
1	Culture Shaping—The Rhetorical Contribution	27
2	Drawing Together—The Role of Talk	47
3	A New Idea Emerges—The Balance of Interests	64
4	New Problems, New Solutions—The Professionalizing of Rhetoric	80
5	Crisis and Confrontation—Determining the Mastery	104
6	Muddling Through—Royalty Restrained	130
7	Elitism—The Rhetoric of Privilege	150
8	The People Find a Voice—The Elder William Pitt	171
9	Concern for the Little Man—Religion and Reform	187
10	The Rights of Englishmen—Debating the American War	207
11	Imperialism on Trial—The Indictment of British Rule over India	234
12	The Specter of Jacobinism—Effects on the Discussable	248
13	The Problems of Ireland—A Rhetorical Battleground	264
14	Scotland—A Rhetorical Highland	283
Epilogue		303
Selected Readings		307
Index		315

Public discussion is the best security
for public welfare, and for the safety
of every good government.
—Charles James Fox

What else is a man to do when he has an idea
. . . but ride it as hard as he can, and leave
it to others to hold it back within proper
limits?
—Charles Pierce

One of the most reliable indices of democracy
has been the variable of freedom of speech, which
is usually the first freedom to go when democracy
declines and the first to reappear when democracy
revives.
—Franklyn Haiman

Preface

Any work of history stems from two sources: the theme or point of view of its writer, and the mass of accumulated data assembled and assessed by the great numbers of prior students of the general field and of its multiplicity of special aspects. The history of Great Britain has been written and rewritten many times. Virtually every aspect of British life has been explored both minutely and extensively—except one. There has been a dearth of writing on the influence of rhetoric on the shaping of Great Britain.

Histories abound on other phases of British life: on painting and literature, on science and economics, on military and naval warfare, on social customs and linguistic differences. There have been histories of British ceramics and coffee-houses and clothing and witchcraft and country inns and church architecture—but not of its richness of public speaking.

There have been many anthologies of political orations and sermons; many essays on particular speakers, or groups of speakers, or styles of speaking; several books on selected portions of the history of public address—notably of Irish oratory, and of preaching; and some general historians have paid generous tribute to specimens of eloquence and occasionally to the effectiveness of particular speeches in turbulent periods, and to the impressive persuasiveness of such individuals as Chatham and Burke and Fox and others.

In attempting this pioneering effort to depict and evaluate the role of rhetoric as a potent influence in the shaping of British history, my indebtedness to both general and specialist prior historians is patent on every page. Citations and bibliographic references are far from adequate to express the depth and extent of this debt. Happily, the factual data in abundance are available, ready at hand, wanting only to be used. As Boswell wrote of Dr. Johnson that he was born to grapple with whole libraries, so are we all, to such extent as we will.

My library experiences extend all the way from the British Museum Library and Oxford's Bodleian and the Library of Congress, on through the libraries of the University of Wisconsin, Pennsylvania State University, New York City, and San Diego, down to such numerous smaller ones as the Kent County Public Libraries and the Clifton M. Miller Library of Washington College in my present hometown of Chestertown, Maryland. Luckily I am even married to a librarian, which is a help as well as a joy. Librarians appear to be a class of people whose unfailing aim is to be cheerfully and instantly helpful. To them I am grateful beyond adequate words.

In working out the general pattern and the interpretations of this history, I am most particularly indebted to the very gracious helpfulness of such acute and knowledgeable colleagues as Carroll C. Arnold, Iline Fife, and Harold O'Brien, of my own Pennsylvania State University; Donald C. Bryant, of Iowa State University; Lloyd F. Bitzer, of the University of Wisconsin; J. Vernon Jensen, of the University of Minnesota; Goodwin F. Berquist, of Ohio State University; John H. Timmis III, of Ohio University; Dr. Katharine Stokes, a retired librarian; Dr. Charles Halstead, of Washington College; and many more through the course of the years—teachers, colleagues, friends, and students—who have helped to develop such critical apparatus as I have. Very special appreciation is extended to Dr. Arnold and Dr. Jensen, whose sustained criticism and encouragement have been invaluable. At Associated University Presses I thank Ms. Diane Grobman, whose painstaking and acute copy editing corrected errors and saved me from various stylistic gaucheries, and Miss Katharine Turok, managing editor, for her considerate and helpful guidance.

Most intimately, I owe grateful thanks to my brother, Dr. Kenneth A. Oliver, formerly of Occidental College, for his general encouragement and specific helpful comments on the initial direction of this work; to my son Dennis M. Oliver, minister of the Ellis High Park Presbyterian Church, in Toronto, for his helpful monitoring of my interpretation of the ecclesiastical trends and speakers; and, above all, to the patience, encouragement, and ever-so-gentle criticism of the work in progress of my wife, Margaret.

No amount of help from others ever absolves the writer from his own responsibilities. I undertook to write this history because I thought somebody ought to do it. The present volume brings the account down only to the start of the nineteenth century; the remainder of the history, down to the present day, is currently nearing completion. My aim is to make clear that discourse which defines issues and circumstances and points a way toward available solutions of problems is one of the significant shaping forces of history. Since it is in discussion and debate that the pros and cons of basic issues are settled, such history points inevitably to what matters most in the shaping of a society and in the lives of its individual members. It is a history of intellectual and emotional struggle. It is my belief that this dimension of history has its own place in the library of human studies and its own claim to the attention of those who care about how our ideas, our ideals, and our institutions came to be.

Introduction
Rhetoric and History—Functions of Persuasion

History is people in motion. Choices have to be made. The fascination of history is to locate the points of decision when policies are debated and one of them is adopted. The course of human affairs takes a turn. Was it for better or for worse? Could it have been otherwise? How was the particular choice that was made brought about? In the Iliad this was one of Homer's concerns. As he told the epic story of the ten years siege of Troy, among his central characters were wise old Nestor and sly young Ulysses, both of whom were counselors rather than warriors, and the advice they gave was even more decisive than the fighting. Homer was concerned with persuasion, and as his account of the fate of Cassandra vividly shows, he knew what it might cost. He also knew what it could win, as shown in Ulysses' success in inducing Agamemnon to adopt the stratagem of the hollow horse. Many a time history is directed by right words, rightly spoken, at right times.

The need to make choices is inevitable. Various possibilities are considered. Available alternatives are examined. Rarely does a particular choice appear so luminously clear, or so inevitably right, as to shut out all doubt as to what ought to be done. The course of human affairs is dynamic. Actions are to be performed. What to do is a matter for judgment, often poised between opportunity and disaster. Present action is demanded even when its results are uncertain. Voices are raised to suggest one action or another. Who speaks, and how, and with what effects are matters of fundamental historical concern. As Macaulay understood, government is 75 percent talk. What persuasive strategies really mean in history is a cardinal concern. They are vastly more than what many critics call "mere talk" or "empty rhetoric."

It is deeply significant that, as Laird wrote in *The Miracle of Language*, "man is the languagized mammal." Humans alone, among all creatures, have the ability to *symbolize meaning*. What we alone can do is to pick out of the booming, buzzing environment around us items to which we ascribe our own interpretation, upon which we act, and by means of which we seek to stimulate, or limit, or guide the conduct of our associates. In this sense, we live in a *pseudoenvironment,* a selective linguistic universe, for better and for worse. What we select and what we transmit to others makes our own great world of difference. This is the special kind of behavior that is peculiarly human. What, then, should we respond to individuals who insist that physical action is preferable to mere talk? Should we not retort as did Sun Yat-sen, the Chinese revolutionist, to his impatient followers: "Action is easy; it is understanding that is difficult"?

Differing circumstances, naturally, call for differing kinds of response. If a child is drowning, it does not suffice to stand on the riverbank shouting words of encouragement (though even that sometimes helps). When people are perplexed, it does not help to command them to do something, without telling them what. There are critical times when words well spoken are the kind of action that matters most. Winston Churchill speaking into a microphone made a vastly greater contribution than he would have if he had taken rifle in hand to stand at the Channel.

Many leaders in English history have been canny in their use of words. Others have been foolish. To point the way is a function of leadership. So is the inspiration of followers, the conversion of doubters, and the refutation of the arguments of opponents. Nor is this all. Speech serves the daily needs of people in their common pursuits as well. And bad counsel, especially when persuasively presented, also has its own often monumental effects.

Freedom of speech is available to only a small portion of the world's population. It is a fair question to inquire what use has been made of it where it exists. Is it worth struggling for? What difference does it make? Answers vary because of the difficulty of estimating the special and particular effects of talk. But this is true also of much else—such as the effects of George III's stubbornness, or of the Corn Laws, or of the invention of the spindle, or of Victoria's fondness for Albert. The tracing of cause to effect in history is as perplexing as it is in a good detective story. What is certain, at least, is that persuasive discourse has played a part, and often a decisive part, in the shaping of human affairs.

Spoken communication has been aptly termed, by Lyman Bryson, "the web of signals and expectations and understandings that make living together possible." For colonies of bees or ants or termites, cooperative society is governed not by ever-shifting understandings but by immutable instinct. Insects survive, but their societies scarcely change. Among human beings, shared meanings are clarified and particular solutions become operative as a consequence of verbal intercourse. This is not less true when proceedings are apparently shaped by force or by impersonal circumstance. Barbarism, both primitive and current, depends upon coercion. Civilization evolves as the accommodation of differences through discussion. This is true in the current management of personal and corporate affairs, and it has been true throughout the processes of history.

It is through dialogue that common understandings are forged. Alternative solutions to sensed problems are examined, and one or another of them is projected into action. New fashions and innovative ideas are proposed, and some of them become guidelines. The ascendance of one view over others is not accidental. An idea or a new system might be implanted by sheer force, but to have lasting effects it must be given projective power. The nature of a society, of a culture, or of a state is determined in part by geography, or by economic interests, or by military power—but its quality and its influence must be sustained by persuasion. Whatever decisions are necessitated in the relations of people must be either fought out or talked out—and even decisions enforced by sheer power also have to be interpreted. The *Magna Carta* derives its great influence in history not from having been imposed upon King John by powerful barons but from having been subsequently discussed and having its implications noted.

The knitting together of individuals and of communities into a nation does not simply occur. It has to be brought about. In part the English nation and the subsequent British Empire were shaped and reshaped through persuasive speaking. As an American student of rhetoric, Herbert A. Wichelns, has insisted, "The effective wielder of public discourse, like the military man, belongs in social history because he is one of its makers."

What is of utmost significance is that we human beings are symbol makers. As such, we live in significant ways in our own fabricated environment. What is *real* is what is formulated in our conceptions. As Walter Lippmann, in his *Public Opinion*, reminded us, "For the most part we do not first see and then define, we define first and then we see." Our definition consists of assessing reality symbolically. As the Hegelian philosopher Hans Vaihinger put it in his *Philosophy of "As If,"* we live *as if* what we feel and believe is in fact true. Our complex patterns of "as if" convictions have all been formulated and entrenched in our processes of symbolic interchanges. We *know* that "out there" exists because we are told that it does, and we at least partly believe it.

What our minds do with facts may fruitfully be compared to and contrasted with what our bodies do with food. We ingest potatoes, swallow them, digest them, sort out the parts that suit our special needs, and utilize them; then we excrete the rest. Similarly, but also differently, our minds "ingest" perceptions, conceive what they mean to us and to our associates, utilize portions of the symbolized items, and consign the remainder to the waste heap of forgetfulness. But even what we try to forget has its own residue of influence. What we retain as conscious guides to our conduct depends to a considerable degree upon social agreements.

As Alfred Korzybski explained in his monumental *Science and Sanity*, it is this kind of "understanding" that makes "time binding" possible. No other creature even begins to approach our ability and our necessity for dealing with circumstances at second hand. It is this secondhand relationship with surrounding factors that makes humanity a special form of creation. It is our most distinguishing feature. A mother hen can cluck to her brood to warn them of a hovering hawk or to summon them to a nutritious find of worms. But she cannot assemble them around her on the warm side of the barn to discuss the predatory evils of life or the provident goodness of nature. Only a person can make a Tuesday evening appointment to deal with community problems. Only a person can consider the social consequences of marriage and divorce or of overindulgence in drink.

Rhetoric is a mode of thought. In Aristotle's phrase, it is "the discovery of the means of persuasion." It is a way of looking at problems. As such it complements and completes the scientific and logical modes of thought. Science aims to depict the nature of reality. Logic undertakes to identify intrinsic relationships among facts. Rhetoric estimates what the facts mean in terms of the relationships of individuals or groups that must deal with them. The rhetorician deals with facts triangularly: considering the accepted nature of facts, the ways in which such facts may be interpreted to serve his own purposes, and the susceptibility of his audience to his chosen way of interpreting them. The speaker must consider what he *can* do with the subject matter, what he *wishes* to do with it, and how he may *induce listeners* to agree with his intent. These three factors shape the thinker's reactions in terms of how he interprets *rhetorical situations*.[1]

And what is a rhetorical situation? Is it when a speaker rises to address an audience that has assembled to hear him? It is this, but it is very much more. A rhetorical situation is any circumstance in which the most appropriate or at least the most effective action that may be taken is the joint enterprise of talking and listening. It may be a conversation around the family dinner table or a secret meeting of politicians who feel the need to make a deal. The essential factor is that *a choice has to be made*, a choice that is not imposed by force but that is induced through discourse. Being in a rhetorical situation is like coming to a crossroads: a choice must be made between going in one direction or another. In some circumstances there is no hesitation or doubt. One member of the party may be strong enough that he has only to state his will and the others must accept it. Or the lights of the distant town may be so plainly discerned that there is no reason for uncertainty. If one road leads downhill and the other up, and if the members of the party are too weak to climb uphill, all they are able to do is take the easier path. The situation becomes rhetorical when alternative choices are feasible and when their respective merits are brought into consideration. The force that proves to be impelling is contrived motivation. A skilled speaker points the way and induces his hearers to follow it. The historical significance of such a process is considerable. Ralph Waldo Emerson chose to devote his life to rhetoric for he believed that "the power of putting things" is decisive. This is a truth that history again and again illuminates.

Successful military commanders realize that mere force is far from enough. General Sir Archibald Wavell, the brilliant victor over Field Marshal Rommel in the North African campaign during World War II, wrote *Generals and Generalship* to clarify this fact. "To learn that Napoleon won the campaign of 1796 by maneuver on interior lines or some such phrase is of little value," he wrote. "If you can discover how a young unknown man inspired a ragged, mutinous, half-starved army and made it fight, how he gave it the energy and momentum to march and fight as it did, how he dominated and controlled generals older and more experienced than himself, then you have learned something."

Multiple factors combine in the making of history. England became first a nation and then a world-girdling empire, which in turn became a group of dominions, through far too complex an accumulation of factors to permit any simplistic determination. The whole panorama must be viewed from one perspective or another. No single history could possibly encompass all that was involved. My present undertaking is to deal with the nature and influence of rhetorical discourse, primarily but not exclusively oral, as a significant source as well as an exemplification of English culture. Talking and listening inevitably have decisive effects. Our aim is to explore what they contributed to the shaping of English society and to the making of the English nation and the British Empire.

From time to time problems become acute that may better be dealt with through talk than by any other form of action. What course should be followed? Feelings of uncertainty and insecurity emerge. What is the difficulty that must be understood and what should be done to alleviate it? A crisis erupts that dramatizes the need for a unified response. How can such a feeling of oneness be generated? On occasion sacrifices are demanded for which acceptable reasons must be presented. There is a need for leadership to clarify problems, to propose solutions, and to stimulate the people for such efforts as may be required. These are all occasions on which speech plays its destined role.

There are still other circumstances in which speech has a national purpose to serve. Events take place that are worthy of being celebrated. Anniversaries offer opportunities to enhance loyalties or to extend or curb or enrich shared expectations, or to convert fears into hopes. Individual and clannish diversities must somehow be knit together into a feeling of commonality. The spirit of nationhood is nurtured both by hopes and by memories. Words well spoken may be either bonds that unite or barbs that stimulate fresh aspirations. Public speaking is a culture-shaping force that helps to accomplish such national goals.

Rhetorical discourse may be either spoken or written. The two processes are distinct. They require different kinds of personalities and they serve different ends. Francis Bacon trenchantly noted a primary distinction when he wrote that the writer must be an "exact" man, the speaker a "ready" man. The writer sits at leisure in his study, with reference works available, to compose guidance for an indefinitely enlarged and generally remote audience of readers. A speaker confronts an immediate circumstance that requires him to draw upon his own resources in confronting doubts and objections as best he can. The differences between the two modes of discourse are manifold, but a major distinction is between the immediacy of speech and the variable time span that separates the writer from his readers. Newspapers and pamphlets lie midway between the two, with characteristics of each. Speeches, even when written, are not intended to be writings. Charles James Fox, noting the distinction, asked, "Did the speech read well?" and then gave his own reply, "Then it was not a good speech."

One of the more oracular interpreters of English history, F. S. Oliver, has stated directly what the generality of historians affirm indirectly through their selection of data that they presume to be important: namely, that public speaking is of small consequence in the shaping of history.[2] "The institution of popular government," he wrote, "seems to be ever haunted by the superstition that a master of the arts of oratory will also prove wise in counsel and vigorous in action." Wise the great speakers have not always been. Yet for many of them, the vigor of their leadership has truly been exerted primarily through their effectiveness in persuasive speech. But in order to support his renunciation of eloquence, Oliver had first of all to misrepresent it.

> Insensibly the anxiety of an eloquent speaker that his hearers should admire his speech will tend to master his first intention, that they should follow his opinion. Half unconsciously, he will adapt or whittle away his opinion in order to win their applause; and he will often choose opinions that fit his style of rhetoric, as a woman chooses clothes becoming to her shape and complexion. He is peculiarly liable to take infection from the mood of his audience, and becomes the proselyte of those he would convert. . . . By the very nature of his trade he is forced to work through the medium of passion and prejudice. Even truth itself, as he states it, becomes untrue; for he must ever be distorting its features and disguising its proportions. Firm resolution, sound judgment, and those other qualities on which statesmanship depends, are merely so many impediments to his artistry.

The basic error of this charge is best refuted in the survey of what speech has meant in the course of British (and human) history. An apt response to it may be cited in the reply made by Isocrates to the similar charge against the Sophists of ancient Athens by Plato.

> Because there has been implanted in us the power to persuade each other and to make clear to each other whatever we desire, not only have we escaped the life of wild beasts, but we have come together and founded

cities and made laws and invented arts; and generally speaking, there is no institution devised by man which the power of speech has not helped us to establish. For this it is which has laid down laws concerning things just and unjust, the things honourable and base, and if it were not for these ordinances we should not be able to live with one another. It is by this also that we confute the bad and extol the good. Through this we educate the ignorant and appraise the wise; for the power to speak well is taken as the surest index of a sound understanding, and discourse which is true and lawful and just is the outward image of a good and faithful soul. With this faculty we both contend against others on matters which are open to dispute and seek light for ourselves on things which are unknown.[3]

A principal weakness in Oliver's renunciation of persuasive speaking is his depiction of it as sheer emotionalism. What he failed to note is that emotions themselves are factors of tremendous social power.[4] Loyalty, affection, hatred, and dread are clearly among history's motivating forces. His dislike of demagoguery must also be put in perspective. The fact that speaking may be used for destructive as well as for constructive effects surely does not render it insignificant. Quite to the contrary. The causes of social disquiet merit fully as much consideration as the impulsions to reform and advancement. Historically, persuasion plays both roles, and both need to be examined.

Equally erroneous is Oliver's contention that eloquence is a weak instrument for the reason that speakers are liable to "whittle away" their own opinions in order to stand as spokesmen for their chosen auditors rather than as leaders of them. Adaptation to the current of prevailing opinion is one of the necessary qualities of leadership. Unless a *speaker* is also a *spokesman*, he may well lose his following. Rhetorical strategy dictates that the promoter of a new vision must establish a viable connection between what he wants and what his listeners want. He must make them feel that he is not only speaking *to* them but also *for* them. Only as this is accomplished can he hope to bring them from their non-sense to his sense. The starting point has to be the juncture of the speaker and the listeners on common ground. After that, what matters is whether he is able to shift them from their erroneous conceptions to the course that he considers to be right. Mastery over the listeners is the ultimate goal, but generally it is most effectually accomplished by comradeship with them. What leadership demands is the ability of transcending the audience while also representing it.

On another plane, the influence of public speaking receives less than its due from the tendency of many recent historians to reject out of hand the importance of the individual. Few now accept Carlyle's insistence that "the history of what man has accomplished in this world, is at bottom the history of the great men who have worked here." *Heroes and Hero Worship* is out of date. Similarly rejected is Emerson's belief that "history is the essence of innumerable biographies," with his consequent conclusion that "an institution is but the lengthened shadow of one man." These views have been rejected because they are manifestly untrue. Equally untrue is the opposing historiography of Arnold Toynbee, to cite one instance, who sought to show in his *Study of History* that mere "human techniques" neither divert nor direct the patterns of development and of decay that are imposed on nations by the very nature of man, of social organization, and of the physical environment. Both the individualistic and the deterministic interpretations of social change are flawed if pursued to their extremes. If Carlyle and Emerson overstated their selected emphasis, so have Karl Marx and Sigmund Freud. Individuals and groups may not have free will, but they tend to think and to act as if they did enjoy the opportunity of choice.

Let it be granted that historical circumstances are complex. What forms public opinion, and how much a leader either guides or is guided by it, and what set of cumulative influences determine the adoption or rejection of specific policies are all such complex questions that they defy simplistic answers. But this does not mean that persuasion has no influence in human affairs. Its influence must be acknowledged even though the specific effects of a particular speech, or of extended debate, are difficult to interpret. So are the effects of the Black Death and of the Battle of Waterloo, yet we readily grant their places among historic forces.

A contemporary student of rhetoric, Harold Zyskind, comes to the point that matters. In his view, rhetoric "is a way of making something in the immediate circumstances, i.e., that it is the start of a process of taking advantage of the chances that offer themselves."[5] As Zyskind explains, each speaker chooses—whether wisely or foolishly—what interpretation he will offer concerning the problem he discusses. He will recommend some possibilities and disregard or reject others. If he has breadth of mind, he creates for his society or his group a frame of reference that thereafter influences its vision of the past, the present, and the future. Of course not all persuasive speakers are also philosophers. Many, even most, of them concentrate upon immediate questions and upon pragmatic strategies. In either instance, they attempt to "take advantage of the chances that offer themselves." By helping to shape the reactions of their listeners they point a way, for better or for worse, with short-range or long-range results. Bolingbroke, for example, directed attention to the nature of the British constitution—even though the influence he exerted was for the most part long delayed. Chatham, for another instance, did much to direct the English people and government to a world view. Neither of them had the special capacity or the opportunity for any prolonged direction of the government. Nevertheless, through their power of persuasion they exercised an influence that has long persisted.

The advent of language came too early in human evolution for us to know how it happened. Before speech could become an effective social influence, a fairly high degree of social organization had to be attained. In this process, speaking and responding had to play vital roles. How groups conducted themselves before individuals began to stand to command attention, to raise questions, to challenge planned actions, and to suggest alternatives, we cannot know. What we do know is that when persuasive speaking and discussions became accepted problem-solving devices, new mind-sets developed that were derived from the kinds of relationships that obtained between speakers and their listeners. Those who spoke had an intention of motivating hearers; those who listened were to some extent conceding the right of the speaker to direct their conceptions. Speaking, even if it be but to ask a question, is an act of instigation that is designed to have an effect upon its auditors. The speaker and his audience have different functions, but these are complementary rather than dissevered. Whether the listener agrees or disagrees with what he hears, he is at least responding. An ideational bond exists.[6] It is precisely this engagement that will be explored as this inquiry into English history proceeds.

The concern of this book is to consider the influence of persuasive speech in the evolving history of England. The overriding questions are these: What was discussable in succesive periods? What could not be discussed? What had to be discussed? Who did the discussing? To what audiences? By what means? And so far as reasonable inference permits, with what results? What I shall attempt to discern are the correlations between discourse and action. To assert that particular instances of rhetoric cause specific actions would be to plunge far beyond the knowable. But to ignore them as a major factor in political life, while emphasizing instead the force of gunfire, results in misdirected interpretation.

Great historical changes that are commonly assessed in terms of military power are often predetermined by shapers of public opinion. There is a trenchant reminder for all historians in a letter written by John Adams, on 13 February 1818, to his friend Hezekiah Niles: "But what do we mean by the American Revolution? Do we mean the American War? The Revolution was effected before the war commenced. The Revolution was in the hearts and minds of the people. . . . *This radical change in the principles, opinions, sentiments, and affections of the people was the real American Revolution.*"[7] And there is truth in the observation of William Norwood Brigance that "whether men shall pursue an immediate want or a remote one, whether they shall accept the satisfaction of a high idealistic desire or of a low material one, has always been, and so long as this planet supports human life, will continue to be, dependent in part on how vividly and impellingly these alternatives are revealed to them by leaders, thinkers, writers, and speakers."[8]

In British history, as elsewhere, a new light, a new impulsion, a new direction in affairs has again and again emerged from leadership exercised through speech. Some of this speaking has been logical analysis, as in Edmund Burke's "On Conciliation with the Colonies." Some has been largely emotional—as in Lord Brougham's denunciation of slavery, Sheridan's portrayal of cruelty in the governing of India, Chatham's exclamation that "if I were an American, as I am an Englishman, I would resist, by God!" and in Churchill's "Solemn hour" appeal. To discount emotion is to renounce the Sermon on the Mount. Emotion, like logic (and often more than logic), is a fact of life. Lord Palmerston noted this when he told the Parliament:

> As long as England shall ride pre-eminent on the ocean of human affairs, there can be none whose fortune shall be so ship-wrecked, there shall be none whose condition shall be so desperate or forlorn, that they may not cast a look of hope toward the light that beams from hence; and though they may be beyond the reach of our power, our moral support and our sympathy shall cheer them in their adversity.

What Palmerston called for with clear insight was leadership through rhetoric—the assertion and reassertion of the ideals of democracy and freedom for which England stands. The influence of which he spoke was not by any means limited to distant lands and peoples. In times of both adversity and prosperity there have been "lights that beam" as guiding principles on the domestic scene and as stimulation to brighten the spirits of the British themselves. Often in the course of English history, that guiding light has been diffused or clouded. Sometimes it has been misdirected. But on many occasions it has spotlighted the way toward progress. It is the history of that diverse set of influences that I shall try to chart.

The general guidelines for this search are such rhetorical questions as:

- What kinds of individuals have been preponderant as spokesmen for ideas?
- What rhetorical means have they employed in pursuit of their goals?
- What barriers to communication have they encountered, and by what strategies did they undertake to accomplish their aims?
- On what kinds of occasions has public speaking been especially utilized?
- What were the listeners like, and how did they respond?
- What discernible or probable effects flowed from the speaking?
- What attitudes toward public speaking have prevailed?
- What rhetorical principles have been advocated and practiced?
- Who have been the effective speakers? What were their roles? What were their leading characteristics?
- What is the nature of effective persuasive speech in public affairs?

These are the central questions. There are other matters that might be dealt with but that in this work are set aside. No history can ever be wholly comprehensive. Choices have to be made. For one thing, this book does not attempt to establish the verbal validity of the published texts of speeches. One reason is that such an endeavor would be literally impossible; the great bulk of the speaking was never reported in precise detail. Much of it has been only sketchily summarized, with its nature and its effectiveness indicated by reactions of listeners. Fortunately for our purpose, whether a speaker actually said precisely those words, in precisely that order, which a printed text represents is far from being essential to the consideration of his persuasive intent and his strategic plans. What matters greatly is why he chose to speak, what purpose he had in mind, and the pattern of motivation he believed would be effective in terms of the general context and the particular expectations of his hearers. Even when the verbal text is accurate, it is only one factor within the pattern of his relations with the problem and with his chosen audience. His character, his reputation, and the position from which he spoke are basic considerations. Was he in office or out? Did he have a cohesive following or was he seeking to forge one? Was there an opportunity to win votes; if not, what other considerations did he have in mind? Such nonverbal factors as the inflections and quality of his voice and the impression made by his physical bearing are also important. Most significant of all is the nature of the bond that united him with his listeners, or of the barrier that separated him from them and that he had to surmount in order to make his influence felt. His motivational appeals, the general features of his style, and his means of adaptation to the circumstances are fundamental; they transcend the question of precise verbal reporting. We do not know what Moses said or how (except for his stutter), but we do know why he spoke and what resulted from his speaking. And so it has been with much of the influential English speaking, especially in the earlier centuries. Even when printed texts of the speeches are available, they often were revised for publication. Many were reported in the second person: "He said that" et cetera. Very few of the effective speeches (before the modern era of radio and television) were read from manuscript. Often they were extemporized in the midst of an ongoing discussion or debate. Whether the available reports of the speeches were accurate or merely approximate is seldom a vital question. The general tenor of the persuasive motivation, of the circumstances surrounding it, and of the responses from its listeners are what I shall seek.

An immensely difficult problem is how to deal with the speaking in the midst of the whole complex of historical developments. How much and what kinds of data need to be presented? Our effort will be, not to deal with the whole of English history, but to identify "rhetorical occasions" in which speech has made a significant contribution. The difficulty in this aim lies in the immediacy of public address. A speaker confronts a particular set of circumstances that determine what he can do and how he can do it. The feelings and the convictions of his listeners both limit and invite what he can say and how he ought to say it. No speech has meaning except in its context, and the context is almost endlessly complex. My guiding principle is to report such aspects of the historical circumstances as appear to be rhetorically vital. It is not a simple principle to apply, for ongoing developments and underlying circumstances all combine to determine the nature of the persuasive problems.

The contribution this work aims to make is not the discovery of new facts but the interpretation of the influence of speaking at critical points. The broad pattern of English history has been exhaustively examined both by specialist scholars and by general historians. On many specific points, historians have sharply disagreed in their interpretations. Some, like Macaulay and Trevelyan, have been frankly partisan. Such "objective" contemporaries as G. R. Elton and A. P. J. Taylor also interpret trends in terms of their own guiding convictions. Historical writing may not be "bunk," as Henry Ford inferred, but it is confusing, as one of Agatha Christie's schoolgirls complains, in that it is "quite different in different books." This need not be troublesome for readers so long as they know what it is that the historian they are reading is seeking to do. In my own extensive and necessary dependence upon the research and interpretations of others, the aim is to remain as steadfastly as possible within the mainstream of agreed-upon facts. On important disputed matters, the reasons for the divergence of views need to be examined and a choice among them needs to be made. What is attempted here is to focus upon the significance of spoken discourse, the modes of its presentation, and the roles of the speakers within the historical context.

The question of what sources to depend upon is paramount. Such primary sources as speech texts, autobiographies, letters, diaries, and histories and biographies written by contemporaries who heard the speeches are essential. But in considering the influence of persuasive discourse, even biased and secondary reports are also to some extent primary, as indicators of interpretations that have persisted.

The notes identifying sources are inserted sparingly. When factual matters are not in dispute, the citation of sources for them would be superfluous. To detail the precise source of every quotation cited or of every factual item would be as tedious as it is unnecessary. When the dependability of witnesses and of critics may need to be evaluated by readers, the references are provided. In still other instances, citations are supplied as guides to a more extensive exploration of significant issues or problems that extend beyond the scope of my immediate inquiry. Like a good map, notes indicate where we are going and how to get there. Beyond this, a plethora of source citations is merely capricious.

It is not the principal purpose of this book to record the "great orators" who have appeared on the English scene. The speeches discussed are not assessed for their literary qualities but for their social and political effects. The preaching of so major a figure as John Donne, for example, had influence far less pervasive than the stylistic revolution induced by his poetry. Among his contemporaries, so minor a preacher and parliamentarian as John Preston stirred listeners more deeply and with sharper effects. A different history of public speaking in Great Britain might seek to validate the texts of speeches; it might present a canon of major speakers; or it might provide systematic rhetorical analyses of selected speeches. The aim in this work is to consider which speakers and speeches, at critical junctures, have made a difference, and what kind of difference, in the nation's development.

In pursuit of this aim, English history is interpreted in humanistic and personalized terms. Articulate leaders—whether in politics, in religion, in the law, or in general public affairs—are often a special breed of individuals who devote themselves to reaching out to cement their relationships with their chosen publics. Their personalities tend to be extraverted and self-consciously assertive. They believe in causes and they accept responsibility, often at great cost to themselves, for promoting them. What they believe intellectually, they also feel emotionally. The interest in their speaking derives partly from their superior verbal skill and partly from their sensitive relation with the needs and aspirations of their listeners. Their importance lies in the positions they assume concerning crucial decisions that have to be made. They are assessed as shapers of attitudes and supporters of policies. Their speeches illuminate the kinds of choices that have been made and the reasons for making them. Their speaking indicates why some courses have proved more appealing, or perhaps merely more expedient, than others. And had they not spoken as they did, different alternatives might have prevailed, with some trends hastened, others delayed, or different courses pursued. In short, they are "makers of history" and as such need to be assessed.[9]

On a concluding personal note, I have undertaken this narrative from my own perspective and with my own interests: I look to the British Isles as a major source from which my own nation has drawn many of its characteristics. I confess to being at least a temperate Anglophile. Much of my professional life has been spent in consideration of how persuasive discourse exerts civic and moral influence. The first book I ever planned to write, almost half a century ago, was a history of public speaking in Great Britain. The project has remained teasingly with me as a debt waiting to be paid.

Samuel Johnson, in one of his melancholy moods, and thinking of his own writings, observed that "a man who merely makes a book from books may be useful but he can never be great." Usefulness is a sufficiently high goal toward which to aim. Whether in this work it is attained, its readers must decide.

Notes

1. See Lloyd F. Bitzer, "The Rhetorical Situation," *Philosophy and Rhetoric* 1 (January 1968): 1–14; and Carroll C. Arnold, *Criticism of Oral Rhetoric* (University Park: Pennsylvania State University Press, 1974), esp. chap. 2, "Rhetorical Situations and Unspoken Contracts," pp. 27–46.
2. F. S. Oliver, *The Endless Adventure: Personalities and Practical Politics in Eighteenth Century England* (Boston: Houghton Mifflin, 1931), pp. 348–49.
3. *Antidosis*, in *Isocrates*, edited by George Norlin, 3 vols. (Loeb Classical Library, 1928–45), 2:254–56.
4. The view that "the display of passion is an essential and widely used tool of rhetoric" is developed by F. G. Bailey in his book, *The Tactical Uses of Passion: An Essay on Power, Reason, and Reality* (Ithaca: Cornell University Press, 1983).
5. Harold Zyskind, "Some Philosophical Strands in Popular Rhetoric," in *Perspectives in Education, Religion, and the Arts*, edited by H. E. Kiefer and M. K. Munitz (Albany: SUNY Press, 1970), p. 380.
6. Carroll C. Arnold explores these relationships in "Oral Rhetoric, Rhetoric, and Literature," *Philosophy and Rhetoric* 1 (Fall 1968): 191–210.
7. John Adams, *Life and Works*, 10 vols. (Boston: Little, Brown, 1865) 10:282. The historical antecedents justifying Adams's view are explored by Stephen Lucas, *Portents of Rebellion* (Philadelphia: Temple University Press, 1976).
8. William Norwood Brigance, "Can We Redefine the James Winans Theory of Persuasion?" *Quarterly Journal of Speech* 21 (February 1935): 24.
9. An early argument for this approach is my own "A Rhetorician's Criticism of Historiography," in *Proceedings of the Eastern Public Speaking Conference* (New York: H. W. Wilson, 1940), pp. 161–72.

The Influence of Rhetoric
in the Shaping of Great Britain

1
Culture Shaping—The Rhetorical Contribution

Among many primitive tribesmen, the leader had to be a speaker. Leadership was not hereditary; it had to be won. Naturally, when a fight or a hunt was in prospect, the men who joined up wanted a chief whom they knew to be brave and resourceful. He had also to be liked and trusted. The men who followed him did so because they wanted to, not because they had to. This was why persuasion was needed. When a foray was planned, the organizer had to explain it and justify it and convince the tribesmen that under his leadership it could be a success. Internal tribal relationships were loose and flexible. Even day-by-day affairs were less governed by force or by rules than shaped by persuasion. On this point anthropologists are agreed. Typical of their conclusions are the words of a specialist in pre-Columbian Indians: "The 'talkers' of the various villages harangued the people from time to time, exhorting them to behave properly, enjoy themselves, get out and rustle food, and prepare it for a feast."[1] It was in this manner that their tribal activities were conducted.

The tribes of England, when they first came under the purview of the Romans, were viewed in a similar way by Tacitus. In his *Germania* he reported that among the Gauls and the Britons public speaking was held in high esteem, and that it helped the tribes to function as effective societies. It is true that his knowledge of their daily lives was scanty. It is also true that he was a prejudiced reporter, for in his day in Rome eloquence was held in high regard and was carefully cultivated. His conviction, as stated in his *Dialogues,* was that "the breastplate and the sword are not, I am well assured, a stronger defense on the battlefield than eloquence is to a man amid the perils of prosecution." He was naturally inclined to look for persuasive skills as the dynamic guiding force in society. And among the Celtic and Anglo-Saxon peoples of England, he found it.

About minor matters the chiefs deliberate; about the more important, the whole tribe. Yet even when the final decision rests with the people, the affair is thoroughly discussed by the chiefs. They assemble, except in the case of sudden emergency, on certain fixed days at a new or full moon.

... Then the king or the chief, according to age, birth, distinction in war, or eloquence is heard *more because he has influence to persuade than because he has power to command.* [Italics added]

"To Lord It over All the World"

To appreciate what persuasive speaking meant to the tribesmen who first settled in the British Isles, it is helpful to recall what they were like. The puzzling question is, What made it possible for them to draw together into a nation?

The early inhabitants of the islands were a strange mix. They differed from one another in race, in language, and in customs. What they chiefly shared was the misery that resulted from their virtually continuous conflicts. In addition to repeated foreign invasions, there was also enmity and warfare across the multiple internal boundaries. Centuries later, Daniel Defoe could find no answer to his derisive question, "Who is the trueborn Englishman?" Samuel Johnson also stressed the long-continuing differences among them, often deriding the Scots and blithely dismissing the Irish with the quip, "They never speak well of one another." Linguists and sociologists find the present population still divided into groups that cling stubbornly to their own separate identities. Yet somehow they united sufficiently to form a nation of such vitality that it spread to become a worldwide empire.

Deep differences still persist. Cockneys and Yorkshiremen, fishermen and farmers, Oxonians and day laborers alike insist that theirs is the type that is "forever England." Even so, as the centuries progressed a feeling of community grew. An inclusive pattern of shared cultural values took form. Despite the odds, they drew together. Common goals were established that invited shared endeavors. The diverse peoples became one people. It did not happen automatically or completely. Persistent distinctions still are sometimes emphasized. Yet a tenuous nationality developed, with loyalty to the whole proving stronger than divisiveness.

The attainment of this result was a difficult, cumbersome, stumbling process; it did not occur accidentally. In it articulate leadership played a significant role. The parts were knit together by interflowing currents of communication.[2] A sense of community, reinforced by feelings of communion, came to be basic values.[3] In large measure, this is because they talked and they listened to one another, thereby establishing communicative bonds. In the creation of such bonds, the persuasive speech demanded of chiefs was less vital than the development of the habit of settling matters by talking about them. As Carroll C. Arnold has made clear, in the establishment of social bonds, "the *collective* character of the speaking may be more important than any individual's speaking."[4] What matters is that through talking and listening, shared ideas became fundamentaly significant. "What I think" was transmuted into "What we think."

How a nation was formed from the mishmash of ethnic groups, languages, and manners remains an intriguing question. Perhaps there was an initial unity that can dimly be perceived from the few signs left from the prehistoric period. Sometime around 1800 B.C there came to England the Beaker Folk—so called because they left behind them many large vessels that suggest they were heavy drinkers. That they were a people of amazing vigor is amply manifest from the impressive monuments at Stonehenge and Avebury. Some centuries afterward they were joined by the Celts, whose language and sturdily independent character left lasting impressions. Among them were the freebooting Picts, who settled mainly in Scotland.

As another thousand years rolled by there came a new inundation from north Germany, attracted (or so the *Anglo-Saxon Chronicle* asserts) "by the cowardice of the Britons and the excellence of the land." As the account continues, "These men came from three tribes of Germany: from the Old Saxons, from the Angles, and from the Jutes." They came separately and they lived separately, having little intercourse except through quarrelling and fighting. "From the Jutes came the people of Kent and the Isle of Wight. . . . From the Old Saxons came the East Saxons, the South Saxons, and the West Saxons. From Angeln, a waste land situated between the Jutes and Saxons, came the East Angles, the Middle Angles, the Mercians, and all the Northumbrians."[5] Despite racial and linguistic similarities, it is the hodgepodge of their differences that the *Chronicle* emphasizes. They came as rival tribes, fighting for land and power. How, then, did they become a nation?

Their conquest by Rome surely was a major reason. For some three centuries prior to the Christian Era they had been known to the Romans, who imported gold from Ireland and tin from Cornwall.[6] Finally it was a Roman invasion, recorded by Julius Caesar and by Tacitus, that brought the islands into written history. This invasion was itself primarily a communicative enterprise—a public relations ploy. Caesar needed heroic news to send home to counter the charge by his rivals, Cassius and Pompey, that his campaign in Gaul had bogged down. After only hasty planning, and with too few reserves, Caesar landed on the Channel coast in August, 55 B.C.This foray was far from being a conquest. But the following summer, much better prepared, Caesar came again, and this time he pushed far inland. This second exploit got for him what he sought—an impressive twenty-day Triumph in Rome.

The Roman populace was impressed, but Caesar's more knowledgeable compatriots were not. Strabo had asserted a hundred years earlier that "there are no advantages in knowing such countries and their inhabitants." Cicero, whose brother was with Caesar, complained to the Senate that the expedition brought back no loot except slaves, whom he termed an unpromising lot.[7] Caesar did not tarry long in England but returned to his principal business in Gaul. It was not until A.D. 43 that the occupation of the island outpost was undertaken—this time by the emperor Claudius, who magnified its importance by assigning to his son the title of Britannicus, as "the first conqueror of barbarous peoples across the seas."

Fiercely though the tribesmen fought, when one of their chiefs, Caractacus was captured and taken to Rome, what most impressed his captors was his dignified discourse. Tacitus, in his *Germania*, credits Caractacus with the first speech by an inhabitant of the British Islands ever recorded. It was a worthy beginning for the rhetorical record: "My present lot is as glorious to you as it is degrading to myself. I had men and horses, arms and wealth. What wonder if I parted with them reluctantly? If you Romans choose to lord it over the world, does it follow that the rest of the world is to accept slavery?" His spirit of bold independence had its intended effect. Caractacus and his family were not executed or even imprisoned, but were allowed to live the remainder of their lives in peaceful respectability.

The actual text of this speech no doubt owes more to Tacitus than to Caractacus. It is also true that Tacitus may have exaggerated the importance of the predecessor of the witenagemot, or witan, the tribal assembly of the earlier Anglo-Saxons. He may well have overstressed its role, having in mind an analogy with the Roman Senate, Nevertheless, the tradition of such deliberative bodies became firmly fixed in England. The reputed "Anglo-Saxon tribal democracy' and the "ancient Anglo-Saxon constitution" became watchwords for the English Whigs. Carried over to America, this tradition helped to shape the first constitution of Pennsylvania.[8] What the witan actually may have been is little known. *The Anglo-Saxon Chronicle* makes no mention of it, nor did Bede, in his *Ecclesiastical History*. But neither of these omissions is either surprising or significant. The *Chronicle* is largely a record of rulers and of battles. Bede's purpose was to celebrate the innovative virtues of Christianity; it was no part of his theme to depict the achievements of paganism. The tradition is firm that the witan was a council composed of civil, military, and in later times ecclesiastical leaders who were summoned by the king to give him such counsel as he felt he needed. It was in no sense democratic and only cursorily deliberative. But this could scarcely have been true of the preceding councils of which Tacitus wrote.

Tacitus may have ascribed to the tribesmen more boldness of spirit than they had. But his claim cannot be lightly brushed aside, for it accords well with what anthropologists have concluded about the role of eloquence among the generality of primitive peoples. Both in peace and in war, they depended on it. It is reasonable to believe that when the king turned to either the early Celtic assembly or to the later Anglo-Saxon witan, he neither did nor could have ignored the "wise men's" advice.

The role of eloquence was also stressed by Dio, in his description of the widowed queen of the Iceni in Norfolk, Boudicca, whom he portrayed as a fiery warrior and orator, who was "very tall in appearance and terrifying," as she urged on her tribesmen by crying out to them that the Romans were but "hares and foxes, trying to rule dogs and slaves." The *Annals* of Tacitus provides additional details.

Boudicca had ample reason to revolt. Her two daughters were raped by Roman legionnaires, and she herself was flogged by order of the Roman governor. Her people also were aroused to hot anger by the unjust seizure of their homes and properties and by imposed taxes that they regarded as outrageously high. In A.D. 60 Boudicca organized the last effective resistance in southern England to Roman rule. Her campaign was climaxed by her capture of Verulaniam, in the suburbs of London, after a battle that, Tacitus reports, resulted in the death of some 70,000 Romans and 80,000 Britons. Although the figures were exaggerated, their citation indicates that Boudicca was no gentle lady. On the basis of firsthand reports from his father-in-law, Agricola, who was on the staff of the Roman governor, Tacitus wrote that "the Britons took no prisoners, sold no captives as slaves, and went in for none of the usual trading in war. They wasted no time in getting down to the bloody business of hanging, burning, and crucifying." Boudicca had little time for enjoying her triumph. Within a year she was dead, from either poison or disease. What is most notable about her is that she was able to raise and to lead a huge army, loosely estimated at 230,000 fighters, and to direct them through a sustained campaign. Undoubtedly her charisma was considerable.

The question remains of how, against all the probabilities, England became a nation. There were Celts and Picts, Saxons, Angles and Jutes, and in later times Danes, Vikings, and Normans. They had little in common except the divisive characteristics of being combative, revengeful, and self-willed. Somehow they learned to talk with one another, to listen, and thus to communicate.

No doubt the conquest by Rome contributed substantially to their emerging unity. For one thing, the Pax Romana subdued their internal struggles. For another, the overlordship of a foreign power gave them a common target for their resentments. Still another factor was that they learned from the Romans how to govern through persuasion.

The way the Romans utilized persuasion is well illustrated in a speech by Petillius Cerealis, reported by Tacitus in his *Annals*. Cerealis was assigned as governor of Britain in A.D. 69, shortly after Boudicca's revolt was subdued. The speech was addressed to Germanic tribesmen, whom Cerealis had been governing in Gaul. No doubt the resentments held by the Gauls were similar to those he was about to encounter in England. The speech reveals how he used persuasion to solve his problems.

He commenced the speech disingenuously: "I have no capacity for public speaking and have always maintained that the worth and excellence of the Roman people lies in its courage and skill in arms, but I feel I must make a few points." Then, having thus reminded his hearers of his military supremacy, he soothingly dealt with their complaints.

> The reasons that some generals and emperors came into your territory and those of the other Gauls was not for gain but at the invitation of your forefathers. They had become so exhausted by internal strife that they were close to collapse. . . . Until you conceded to us the right to govern you, there were wars constantly among you and and local despots in command all over Gaul. Yet, though we have often been provoked, we have used our victories to impose only those burdens which are unavoidable if peace is to be preserved. Peace cannot be maintained without armies; armies need paying, and that means taxes. Everything else is shared with you. . . . You are not excluded from anything. In fact, in one way you benefit especially; the good that flows from popular emperors reaches everyone, far and near alike, but the evil wreaked by tyrants falls on those closest to them. Just as you put up with natural disasters such as too much rain or poor harvests, so should you look upon extravagence and greed among those who have power over you. There will be faults as long as there are men, but they are not with us all the time, and better times compensate for the bad. . . . At present, victor and vanquished enjoy peace and the imperial civilization under the same law and on an equal footing. Let your experience with the alternatives prevent you from preferring the ruin that will follow on revolt to the safety that is conferred by obedience.

The speech thus concluded as it had begun, with the reminder that resistance was useless. The motivation Cerealis offered consisted more of rationalization than of sound reasoning. Yet in its seeming plausibility, it must have been effective to its listeners, as it would be to many modern audiences. Its pattern of development shows that sophistication in governing is not a modern invention. *Submit because you have to; it is not so bad* is a theme that was as suitable for Cerealis's new role in Britain as it had been in Gaul.

"Nothing to Prevent You from Converting All You Can"

Roman rule did not unify the tribesmen, but it did provide them with means of achieving an effective pattern of communication. Local leaders were elevated as landed aristocrats and were encouraged and assisted to maintain order. Roads were built. Twenty or thirty substantial towns were constructed. London, as the commercial center, reached so high a degree of urbanity as to have more stone buildings that it would ever have again until after the Great Fire of 1668. A system of sanitation was created that provided more baths per capita than London would have again until the age of Victoria. When, some four centuries later, the Roman legions were withdrawn, internal separation and warfare broke out again. Meanwhile, an example had been given in which a dozen successive generations experienced what unity could mean.

It was 597 before another source of unification was provided, and this time also it came from Rome. The new impulse was through Christianity, from the papacy. It came not by military conquest but by preaching aimed at winning converts.

Gregory the Great, long before his elevation to pope, yearned to go to England as a missionary. According to his first biographer, a monk of Whitby, Gregory was entranced by his first view of fair-haired English slaves offered for sale in the Roman market. "These are not Angles," he was supposed to have exclaimed, "but Angels." As pope he was heavily burdened, but he did not forget England. Persisting in his intention to evangelize the islanders, he selected a monk named Augustine, who was enjoying a good life in the monastery of Saint Andrew in Rome. Augustine begged to be excused, but Gregory wrote to him, "Let not therefore the toil of the journey, nor the tongues of evil-speaking men deter you."[9] Thus the evangelical campaign was launched, reluctantly headed by an unwilling chief. Its consequences proved to be enormous.

The rhetorical circumstances when Augustine arrived were favorable.[10] King Ethelbert of Northumbria had employed his Jute warriors to bring under his rule the Saxons of Middlesex and Essex and the South Folk (or English) of East Anglia and Mercia. In so doing, he created the core that became England.[11] At least a basis for nationhood was established. More relevant to Augustine's mission was the fact that Ethelbert had married a Frankish princess named Bertha, who was a Christian, and who, as part of her marriage contract, brought with her a Christian priest. It was these two factors of broadened political control and a receptive attitude toward the Roman religion that assured Augustine a favorable audience.

Augustine preached his first sermon to the court in Kent. He spoke it in Latin, which was translated into Saxon piecemeal as he spoke. King Ethelbert, with sensible caution, responded: "Your words are fair, but they are new and of doubtful meaning." Nevertheless, probably nudged by Queen Bertha, he added: "Since you have come to us from a distant place, and since I seem to perceive that you believe the concepts you wish to impart to us to be true and ennobling, we wish that no harm befall you; rather, we wish to receive you with warm hospitality and to bestow upon you whatever is necessary to your well-being; moreover, we shall do nothing to prevent you from converting all those you can to the truth of your religion."

Thus was the momentous event depicted by the Venerable Bede. Its effect was indeed to launch the beginning of a new era. Augustine was named the first archbishop of Canterbury, and a much later successor to that same office found another kind of significance in the occasion—one that reflected not the speaking but the listening. After reporting Ethelbert's reply to Augustine, the later interpreter concluded:

> Such an answer, simple as it was, seems to contain the seeds of all that is excellent in the English character. . . . There is the natural dislike to change, which Englishmen still retain; there is the willingness at the same time to listen favorably to anything which comes recommended by the energy and self-devotion of those who urge it; there is, lastly, the spirit of moderation, and the desire to see fair play, which is one of our best gifts.[12]

Whether this interpretation truly depicts basic English traits, and to whatever extent it accurately characterizes Ethelbert, what is surely significant is that Ethelbert's hospitality assured to Augustine the opportunity to conduct his mission. As archbishop of Canterbury, Augustine set about devising a countrywide administrative system. He sent his priests throughout the surrounding areas as evangelists, with the result, as related by Bede, that "greater numbers began daily to flock together to hear the word, and forsaking their heathen rites, to associate themselves by believing, to the unity of the Church of Christ."

Thus in the cooperative enterprise launched by Ethelbert and Augustine there commenced the virtual partnership of the English throne and the Christian church that has persisted as a central theme in the history of the nation. Augustine's mission continued for seven years, until his death in 604. What he harvested was not only converts to the faith but also a new spirit of national unity. One of his most influential measures was to create a set of administrative dioceses, all united into a national church. As a result of these evangelizing and organizational programs, the seventh century proved to be a time of complementary development in the Christianizing of England and the substantial nurturing of an enlarged civil society. It did not all come from Pope Gregory's vision and Augustine's sermon at Ethelbert's court, but they started it.

Under King Eadwine (617–33) the center of power shifted to Northumbria. He maintained such social orderliness that, as Bede wrote, "in Eadwine's time, a woman with a babe in her arms might walk safely from sea to sea." Such stability provided another favorable rhetorical circumstance, under which evangelistic preaching flourished. As Bede reports, an elder at the court produced a speech with an image so beautiful and suggestive that it has often been quoted: "So seems the life of man as a sparrow's flight through the hall when you are seated at meat in the wintertide, with the warm fire lighted on the hearth, but the icy rainstorm without. The sparrow flies in at one door and tarries for a moment in the light and heat of the hearthfire, then, flying forth from the other, vanishes into the wintry darkness from which it came. So tarries for a moment the life of man in our sight. But of what went before it and after it, we know naught. If this teaching tells us aught of these, let us follow it." The literal-minded might complain that sparrows are not abroad at nighttime in midwinter and, in any event, would not be likely to fly into a lighted and bustling hall. But the rhetorical function is far from limited to the reporting of facts; its business is interpretation, for the creation of attitudes, feelings, and beliefs.

Another elder at the court, a priest named Coifi, seized upon the occasion to speak decisive words. "None of your people, Eadwine," he exclaimed, "have worshiped the gods more busily than I, yet there are many more favored and more fortunate. Were these gods good for anything, they would help their worshipers." He concluded his speech by throwing his spear dramatically against the pagan monument in the hall, with the result that more converts embraced the new religion.

In this time Catholicism was spread all across Europe, except Germany, from Italy and Spain on up to the British Isles. It was in Ireland, through the preaching of Saint Patrick, that it became most deeply rooted and attained to high scholarship as well as to evangelical zeal. It also helped decisively to create a strong bond between the Irish and the English.[13] The center of European scholarship, both biblical and scientific, came to be in the new Irish monasteries, especially those at Darrow and Armagh. Irish intellectualism swept over the Continent, from Burgundy all the way down to and across the Apennines.

The Irish influence also penetrated into the northwestern Scottish Highlands. On a barren island off the coast, a monk named Columba founded the monastery of Iona. In it a Northumbrian prince, Oswald, spent his youth and was profoundly influenced. When he became king he set out to reestablish the realm of Eadwine, and he undertook to do so not by the sword but by sending missionaries out to preach to the unconverted. Moreover, he sought to seal this new kind of conquest with kindness and generosity. When he was told that outside his court the poor were assembled in want and hunger, he ordered that the food from his table and the silver dishes in which it was served be distributed to them.

Meanwhile, to a school established in Selwood Forest by an Irish missionary named Maelduib there came a young man called Aldhelm, whose influence was to spread widely from the monastery he later established at Malmsbury. "Already," in his student days, it was said, "he must have been dreaming of words—words that could reveal or hide, as one wished, the thoughts in one's mind; words chosen out of a multitude that lay at hand, used for their own sake, alone and in companies, marching and meeting in complex regiment and line, marshalled, each in its appointed place, all under one's own individual control."[14] As he matured, his eloquence won for him Continental as well as provincial fame. From an Irish abbot in France came a letter to Aldhelm testifying to the power he exercised: "To my ignorant ears there has come as it were on the wings of praise the fame of your skill in Latin, such as the ears of sensitive readers can hear without a shudder; no caricature or feeble imitation, but endowed with the beauty of true Roman eloquence."[15] Pompous and pedantic though his style has been termed, nevertheless he proved effective in spreading the vision he entertained of the orthodoxy of Rome and the rich imaginative imagery of Ireland, combining the best insights of the Italian and Celtic minds.

An even greater influence was spreading in this same period from Bishop Wilfrid of York, who managed to divert leadership of the new religion from Ireland to England. This was a shift that was to have a profound effect on the history of both islands.

Until the middle of the seventh century, the supremacy of the Irish churchmen was seldom questioned. But differences developed, in both the ritual and the mode of organization, between the Irish and English churches. By which form should the newly converted Christians be bound? To settle this question, a convocation was held at Whitby in 664. The Irish church was represented by a priest named Colman: the English by Wilfrid of York. Wilfrid's early education had been under Irish monks, in the monastery of Lindisfarne, which was an offshoot of the Iona group. There he lived a life of strict asceticism, dressing poorly, eating little, and spending his long days in prayer and in solitude, according to the Celtic tradition. At the age of nineteen, in 652, he transferred to Canterbury, where he found the church administered with richness of ritual by monks who enjoyed the luxuries of good living. Perplexed and eager to find the right mode, he developed a passionate desire to make a pilgrimage to Rome. This he was enabled to do, and in Rome he came under the influence of the great scholar and evangelist Boniface. By the time the Convocation of Whitby was convened, Wilfrid was not only well prepared to represent the English system but was also unchallenged as its spokesman.

As happens often in political and ecclesiastical controversies, the basic issues were confused by trivialities. Colman argued for the Irish fashion of the tonsure, which the English derided. Colman also insisted upon the Irish date and method of celebrating Easter, Wilfrid upon the mode and the date set by Rome and accepted by Canterbury. The fundamental question was whether ecclesiastical authority should flow from Rome through Iona or through Canterbury. The vitality of this issue arose from the fact that the Irish church was relatively decentralized, with its supervisory functions distributed among the great clans, whereas the English church had the authority over its bishops clearly fixed in the Archbishopric of Canterbury. In Ireland, ecclesiastical controversies were enmeshed in clan rivalries; as a consequence, its priests had secular as well as churchly duties and privileges. Divisiveness and disorder were inevitable. There were disputes as to whether the church or the clans had ultimate authority.

Had Colman prevailed in the debate at Whitby, disunity would have become entrenched in England also. Wilfrid, however, was successful in his argument for the close union of Church and State. Loyalty to the Established Church he equated with submissiveness to rule by the king. After Whitby, this concept of Church-State partnership prevailed and became a dominant force in the shaping of Great Britain. The forensic ability of Wilfrid was not the only reason for the success of the English view, but it was the cutting edge by which the decision was reached.

"Let Him Build the House of His Mind"

The sequential shaping of England into a nation was substantially aided by three notable men: Theodore of Tarsus, the Venerable Bede, and King Alfred. In their separate ways they made enormous contributions: Theodore's, organizational; Bede's by scholarship; Alfred's through providing an impressive image of patriotic leadership.

In 668 Pope Vitalian appointed Theodore of Tarsus as the seventh archbishop of Canterbury, with instructions to take full advantage of the decisions that had been reached in the Convocation of Whitby. Reaching England in May of the following year, Theodore immediately set out on a tour of the whole of Anglo-Saxon areas, giving instructions to the abbots, correcting abuses in the conduct of the clergy, and establishing Easter as the principal Christian annual event. As Bede relates in his *Ecclesiastical History*, Theodore was the first archbishop to whom the whole "church of the Angles" submitted.

This was just the start of Theodore's contributions. He also disavowed the subordination of the church to the Monarchy, insisting that their association was coordinate, not that of subordinate to superior. In order to secure the church's position of equality, he took care to insure an independent and adequate ecclesiastical income. Tithing was imposed, properties were acquired, and a code of penance was established whereby sinners paid money to the priests for absolution. Most lastingly significant was his supplanting of the wandering evangelists with clergy settled in the communities. From that time, England was encompassed with a closely knit framework of ecclesiastic communication, flowing to and from Canterbury.

Two vital consequences flowed from these innovations. One was that the means of government in churchly matters derived not from force but through moral suasion—which set the example for secular rule by law. Secondly, the effective centralization of ecclesiastical authority encouraged acceptance of a single authoritative monarchy. Both factors were effectuated by direct, consistent, and controlled communication. The society was becoming nationally structured. The process of knitting together a sense of unity was well under way.

Strengthened by this new unity and also by the direct influence of the settled and educated clergy. England quickly replaced Ireland as the literate and scholarly leader of Europe. Its supremacy as the schoolmaster of the times was enhanced from two great monasteries,—the one Wilfrid developed at York and another at Jarrow, under the leadership of a great scholar named Baeda, who came to be known in history as the Venerable Bede.

Bede was a recluse but far from being provincial, either in his interests or in the extent of his influence. Through preaching, teaching, and writing he spread his enormous knowledge and the strength of his ideas throughout the islands and the Continent. "I have spent my whole life in the same monastery," he mused in his latter years, "and while attentive to the rule of my order and the service of the church my constant pleasure lay in learning, or teaching, or writing." From his earliest youth on to the end of his life, his goal was clear—not to innovate, but to propagate. As a schoolmaster, he found his classrooms crowded with some six hundred resident monks, to which audience was added a steady stream of seekers from outside who came eagerly to get his guidance. To them he taught that the tongue is all-powerful—and also dangerous. "It is safer to hear the truth than to preach it. For the hearer saves his humility; scarcely will the preacher escape, be it but a little boastfulness." Heresy, and especially the teaching of heresy, was in his view, the greatest of sins. Authority was to be respected. "There is nothing said that has not been said before."[16]

Throughout his lifetime, from around 673 until his death in 735, Bede fortified his comprehensive mind with enormous industry and purposiveness. He mastered Greek literature, the sciences, and classical and biblical scholarship. As Edmund Burke was later to affirm, he became "the father of English learning." With no secretary, no research assistants, and only minimal library resources, he completed the prodigious body of forty-five books. Many were treatises on books of the Bible. Others were textbooks on astronomy, meteorology, physics, music, philosophy, grammar, arithmetic, medicine, and rhetoric. One of his great contributions was the popularization and the improvement of the English language. From his labors he never rested. Even in his last illness he continued to teach, asserting, "I do not want my boys to read a lie, or to work for no purpose after I am gone."

On the last day of his life he urged the students gathered around his bed to "learn with what speed you may; I know not how long I may last." On that day he dictated the last of the final chapter of his last book, a rendering of the Gospel of Saint John into English. As evening approached, the scribe who was copying his dictation informed him, "There is one last sentence unfinished." "Write it quickly," Bede urged. When the scribe comforted him with, "It is finished now," Bede agreed: "You speak truth, all is finished now." He died chanting his favorite prayer, the Gloria.

Actually, all was far from finished. Bede's influence lived on, little diminished by his death. England's scholarly dominance reached new heights in the century that followed. Boniface, one of Bede's disciples, conducted extensive evangelical campaigns in Germany. Alcuin, another, established a center of learning at the court of the French king, Pippin, and his successor and son, Charlemagne. Many princes from England's major tribes went for study to Alcuin's school, established in the abbey of Saint Martin at Tours. The greatest of these was Egbert, of the West Saxons, who in 815 extended his mastery throughout England, so that for the first time the English were brought together under a single rule.

The continent was astir with freebooters taking to the sea to explore, to loot, and to conquer. In 787, as the *Anglo-Saxon Chronicle* attests, there came "the first ships of the Danishmen, which sought the land of the English nation." Concurrently, Norsemen invaded and occupied Ireland and all the northwestern area of Great Britain. It remained for a greater man, Alfred—a grandson of Egbert—to lay the true foundations of the English nation. His methods necessarily were in part military. But even more significantly, he undertook to restore the primacy of learning. After the Peace of Wedmore in 878, he was granted a span of some fourteen years of peace in which to pursue his aim of restoring the cultural primacy that had declined during the wars against the Norsemen.

King Alfred proved to be notable both as an author and as an editor. So far as the record shows, he had neither occasion nor special skill as a public speaker. But he was very much aware of the English populace as an audience and he was deeply concerned with what a ruler might do to influence it. He personally translated Bede's *Ecclesiastical History*, aiming to strengthen his people's knowledge of and pride in their country's past. He oversaw the translation and revision of a Spanish work, *History of the World*, and wrote a preface for it in which he said that "in old times men came hither to seek for instruction; and now, if we are to have it, we must get it from abroad." He supervised the revival and continuance of the *Anglo-Saxon Chronicle*. He translated Pope Gregory's *Pastoral Care*, explaining that his purpose was to "turn into the tongue that we all can understand certain books that are necessary for all men to know." Knowledge, he realized, is power, and it was this power that he sought to leave as his legacy for his countrymen.

When he turned to translating Boethius's *Consolation of Philosophy*, he sought to shape English culture by inserting into it such passages as:

> He that will have eternal riches, let him build the house of his mind on the footstool of lowliness, not on the highest hill where the raging winds of trouble blow or the rain of measureless anxiety. . . .
>
> A man will not be the better because he hath a well-born father, if he himself is naught. The only thing which is good in noble descent is this—that it makes a man ashamed of being worse than his elders. . . .
>
> To give money to a school is to give to God. . . .[17]

Rhetoric played its part in King Alfred's contribution of unifying England in another and curious way: by the creation of legends about him. Someone invented a story that after a major defeat by the Danes, while his army was scattered, King Alfred took refuge in a poor cottage. The housewife, not knowing who he was, left him alone to watch the cakes baking beside the fire. Lost in thought, Alfred allowed the cakes to burn. Such a story illustrates how rhetoric may embellish facts, or interpret them, or substitute for them. The effect of this tale was to disseminate an image of Alfred as being willing to dwell humbly with the poorest of his subjects while being so intent upon his kingly responsibilities that he allowed trivial matters to go unnoticed. Such a legend is akin to that of later times, in which Robert of Bruce, disconsolate and about to abandon his fight for Scottish liberties, was heartened while resting in a cave by watching a spider try and try and try again before successfully anchoring a filament, from one wall to another, as a basis for spinning its web. It is like the story Parson Weems invented concerning George Washington: that when his father asked him who had cut down a cherry tree, he replied, "I did it; I cannot tell a lie." Along with battles, and literary production, and other great deeds, legends also help to build reputations and shape attitudes, and thereby assist in the development of nations. To some degree, Alfred was a product of rhetoric, as well as a master of it.

The persistently rhetorical cast of Alfred's mind is what made him a teacher and a reformer. His purpose, as he saw it, was less to build a domain than to resuscitate a civilization. In his court, he set up a school for young nobles. Through it he sought to fulfill his desire that "every youth now in England, that is freeborn and has wealth enough, be set to learn"—and most particularly to learn to use his own English language. It was from the influence of this school, and from Alfred's general encouragement of learning, that "the tide of literary fashion suddenly turned. English prose started vigorously to life. Theology stooped to an English dress. History became almost wholly vernacular. . . . A national literature, in fact, sprang suddenly into existence which was without parallel in the Western world."[18]

Alfred's own practice set an example for his subjects. When time permitted, he read books; when he was too busy to read, he listened while he had them read aloud. What he advocated, he did. Under his tutelage, England once more turned toward becoming literate. Moreover, through his influence it was also becoming unified, with a strong attachment to its own traditions, culture, and aspirations.

"They Must Will What the King Willed"

The social organization of the time of King Alfred also took form in a hierarchal structure that determined the flow of communication. It was not democratic, though in some respects it seemed so, since the population was all devoted to agriculture and only a few were more prosperous than their neighbors. A structure of class differences existed that was to continue, with significant modifications by the Normans. It was not equality but rank distinctions that were taken for granted. Rising above the agricultural base were two dominant professions; the military and the ecclesiastical. These were the true professionals, supported by the public purse.

The secular society was divided into four classes: at the top the noblemen, or *eorls;* then the freemen, or *ceorls;* at the bottom the slaves, or *thralls;* and just emerging, to increase rapidly after the Normans came to rule, the serfs or *villeins.* Under the eorls were assembled a growing body of *thanes,* professional soldiers, who were rewarded with grants of land. Largely from the influence of the Danes, who drew attention to the sea and developed trading as a substitute for plundering, there developed gradually a new and influential body of merchants. The ceorls of that time were small landowners who led the militia, or *fyrd,* and were always ready to be called out in time of war. In Alfred's time, the ceorls were numerous and respected. In later times they became divided into two groups, one rising to the nobility, the other subsiding as serfs, who were rewarded with security but were bound to remain on the large estates they served. Individuals knew their places, their duties, and their rights.

The communal life was simple but was generally more comfortable than that on the Continent. The farm villages into which most of the inhabitants huddled were composed of barren huts without windows or chimneys. The farming methods were exceedingly primitive and were destructive of the natural fertility of the land. Each freeman was entitled to some fifteen to thirty acres for his own cultivation, but these plots were assigned to him annually and changed from year to year. In consequence, much time was wasted walking to and from scattered fields, and no freeman had motivation to improve land that would be his for only a year or two. It was not until the eighteenth century that improved agricultural methods became prevalent. By modern standards the inhabitants were impoverished, but the comparison is misleading. What is notable about Alfred's time was the amount of its wealth—sufficient to provide amazingly large payments of "Danegeld"—far greater than that in Europe.

Another distinctive characteristic of the populace was pride. Each village was largely self-sufficient, producing its own food and cloth. The villagers had no taste for being governed any more than was required for their protection. This pride in independence is a major reason that the English developed no written constitution. What they did develop was a system of common law. Orderliness rested primarily upon a common sense of what was proper, traditional, and just. Civil organization was minimal; it was also participatory. Problems were settled largely by discussion.

At the apex of the society was the king, who was assisted by the witan, or the king's council. It was not elected but consisted of nobles, bishops, and other leading men who were chosen by the king. This body had little authority under a strong king, but when the monarch was weak the "wise men" assumed a leading role in establishing policies. Upon the death of a king his successor was chosen, or more often confirmed, by the witan. At least the principle was accepted that the minds of many are a wiser guide than the mind of one.

The kingdom was divided into shires, many of which were remnants of earlier kingdoms, with a strong sense of local identity. Each shire was headed by an eorl, who organized defensive forces that were funded by the "third penny" of fines levied in the shire courts. The eorl also presided over the shire assemblies. Associated with the eorls, and as time passed coming to exceed their authority, were sheriffs, or *reeves*, who were appointed by the king and served as his direct representatives.

Who, then, were the community spokesmen? The spokesmen for the villagers were the eorls and the bishops. Those who brought to them orders and guidance from the monarch were the sheriffs. But between these spokesmen and the people were the shire assemblies, which served as clearinghouses for local affairs. Meeting twice a year, these assemblies served as appeals courts for cases that were left unsettled in the local moot courts. They also considered such public business as needed attention. In theory, all freemen were entitled to attend the shire assemblies and take part in their discussions and decisions. In practice, such participation was limited to the thanes, for few except them had time for it. Under Alfred the shire and court meetings were held with fair regularity and attained importance. Through this means, the English gained far greater experience in managing their political affairs than existed on the Continent.

Some of the laws were ill defined, but the majority of them were too precisely detailed to have general applicability. What was legal, in consequence, came to be considered what the community felt to be just. In the moot trials, the defendant had the burden of proving his innocence. Testimony was taken under oath. When the accused and his accuser contradicted one another, the case was settled by the ordeal of fire—the holding of a piece of red-hot iron, or the plunging of an arm into boiling water. If the flesh did not heal by the third day, it was presumed that God had judged the man guilty. It was a harsh system, but it worked because the communities were small, the people knew one another, and they understood that mutual rights must be protected. Most significantly, the system was under local control, among neighbors, and it nurtured the feeling that justice was theirs to preserve.

And what did they talk about? Religion certainly, for theirs was indeed an age of faith. Also of war and its threat or aftermath, for battles were frequent and raids even frequenter, with few families remote from the effects. The weather, naturally, and what it meant to crops, for too much rain or a drought, or an overly cold spring, or too hot an August meant deprivation at the table. Of neighborhood affairs, for despite the scant population the towns were so close together that almost no one lived so much as half-a-day's walk from other families. More than one might think, they also talked of international affairs, for the Continental ties with Italy, Spain, France, Germany, and Scandinavia were close. Surviving literature deals with all such topics and is especially rich in pre-Christian legends like *Beowulf*, in lives of saints and in miracles, in such folklore as is enshrined in ballads, and in tales of distant lands and distant times. Festivals, fairs, and market days brought them together often and encouraged exchanges of pleasantries.

We know that "fair speaking" was valued, for it was often praised. We know from the richness of the riddles that have come down to us that they enjoyed wit and playfulness with words and ideas. If their talk was anything like their surviving literature—as it must have been—they delighted in analogies, similes, comparisons, and all manner of periphrases. Their use of language was anything but simple. In their everyday speech, the body was the bone chamber, the heart the treasure chamber, their thoughts the breast treasures. The sword was likened to lightning, the sea was the whale's way or the path of sails, and darkness was the helmet of the night. Metaphor was their habitual mode.[19]

After the death of King Alfred about 900, the knitting together of the land into one kingdom was pursued even more successfully by his son, Edward the Elder, and his grandson, Athelstan. Then came both unification and empire under the Danish warrior-king Canute, who ascended the throne at the age of twenty-two, and who until his death in 1035 ruled not only all England but also the bulk of Scandinavia.

Eight years later, in 1043, the crown was inherited by another Anglo-Saxon, Edward, called the Confessor, who was near forty years of age and reigned for twenty crucial years. He was a reluctant candidate for the throne, preferring the religious life to which he had been reared during his youth in Normandy; but he was the choice of the great Earl Godwin and was joyously received by the English as one of their own.[20]

It was during his reign that the Normanization of England took firm root. He yielded himself largely to the guidance of Norman monks. One of them, Robert of Jumièges, he named first to be bishop of London and then archbishop of Canterbury. Edward also placed all the great Channel ports under Norman control, and Norman barons were appointed by him as guardians of the border with Scotland.

The only effective barrier to the full Normanization of England was Earl Godwin, who lived to regret his choice of Edward for the throne. It was Godwin who organized resistance to the Norman administrators, and he defeated their armed forces in a brawl near Dover. To the Saxon populace, Godwin was the champion of their liberties. For a brief time, the Normanization processes were suspended. Robert of Jumièges was deposed from the Canterbury archbishopric and a Saxon, Stigand, was appointed in his stead. The people of England united under the slogan Live or Die for Earl Godwin! Then, in the very year of his triumph at Dover, Godwin died. His three sons succeeded to the major earldoms, dividing England into three parts, of which the strongest was Wessex, governed by Earl Harold.

The disunity and disheartenment of England was compounded by the strange behavior of Edward the Confessor. On the very day of his marriage (or so at least it was widely reported), he took a vow of chastity—thereby depriving the throne of a legitimate successor. When he died in 1066, the witan promptly named Earl Harold of Wessex to be the new king.

Duke William of Normandy, however, also claimed the throne, declaring that it had been promised to him not only by Edward but also by Harold, when he was shipwrecked on the French coast, captured by the Normans, and to secure his freedom swore a solemn oath to support William as heir to the throne. English loyalties were sadly divided. Harold's two brothers, jealously defending the autonomy of their own earldoms, refused to accede to his election as king. The devout Christians of south-central England were distraught by the report that Harold had abjured his oath to support William. As a result, when the few thousand Normans under William's banner landed on the English coast, the million inhabitants of England were unequal to the task of repelling them. A few miles north of Hastings, on a day in mid-October 1066, Harold's men fought a brave but losing battle, and Harold himself was slain. Duke William tarried for a few weeks to give the English time to realize their helplessness, then on Christmas Day entered London. In Westminster Abbey, he took the crown as England's legitimate king.

The fighting had been minimal. The English had been accustomed to imposed rule, and William won support by promising wisely that he would leave undisturbed "the law of King Edward as to lands and all other things." The transition might have been peaceful had not William left England too quickly in order to attend to the pressing duties of his Norman dukedom. Upon his departure, revolts broke out, particularly in the north. William determined to teach the English a lesson they would not forget. He laid waste broad areas so that none was left "to bury the dead, for all were wiped out, either by the sword or famine."

Thus for the last time England was conquered by a foreign invader. A sermon by Wulfstan, bishop of York, spoken during the Danish invasions, suggests reasons for the failure of Saxon England. One factor, according to Wulfstan, was the virtual loss of the educational impulse that had been reactivated by King Alfred. Another was the decentralization resulting from the rival earldoms. Such conditions were unfavorable to the evolution of a national forum in which problems could be talked into solution. In Wulfstan's terms, "passivity" and "ignorance" came to be more characteristic than "independence" and "inquiry." Local interests predominated over national loyalty. England fell apart largely because of failure to build on the sound foundations laid by Wilfrid, Bede, and Alfred. The unity that was just emerging was too frail to stand. Communication broke down because there was not just one audience but many. And it is not fanciful to conclude that the failure of communication was what brought about the downfall of Saxon England.

As resistance ended, a new era of imposed unification commenced. In the words of a contemporary chronicle, "the rich complained and the poor murmured, but . . . they must will what the king willed." Thus the history of Saxon England closed. The new era of Norman England began. And the language under which the people were ruled was French.

The difficulties that persisted were largely derived from this: that those who spoke with governmental authority did not do so in the language the people treasured and trusted as their own, but in a foreign tongue, which usage emphasized the gulf between the rulers and the ruled.

Notes

1. Harold E. Driver, *Indians of North America* (Chicago: University of Chicago Press, 1961), p. 328. In the course of his book, he cites numerous similar instances of the shaping of behavior through persuasive speaking (cf. pp. 86, 238, 242, 337, 346, 368, 373, 381, 402, 427, 451, 463, 471, 475, 502, 535, 541, and 557).

2. For a cogent demonstration of the essentiality of controlled communicative flow in order to maintain any large organization, see Phillip K. Tomkins, "The Functions of Human Communication in Organizations," in *Handbook of Rhetorical and Communication Theory*, edited by Carroll C. Arnold and John Waite Bowers (Boston: Allyn and Bacon, 1984).

3. Robert T. Oliver, "Community, Communion, and Communication," in *Communication Quarterly* 15 (November 1967): 7–9.

4. Arnold, *Criticism of Oral Rhetoric*, p. 246.

5. *The Anglo-Saxon Chronicle*, edited by Dorothy Whitelock (New Brunswick, N.J.: Rutgers University Press, 1961).

6. H. C. Darby, ed., *An Historical Geography of England before A.D. 1300* (Cambridge: Cambridge University Press, 1963), p. 23.

7. F. S. Cowell, *Cicero and the Roman Empire* (New York: Chanticleer Press, 1948), p. 231.

8. Bernard Bailyn, *The Ideological Origins of the American Revolution* (Cambridge: Harvard University Press, Belknap Press, 1967), pp. 80–85.

9. Bede, *The Ecclesiastical History of the English Nation*, translated by Vida D. Scudder (London: J. M. Dent, 1910), pp. 33–35.

10. Bitzer, "Rhetorical Situation," defines rhetorical circumstance as follows:

If someone says, That is a dangerous situation, his words suggest the presence of events, persons, or objects which threaten him, or someone else, or something of value. If someone remarks, I find myself in an embarrassing situation, again the statement implies certain situational characteristics. . . . When I ask, What is a rhetorical situation? I want to know the nature of those contexts in which speakers or writers create rhetorical discourse. . . . In short, rhetoric is a mode of altering reality, not by the direct application of energy to objects, but by the creation of discourse which changes reality through the mediation of thought and action. . . Let us regard rhetorical situation as . . . an exigence which strongly invites utterance. . . . Every rhetorical situation in principle evolves to a propitious moment for the fitting rhetorical response. (P. 1)

11. Peter Hunter Blair, *An Introduction to Anglo-Saxon England* (Cambridge: Cambridge University Press, 1966), p. 11, reports that Tacitus used the term *Anglii*, but the term *Engleland* was not to emerge for another four hundred years—that is, at around the end of the Roman occupation.

12. Arthur P. Stanley, *Historical Memorials of Canterbury* (London, 1875), p. 34.

13. "The spread of Christianity in Ireland after the successful mission of St. Patrick transformed the old hostility between the inhabitants of Celtic Britain and those of Ireland into a close and friendly relationship both cultural and economic" was the conclusion of D. J. V. Fisher, *The Anglo-Saxon Age, c. 400–1042* (London: Longmans, 1973), p. 12.

14. Eleanor Shipley Duckett, *Anglo-Saxon Saints and Scholars* (New York: Macmillan, 1947), p. 19.

15. Ibid., p. 77.

16. This summation is from ibid., pp. 217–336.

17. Cited from Eleanor Shipley Duckett, *Alfred the Great* (Chicago: University of Chicago Press, 1956), which sifts out the realities from the myths that enshroud Alfred's life.

18. John Henry Green, *A Short History of the English People* (Chicago, 1883), 1:72–78.

19. See Emile Legouis and Louis Cazamian, *A History of English Literature*, rev. ed. (New York: Macmillan, 1929), esp. 1:18–23.

20. Earl Barlow, *Edward the Confessor* (Berkeley and Los Angeles: University of California Press, 1970).

2
Drawing Together—The Role of Talk

Under the tight rule of William of Normandy, the old patterns of local and national communication were broken and replaced. New earldoms were created, with a French-speaking aristocracy in control. The form of English society was reshaped. What was accomplished owed much to the exceptional leadership abilities of the new king. His qualities were neatly summarized by a monk of the abbey of Caen, who knew him well. Since this monk was a loyal Norman, well disposed toward William, his account was biased. Nevertheless, an able recent biographer of the Conqueror considers it to be "a remarkable description" by "a man who was in a position to know the facts."[1] What the monk stressed was William's capacity to size up situations and to induce people to accept his interpretation of them.

> So skilled was he in the appraisal of the true significance of events, that he was able to cope with adversity, and to take full advantage in prosperous times of the fickle promise of fortune. . . . In speech he was fluent and persuasive, being skilled at all times in making known his will. If his voice was harsh, what he said was always suited to the occasion.

Even when "the people murmured" about his severity, his person and his personality made him an attractive figure, able to inspire and to build upon loyalty. More to the point, his words, and only his, were decisive.

The defeat of the Saxons had stemmed from the decentralization of their ancient system of relationships. They were without a solid focus for nationalistic sentiments. After the death of Earl Godwin, there was no Saxon voice that could inspire the people with unified loyalty. Local deliberation concerning policies could not suffice. The network of national communication was sundered. The quick and easy success of the conquest has rightly been attributed to two factors. First was "the lack of any common purpose among the insurgents whose efforts were made in isolation and without any contact with one another," thus rendering their efforts uncoordinated and futile. Second, "there was almost from the first a substantial body of opinion which was favorable, or at least not actively hostile, to the new regime."[2] What the conquest indicated was that England was dismembered. This much had Saxon rivalries and the Normanization policies of the Confessor accomplished.

"No Longer French, nor Anglo-Saxon; All Are English"

What above all William brought to England was a new system of organization that bound the parts together into a single administrative whole, comparable to the ecclesiastical system that was initiated by Augustine and cemented by Archbishop Theodore. Under William, new channels of communication were established between local communities and the Court. It was this, even more than the flow of new ideas from the Continent, that set England upon a new course.

William's success is all the more remarkable in that he did not, as he had promised, "leave undisturbed the land and all other things." Far from it. He set about to impose upon the society a new system of feudalism. Its most grievous aspect was that his own Norman followers were granted ownership of the manors and the fields that had been Saxon. Its most lastingly influential effect was that this feudal system provided a set of all-encompassing communicative bonds. The transformation of the country was commenced by military power, but it developed through a tightly knit pattern of communication. This was the superstructure, and it mattered. Even so, the old local institutions also persisted. As Esme Wingfield-Stratford concludes, "The method of local government by moots or assemblies. . . . though somewhat roughly handled in the first stages of the Conquest, was too strong to be uprooted, and the Norman could do no more and no better than to take it substantially as he found it."[3]

The Normanization of England has been described so negatively and so vividly by Sir Walter Scott in such novels as *Ivanhoe* and *Kenilworth* that a more balanced interpretation is rendered difficult. Ample credit has been given by most recent historians to the beneficial effects of the survey of lands, property, and population presented in the Domesday Book. What King William's reign accomplished was a start toward the melding together of the jigsaw puzzle of the areas and the ethnic identities into a coherent pattern—this was his most fundamental contribution. The evolution of an English culture required the operation of channels of communication as well as the exercise of power. The process could not be completed quickly. It required the time span of several succeeding generations. Somehow there had to evolve a body of traditions and a concept of commonality to form the generalized concept of *Englishman*.

The new breed of English did not assume recognizable form until about the lifetime of Geoffrey Chaucer. In the judgment of G. M. Trevelyan, as set forth in his *English Social History*, it was not until the fourteenth century that "the English people first clearly appear as a racial and cultural unit." It was not until then, he concluded, that "the upper class is no longer French, nor the peasant class Anglo-Saxon; all are English." This long it took for the islanders to advance beyond "Norman ideas" and "French models" to formulate their own types and customs.

Actually, the transformation of England from primitive tribalism into a true sense of nationalism extended through a full forty-five generations, dating from the time Julius Caesar led the first Romans ashore. Some nine or ten of these generations succeeded one another after the Conquest before Chaucer described the new citizenry that was developing. During the long interim, internal pacification was generally imposed in part by military force but even more fully by changes in administration, which resulted in changes in communication.

What needs to be understood is that administration *is* communication. Facts, ideas, and policies need to be shared and shaped through accepted institutions. Organization does not simply contain channels of communication; it consists of them. It is the flow of communication that vitalizes the structure of authority. Unless ideas are broadly shared, there is no audience beyond the clannish limits for literature or for speech. There has to be a sense of general identity, of shared heritage, and of pragmatic goals and interests that encompass the whole people before they can have either the forms or the feelings of community. There must be awareness among the people that even the distinct social classes and the localities with a long history of enmity have a need to stand together to protect their common rights and to pursue their common aims.

"Our Heroic Ancestors"

Such a feeling of relatedness developed among the English from two different sources. One was the enshrinement and enrichment of memories. The other was the method by which they were governed.

Gradually there grew a common loyalty to "our heroic ancestors." The result was akin to that which (later and in a different land) led the diverse bodies of immigrants who poured into America from all parts of the world to revere, however incongruously, "our colonial ancestors." National memories have to be clarified; they have to be imbued with emotional fervor; and they have to be internalized in order to serve both as traditions and as guiding principles. Such epics as *Beowulf* and the Arthurian legends of Camelot came to be esteemed as a common heritage. Such names as Alfred and Bede and Harold came to be generally celebrated. There also was a sharing of proverbs, of folktales, of legends, and of remembered (or invented) heroic exploits. Shaping the feelings of the people were tales of the moralistic knights assembled by the selfless King Arthur to rescue the victims of evil and to seek the Holy Grail; of King Alfred brooding over battle plans while he let the cakes burn in a peasant's hut; of King Canute illustrating limits of authority by his inability to hold back the tide. Memories enriched by inventiveness also glowed with emotional power: about how King Richard proved himself the ideal knight in battling the Saracens, and how the Lincolnshire bandit Robin Hood derided and deceived the haughty Sheriff of Nottinghamshire to rescue Maid Marian. Pride and pleasure alike were enriched by ballads and folk dances, by deer poaching on the estates of aristocrats and by besting the French with superior archery.

Equally influential was the fabric of feudalism. Just as truly as the caste system of India and the family system of China determined the nature of communicative possibilities and processes in those areas, so did feudalism in England.[4] Such social systems may fruitfully be considered as *rhetoric in being*. Channels are established through which authoritative intercourse flows. What is discussable and how it is discussed are predetermined by the social structure. There is a clear identification of who *can* speak and of who *must* speak. Rhetorical occasions are identified. The audience, the modes of discourse, and what it is acceptable to say are all subject to recognized constraints. Such was the political pattern. And it was complemented by a similarly standardized structure of the church, with its authority extending into every hamlet and supported by a sincere and unquestioning faith—even while its miracles and relics and sales of absolution for sins yet to be committed were subject to ridicule and resentment.

Authoritarianism, however, whether from feudal lords or bishops, was not so rigid as to prevent the give-and-take of participatory discussion. The right to talk together about their common problems and to seek solutions through consensus was traditionally supported in the shire assemblies, the moot courts, and the proceedings of English common law, with its emphasis upon circumstances and precedents. The moot courts considered not only specific behaviors but also what was held to be just in other localities. The emphasis upon participation encouraged a sense of civic responsibility, and the tendency to base decisions on comparable factors strengthened the sense of association. Only through such processes could the strangely assorted Canterbury pilgrims described by Chaucer be indisputably English, one and all. Trueborn the English might not be; even so, out of their disparate backgrounds there arose a common culture. What this means above all else was that they developed an interflow of communication, based on beliefs and attitudes that were broadly shared.

The handicaps that had to be overcome are still residual, even into this century. *Coherence* was attained, but not *sameness*. Class distinctions still form a layered society. Ethnic and geographical compartmentalisms persist. Not only the Irish, the Scots, and the Welsh, but also the Cornish, the Northumbrians, the Yorkshiremen, and still others cling to their particularized characteristics. To be a Lancastrian or Cambridgean remains a matter of special pride. Graduates of the prestigious public schools and the great universities continue to regard themselves and to be regarded as forming a distinct group. So do the Cotswoldians and the Cockneys. Regional dialects are strongly distinctive, and separate languages are cherished in Ireland and in Wales. Yet from one end of England to the other, a sense of collective involvement is felt.

A strong impulsion toward both unity and change came from foreign relations. Successive waves of foreign invasion confronted the islanders with common enemies and encouraged unified efforts to resist. But there was also the contrary effect of outside influences that required continuing adjustment. For many centuries not only the geographical but also the psychological ties of Englishmen reached into large portions of the European mainland. Ideas from across the Channel penetrated both widely and deeply. In many ways and through many generations the southern and midland peoples were more closely allied with France and the Low Countries than with the remoter parts of their own islands. Even as late as the eighteenth century, Scottish interests identified in significant ways more closely with Paris than with London. Even more fundamentally, Irish interests took their own separate course. Differing modes of thought and of behavior developed. So, too, did receptivity to change. Both of these factors worked against a commonality of tradition-rooted culture.

But despite the impediments, a great nation was taking form—great enough to give to the world one of its finest bodies of national literature, the ideal of democracy, and eventually an impetus to global colonization. The inmost nature of English culture may even now remain subject to question. From the outside view, the England depicted by Jane Austen and by Charles Dickens, by Sir Walter Scott and by Oscar Wilde, by Alexander Pope and by Jonathan Swift, by Robert Burns and by Alfred Lord Tennyson, seemingly presents more differences than similarities. So do the Dissenters and the Anglicans, or the Lord Chesterfields and the Samuel Johnsons. Yet even while the divergent groups of islanders appear to be standing separate from one another, they also constitute a recognizable national type. Such contrarities as Samuel Pepys and David Hume, or Winston Churchill and Clement Attlee, are stubbornly representative of John Bull. Even when such distinctive individuals are out on foreign strands, in the words of the poet Rupert Brooke, there is "forever England."

"Freynsch into Englysh"

How did it all come about? Through the centuries spoken communication undoubtedly played a large and probably a decisive role. Writing and reading came late and exercised their greatest influence only after Gutenberg. Newspapers and other periodicals nurtured writing as a major profession only in and after the seventeenth century. Much earlier, the flow of spoken communication,—the saying and the listening concerning common ideas,—helped to bind the many into the one. This it was, in the trenchant phrase of Carroll Arnold, that created a "community of engagement."

The emergence of true nationality was largely shaped by three factors: by basic changes in the political structure of the society; by development of the unifying power of shared traditions; and by the general usage of common language. The significant constitutional changes were chiefly the work of four strong kings and their appointed agents. William the Conqueror implanted the feudal structure, which was political, social, and economic. Henry I effectively centralized the governmental apparatus and practices. Henry II gave new shape to the legal system. Edward I accomplished additional legal reforms and contributed to the formation of the Parliament. Such structural changes meant the infusion of new modes of inclusive communication. As indicated above, a second influence was the evolution of a folk heritage that was broadly encompassing. And third, also essential for the operation of societal processes, the national language came into general use.

For several generations after 1066, communication was cumbersomely tripartite. Latin was the universal language among scholars and clerics, both in England and on the Continent. The French language was dominant in the Court and among the nobility; it served also the needs of maintaining the extensive relations between the islanders and the Continental domain that was fought for by successive Norman-English kings. Meanwhile, among the great masses of the peasantry, the Anglo-Saxon tongue alone prevailed.

Such linguistic divisiveness was worse than cumbersome; it was also self-defeating. More than denying the existence of social cohesiveness, it also encumbered its growth. The enforcement of laws, the collection of taxes, the conduct of trade, and even the direction of military operations all depended for their efficiency upon attaining effective communication. Despite the problems inherent in linguistic divisiveness, its elimination was delayed by an aristocratic pride in self-conscious superiority. The learned were reluctant to surrender the special distinction of being the ones who mastered Latin, which they held to be vastly better for their elaboration of ideas than the vulgar dialects. The powerful felt keenly their special mark of speaking French. But a change had to come. Since the peasantry would not—and indeed could not,—accomodate themselves to Latin and French, their betters had no recourse except to speak with them in their own language. In this respect, the superiors were forced to yield to their inferiors.

The transformation began in the fourteenth century. In 1350 one John

Cornwal, "a maystere of gramere, chaunged the lore of gramere schole and construction of Freynsch into Englysh." Like most educational innovations, this was less the precursor of change than an acceptance of its inevitability. As in the legend of King Canute, this was a tide that could not be held back. In 1362 English was ordained the language of the law courts. In 1363 the chancellor opened Parliament with a speech in English for the first time. In 1384 the City of London issued its first English-language proclamation. In 1399 Henry of Lancaster delivered his coronation speech in English.[5]

Particularly influential in the universalization of English were the preaching friars of the Dominican and Franciscan orders. Saint Dominic and Saint Francis founded these orders with the aim of restoring the simplicity and directness of relationship of the people with their church that had been diminished through the reclusive and inward-turning character of the monasteries. A small band of Dominicans first came to England in 1221; three years later an even smaller band of nine Franciscans arrived. With devotion and zest they set about their mission to evangelize the peasantry. In doing so, they spoke, as they had to, in the language that the rural folk understood. And they were warmly welcomed.

The Christian religion was not only revitalized but was also considerably altered by this new mode of preaching in the vernacular. The settled clergy of the time did only minimal preaching; their church services were largely ritualistic. The monks in their monasteries taught only by the example of their pietistic living—except in their schools. The friars, traveling individually, went out into the villages and small towns. Each friar found for himself some kind of shelter, often an abandoned hut on the outskirts of town. Then he commenced to preach, and he did so in a manner that emphasized not the social distance between priest and parishioners but the closeness of the bond that united them. This was accomplished first of all by putting the sermons in the language that belonged to the people, that was theirs by inheritance and by their community traditions. Such a speaker-listener relationship brought to the church a meaning it had long lost.

The effect was little short of magical. As a student of the period reports, "It is no exaggeration to say that the eloquence and sincerity of the friars swept men of all classes under their influence . . . [for] the friars offered something men had never experienced before, the exhilaration which can come from listening to a trained speaker preaching from both heart and head."[6] But much more than mere pleasure resulted. The people could take home with them the ideas of the preachers, to discuss them among themselves, without the strain and uncertainty of translation. Spiritual concepts were democratized. Political and social views also were affected. If parishioners could take home ideas of God's grace to discuss with their friends, how much more could they examine and judge the practices of their lords, and even of the king. Social and religious relationships were interwoven. As preaching came to complement ritualism, and most especially as it was done in the vernacular, it had an impact that was new and decisive.

Testimony about the effects of the preaching friars abounds. It has been summed up well by the scholar George Holmes, who called them "leaders of intellectual life," who had "enormous attraction" and "exercised a great influence."[7] He explained further:

> Their own ardour and the admiration of their contemporaries quickly made them outstanding bodies within the Church. They were exempt by papal bulls from the ordinary jurisdiction of bishops. . . . They were much suspected by many of the secular clergy but eagerly sought by many of the laity. . . . In both the universities, where they quickly penetrated and took the lead, and the ordinary urban parishes, they were easily the most vital force in the thirteenth century Church.

Although these comments were made about the friars on the Continent, they apply with equal force to those in England. In both areas, they instigated "the philosophical ferment which would be true both to the logic of the human mind and to Christian beliefs."

Increasing use of the Anglo-Saxon language was further stimulated by anti-French sentiments, which were in evidence during the Hundred Years' War. Inevitably the French language came into deeper disfavor. Even so, the scorn of the nobility and of the scholars for the vernacular, which they considered fit only for women, children, and uneducated yokels, was a formidable barrier against linguistic change. Fortunately, the popular tongue was given respectability by three men who came to be held in high repute: John Wycliffe, William Langland, and Geoffrey Chaucer, all born between 1314 and 1340. Their rhetorical influence was similar, and it was enormous.

The least among them, perhaps, was Langland—yet in his own time, the influence of his massive, disorganized, and often incoherent poem, *Piers Plowman*, was shattering. "How national it is!" we are told, "How near the people!"[8] The author was a legal scribe who was deeply versed in Latin, but his sympathies were all with the common people. This long and rambling poem was his principal work, appearing first in 1362, when he was just past thirty, and twice thereafter extensively revised, prior to his death at the end of the century. In spirit it is a socioreligious satire that boils with indignation against the society that calls itself Christian yet was viciously un-Christian in its practices; it proceeds to portray what English life could be if it should become Christian in fact. To accomplish this transformation, Langland recommended a parliamentary government under which the king and the House of Commons should work together to serve the genuine needs of the people. With irony and great forcefulness he urged ideas that were astonishingly novel in his time. Despite the savagery of his satire, he tried to avoid anatagonizing the church by insisting on the vitality of its asserted doctrines rather than attacking them; what he pleaded for was that they be brought into effect. He also stopped short of preaching rebellion against the political authorities. Instead, he feelingly detailed the miseries and harshness of the life of the poor, and he encouraged the assertion of basic rights in a spirit of independence. In doing so, he wrote in the vernacular, thus making his ideas and feelings immediately available to the people's understanding. His choice of a plowman as hero made his message particularly appealing to the peasants. He insisted that they were far more closely related to Christ than were the idle and luxury-loving aristocrats. He was a superb rhetorician who knew his audience and knew how to reach them with pragmatic and democratizing impact.

Far superior to Langland in literary skill, and much more influential in giving the emergent English language an aura of respectability, was Geoffrey Chaucer. Unlike Langland, Chaucer had the advantage of membership in the ruling circle. He enjoyed the patronage of the powerful John of Gaunt, whose sister-in-law he married. And he proved his worth in the course of a distinguished career as a diplomat on the Continent. Upon his return home he was appointed first the comptroller of customs and afterward to the highly important post of clerk of the king's works, which latter position gave him broad responsibility for the construction of roads, bridges, and public buildings. Somehow he also found time for the writing of volumes of exquisitely effective poetry, in which he did much to clarify and to guide the cultural changes that were taking place.

Chaucer's most effective rhetorical influence stemmed from his *Canterbury Tales*, which present a wide assortment of fourteenth-century types who differed from one another in many ways yet who were all truly English. From the Knight to the Oxenford Clerk, and from the Wife of Bath to the Miller, they understood one another, shared common feelings, and felt comfortable in their comradely journeying. They shared a commonality of manners and of moods, of morals and religious devotion, and also of a fruitful skepticism concerning the reverence for relics and miracles. Among them was vividly represented the frailties of the nobility and the ecclesiastics, along with the warm friendliness and generosity of the commoners. As a group they represented the emergent community values of individuality combined with a strong sense of their coordinate unity. Above all, they were neither French nor Anglo-Saxon but simply English. And it was in their own English language that they discussed their interests, their problems, and their ideals. As enduring literature, this collection of narrative poems is among the best in any language, and its rhetorical influence—in shaping the sense of oneness of the people, and in manifesting the flexibility and vividness of the vernacular tongue—was considerable.

"Religious Roundsmen, along the Winding Muddy Roads"

Great as were Langland and Chaucer, the influence of John Wycliffe upon his time was even greater. In effect, he was the founder—however partially and indirectly—of English Protestantism. He was and he remained a priest of the Roman Catholic church; but he developed and popularized the view that the church is a "community of believers" rather than a system of "ecclesiastical authority." Wycliffe denied the cardinal principle that the church is the sole custodian of the keys of Heaven and of Hell. He insisted that it is not the church but the Bible that is the true expression of God's will. To enforce his preachings he translated large portions of the Bible into English, calling it "a charter written by God" and the "marrow of all laws." It was by following the example of Christ, he proclaimed, that all might find their way to salvation. In sum, he "denied authority to the pope and the hierarchy, and overthrew the accepted notions of monasticism, excommunication, the mass, and the priesthood—in short, of the whole structure of the medieval Church."[9] The rhetorical effects of his teachings can scarcely be subordinated even to the work of Luther.

The most revolutionary influence of the transformation he instituted was to broaden extensively the discussable range of religious questions. The Bible needs to be interpreted, and interpretations differ widely. For Christ to be the great exemplar requires that his sayings and his acts be considered in terms of immediate circumstances. Since ecclesiastical authority was not to govern, individual and local judgments became essential. Instead of being merely accepted, religion was propelled into a new era of being discussed, argued about, and evaluated. More than ever before, the people were impelled to participate in their own quest for salvation. These ideas Wycliffe took with him to Oxford University, where he was named master of Balliol College. In the philosophical disputations that enlivened the university, he was the dominant influence, and his lectures were crowded with eager listeners.

His immediate rhetorical influence was chiefly among his fellows at Oxford until after his writings were published and came to be heatedly discussed not only throughout England but also all across Europe. The rhetorical circumstances were sufficiently favorable to save him from prosecution for his heresies. For one thing, the seat of the papacy was removed by French power from Rome to Avignon, thus lessening its attraction for the English. For another, he enjoyed the patronage of the great political figure, John of Gaunt, not (as did Chaucer) for personal reasons but because Gaunt was strengthening his own power base by opposing the French pope. For yet another, he carefully avoided political and social controversy. He urged the peasants to "live in meekness and truly and willfully serve their masters"; concurrently, he won popular support by arguing that the lords of the manors should "govern well their tenants and maintain them in right and reason, and be merciful to them in their rent, and suffer not their officers to do them wrong." These preachings, too, raised questions that invited discussion and debate on their own merits, while preserving him from attack. Radical as many of his ideas were, his presentation of them was moderate.

Even more rhetorically effective was his perception that to make his ideas effective he should organize a body of spokesmen to carry them directly to the people. To this end Wycliffe enlisted a set of unordained "poor priests"—who were derisively termed Lollards by their critics, as being grumblers and mumblers in the vernacular. As. H. B. Workman, Wycliffe's major biographer, attests, these Lollards set forth "clad in russet robes of undressed wool reaching to their feet, without sandals, purse, or script, a long staff in their hands, dependent for food and shelter on the good will of their neighbors, their only possessions a few pages of Wycliffe's Bible." Their dress, their behavior, and their mode of living identified them with the peasants whom they sought to influence, rather than as a distinct and separate order of priests. Their closeness with their listeners was enhanced by their preaching in words derided by the settled clergy as little better than the "grunting of pigs," but that seemed to its auditors as true talk rather than ecclesiastical pronouncements. These Lollards were religious zealots who staunchly refused to submit to the authority of either the pope or the archbishop of Canterbury. They undermined the status of the settled clergy, whom they denounced for their lechery and their luxury. They further appealed to the sentiments of the people by emphasizing the bad effects of the flow of English wealth to the papacy. And they heightened existing resentments by repeating the old saying that the English are good asses, for they carry well the load laid upon them. Most important, they provided for Wycliffe hundreds of tongues that spoke directly to the people, in face-to-face meetings, and who continued to spread his message throughout the countryside for more than a century after his death. If it is true that many hands make light work, it is even truer that many voices magnify the effect of what is said, for the more who say it, the greater is the credibility. Han Fei-tzu, the third-century B.C. Chinese philosopher, put it well when he noted that if one man says there is a tiger in the courtyard, no one believes him, nor do they believe two or three men who say it. But if many say it, it will be accepted as a fact—even if there is no tiger. What Wycliffe's Lollards were saying was startlingly new, and as the campaign went forward its effects became evident.

One effect of the preaching by the friars and the Lollards was to stimulate in the villagers a sense of belonging to a larger community. As Trevelyan's *Social History* notes, "The religious roundsmen, on foot and on horseback, were always on the move along the winding muddy roads of England." Their religious mission assured for them a ready welcome, as did their popular protests against ecclesiastical abuses. Along with their evangelism, they brought to the villagers and townspeople a fresh flow of news from the world out beyond their locality. As J. J. Jusserand puts it in his *English Wayfaring Life in the Middle Ages,* these preachers from afar came as "microbes, infecting the stationary part of the population with the ideas of a new age and a larger world."

For this and other reasons, localism was far from being characteristic of even the remote rural areas. The continuing wars with France directed English attention to the Continent. So did the growing trade with Flanders. The Crusades never engaged the English so fully as they did the countries of Europe; nevertheless, as they continued for some two centuries, they impelled serious consideration of distant lands and of infidel beliefs and customs. Inside England recurrent conflicts continued, with the effect of bringing diverse communities into contact with one another. As a cliché of the time phrased it, "Wales was conquered, Ireland partly conquered, and Scotland resisted conquest." But from even the warfare, names of such later heroes as William Wallace and the even more popular Robert of Bruce inspired legends that helped to nurture ideals of independence, initiative, and equality. From every village, sons and husbands were pressed into military service, and the survivors returned home with tales of faraway lands and peoples. The regular meetings of the shires and the hundreds, which were local courts with jurisdiction often embracing several villages, and the trials in the moot courts led to a "great deal of wrangling and jockeying," as Jusserand put it, in the argumentative processes of reaching decisions—while people searched for precedents drawn from similar cases tried in other localities. All such factors were mind-stretchers that built wide-ranging interests. Meanwhile, there were also the sheriffs, as agents of the king, to remind them of the authority and the demands of the nation.

"Matters Goeth Not Well to Pass in England"

Then, in 1349, there commenced a great plague, the Black Death, which proved to be a turning point in English history. Indeed, George Holmes ranks it along with the battles of Hastings and of Saratoga as one of the three most momentous events that have shaped the course of British history. For the great plague, in his estimation, "initiated a long period in which the basic material forces working in society were different from what they had been in the central Middle Ages, and this change had profound effects on almost every aspect of history in the century after." What should be added is that the "profound effects" flowed less from the tragedies caused by the plague than from what agitated and eloquent speakers said about it. As Walter Lippmann convincingly illustrated in his book *Public*

Opinion, people do not first see and then define; they define and then see. What the plague meant, what its implications were, and what new options it provided for the people were not self-evident; they were things that had to be pointed out in order for them to become effective.

The miseries that resulted from the Black Death were themselves evident enough; no one needed to be told about them. In less than three years, the population of England was incredibly reduced from four million down to a mere million and a half—five dead from every household numbering eight. Despair struck into every hamlet and home. Farmlands were abandoned, left untended and unproductive. Prices of food and of every other necessity skyrocketed, yet there was little money with which to buy, for unemployment was widespread because of the disruption of trade and all normal pursuits. Cold, hunger, and every imaginable hardship afflicted the minority who survived. Out of despair came a spirit of angry rebelliousness. What seemed clear enough was that neither government nor religion had adequate solutions for the grievances of the people. Everyone felt that something had to be done—but what?

In many localities voices were raised to express the rage that the people felt. In Suffolk their spokesman was one John Wrawe, of whom almost nothing else is known. In Norfolk a dyer of woolens named Geoffrey Lister assumed the grandiose title of King of the Commons and aroused the people to state their grievances in petitions addressed to the king. In still other localities there were others who spoke out, for the depth of the distress demanded that it be discussed. But among them all, the voices that were most widely heard and heeded were those of John Ball and Wat Tyler.

John Ball, who came to be known as the Mad Priest of Kent, was the master agitator of the time. What his speaking accomplished is left uncertain by the fact that the chroniclers were paying small attention to the doings of any but the great. Nevertheless, out of the murk emerges undoubted evidence that this obscure man became a national rallying point. Across England there spread through constant repetition a couplet expressive of his conviction that society as it was organized simply did not work:

> When Adam delved and Eve span,
> Who was then the gentleman?

What is known for certain about John Ball is that he busily carried his agitation from place to place—and that his eloquence inflamed the feelings of the crowds who heard him. John Ball was a priest, and the privileges accorded to clerics helped him in his struggle to survive. He was a mere child during the years of the Black Death, but the impressions it burned into him, and into the people generally, were persistent in the years of his maturity. He became an itinerant, hurrying to meet the dismayed worshipers as they left the massive cathedrals, to speak to them in the cloisters and in the open town squares. For his denunciatory incitements, he was twice imprisoned on orders from the archbishop of Canterbury. But he could not be quieted. Each time after his release he set about his preaching again. He burned with a sense of personal responsibility to "point the way" toward improvements that were not only urgently needed but that could be attained if only the people would unite to insist upon them. And scanty as the record is, it is clear that Ball won the response he sought. His limitations were that he had neither the skill as an organizer nor the national status that was needed to build discontent into rebellion. What he did accomplish was to bring into sharp focus feelings and ideas that, far from being primitive, sound strikingly similar to the reformist appeals of much later centuries.

His sympathy for the poor gave him a dynamic force that initiated his preaching in 1366 and kept him at it for fifteen years. We know little of his manner of speaking. But his influence was great enough to attract the notice of Jean Froissart, the master chronicler of the time whose loyalties were all to the aristocracy (and whose *Chronique* was to provide Shakespeare with substance for many of his plays). Froissart preserved the text of John Ball's standard sermon, which he delivered again and again. In the translation by Lord Berners, this speech reads as stirringly today as it sounded in the ears of Ball's listeners. We can readily conceive the eagerness with which the impoverished peasantry listened as their champion exhorted them.

> Ah, ye good people, the matters goeth not well to pass in England, and shall not till everything be common, and that there are no villeins nor gentlemen, but that all be united together, and that the lords be no greater masters than we be.

His point was an electric charge, upon which he built a call to rebellion.

> What have we deserved, or why should we be kept thus in servage? We be all from one father and mother, Adam and Eve; whereby can they say or shew that they be greater lords than we be, saving that they cause us to win and labour for what they dispend? They are clothed in velvet and camlet, fringed with grise, and we be vestured with poor cloth; they have their wines, spices, and good bread, and we have the drawings out of the chaff and drink water; they dwell in fine houses, and we have the pain and travail, rain and wind in the fields; and by that that cometh out of our labours they keep and maintain their estates; we be called their bondsmen, and without we do readily their services, we be beaten; and we have no sovereign to whom we may complain, nor that will hear us to do us right.

Then he proposed the only solution that was available at the time.

Let us go to the king, he is young, and show him what service we be in, and show him how we will have it otherwise, or else we will provide us of some remedy; and if we go together, all manner of people that be now in bondage will follow us in the intent to be made free; and when the king seeth us, we shall have some remedy, either by fairness or otherwise.

How this speech affected Ball's listeners was also reported by Froissart: "Whereby many of the mean people loved him, and such as intended no goodness said how he saith truth; and so they would murmur with one another in the fields and in the ways they went together, affirming how John Ball said truth." Froissart further reported that copies of Ball's speech were widely circulated. Their impact was increased as the peasants talked with one another of the resentments they all felt. The culmination came through the leadership of Wat Tyler, of whom so little is known that it is uncertain whether he came from Sussex or from Kent. What is known about him is what he did.

A revolt of the peasants broke out in May 1381, aroused by the speeches of the various agitators. Tyler led an assault by a small and disorganized band against the great fortified city of London. From their encampment outside the walls, Tyler haughtily sent in to the court a set of demands that, according to the contemporary *Anonimalle Chronicle*, concluded with a call for seizure of the ecclesiastical lands, "which should be divided between the commons, saving their reasonable sustenance from them; and that there should be no villeins in England or any serfdom or villeinage, but that all [are] to be free and of one condition."

The Council of the City of London urged the young king, Richard II, who was only fifteen, to ride out to confront the mob. This Richard did, with great boldness, shouting out to them that he came as their leader. The confrontation came in Smithfield, where miscreants were hanged. There, as some observers declared, Wat Tyler displayed his naked dagger and seized hold of the bridle of the king's horse. Whether this was true or only an invented excuse, the king's guards pulled Tyler from his horse and killed him. King Richard pacified the mob by promising a series of reforms. Here was something truly startling—a sharp contrast to, and more significant than, the Magna Carta that the barons had exacted from King John a century earlier. Then it was, as it almost always had been, a jousting for more power among the powerful. Here on the field of Smithfield, it was the people confronting their king, to demand and to receive concessions, in acknowledgment that they had been abused, that they had inalienable rights, and that they had the means of securing those rights. This was revolution indeed.

It was not, however, the kind of revolution that comes with a big bang. On the contrary, it was so inconspicuous that its effects were scarcely noticed. Wat Tyler had built no national organization; in consequence, the rebellion turned out to be little more than a demonstration. The Lords and Commons of Parliament assembled and declared that they would rather die than surrender their traditional rights. The most they would concede was to advise King Richard to pursue policies of clemency and conciliation. Even this gesture was soon forgotten. Richard II, whose youth was so promising, matured badly, sacrificing his talents to his love of luxury and insisting upon autocratic powers that he lacked skill in exercising. The one major reform that he did put into effect backfired. He bravely took away from the nobles their feudal right to maintain private armies. But this simply led to a period of chaotic lawlessness, for the disbanded soldiers formed bands of freebooters that ravaged the countryside. The Irish rose in revolt, and Richard made the mistake of going over to subdue it in person. Before he could return, Henry of Lancaster, son of John of Gaunt, returned to England from France, and thousands of disbanded soldiers rallied under his leadership. When Richard was able to come back from Ireland, Henry arrested him, and Richard abdicated.

The Peasants' Revolt sputtered to a futile end within a month of its outbreak, but the spirit that led to it was another matter. The fourteenth century was marked by changes so momentous that they swept away much of the history that preceded it. The patterns of English communication were recast in a new mold. The nation found a new unity in its use of a common language; notably, it was the language not of the overlords but of the people. Within the national unity there had emerged yet another base of segmental unity—the development by the poor and dispossessed of a strong sense of their own identity, of resentment against their ancient wrongs, and of a determination to have those wrongs redressed. The rhetorical influences flowing from the preaching of the friars and the Lollards, from the teaching of Wycliffe, from the inciting anger of Langland, and from the new communicative possibilities enlarged through usage of a single language combined to change the nature of society—the kind of change that made possible the poetry of Chaucer and that is depicted in it.

England became a new kind of nation. The class identification of the peasantry led to new demands for justice and for equality. Through the itinerant priests and the speaking by the agitators, the people found voices of their own. The groundwork was laid for another period in which decisive changes could be won. This new feeling, far more than the much-celebrated Magna Carta, provided the dynamism for the time that lay ahead. The calendar was turning away from the years of dominance by mailed nobles with swords in hand mounted upon horses. There was a dawning of an age to come, of the Renaissance, of the period of new birth. It was vibrant with ideas that needed to be discussed. Such changes produced a new type of personality, marked by assertive individuality, which made it a veritable age of talk.

Notes

1. David C. Douglas, *Willliam the Conqueror: The Norman Impact upon England* (Berkeley and Los Angeles: University of California Press, 1964), pp. 370–71.
2. Ibid., p. 215.
3. Esme Wingfield-Stratford, *The History of British Civilization* (London: Routledge and Kegan Paul, 1928), p. 119.
4. Cf. Robert T. Oliver, *Communication and Culture in Ancient India and China* (Syracuse: Syracuse University Press, 1970).
5. Legouis and Cazamian, *History of English Literature*, 1:78, discuss the "compromise effected between the two languages," whereby "the words which the Normans found the most difficult, in meaning or in pronunciation were gradually dropped and replaced by their own words." The completeness of the change is indicated in the fact that E. F. Jacob, *The Fifteenth Century, 1399–1485* (Oxford: Oxford University Press, 1953), found no occasion to comment on the language usage.
6. Doris Mary Sheldon, *English Society in the Early Middle Ages* (London: Penguin Books, 1952), p. 243. See also Beryl Smalley, *English Friars and Antiquity in the Early Fourteenth Century* (New York: Barnes and Noble, 1960).
7. George Holmes, *The Later Middle Ages, 1272–1485* (Edinburgh: Thomas Nelson, 1962), pp. 46, 57.
8. Legouis and Cazamian, *History of English Literature*, 1:116.
9. Holmes, *Later Middle Ages*, p. 171.

3
A New Idea Emerges—The Balance of Interests

As a new humanistic learning swept up from Italy through Europe and on into England, one of its most significant effects was that it changed and greatly expanded the topics that were discussable. Religious faith remained vital, but it came to be newly conceived in ways that had to be threshed out. What to believe was seldom challenged, but how to believe became subject to lively debate. The universities, and also the school system generally, became forums for discussion, in which what had long been unthinkable came to be thought about and to be talked about.

Politics was far from being immune to the effects of such changes. For centuries the King's Council was viewed in much the same way as had been the old Saxon witan—that is, as a group of wise men selected by the king to give him such advice as he asked for, to be accepted or rejected at his own will. During the period of change a new concept slowly developed of a Parliament that derived not from royal power but from the communities of England, with the aim and with the independence to represent their wishes and their needs. Concurrently, the meaning of law, and its operations, came into new consideration, with a new national consistency and clarity emerging.

The changes were evolutionary rather than revolutionary. Their course was not marked by climactic crises but by multiple bumps and nudges. The general tendencies are far more evident from the perspective of history than they were to the people who participated in them. The influences that altered the nature of the society were complex, and their results were interwoven. There is no simplistic pattern, either chronological or topical, that can be imposed with full conformity to all the relevant facts. To view what was happening, it is necessary to shift backward and forward in time, and from one type of inquiry to another.

What is evident is that new ideas gained influence. Insitutional changes were astir. Fresh leadership came from scholarly intellectuals. Attitudes and customs that had grown from the militaristic and land-tenure aspects of feudalism came to be challenged and to be changed. Society became more flexible. Individuals came to be more conscious of their rights and of the opportunities. A wider array of options came into consideration. As an animating and directing force, persuasive discourse assumed new importance in the rhetorical circumstances that these conditions brought about. Such happenings did not occur in sudden bursts of clarity. Points of decision were not so much cataclysmic as they were continuous. They did not so much resemble a particular crossroads at which a decisive choice of direction must be made as they did a maze of interconnecting footpaths through which a general direction could be maintained. This was difficult, for there had to be much turning aside and some turning back as well as going forward. As new goals gradually emerged, there was natually much questioning as to what their effects would be. There was much to talk about, many voices raised, and inevitable uncertainty as to what to say and how to respond. In all stages of history, hindsight is far clearer than foresight, even if not always more correct, and for the period known as the Renaissance this is particularly true.

The shifting of feelings and beliefs to new bases gave to speech a new importance in sharpening awareness and in defining the relationships among contending ideas and among people. Institutions that governed religion, civic affairs, and the manner of living had to be reshaped, redirected, and explained. They also had to be rendered acceptable. Traditional spokesmen offering traditional messages no longer sufficed. The power centers that had long dominated English life—the throne, the nobility, and the church—were joined by intellectuals speaking for themselves, to utter truth as they conceived it, and by the Parliament, that to some degree and in some ways began to serve as a voice for the people. More than heretofore, persuasion became a pervasive social force. This shift was one of the fundamental characteristics of the new society of the Renaissance.

"The Common Advice in the Premises"

Historic roots commence as tiny tendrils that only gradually attain strength and depth. One such emerged as early as 1272, when Edward I became king at the mature age of thirty-five. He came to the throne with a reputation already well established as a crusading warrior who "bore the best lance in the world." He was so handsome, as chroniclers of his time attest, that "he stood head and shoulders above the rest." He was deeply religious, which his subjects found reassuring. He was also merciless toward his enemies in ways that Machiavelli was later to recommend. Since his reign was beset by constant warfare, he was always in need of funds. With a realization that taxation should have some popular acceptance, King Edward took the crucial step of establishing Parliament as a legislative body. On 3 October 1295—a date important in constitutional history—he sent this message to his sheriffs:

> ... We strictly require you to cause two knights from the aforesaid county, two citizens from each city in the same county, and two burgesses from each borough, of the more discreet and capable, to be elected without delay, with full and sufficient power . . . to do what shall be ordained by the common advice in the premises.

As a result of this decree, there assembled in Westminster Hall the Model Parliament, which was to develop slowly and haltingly into an instrument of the popular will. Its power initially was as carefully limited as was the electoral process that limited its membership to those whom the sheriffs deemed to be the "more discreet and capable." The true significance was that the chosen members were "to do what was ordained by the common advice in the premises." This was the decisive factor that commenced a movement toward popular government. More centuries were required for anything like democracy to mature, but once a parliament was convened, with authority to reach decisions of its own, a process was begun that could not afterward be abandoned. The new legislature was not very representative, but it was recognized as being participatory in governing the realm.

In its beginnings, the Model Parliament was far from being impressive. Some forty shires or counties sent two knights each to Westminster, along with two burgesses from each of the chartered cities and a larger group from London. No more than eighty boroughs actually sent members to the House of Commons. And these went not eagerly, but reluctantly, as some citizens respond when called upon to serve on a jury. There were no obvious advantages from their role. The duty they were called upon to perform was the unpopular one of raising taxes. Moreover, the members received no remuneration beyond their actual expenses. When they arrived in the Parliament they were overawed by the nobles and the bishops. Despite these handicapping factors, the essential legislative functioning of the Parliament was quickly given added impetus. In 1297, when King Edward was urgently in need of more funds, he granted a "Confirmation of the Charters," whereby he agreed not to exact any special taxes or to seize properties, "without the common consent of the realm."

Several factors aided in the future strengthening of public influence within the Parliament and also its independence. For one, the bishops, in a jealous insistence upon their superior status, voluntarily withdrew from the Commons to sit with the Lords. In the Commons, the knights aligned themselves with the burgesses, since both groups represented local interests and felt the pressure of public opinion. Even more significantly, freedom in debate was bolstered by a provision protecting the members from arrest while they were performing their duties. A climax came in 1311, when with great boldness the parliamentarians proclaimed to King Edward

II that their "oath of allegiance relates more to the Crown than to the person of the king, and is more tied to it than to the individual."

This was a vital claim for parliamentary independence. To "parley," or to discuss and debate governmental affairs, was the idea whose time had come. Eventually, by fits and starts, with many delays and slippages, it came to be established. Fulfillment in practice lagged far behind the theory. But what is once granted cannot easily be taken away. Government by the people was a notion not yet conceived. But a seed was planted; government by discussion was envisioned; roots slowly developed; and at long last, in the seventeenth century, the predominance of Parliament would finally be demonstrated.

"Boys Who Are Studying Rhetoric"

During the fourteenth century a new set of rhetorical circumstances gave enormous impetus to the role of public discussion. As was noted in the preceding chapter, by French power the seat of the papacy was removed in 1309 from Rome to Avignon, and it continued there until 1377. After that, for yet another generation, the church was headed by two, and at times even by three, rival popes, until this Great Schism was finally healed by the Council of Constance in 1418. The effects upon the religious feelings of the people of England were enormous. Religious zeal seems not to have been diminished. Christian belief remained vital. But the authority and the functioning of the Church naturally came into frequent and heated discussion as true believers were uncertain where their duty lay. The authority of the church could no longer be taken for granted—it had to be examined.

The ecclesiastics, deeply shaken by the disunity of the Great Schism, made new efforts to liberate the English church from domination by the newly ill-defined See of Saint Peter. Meanwhile, they had to fend off attacks upon orthodoxy that were coming not only from the preaching of the Lollards and other undisciplined itinerant priests but also from the intellectuals in the universities. Among the most influential of these were Reginald Pecock, John Colet, and Sir John Fortescue. Their leadership was effective because of the rapid expansion of the educational system.

Traditionally, the schools were exclusive and seclusive ivory towers, remote from popular control and from public affairs. Even so, the educational processes were far from being passive. As early as in the twelfth century, according to a contemporary account, regular "speech days" were established, at which times the students were required to set forth and to defend their own ideas. One William Fitzstephens provided an enlightening view into how they operated.

> On high days, the masters gather their pupils at the churches and there the scholars engage in disputations. Some present an argument. Some

dispute a thesis by means of question and answer, or in syllogisms. There are those who play to the gallery, those who seek the truth, those who hope to make an impression by sheer volume of words, and those who rely on verbal artifices. Boys who are studying rhetoric use every art they know to present a case persuasively.[1]

The rhetorical sophistication of Fitzstephens, in his detail of the various "hidden purposes" the student speakers represented, is impressive. It is evident from his account that, within the schools, debate and discussion were recognized as prime tools of learning, by means of which individual understanding and conviction might be both developed and examined. It is also evident that skill in speech was deemed to be an important means for winning leadership roles and exercising influence. This same point is manifest in the nature of the curriculum. Grammar, logic, and rhetoric constituted the *trivium* that was the central focus of study. All three were concerned not with what to know—for this was predetermined by the church and by political and social tradition—but with how to make knowledge effective. The aim was to teach the students to be persuasive in their discourse, both in their writing and in their speaking.[2]

What the schools aimed particularly to accomplish was to train leaders, especially ecclesiastics. What leadership required, in the view then held (which seems to be strikingly modern), was the ability to think clearly and to communicate ideas accurately and influentially. The idea was similar to that which Tacitus had stated: A leader will be followed more because he has influence to persuade than because he has power to command. The aim was much like that restated in later years by Francis Bacon, in his *Advancement of Learning:* to cultivate ability to make "rational knowledge" transitive; or, in Bacon's words, to develop skill in "the spreading or transferring of knowledge to others."

"They Could Learn from Nobody Else"

Since scholarship at that time was both promulgated and preserved by churchmen, it was the ability to preach effectively that chiefly concerned them. A historian of the fifteenth-century English church points out that the preachers were far from being founts of wisdom, just as their parishioners were not seekers for knowledge. The conditions imposed constraints upon both speakers and listeners. "The priest grappled with his vocation in a society of unrestrained passion and unseemly violence; not only was he surrounded by his context, he himself sprang from it; he was no alien to its emotions and traditions and his task was harder, in some ways, than the missionary's, for he had to seek detachment, moral and emotional, in two dimensions—from himself as well as from his parish."[3] In short, the problem was to represent Christianity in a society that was notably un-Christian and without true interest in spiritual or moral concerns. The real problems were how to survive in an impoverished and violent society.

The preaching was done by two very different kinds of priests: the settled clergy, who were subject to the discipline of Canterbury, and the itinerants, who represented various types and degrees of heresies. What they had in common was their function of providing the means for eternal salvation—by the settled clergy through hearing confessions, officiating at the Mass, and providing absolution for sins; and by the Lollards and similar independent preachers by portraying the example of Christ and the teachings found in the Bible.

For the settled clergy, their profession provided a livelihood. Their functions were clearly prescribed. The operations of the church were organized and supervised somewhat like a modern multinational corporation. The English church was a branch of the Church Universal. Bishops and archbishops were appointed by the pope, with or without the counsel and consent of the king. Local parishes had no voice in the choice of their priests. The church and the people were separated. The duty of the officiating clergy was to speak *to* the people, not *with* them. They were expected to maintain the obedience of submissive recipients of the sacraments. One means of stressing the separate character of the priests was the architectural change in the fifteenth century of placing the pulpit apart from and above the congregation. The social distance between the priests and the parishioners was emphasized. The conduct of the services was formal and impersonal. Yet neither in their learning nor in their character and personality were the priests notably superior to their listeners. Even so, their influence was considerable—the massive prestige of the church supported them.

In comparison with their parishioners, the settled clergy were well-to-do. During the fifteenth century, the number of benefices administered by the church has been estimated at 9,500. Many of these were further subdivided into portions. For example, in the archdeaconry of Lincoln, some twenty-six of the parishes were divided into halves, five into thirds, two into quarters, and three into even smaller units. The money with which to support them came from tithes and from special fees that were demanded from time to time.

But the very factors that brought them material advantages also led to a growing resentment against them. They were too much separated from the people to win a willing adherence. As was noted by Thomas Gascoigne, an Oxford professor with heretical inclinations, "There are three things that make a bishop in England: the will of the king, the will of the pope or the court of Rome, and money paid in large quantities to that court." As he added somberly, the amounts exacted contributed "to the impoverishment of the realm."[4] The church was becoming increasingly an institution pursuing its own ends. The "will of the king" was often disregarded in appointments to bishoprics. The wealth of the church helped to set it aside from the people. In contemporary accounts, bishops were typically portrayed as being dressed in ermine and attended by many servants. The vow of poverty had become a lie.

Despite such problems, the claim by the church to a monopoly over the means to salvation gave it great authority. Without its sanction, orthodoxy taught, even devout believers had no prospect of avoiding the terrors of Hell. In that age of faith, such authority was of tremendous import. Living conditions were so harsh that they were bearable only when viewed as a transitory prelude to eternal bliss. Authority flowed from the top downward and was little restrained by either compassion or respect for human rights. The spirit essentially was, "Let him take who can and let him suffer who must." The general structure of the society was established and governed by the Crown, the Church, and—gradually even though in lesser degree—by the Parliament. But it was the settled clergy on the local level that held the key to such orderliness as was maintained.

> The parish was then the fundamental unit, as real and, in an age of subdivided townships, more unified than the manor; and the incumbent of its church, who had the cure of souls . . . had a charge which was both spiritual and material. He had to preach the faith along lines prescribed . . . for his flock's instruction, he had the power of absolution which no bailiff or secular officer possessed, and he had to vindicate his claim to receive from his parishioners the tithe, great or little, to which he was entitled.

In the view of Jacob, this necessity to "vindicate his claim" to receive the tithes meant that the status of the settled preacher depended in no small degree upon his power of persuasion, for "he had to teach his congregation the meaning of reverence and the simple essentials of manners in rude environments where they could learn from nobody else." In order to accomplish his goals, the priest had to hold the attention of his listeners and to guide their responses. "The medieval countryman," Jacob reminds us, "easily fell asleep, and his attention had to be held. Hence the priests had to employ colour, illustration, and the techniques of modernization, to present the saints and local heroes in a 'live' way."[5] The rituals of the church were a form of theatre; the sermons, enlivened with anecdotes, were virtually the only pleasurable stimulants the peasants had available to them. Such were the duties, the responsibilities, and the opportunities of the settled clergy.

Much more appealing to the villagers were the periodic visits and the vivid exhortations of the itinerant preachers. They brought news from adjacent areas, and they provided entertainment. As Wycliffe related, they also augmented their income by serving as peddlers—bringing in trinkets, spices, silk cloth, and other novelties that brightened the lives of the people. More important, to the great annoyance of both the church and the local aristocrats, they also instigated discontent. As Jusserand found, in preparing his study of the time, these wandering preachers "knew what was the condition of the people; they knew the miseries of the poor, which were those of their father and mother and of themselves; and the intellectual culture they had received enabled them to transform into precise conceptions the general aspirations of the tillers of the soil."[6]

Here, precisely, was the dilemma that confronted the Established Church. It was facing competition for influence from wandering and undisciplinable preachers who were far superior to their own clerics in winning popular approval; yet the organizational methods by which its own priests were educated and appointed were too rigid to offer any ready means of securing more effective preachers. As the church authorities considered the options available to them, they did not decide to change the system; instead, they sought a very different remedy. No longer would they leave sermonizing to chance.

As early as 1483 a book of four basic sermons, *Quator Sermones*, was ghostwritten for the church and became one of Caxton's early printings. Since the church urged its use, and since the settled clergy were ill-prepared to compose their own messages, this book proved so useful that in twenty years it was reissued eleven times by Caxton and was further pirated by all the other major English printers. Even so, the effect did not succeed in winning the approval of the parishioners, for while the sample sermons carefully detailed the principal articles of the true faith, they were wholly lacking in illustrative examples and in direct application to the practical problems of the listeners. In an effort to rectify these weaknesses, a scholarly cleric named John Myric, in that same year, prepared another series of illustrative sermons that he entitled *Festial*. This work was even better received by the preachers, going through nineteen editions within two decades. But once again, these sermons by Myric also failed to please the congregations. Like the *Quator Sermones*, they lacked any consideration of the problems of daily living of the peasantry. The merit they did have lay in the vigor of their "crude and sensational anecdotes." Their style, however, was turgidly scholastic: "tropological, analogical, and allegorical, rather than literal." Moreover, "their emphasis is morbidly ascetic and their tone extravagently minatory."[7]

Still another effort sponsored by Canterbury was a collection of seventy sample sermons, entitled *Speculum Sacerdotale*, which was little better. Instead of pragmatic discussions of Christian virtues, they deal with such themes as "saintly victories over dragons." The single exception among them is the Easter sermon, which insists that salvation depends upon contrition, confession, and good deeds. It warns that continuance in even one sin is "like unto a shipman that stoppeth all the holes in the ship except one, at the which all the water cometh in and drowneth the ship." In it, forgiveness of enemies is urged. Stress is also placed upon good manners for, since the body is the temple of the soul, there should be no spitting, belching, or sneezing—at least not in church. As Heath evaluates this sermon, "its basis leaves little to be desired; if its explanations are curious, they are adequate, and if its tales are crude their point is wholesome. Comprehensive and systematic, it makes clear what Easter is all about, and what part in it confession and communion should play; above all, it is about the mercy of God." One good sermon, however, was far from sufficient weaponry with which to wage the rhetorical war against heresies.

The weakness of the Established Church was highlighted by John Colet, another Oxford professor, when he mourned that "the brode gate of holy orders opened, and every man that offered hymselfe is all where admytted without pullynge back." The method by which settled clergymen were appointed did not weed out the ignorant. As late as 1551, John Hooper, the bishop of Gloucester, found to his dismay that the parish priests were so uneducated that many of them could not repeat the Ten Commandments, and more than a few of them did not know their source in the Bible. Others could not even recite the Lord's Prayer, and an occasional one among them did not know its author.

"If by Chance I Have Gone Too Far"

As was noted a few pages earlier, these problems that greatly disturbed the church came under special scrutiny in the great universities. Philosophically minded professors searched for answers that rested upon verifiable certainties. Many of them were particularly incensed that influence of the broadest social extent and of the deepest spiritual significance was exercised not by their own intellectual profession but by a body of clergy that was so manifestly unfit. Oxford was the principal source of the intellectual rebellion that developed, and several of its professors became the leading spokesmen.

John Colet set out to reform these conditions as best he could. He attained a status from which to exercise influence by winning appointment as dean of Saint Paul's. Neither his scholarship nor his literary ability was notable. Even so, "by sheer force of personality . . . he influenced his age; he went about London and Oxford and Canterbury with the same uncompromising determination as Bunyan's pilgrims amid the booths of Vanity Fair to purchase the truth, and nothing else." Like Wycliffe, he appealed from the authority of the church to that of Scripture. But in his view, the Bible itself was in need of rational criticism. The story of Adam and Eve, he asserted, was not literal but poetic. He daringly sought to reinterpret the teachings of both Moses and Paul in terms of contemporary conditions and needs. In his preaching in Saint Paul's Cathedral he denounced the worldliness and the corruption that had brought the church into disrepute. In all his preaching, he insisted that he was a loyal churchman, for which reason he escaped being charged with heresy. The tone of his preaching is well illustrated in a sermon in which he acknowledged: "If by chance I seem to have gone too far in this sermon—if I have said anything with too much warmth—forgive it me, and pardon a man speaking out of zeal, a man sorrowing for the ruin of the Church, and bend your whole mind to its reformation. Suffer not, fathers, suffer not this so illustrious an assembly to break up without result."[8]

The result toward which Colet aimed was sufficiently muddled that only his charismatic personality could have won for him the high esteem in which he was held. He was highly dubious of the value of human reason, which he called "the enemy and opponent of grace." He was also unwilling to accept Scriptures as the Word of God, for he found them to be interspersed with "the bait of a high and holy fiction" that had been written to entice people into God's service. When he studied the Bible historically, seeking to interpret it according to the tenor of the times in which the various books were written, he failed to find an evolutionary process toward a higher morality, or a purer spirituality, or increasing insight into reality; but instead, "little more than aimless mutability." What he concluded is that mankind is condemned to deal constantly with problems that are often misunderstood and that are, indeed, beyond the possibility of human comprehension. The only recourse we have is faith, the "faith that passeth understanding," a faith that each individual must cling to for himself and in his own way. It is this faith that is our only guide to salvation. Such views, while stressing individualism and humbly acknowledging the overlordship of God, also renounced the institutional authority of the church. The wonder is that his personality was so attractive that Erasmus found him to be a very Plato, and that he escaped being tried for heresy. He did not succeed in his desire to reform the church, but he did win an admiring following of intellectuals.[9]

Reginald Pecock, another of the Oxford intellectuals, devoted his enormous abilities to the defense of orthodoxy, but his rhetorical strategies were so badly mismanaged that he was finally brought to trial for advocating heresy. When he was named bishop of Chichester, he set himself the task of combating the threat of Lollardism. Yet in part he agreed with its tenets. He conceded to the Lollards that reported miracles should always be suspect, for human testimony is notoriously fallible. In his own conversations, he said, he never knew three or four men, returning from the battlefields of France, who agreed in their reports of "how a town or a castle was won in France, or how a battle was fought there, though these men were held right faithful men and true, and though each of them would have sworn that it was true what he told and that he was present and saw it."

In short, human testimony is never to be merely accepted; it has to be objectively validated with dependable facts. Furthermore, he also agreed with the Lollards that the ultimate authority for God's will is the Bible, but he refused to accept their contention that Wycliffe's interpretation of the Scriptures was to be accepted. Far from it. Since the Scriptures are a diverse body of writings gathered from many eras and recorded by many different individuals, they naturally include many contradictions. These, like any body of historic documents, have to be interpreted by human reason. And since the various books of the Bible were composed in specific circumstances, designed to explicate particular conditions, they are always in need of being reinterpreted in accordance with the needs and the nature of local and immediate circumstances. It does not suffice to depend upon the history of ecclesiastical pronouncements for guidance, for all history is legend that is shaped in some part by "untrue fables." Of course the scholarship of sincere churchmen is to be respected—but it cannot simply be accepted. The ultimate authority essentially has to be *reason* as the final determinant of what is most probable amid all the bewildering, diverse reports. In sum, even as Pecock assailed the Lollards for their dogmatic assurance of their own certainties, he also gave support to their rejection of the church as the ultimate authority. This was the heresy for which he was condemned. He escaped martyrdom at the stake only by publicly recanting his views.

The major rhetorical difference between these two intellectuals was that Colet avoided entanglement in the controversy over Lollardism. His appeal was primarily to the small minority of scholars and was therefore not broadly damaging to the church. The freedom of discussion in which he engaged was not viewed as a threat to the establishment. The "available choice" that Colet chose for himself was to think freely but to avoid becoming an agitator. The ivory tower within which he confined himself kept him secure. Pecock more daringly ventured into the public forum and paid the consequences. But both of them stressed the conviction that every individual must interpret what religion means to him. This was their major contribution to the considerable enlargement of the "realm of the discussable."

"Hearken Amiably to One Another"

The rhetorical circumstances were shaped fully as much by political developments as by the new inquiries into the foundations of religion. When Henry IV seized the throne from Richard II in 1399, he had only an uncertain claim to the throne by "divine right of inheritance." Lacking this, he had to win the support of Parliament. Because his reign was beset by local rebellions and also by threat of invasion from France, he was always in need of funds that only Parliament could grant. For such reasons, "Parliament was so much the master of the King as to render his position farcical."[10] Disorders were still further aggravated by King Henry's efforts to win support from Canterbury by a merciless prosecution of the Lollards. For a time, matters seemed better for England when his son and successor, Henry V, won a great victory at Agincourt—but it was rendered futile by Joan of Arc's arousal of French patriotism. The war dragged on for another forty years.

During this time the influence of the House of Commons, in which money bills to support the war had to originate, considerably expanded. Before granting funds, the Commons demanded that the king respond satisfactorily to the petitions that they submitted to him requiring various redresses of grievances. This did not mean that the people were gaining representation, for the selection of its membership was still controlled in part by the king and in even larger part by local aristocrats. What it did represent, however, was an increasing influence in the government and of a kind that reflected local interest.

What significant role debate played in Parliament's proceedings is uncertain, for no journal was kept. One small but enlightening glimpse into its discussions is preserved in a sermon that was preached at the opening of King Edward V's first Parliament, on 23 January 1484, by John Russell, bishop of Lincoln, who was held to be "a wise manne and good, of much experience and one of the most learned men, undoubtedly, that England had in his time."[11] Right government of the kingdom, Bishop Russell urged, required that the members listen to "the common voice grounded in a reasonable precedent"; and he pleaded with them to "hearken amiably to one another." Amiable or not, the members intended to deal seriously with grievances spelled out in the petitions, and they took full advantage of their power over the king's purse.

The consequence was, in the opinion that S. B. Chrimes stated in his *English Constitutional Ideas in the Fifteenth Century*, that the binding force of parliamentary legislation came to be based "less from the fact that it had the sanction of the king in his court and more from the fact that every man in England was party and therefore privy to it." Jacob agreed, in his *History of the Fifteenth Century*, summarizing the tendency of the time as "the acceleration of the processes by which on the one hand the commons were gaining the initiative in parliament and on the other the secular lords, or a group of them, were developing a faculty for government and administration."

The gradual strengthening of the ability of the people to win consideration of their needs was aided by the growth of the colleges in the universities of Oxford and Cambridge and by the rapid increase in the number and quality of local grammar schools. The invention of printing accelerated literacy and encouraged learning. Education was coming to be conceived in more pragmatic terms as trade enhanced the need of merchants for managerial skills. The universities were induced to permit wider enrollment for middle-class families. The educated class was broadening, with the inevitable result that public opinion came to have more effect.

A major interpreter of the political changes was John Fortescue, a scholarly lawyer, who produced an influential work entitled *The Praise of the Laws of England*. In effect, he not only praised the common law but also considerably revised it. He served as chief justice of the King's Bench under Henry VI, and then, for his loyalty to the fallen house of Lancaster, he was exiled to France, where he made a close study of Roman law. Fortescue's devotion to the traditions of English common law led him to appreciate the great advantages of a constitutional, as opposed to an absolute, monarchy. The superiority of the English over the French, he concluded, lay primarily in the fact that in England the supremacy of law rests not on the royal will but upon the assent of the people. In his view, "the King exists for the sake of the kingdom and not the kingdom for the sake of the King. The politic King looks upon the exercise of his power as a duty, and actually glories in its limitation."[12]

Fortescue was not content, however, merely to celebrate English law; he also saw the need to change it and to change attitudes toward it. The major weakness of the common law was what was also the chief source of its strength—namely, its close dependence on local conditions, customs, and opinion. Juries were too little inclined to vote for the guilt of neighbors and friends. The reliance upon precedents led to interminable delays in searching them out and to increase the power of attorneys, who interpreted them. Too many of the guilty were going free, and the courts were clogged with cases awaiting trial. Because of such manifest problems, some advocated scrapping the common law to replace it with the Continental Justinian code. Fortescue argued successfully for solving the difficulties by establishing "prerogative courts" of superior jurisdiction, that would be unfettered by local prejudices. This was the origin of the Star Chamber and similar Chancery courts in which prompt judgment could be obtained.

Even more fundamentally, in chapter 13 of his massive work, Fortescue sought to clarify the essential function of law as the chief preservative of civilized society.

> The law, indeed, by which a group of men is made into a people, resembles the nerves of the body physical, for, just as the body is held together by the nerves, so this body mystical is held together and united into one by the law, which is derived from the word *ligando*, and the bones and the members of this body, which signify the solid basis of truth by which the community is sustained, preserve their rights through the law, as the body natural does through the nerves. And just as the head of the body physical is unable to change its nerves, or to deny its members proper strength and due nourishment of blood, so a king, who is head of the body politic is unable to change the laws of that body,

or to deprive that same people of their own substance, uninvited or against their wills. You have here, Prince, the form of the institution of the political kingdom.

Fortescue's arguments fitted the temper of the people and the distinctive qualities of the common law were preserved. In effect, "it stood for the best as well as the worst elements in the national character. It was disorderly and illogical, it eschewed generalization, but for all that it started not from the abstract privilege of the sovereign but from the concrete liberties of the individual."[13] It proved to be a balancing element that satisfied the people's needs.

The paragraph cited from Fortescue summarizes much of what was accomplished in political organizations as England emerged from medievalism, through the Renaissance, and on into the new age of the Tudors. Legality was enshrined as a set of rules that are implicit in nature and that are essential for the operations of society. Since law is a social necessity, it must not be violated—not by the king, not by the Parliament, not by the people. As Pecock and Colet had also done, Fortescue traced the basis for law to the Word of God, as found in the Bible, and as spelled out most explicitly in the saying by Jesus that "whatsoever ye would that men should do to you, do ye also unto them." This concept, Fortescue argued, is the "law of nature," and is therefore the foundation of equity. He might have added, as his work indicates, that it was also the guiding principle long established in the moot courts in which neighborhood disputes were settled. Most fundamentally, it described a structure within which problems were solved not by force but through discussion and concurrence. This is the "solid basis of truth by which the community is sustained."

In concluding this survey of the period, it was a time of ferment that liberated minds and of legislative developments that at least initiated the idea of representative government. It was also a time of turmoil and uncertainty. If Shakespeare was right in asserting that Agincourt represents the high tide of English patriotism, it was a tide that quickly receded. The successive Lancastrian and Yorkist kings who fought the Wars of the Roses were unable to maintain order or to nurture prosperity. In the opinion of one distinguished historian, it is "hard to escape the conclusion that in the fifteenth century England displayed the characteristics of a stagnant and declining civilization."[14] Another details some of the reasons, all stemming from governmental weakness: "The Justices of the Benches were retained in private interests, the justices of the peace were being made helpless by maintenances, the livery statutes were not kept, the elections of shire knights were corruptly managed, assize jurors were bought, the sheriffs were the tools of greater men, and, through their powers over juries, the law of the country was at their mercy."[15] In this kind of summation, it was a time of decay.

A far different interpretation arises from viewing the time rhetorically. It is true that politically the century was marked by failures. But it was a time of great success in the realm of the mind. Literacy was greatly expanding. There developed a growing spirit of individual assertiveness. The people were coming to believe that the problems that oppressed them were amenable to solution, if and only if they could be identified, understood, and submitted to the people's will. A cardinal fact that stands out is that never, after this time, was the legislative role of Parliament effectively denied. The Tudors worked with and through Parliament, rather than trying to avoid it. For a brief time the Stuarts were to try a different tack, which resulted in civil war and a parliamentary victory. The spirit of John Ball, on through the rising led by Jack Cade, was alight and could not be denied.

It was the saving grace of the period of transformation that in it developed the new view that not centralized and imposed rule but instead the common sense of what is just and right should and eventually would prevail. In essence, the period was preparatory for much that would follow. Contrary views were widely and earnestly discussed. The general opinion took on a new force. Even if means for accomplishing desired reforms were not available, at least a groundwork in public sentiment was being laid. This was the promise of that time to the future. This was its liberating rhetorical effect. In this sense, it was not a time of gloom but a prelude to hope. The king remained. The aristocracy remained. But the people, too, were coming to be heard. This was the balancing in interests that emerged.

Notes

1. Cited by Jacob, *Fifteenth Century*, p. 406.
2. According to D. L. Clark, *Rhetoric and Poetry in the Renaissance* (London: Russell and Russell, 1963), p. 68, the study of rhetoric as it had been shaped by Aristotle, Plato, Cicero, and Quintilian did not enter the schools until the seventeenth century; but a less formalized rhetoric, following the counsel of Augustine and Bede, was firmly entrenched in the fifteenth century (see Wilbur Samuel Howell, "Renaissance Rhetoric and Modern Rhetoric," in *The Rhetorical Idiom*, edited by Donald C. Bryant [Ithaca: Cornell University Press, 1958]).
3. Peter Heath, *The English Parish Clergy on the Eve of the Reformation* (London: Routledge and Kegan Paul, 1969), p. 8.
4. Jacob, *Fifteenth Century*, p. 269.
5. Ibid., p. 280.
6. J. J. Jusserand, *English Wayfaring Life in the Middle Ages*, translated by Lucy Toulmain Smith, 4th ed. (New York: Barnes and Noble, 1950), p. 159.
7. Heath, *English Parish Clergy*, pp. 70–73.
8. The quotations are from Wingfield-Stratford, *British Civilization*, pp. 342–43.
9. This interpretation of Colet, and also of Pecock, is supported by Arthur B. Ferguson, *Clio Unbound: Perception of the Social and Cultural Past in Renaissance England* (Durham, N.C.: Duke University Press, 1979), pp. 146–49, and 137. It is a significant revision of the admiring depiction presented by Seebohm's *Oxford Reformers*, which was long held to be the standard view.
10. Wingfield-Stratford, *British Civilization*, p. 271.

11. From a contemporary account, quoted by Jacob, *Fifteenth Century,* p. 630.
12. Wingfield-Stratford, *British Civilization,* p. 327.
13. Ibid., p. 329.
14. G. E. Elton, *England under the Tudors* (London: Methuen, 1962), p. 9.
15. This is the gloomy summation of J. E. A. Joliffe, *The Constitutional History of Medieval England* (Toronto: Macmillan, 1937).

4
New Problems, New Solutions—
The Professionalizing of Rhetoric

During the Tudor period, writers and speakers confronted rhetorical circumstances that challenged them with new problems and also with an enlargment of available solutions that they might fruitfully and sometimes safely discuss. The meanings that mattered both to individuals and to the society—mentally and emotionally—were changing swiftly. The need for interpretative guidance, the need to tell people what it all meant, became urgent. In consequence, there was an explosion of great literature and of meaningful discussion, debate, and persuasive discourse.

America was discovered, opening a whole New World to exploration and exploitation. Copernicus made a discovery of a different sort—that this earth is not the center of the universe—which demanded reconsideration of the traditional conviction that our planet is God's special and central concern. The consensus that had lasted with only modest variations since history began was shattered. A host of new problems had to be talked about, and old ones had to be reexamined. A new commonality of understandings had to be attained. This was the rhetorical challenge. For meeting it, a host of new facts had burst into awareness. New modes of thought were required. Some were accepted, some rejected, as renovation and traditionalism posed conflicting demands. Social values were essentially in flux, with new certainties desperately needed to replace old ones that were lost.

Waldo Frank, in his effort to dramatize the problem, pointed to the contrast offered by Dante's *Divine Comedy* and Cervantes' *Don Quixote*. (He might as well have noted the change from medieval miracle plays to the Elizabethan dramas.) "Note in Dante's story," he wrote, "*the lack of dissonance between the hero and his world*. Note it well, for in the centuries to come you will not meet with such harmony again. Suffering, struggle, and defeat there are; [but for Dante] they fuse into a general accord." The accord was such an absolute certainty of established belief that even the unfortunates who were condemned to an eternity of torture in hell fire accepted their fate as being both inevitable and just. No such consensus persisted when the old patterns of feudalism and orthodoxy broke apart. *"Don Quixote* is a tale of discord . . . between the hero and his world, between God and man, between Christian ideals and the human order."[1] The woeful knight tilting at windmills was not at home in his world. He could neither accept it nor change it. His own hell was within himself. His fate was not to be divinely damned but to be socially ridiculed and to feel himself to be morally and physically futile. The only recourse left to him was to dream imposible dreams and fight unbeatable foes. But since man can not live in a miasma of inevitable defeat, new goals had to be set and new methods for reaching them had to be devised. Articulate leadership was urgently required.

Historians have stretched their ingenuity to explain the depth and the spread of the changes that were taking place.[2] Man was in danger of being dehumanized, stripped of his pride of being a unique creation, forced to turn from the church to experience and to reason as his guides. The ideal of stability was challenged by a new ambition for progress. It was a search in which many could take part, for the treasure of knowledge, to which only the learned had held the key, became through print widely available. The impetus to a new kind of society was not only religious and philosophical but also economic and political.

Capitalism and commercial enterprise came to shake apart the ancient land-tenure relationships. Robin Hood as a popular hero was succeeded by Dick Whittington, who set out with his cat to win wealth abroad. The Horatio Alger saga of the rise from poverty began to be dreamed. The inevitability of privileges for the few came to be challenged. This challenge was posed by Sir Thomas More, in his *Utopia*, with a directness that matched the later advent of Marx and Lenin. "I can conceive nothing but a conspiracy of certain rich men," More wrote, "procuring their own commodities . . . while in the meantime poor laborers . . . should get so poor a living and lead so wretched and miserable a life, that the state and condition of the laboring beasts may seem much better and wealthier." Self-interest was emerging with a centrality such as had been formerly held by religious faith. New and different demands were being made upon the monarchy, the nobility, the Parliament, and the ecclesiastics. Such new ideas led to a new vigor of debate.

"Earthly Salvation through Endeavor and Reform"

The political structure responded to the changes not cataclysmally but gradually, and at best only partially. The first of the Tudors—Henry VII— who seized the throne from Richard III on the bloody battlefield of Bosworth, took up the discarded crown that Richard had dropped under a hawthorn bush and set it upon his own head with his own hands, not waiting for the consent of either Parliament or the church. But what he started with a battle, he cemented with reforms of administration. To bring orderliness out of the distractions of the long Wars of the Roses, he made peace with the aristocracy and sought to mollify the distraught populace. In significant ways, he was a Renaissance man. His complex personality combined Machiavellian cunning in controlling the aristocracy with a liberalizing encouragement of the spread of new ideas. His frugality in governing the kingdom was in sharp contrast with his love of luxury and his recognition of the value of conspicuous splendor as a means of emphasizing his role as leader. Instead of denying the right of Parliament to a role in government, he chose to dominate and to use it. He thereby set a pattern that the Tudor dynasty sought to maintain. His character was well summed up by the contemporary anonymous author of *Anglia Historia,* who concluded: "His mind was brave and resolute. . . . Withal he was not devoid of scholarship. . . . No one dared [to try] to get the better of him through deceit and guile." His quarter-century reign commenced a new orderliness, within which opinions contended actively.

How this new England appeared to the Dutch scholar Erasmus newly come over to Oxford, was described in a letter he wrote in 1499 to his friend Robert Fisher.

> Well, you will say, "how does our dear England suit you?" If you have any confidence in my word at all, dear Robert, pray believe me in this, that nothing ever pleased me as much. I found the climate here [meaning the intellectual climate] so very mild and healthful, and so much refinement and erudition, not of the trite and commonplace, but of the abstruse, accurate, and classic, both in Latin and Greek, that now I no longer sigh for Italy, except to visit it simply. When I hear my friend Colet I seem to be listening to Plato himself. Who dares not admire in Grocyn his absolute mastery of the sciences? What judgment more acute, more lofty, more penetrating than that of Linacre? Has nature ever created a gentler, sweeter, or happier character than that of Sir Thomas More? But why need I go over the rest of the catalog? It is wonderful to say what a widespread and dense crop of classical literature is flourishing here.

Among the Oxford humanists, whom Erasmus joined, animated talk was the way of life. Nor was such stimulating discussion confined to intellectual circles. The whole of Tudor England, through all its social classes and throughout its eleven decades, was a time of such innovative cultural changes as to invite a long, lingering look. Of course it was not all progressive. As is true of all times, there were crosscurrents and retrogressions, along with the advances. As A. L. Rowse, the overly enthusiastic biographer of Shakespeare and celebrator of the Age of Elizabeth, felt obliged to confess, "Since the times were harsh and treacherous," so too were the contenders for power and privilege "harsh and treacherous." Along with the brilliance of achievement, Rowse could not discount such negative factors as "the constraint, the watchfulness, and the latent savagery of the time."[3] No more than in the Athens of Socrates nor in the

Concord of Emerson was Tudor England without deep flaws. Nevertheless, the period was the breeder of such transcendent spirits as Christopher Marlowe and Philip Sidney, of William Shakespeare and Francis Bacon, of Thomas More and Walter Raleigh, and of such canny politicians as the Earl of Leicester and the Earl of Essex, along with the succession of such strong-willed and able monarchs as Henry VII, Henry VIII, Mary, and Elizabeth. It was a time of both fruition and exploratory innovation.

It is neither accidental nor incidental that the age stimulated exuberant ideas that reached for expression beyond the defensive boundaries of conservatism. Nothing nurtures assertive talk more surely than new visions that contend against reactionary constraints. Debate and evangelistic fervor flourished. Amid religious revolutionism, martyrdom became an honored way of death, as Catholic and Protestant antagonists shared the ardor illustrated in the words with which Hugh Latimer comforted his fellow sufferer, Nicholas Ridley, while they both burned in the town square of Oxford: "Be of good comfort, Mr. Ridley, and play the man! We shall this day light such a candle, by God's grace, in England, as I trust never shall be put out."[4] In many ways, on many fronts, and at great cost, the spirit of greatness was lighted in England during this glowing century.

In the broadest sense, it was a season of blossoming and of opening. A new literature and a new religion sprang into being. For the first time, stimulated by the writings of Amerigo Vespucci, English seafaring commenced its preliminary extensions into the New World of America and into the Far East. The theatre attained a height never before achieved and never afterward surpassed, in the richness of its variety surmounting even the Athens of Aeschylus, the France of Molière, and the London of George Bernard Shaw. The writing of poetry became an expected avocation even of statesmen. The urge of social reforms found advocates. The spirit of individualism opened new vistas for better living. As the long wars with France ended in retreat, the English looked with new zest toward the opportunities of the world across the seas. As the expansion of publishing provided both an impetus and a medium, intelligence grappled with new ideas. Minds expanded with new knowledge and were stimulated with fresh challenges. Parliament groped toward its eventual function of being the people's voice; happily, its debates were coming to be at least sketchily recorded. It is not improper to conclude that the long period of English adolescence was at last ripening to maturity.

"To Be Much Spoken of and Appreciated"

Utopia was envisioned. This book by Sir Thomas More, published in 1516, was written in Latin, for he sought to avoid trouble by addressing it solely to scholars. But the ideas in it were too revolutionary to be narrowly confined. It contained, as has been noted, not only a renovating protest denouncing "the conspiracy of the rich against the poor," but such shattering ideas as a call for the sharing of property and the limiting of the workday to nine hours. Nor was this all. Calling soldiers "men-slayers," he expressed a new hatred for war. With equal anger, he denounced the harsh old penal laws. Underlying this utopian vision was a belief in the innate goodness of man, which renounced the orthodox insistence upon original sin and thereby weakened dependence for salvation upon the concept that God had "mercifully" sacrificed his son to provide a medium of redemption. What More offered, instead, was the idea that mankind could and must seek to attain earthly salvation through endeavor and reform.

The new ideas were not only finding a wide audience, they were also encouraging a professionalization of rhetoric. Ideas were not only to be discussed, but the discussion should be with an orderliness and an artfulness that would make them effective. The old rhetoric of Aristotle, Cicero, and Quintilian had already come back into notice. As early as 1431 Aristotle's *Rhetoric* was listed among the books studied at Oxford. Richard Murphy's *Rhetoric in the Middle Ages* cites evidence that it was being read even earlier. He also points out that Aristotle's *Organon* had long been influential in Europe and that as far back as 1159 John of Salisbury was praising Aristotle's *Topica*. But it was in these Tudor times that Englishmen began developing rhetorical ideas of their own as an aid to solving the problems that abounded.

The initial efforts were at best cursory. In 1528 Tyndale started the trend with his book, *The Obedience of a Christian Man and How Christian Rulers Ought to Govern*. Roger Ascham followed, in 1545, with his *Toxophilus*, in which he argued for the general use of English that would be aimed at enhancing "the pleasure or commodities of the gentlemen and yeomen of Englande." The new trend led to the genuine professionalism of Thomas Wilson's *Art of Rhetoric*, published in 1553, in which he urged development of a direct and simplified style that would abjure "inkhorn terms" and "outlandish English" in favor of the simplicity and directness of Chaucer. More significantly, he recommended an active, correct, and artful mode of speaking by parliamentarians, preachers, and the rising class of businessmen as a means of influencing the responses of their listeners. In 1577 appeared Henry Peacham's *The Garden of Eloquence*, discussing devices of rhetorical style.

Actually, the new movement had commenced even earlier, chiefly as an attempt to teach the English to improve their manners, and was based upon Italianate models. The pleasures and the methods of social conversation were recommended in an outpouring of books that included *The Boke of Courtesye* in 1478, Erasmus's satiric *Praise of Folly* in 1511; *The Myrrour of Goode Manneres* in 1523; John Elyot's influential *Boke Called the Gouvernour* in 1531; Thomas Hoby's *Courtier* in 1561; and the better-remembered *Apologie for Poetrie* and *Arcadia*, by the "most perfect knight," Sir Philip Sidney.

The apex of these developments of rhetoric came in the *De Augmentis*

Scientiarum, by Francis Bacon, in which a complete system was presented for the first time. In it he depicted the art of inquiry or invention, the art of examination or judgment, the art of memory, and the art of elocution. All of these cumulated in the art of transmitting—"of producing and expressing to others those things which have been invented, judged, and laid up in the memory . . . This art includes all the arts that relate to words and discourse." He went on discuss such types of demonstration as the syllogism and the example, and above all, the imaginative appeal, which he believed to be the special function of rhetoric. Much of Bacon's influence came later and will be later discussed. But the spirit that animated him was very much alive even in early Tudor times.

As all these books attest, personal appearance, social manners, and behavior that aims to win approval and to exert influence were becoming increasingly important. "Henry VII likes to be much spoken of and to be highly appreciated by the whole world," the Spanish ambassador to the king's court wrote home to his own sovereign.[5] He might well have added that this desire had become quite general. It certainly was to prove characteristic of the successive Tudor monarchs, of their courtiers, and more broadly in other social circles. Sparkle, style, and sumptuous display were all means of communicating importance. And not only in the conniving atmosphere of the Tudor court but also among the middle-class merchants, seeming to be important was helpful to advancement and to self-defense.

The prevailing traditional sociopolitical theory was that God had created a natural order—the Great Chain of Being—within which everyone had an ordained place and function. This theory enshrined subordination, but also coordination. Superiors had privileges but also responsibilities. Harmony was valued as the basis for justice, with the guiding rule being to leave well enough alone. It was in this spirit that the robust and brilliant Henry VIII opened the Parliament of 1543 by assuring its members that "we at no time stand so high in our estate royal as in time of Parliament, wherein we as head and you as members are conjoined and knit together into one body politic." The image was in close accord with that employed a century earlier by Fortescue when he pictured the political structure as a body in which the musculature was directed by the nerves. In this image the central nervous system is supreme; even more significant, however, the whole body politic is a unity within which each part in its own functioning is essential to the health of the whole. The animating theory was stated by Tyndale in his *Christian Obedience:* "Be as fathers to your tenants, be unto them as Christ was unto us." No part of the social body could benefit except as all benefited. This was the theory, though the practice fell far short.

"If a Lion Knew His Strength, Hard Were It for Any Man"

The role Parliament played in this scheme of governance evolved slowly. Until well into the later Tudor period, it was customary to speak not of *the*

Parliament but of *a* Parliament. Its convening came at the call of the king, it came into being only by his request, and it ended when he dissolved it. During the reign of Edward III the sessions had been almost annual: forty-eight in a fifty-year span. During the Wars of the Roses, and on until after the death of Henry VIII, intervals of six to eight years passed between parliamentary sessions. The members were brought together only when the king needed what they—and they alone—could provide. What held the country together was a sense of commonality of interests that was both spiritual and temporal. As the Duke of Somerset asserted in 1549, seeking to surmount the disorders of the brief reign of the sickly boy, Edward VI, "society in a realm doth consist and is maintained by means of religion and law." Englishmen had for many centuries felt themselves bound by both of these sources of authority. The two were closely united, for law was derived from the basic moral precepts of the Christian faith as interpreted by the church. But the stresses precipitated during the reign of Henry VIII challenged this theory with its most vital test. Both law and religion were challenged. And religion, as the foundation and source, posed the central problems that had to be solved.[6]

Henry VIII was both a brilliant scholar and a good Catholic. When Martin Luther dissolved the ecclesiastical and political partnership of past centuries with the heretical pronouncements of his Ninety-five Theses, King Henry responded by writing a book, *Assertio Septem Sacermentum*, which stated the case of Catholicism so cogently that the pope hailed him as Defender of the Faith. Trouble for England developed when Henry's queen, Catherine of Aragon, failed to produce an heir, and Henry fell in love with Anne Boleyn. After she became pregnant, thus assuring the heir that he and his subjects urgently wanted, Henry determined to divorce Catherine and marry Anne. It was a simple matter that might well have been easily managed, had not international politics interfered. Popes had customarily allowed kings to change wives when this seemed necessary to procure a male heir. But the regnant pope, Clement VII, was virtually an instrument of Emperor Charles V, who was Catherine's nephew. Even so, a crisis could have been avoided had Cardinal Wolsey acted quickly, on his own authority, to sanction the divorce. But Wolsey, fearful of the political effects upon his own fortunes, determined to protect himself by passing the decision on to the pope. The ingredients of the problem were melodramatic, but the results shook England to its foundation. Wolsey was stripped of his political office as lord chancellor and escaped beheading by a timely death. In his place Henry appointed the highly respected Thomas More, but More disappointed the king by sturdily refusing to agree to the divorce. Henry not only went on with his plan to marry Anne but also tore the English Church away from its subordination to Rome. He indicted some fifteen leading clergymen and denounced the whole ecclesiastical establishment. To accomplish his aim, Henry turned for support to an obscure but scholarly Oxford don, Thomas Cranmer, who obediently sought to win approval from the English and European theologians for granting the divorce. As his reward, Cranmer was named archbishop of Canterbury. Henry named as lord chancellor a commoner, Thomas Cromwell, who was a merchant, a member of Parliament, and an aide to Wolsey. Pope Clement bowed to necessity and agreed to the divorce. Cranmer declared Henry's marriage to Catherine annulled, thereby permitting him to marry Anne Boleyn just in time to make their daughter, Elizabeth, legitimate. Thereupon, Cromwell energetically set about dismantling and reorganizing the English church, with Henry VIII as protector and supreme head of the Church of England and its clergy.

Religion was a vital force in the life of the people, and the nationwide discussion that broke out was animated and vigorous. In Cambridge the dons met in the White Horse Tavern to discuss the issues. Parliament obediently acceded to the reshaping of the church and the transfer of its revenues to the Crown. But opposition was organized, first by Thomas More, then by John Fisher, the bishop of Rochester, and the king's own cousin, Reginald Pole. King Henry mercilessly exercised the power he possessed. Pole escaped to the Netherlands; Fisher and More were imprisoned and were finally executed in 1535, almost a decade after the turmoil commenced; and scores of monks and friars died under torture for their stubbornness in clinging to their faith. The basic fact was well stated by Thomas More: "If a lion knew his strength, hard were it for any man to rule him."

During the next twelve years Henry VIII found reasons for more marriages, more divorces, and more executions. He also consolidated the power of the throne, submerged the vast public discontent, and maintained general stability. He dominated the Parliament, though without denying its right to function. As G. R. Elton concludes in *England under the Tudors*, these were the circumstances that "began the long struggle of the Commons for control over their own privileges and for the power of a court in ordering their own affairs."

"Too Few, Too Few, and Never So Few as Now"

The succeeding years were a time of bloody persecution but even more of rhetorical contention to search out a solution. The bulk of the populace had long been so resentful of the domination of the clergy over their lives that they accepted the shift of churchly authority from the pope to the king with little overt opposition. For the clergy themselves, the circumstances were tragic. Henry's successor, the young Edward VI, yielding to the strong influence of the Duke of Northumberland, undertook to root out Roman Catholicism with two successive Acts of Uniformity that were stringently enforced. After his death, the general populace, revolted by the tyrannical cruelty of Northumberland, readily gave support to Catherine's daughter, Queen Mary, as she set about vindicating her mother's reputation and returning England to the Catholic fold. One of her first acts was to prohibit the preaching of any sermons whatsoever pending enactment of new laws by Parliament to reestablish the Roman connection. She recalled Reginald Pole and made him archbishop of Canterbury. She convened successive annual Parliaments, which yielded to her demands to return the church to papal control. But the Parliament refused to restore to the church the properties that had been confiscated, for this would have required more taxes to replace the revenues the Crown would thereby have lost.

The queen also commenced a rooting out of heretics with a severity that caused her to be known as Bloody Mary. Among those who were burned at the stake for their faith, the most notable were John Rogers, who had edited Tyndale's translation of the Bible; John Hooper, who was ousted from his appointment as bishop of Worcester; the Oxonians Latimer and Ridley; and Archbishop Cranmer.

Illustrative of the rhetorical perils of the dilemma that confronted them, and others who could not avoid their leadership of speaking out, were the experiences of Hugh Latimer and Thomas Cranmer. Their importance is not that they were unique but that they were representative of the problems that devoted defenders of the faith could not avoid. To interpret rightly the rhetorical situation, it must be kept in mind that the price they had to pay in order to speak their minds was not merely the possibility that their persuasion might fall short of convincing their listeners, which is the chance that all speakers must take, but the virtual certainty that by becoming advocates they would lose their lives, and that their deaths would be miserably painful and under the imputation of social shame. Death at the stake was their only real prospect. Facing all of this, they still refused to acquiesce in proceedings that they believed were inimical to the will of God.

Hugh Latimer, a graduate of Cambridge University, grew to his maturity in the midst of theological debates—such as those that animated the evening meetings in Cambridge's White Horse Tavern. His troubles began when he chose to side with the king against the church, by arguing in favor of Henry VIII's right to divorce Catherine. For this he was condemned by the Catholic convocation and might have paid with his life had not the king interceded to protect him. The reward Henry granted to him was appointment as bishop of Worcester. But in this post he felt his responsibility to protect ecclesiastical rights that Henry's new dispensations were taking away, and this time he was in danger of secular indictment. To safeguard himself from prosecution he subsided into silence, doing no preaching for the next six years. His opinions, however, he refused either to renounce or to conceal, with the consequence that just before Henry's death he was arrested and imprisoned in the Tower of London. Edward VI pardoned him; then, in 1553, after Queen Mary's accession, he was again imprisoned. There ensued three years of disputation concerning his fate. The charges against him were based on heretical views that he had set forth in four sermons, the most notorious entitled "On the Plow," all preached in the conspicuous pulpit of Saint Paul's Cross in London, during the year 1548, during the reign of Edward VI.[7]

The tangled sequence of events reveals several significant factors affecting the rhetorical circumstances that ensnarled the clergy. For one thing, it was difficult to accommodate their views or their public declarations to the rapid and fundamental shifts of political control over the church. What was acceptable in one reign was treasonous, even retrospectively, in another. Perhaps even worse were the effects upon the minds and the consciences of devout ecclesiastics. Every effort they might make to be politically reasonable was not only liable to be futile but was also personally anguished as they felt their own inconsistency and resulting lack of integrity. Both of these difficulties oppressed Latimer and imposed upon him a necessity to try to explain his convictions and his public stands not only to the public but also to himself. These are the kinds of problems he wrestled with in his widely discussed sermon, "On the Plow."

Opening his sermon, Latimer told his congregation, "I purposed to declare unto you two things. The one, what seed should be sown in God's field, in God's plow land; and the other, who should be the sowers." The analogy was crude, and Latimer felt the need to justify it. His likening of preaching to a plowman's labor he defended as being comparable to Christ's comparison of faith to a mustard seed. No offense should be taken for, "as preachers must be wary and circumspect that they give not any just occasion to be slandered and ill-spoken of by the hearers, so must not the auditors be offended without cause." He further justified his analogy by pointing out that preachers and plowers alike must work at all seasons and do many kinds of work. The evil that oppressed him was that "few of them there be throughout this realm that give meat to their flocks as they should do. . . . Too few, too few; the more is the pity, and never so few as now."

This sense of his duty he had come to see only gradually and reluctantly, but by now he felt certain of where it led him. He could not avoid speaking out to denounce the evils of political interference with the church. He could no longer evade his responsibility to do his best to try to salvage the sanctity of sincere faith. With this new clarity in his own understanding, he set forth what he believed directly, with no subterfuge, realizing fully the price he would have to pay for his seditious words:

> But this much I dare say, that since lording and loitering hath come up, preaching hath come down, contrary to the apostles' times; for they preached and lorded not, and now they lord and preach not. For they that be lords will go ill to plow; it is no meet office for them; it is not

seeming for their estate. Thus came up lording loiterers; thus crept in unpreaching prelates; and so have they long continued. For how many unlearned prelates have we now at this day! And no marvel: For if the plowmen that now be were made lords, they would clean give over plowing; they would leave off their labour, and fall to lording outright, and let the plow stand; and then with plows not walking, nothing should be in the commonweal but hunger. For ever since the prelates were made lords and nobles, the plow standeth; there is no work done; the people starve.

So much for his charge. It was clearly stated. Too many churchmen had forsworn their spiritual leadership. Too many had sold out in order to gain benefits for themselves. But far from leaving it at this, he launched into a veritable frenzy of denunciation, partly to relieve his own conscience for his own six years of quiet acquiescence, and partly to emphasize his point so urgently that it would be remembered and might have effect.

Well, well, is this their office? Is this their calling? Should we have ministers of the church to be controllers of the mint? Is this a meet office for a priest that hath cure of souls? Is this his charge? I would here ask one question: I would fain know who controlleth the devil at home in his parish, while he controlleth the mint? . . .
Oh that our prelates would be as diligent to sow the corn of good doctrine, as Satan is to sow cockle and durnel! And this is the devilish plowing, the which worketh to have things in Latin, and letteth the fruitful edification. But here some men will say to me, What, Sir, are ye so privy to the devil's counsel, that ye know all this to be true? Truly, I know him too well, and have obeyed him a little too much in condescending to some follies.

Having thus salved his own troubled soul by this admission, and well knowing the heavy cost of taking so resolute a stand, Latimer launched forthrightly on to his conclusion.

Wo worth thee, O devil, wo worth thee, that hast prevailed so far and so long; that hath made England to worship false gods, forsaking Christ their Lord. Wo worth thee, devil, wo worth thee, devil, and all thy angels. If Christ by his death draweth all things to himself, and draweth all men to salvation, and to heavenly bliss, that trust in him; then the priests at the mass, at the popish mass, I say, what can they draw, when Christ draweth all, but lands and goods from the right heirs? The priests draw goods and riches, benefices and promotions to themselves. . . . These be the Italian bishop's devices, and the devil hath pricked at this work to frustrate the cross of Christ.

This sermon, which was printed and came into wide discussion, clarified and sharpened issues that had to be understood and confronted before they could be solved. Was ritual or was preaching the proper function of the church? Should ritual and preaching be in Latin, thereby demanding acceptance without understanding, or should it be in the vernacular? Should Englishmen be subject to Italianate methods and controls? Above all, were matters of religion available for discussion? Should they be debated and examined by the people? Might ecclesiastics properly devote their learning and their talents to government, thereby receiving very tangible and considerable benefits for themselves, or should they remain stubbornly resistant to political pressures and scornful of political rewards? Such was the broadening of the range of religious discussion that Latimer demanded—and this at the very time when the severest of penalties had to be paid for any deviation from religious views and forms that the government ordained. And these claims he continued to insist upon, even after the restoration of Catholicism during the reign of Queen Mary. He continued in his defiant independence even while bound to the stake, where he was burned to death on 16 October 1555. To him England is indebted for his defense of the liberty of conscience and of freedom to discuss whatever an individual believes, however unpopular or even unlawful it may be.

Thomas Cranmer was among those who watched, from the rooftop of Bocardo jail, while Latimer and his companion Ridley suffered their painful deaths. As has been noted earlier, Cranmer supported Henry VIII's break with Rome and was rewarded with appointment as archbishop of Canterbury. When Edward VI died, Cranmer supported Lady Jane Grey, the Protestant claimant to the throne. Two months after the accession of Queen Mary, Cranmer was arrested and confined in the Tower. His trial was delayed for two and a half years, while he was allowed to defend himself and was urged to recant his heretical views. In February 1556, he was stripped of his title of archbishop and condemned to the flames. His contributions to the Reformation had included his preparation of the Book of Common Prayer and his sponsorship of the Great Bible in the 1539 translation. He had interceded as best he could to try to prevent the execution of Latimer, Sir Thoms More, and Bishop Fisher. His greatest failure, as he himself came to believe, had been his advocacy of the supremacy of the State over the Church. His views included a commingling of contrarities, which are sometimes interpreted as an effort to keep himself safely on the winning side in the convolutions of change.

When he came to his own execution, he was permitted to speak for himself from a platform erected in Saint Mary's Church, a few steps from the place in Oxford's Broad Street where he was shortly to be burned. The speech he gave was brief, for it was rudely interrupted, but in the few words he was allowed to utter he attempted to justify the mixture of his words and his acts that represented a confusion shared by many in his time. What was right and true and holy under the turbulent circumstances was not easily to be understood.

During the long course of his trial, Cranmer had drawn up and signed "six recantations" of his errors. The permission granted to him to speak before his execution was in expectation that he would confirm this concession, thereby justifying the sentence of death passed against him. At first he seemed to be doing as his prosecutors desired. He urged the people "to obey your king and queen willingly and gladly, without murmuring or grudging; not for fear of them only, but much more for fear of God, knowing that they be God's ministers." Next he pleaded for all to live in brotherly love, forbearing "contention and hatred." So far he satisfied his jailers, saying what they wished. Then his speech took a different turn.

> And now, forasmuch as I am come to the last end of my life, whereupon hangeth all my life past and all my life to come, either to live with my Master Christ for ever in joy, or else to be in pain for ever with wicked devils in hell, and see before mine eyes presently either heaven ready to receive me, or else hell ready to swallow me up; I shall therefore declare unto you my very faith, how I believe, without any colour or dissimulation, for now is no time to dissemble, whatsoever I have said or written in times past.

This much his judges could hear without offense. But then Cranmer hurried on, seizing the slim chance he had to leave his legacy of renunciation of the conformity that had won for him the ermine robes of the archbishopric.

> And now I come to the great thing that so much troubleth my conscience, more than anything that I ever did or said in my whole life, and that is the setting abroad of a writing contrary to the truth; which now here I renounce and refuse.

In the few more words he was allowed to speak, he abjured the recantation he had written in the Tower. And since his hand had written it, "contrary to my heart," he promised that his right hand should first of all be burned. As this meaning emerged, Cranmer's principal jailer, Henry Cole, provost of Eton, cried out, "Stop the heretic's mouth, and take him away!" At the stake, true to his word, Cranmer steadfastly held his right hand in the flames until he died.

Such was the cost of speaking out against the dominance of the State over religious beliefs. Just as both Latimer and Cranmer came only hesitantly to the dangerous and costly public assertion of their true convictions, and just as both of them wrestled internally with themselves concerning what they should believe and whether they dared to espouse it, so too was the problem as it confronted many clergymen during this period of cataclysmic changes from Catholicism to Protestantism, then back to Catholicism, and once more to Protestantism, all within the space of a single generation, and all under the stern control of a monarchy that exacted the hardest of punishment for refusal to shift as the State shifted.

What should, and what could, the preachers say? How could they adjust to the puzzled and mixed expectations of their congregations? Far more than on the Continent, the meaning of religion had been brought to the bar of reason and of personal interpretation. A Pandora's box had been opened, to unleash individualism, vernacularism, and the democratization of knowledge. Once these forces were let loose, they created a cultural diversity within the country that threatened to tear apart the sentiments of nationalism. To the great credit of Englishmen, they somehow found a preservative middle way. The church would remain catholic, but at its head would not be the pope but the king. The rituals of the church service would largely retain their old familiar forms. What was to be followed would be, as it had been, the way of Christ—carefully subject to interpretation by the priests, thereby safeguarding their basic function. Still, the solution was far from neat or clear; the rational, personal, and democratic tendencies that had been introduced led into a new era in which the struggle would not be between the Established Church and the Church Universal, but would become a spiritual civil war among contending sects.

During and after the long reign of Elizabeth I, religious controversies raged unabated: not between Catholic and Protestant, but as disputes among rapidly evolving devout, and even fanatic, denominations. For another two centuries Catholicism was driven underground, but still doctrinal differences remained acute. Henceforth, the English pulpit would have two quite diverse functions. One was, as of old, to superintend the salvation of believers. The other was to define and to defend the very nature of belief. Different interpretations led to bitter divisiveness. Shepherds of the Faith became Warriors of the Word. Religion became a battlefield on which hatred was often more evident than love. This was Reformation with a vengeance.

"No Orator as Brutus Is"

Along with the Reformation, it was chiefly the Renaissance that led the English into changes that created greatness. Translations abounded, not only of classical Greek and Latin works but also of contemporary European writings. Much was learned from the past and from abroad, but there was also a great fruition of native traditions. "The English character was . . . too definite and too insular merely to reflect a foreign country."[8] The means by which translations assisted, rather than dominated, genuinely English attitudes is well illustrated in the plays of William Shakespeare. He utilized the materials of others—but in ways that were superbly his own and typically English. This, too, was part of the middle way that emerged.

Shakespeare's contributions to the professionalizing of rhetoric were considerable. He realized and crystallized the cardinal fact that public address is of enormous consequence in the direction of affairs. And he also illustrated the kinds of persuasive skills that were available and showed vividly the kinds of effects that they produce. Few rhetoricians have understood better than he the nature of rhetorical situations, and still fewer have so vividly and convincingly manifested the effects that sheer persuasive skill may produce. Again and again his plays present circumstances in which words well spoken were the best, if not indeed the only means for solving problems.

Not unnaturally, his *Julius Caesar,* set in the time of Rome's greatest oratorical period, showed how in a crisis it was not by force but by eloquence that the course of events was decisively determined. It was not the slaying of Caesar or the massing of military forces, but the debate between Brutus and Antony that shaped the circumstances that prevailed. With full confidence in his own powers of persuasion and in the justice of his cause, Brutus accepted Antony's request to discuss in the Forum the merit of what the conspirators had done.[9] The debate that ensued illustrated the sophistication of rhetorical skills that had come into development. It merits detailed analysis.

Brutus stated his justification of the assassination only casually and briefly, confident of the public approval with which it had been immediately rewarded: "Not that I loved Caesar less, but that I loved Rome more." Like all Romans he admired Caesar; more than this, he and the general-turned-dictator were personal friends. "As Caesar loved me, I weep for him; as he was fortunate, I rejoice at it; as he was valiant, I honour him; but as he was ambitious, I slew him." That was his case; and as all Rome knew, it was a good one.

Then enter Mark Antony—and Brutus made the fatal mistake of allowing Antony to speak. What persuasion can accomplish Shakespeare manifested through an ingenious motivational sequence. It commenced with the speaker identifying himself wholly with his listeners, including the patriotic assassins: "I come to bury Caesar, not to praise him." The circumstances were clear, with nothing controversial.

> The evil that men do lives after them,
> The good is oft interred with their bones;
> So let it be with Caesar.

But then he interjected just a touch of doubt, a mere shadow of questioning, even a hint of sarcasm, yet still nothing controversial except for an intriguing "if".

> The noble Brutus
> Hath told you that Caesar was ambitious;

> If it were so, it was a grievous fault,
> And grievously hath Caesar answer'd it.

But let it be; the "if" was no more than tantalizing; Antony quickly brushed it aside, with a word of praise for the slayers.

> Here, under leave of Brutus and the rest,—
> For Brutus is an honourable man;
> So are they all, all honourable men,—
> Come I to speak in Caesar's funeral.

What came next was a swift but very natural transition—from what any friend would say of another to a cogent reminder of the debt that all owed to their leader who had been slain.

> He was my friend, faithful and just to me:
> But Brutus says he was ambitious;
> And Brutus is an honourable man.
> He hath brought many captives home to Rome
> Whose ransom did the general coffers fill;
> Did this in Caesar seem ambitious?

If Brutus had remained on the scene he might well at this point have stepped forward to pluck Antony by the sleeve and to suggest that he had said enough; but overconfidently Brutus had left the Forum to Antony, to deal with the citizens as best he could. Antony had established the ground he wanted and confidently went forward on it.

> When that the poor have cried, Caesar hath wept;
> Ambition should be made of sterner stuff:
> Yet Brutus says he was ambitious;
> And Brutus is an honourable man.
> You all did see that on the Lupercal
> I thrice presented him a kingly crown,
> Which he did thrice refuse; was this ambition?
> Yet Brutus says he was ambitious;
> And, sure, he is an honourable man.
> I speak not to disprove what Brutus spoke,
> But here I am to speak what I do know.
> You all did love him once, not without cause;
> What cause withholds you then to mourn for him?

No more than a doubt had been suggested—a doubt whether the conspirators had been entirely wise, along with the reminder that their long-held devotion to Caesar had not been without sound reason. Antony paused, to allow time for this reaction to crystallize. Then thoughtfully he continued.

> But yesterday the word of Caesar might
> Have stood against the world; now lies he there,
> And none so poor to do him reverence.
> O masters!* If I were dispos'd to stir
> Your hearts and minds to mutiny and rage,
> I should do Brutus wrong, and Cassius wrong†
> Whom you all know are honourable men.
> I will not do them wrong; I rather choose
> To wrong the dead, to wrong myself, and you,
> Than I will wrong such honourable men.

By this time Antony sensed that the way was prepared for a major transition—and he made it boldy through an appeal to simple greed.

> But here's a parchment with the seal of Caesar;
> I found it in his closet, 'tis his will.
> Let but the commons hear this testament,—
> Which, pardon me, I do not mean to read,—
> And they would go and kiss dear Caesar's wounds,
> And dip their napkins in his sacred blood,
> Yea, beg a hair of him for memory.
> And, dying, mention it within their wills,
> Bequeathing it as a rich legacy
> Unto their issue.

Inevitably the listeners demanded to have the will read; Antony, holding it back from them, continued to intimate its contents, as a stimulus to their imaginations. Finally, after yielding to their demand to know of Caesar's generous bequest, he came to his emotionally climactic conclusion.

> If you have tears, prepare to shed them now.
> You all do know this mantle; I remember
> The first time ever Caesar put it on:
> 'Twas in a summer evening, in his tent,
> That day he overcame the Nervii:—
> Look! on this place ran Cassius' dagger through:
> See what a rent the envious Casca made:
> Through this the well-beloved Brutus stabb'd;
> And as he plucked his cursed blade away
> Mark how the blood of Caesar followed it.

The whole tone of the speech was transformed. From being honourable men, the assassins were degraded into simple murderers, envious betrayers of the leader who had loved as well as led them. Antony stepped

---

*A sharp reminder that it is they, not the conspirators, who have the right to judge.
†Another reminder—that the noble Brutus had associates of lesser nobility.

back, withdrew, and then once more plunged ahead, knowing that he had now won his audience.

> I come not, friends, to steal away your hearts;
> I am no orator as Brutus is;
> But, as you know me all, a plain blunt man,
> That loves my friend: and that they know full well
> Who gave me public leave to speak of him,
> For I have neither wit, nor words, nor worth,
> Action, nor utterance, nor any power of speech,
> To stir men's blood; I only speak right on:
> To tell you that which you yourselves do know,
> Show you sweet Caesar's wounds, poor poor dumb mouths,
> And bid them speak for me; but were I Brutus,
> And Brutus Antony, there were an Antony
> Would ruffle up your spirits, and put a tongue
> To every wound of Caesar, that should move
> The stones of Rome to rise and mutiny.

Shakespeare knew well his Elizabethan audience: knew their mingling of admiration for eloquence and also their suspicion of it; knew that they would respond to persuasion while preferring to believe that they were superior to it; knew that one way of winning their assent was by asserting that the eloquence lay all on the side of the opposition and that what they responded to was not oratory but simple reason and fact. And he knew also the nature of rhetorical circumstances, wherein the only kind of action that is truly effective is the skilled use of motivational speech. These kinds of insight led him to highlight dramatic climaxes again and again in his plays with effective emotional appeals: with Henry V's arousal of his men at Agincourt, with Portia's plea in the defense of her lover, with Hamlet's sly stimulus that turned the Danish court against his mother and stepfather, with Coriolanus's justifications of his tyranny. In play after play, in the comedies and tragedies and histories alike, the popular Avon dramatist demonstrated repeatedly how decisively and how frequently the course of affairs is shaped by eloquence. What he most clearly showed was the professionalization that rhetoric had attained. The rhetoricians explained the processes; Shakespeare illustrated them.

"To Maintain the Freedom and Consultation of Speech"

The role of persuasion during the Tudor era is well exemplified in a speech that was delivered by Peter Wentworth, in the House of Commons, on 8 February 1576. Wentworth was a Puritan, one of the new breed of Dissenters whose aim was to enlarge civil liberties and particularly the liberty of conscience. The speech he gave was one that, as he said, he had been preparing through a course of some three years. Its theme was the necessity of defending at all costs the freedom of debate in Parliament. "I will never hold my tongue," he commenced, on any occasion "wherein God is dishonoured, the Prince periled, or the liberties of Parliament impeached."

His introductory statements were blunt. "Sweet is the name of liberty, but the thing itself is above all estimable treasure." He had been a member, he pointed out, for only two sessions—"at both of which times I saw the liberty of free speech, the which is the only salve to heal the sores of this Commonwealth, so much and so many times infringed . . . as hath much grieved me." The goal he urged the members to pursue was to insure that "all things that do hinder it [be] removed, repulsed, and taken away." Such counsel, he pointed out, was not rebellious, for "loving subjects" will always support what is helpful to the State and will oppose what threatens to harm it. But what of others not loving—what of evil or irresponsible speakers who might urge a course that is perilous? Even they should be heard without restraint. For, "a wicked purpose may the easier be prevented if it is known." The issue he raised was fundamental. Unless there is freedom of discussion, "it is a very scorn and mockery to call it a Parliament House, for in truth it is none but a very school of flattery and dissimulation."

With typical Puritan vigor, Wentworth plunged on. There are, he said, two things that "do great harm in this place . . . Take heed what you do; the Queen likes not such a matter . . . The other: sometimes a message is brought into the House, either of commanding or inhibiting." Concerning both factors, "I would to God, Mr. Speaker, these two were burned in hell—I mean rumors and messages, for wicked they undoubtedly are." To resist the demands by the Crown, he went on, is sometimes the highest form of patriotism. "Many a time it falleth out that a Prince may favor a cause perilous to himself and the whole State. What are we then if we follow the Prince's mind? Are we not unfaithful unto God, our Prince, and State? Yes, truly; we are chosen of the whole realm, of a special trust and confidence by them, reposed in us, to foresee all such inconveniences." Blind loyalty was false to their function. "Love, even perfect love, void of all dissimulation, will not suffer me to hide them to Her Majesty's peril, but to utter them to Her Majesty's safety. . . . And then Her Majesty will stand where her enemies have fallen: for no estate will stand where the Prince will not be governed by advice." With great clarity he restated his theme: "It is a great and special part of our office, Mr. Speaker, to maintain the freedom and consultation of speech; for by this good laws that do set forth God's glory and for the preservation of the Prince and State are made."

Wentworth's speech is a landmark in the development of the nation—more assertive of the responsibility and the right of parliamentary participation in the shaping of policy than had previously been claimed. The freedom of debate upon which Wentworth insisted was not yet granted. Before he was ready to conclude, he was shouted down and forced to desist. But the influence of his speech spread. A text of it was preserved and was printed, finally, in 1682, in Sir Simonds D'Ewes's *Journal of all the Parliaments during the Reign of Queen Elizabeth*. The issue that he raised was clear-cut: When there was a conflict of views between the king and the Parliament, which should prevail? The settlement of the issue was postponed for some two generations, and even after the Puritan Revolution the question remained uncertain for more than another century. But it remained a theme that had to be discussed.[10]

Only eight years after Wentworth was forced to step down, the issue again became central, at the opening of a new Parliament in December 1584. The nation was by then so distraught by religious turmoil that Parliament was determined to assert a role in curbing it. After weeks of maneuvering, on 27 February, a parliamentary delegation visited Queen Elizabeth to present their case. Elizabeth was ready to meet their challenge. As is amply shown by J. E. Neale, in his two-volume study, *The Elizabethan House of Commons* and *Elizabeth I and Her Parliaments*, Elizabeth was herself shrewdly persuasive, and she was well aware that persuasion is a better instrument of government than is force.

In her colloquy with the parliamentary delegates she demonstrated both her knowledge and her rhetorical skill. In this, as in her many other speeches, she utilized persuasiveness as a principal bulwark of the Crown. With canny skill she parried their arguments and reinterpreted the admitted facts in a way that suited her needs. The ills of which they complained were real; she not only admitted them, she confirmed them. But where lay the fault? It was not, she insisted, with the monarch but with some members of Parliament, who were not being sufficiently restrained by the loyal and sensible majority. This was the root of the problem that she, as well as they, felt the need to remedy. Let the Parliament pass laws of greater severity to enforce conformity, and all would be well with the realm.

> Again you suffer many ministers to preach what they list and to minister the sacraments according to their own fancies, some one way, some another, to the breach of unity; yea, and some of them so curious in searching matters above their capacity as they preach what they wot not what—that there is no Hell but a torment of conscience. Nay, I have heard there be six preachers in one diocese the which do preach six sundry ways. I wish such to be brought to conformity and unity; that they administer the sacraments according to the order of this Realm and preach all one truth; and that such as be found not worthy to preach, be compelled to read the homilies . . . for there is more learning in one of those than in twenty of some of their sermons. And we require you that

you do not favor such men, being carried away with pity, hoping of their conformity, and inclining to noblemen's letters and gentlemen's letters, for they will be hanged before they will be reformed.

What Elizabeth was saying—and the fact that she was saying it as persuasion rather than as a royal command—provides an enlightening view into what had come to pass in England during the Tudor times. The Parliament to which she addressed herself was not hers but the realm's. Moreover, the unleasing of a diversity of opinions, and the public discussion of them, had led to a new spirit of self-assertiveness and to a pluralistic society. Even though she used the phrase "we require you," it is clear that the relationship between the throne and the legislature had become such that she had to induce rather than demand obedience to her will. She had to adduce reasons that would be convincing. She did not send a simple command to the Parliament, but rather received its delegation, listened to its arguments, and replied with arguments of her own.

In the last of Elizabeth's Parliaments, convened on 27 October 1601, the role of persuasive intercourse had come into even sharper focus. William Cecil, whose wise counsels had served the kingdom well, was dead. The self-willed Earl of Essex had been executed. Ireland was again in revolt and this time was assisted by a Spanish army that had landed on its coast. Elizabeth was near seventy, in ill health, and well aware that she had not much longer to live. In order to repel the Spanish invaders, she needed money, and Parliament was determined to strengthen its own authority before granting it. John Croke, newly elected Speaker of the Commons, opened its session with an ornate speech of fawning adulation, assuring the queen that "God hath placed you by Himself." These opening remarks were followed by a similarly obsequious speech by the lord keeper, Thomas Edgerton, who tried to reconcile the freedom Parliament exercised with the ultimate authority of the Crown.

> For freedom of speech, her Majesty willingly consenteth thereunto, with this caution: that the time be not spent in idle and vain matters, painting the same out with froth and volubility of words. And her Majesty commandeth that you suffer not any speeches made for contention or contradiction sake, maintained only by a tempest of words, whereby the speakers may seem to gain some reputed credit by emboldening themselves by contradiction, and by troubling the House to no purpose, with long and vain orations, to hinder the proceedings in matters of great and more weighty importance.

The effort to control the freedom of discussion that had been won was in vain. More speeches followed, spoken by members who insisted upon the right to speak their minds. Bills were introduced to limit the Crown's control over monopolies. Then Francis Bacon arose. He pleaded for moderation, reminding the members that the Queen "hath power by her patents to set at liberty things restrained by statute-law or otherwise." Do not, he urged, force a confrontation between themselves and their monarch. Instead, he recommended pleading for the reforms they wanted rather than demanding them.

The essential fact was clear: that parliamentary restraints had to be argued for rather than commanded. Nor did the Parliament surrender the independence it had won. John Bennet, member for York, replied to Bacon that "as I think it no derogation to the omnipotency of God to say that He can do ill, so I think it no derogation to Her Majesty or person of the Queen to say the like." Francis Moore, a lawyer who represented Reading, sought to bring the debate to a practical point.

> I cannot utter with my tongue or conceive with my heart the great grievances that the town and country for which I serve suffer from some of these monopolies. It bringeth the general profit into a private hand; and the end of all is beggary and bondage to the subject.

The debate continued for a full month, often becoming acrimonious. At its conclusion a compromise was adopted: The authority of the Crown to establish monopolies was confirmed, but the queen must promise that they would be curtailed. On 30 November a delegation from Parliament assembled before the queen to hear what became known as her Golden Speech, by which she sought to restore unity and to strengthen loyalty. Her remarks were delivered extempore, with great skill in both their composition and their presentation. Like Shakespeare's Mark Antony, Elizabeth began conciliatorily, seeming to submit. Then, through a fine motivational sequence, she proceeded to her affirmation that the authority of the monarch was beyond the reach of parliamentary control. On the queen's authority, her speech was published, to give it a wider audience. It continued to be cited often during the disputes that marked the succeeding generations. Her persuasive appeal was carefully patterned: from conciliation to self-justification, to admission of Parliament's basic reasonableness, and on to more self-justification.

> I do assure you there is no prince that loves his subjects better.... There is no jewel, be it of never so rich a price, which I set before this jewel: I mean your love.... Therefore, I have cause to wish nothing more than to content the subject; and that is a duty which I owe....
>
> Of myself, I must say this: I never was any greedy, scraping grasper, not a strait, fast-holding Prince, nor yet a waster. My heart was never set on any worldly goods, but only for my subjects' good. What you bestow on me, I will not hoard it up, but receive it to bestow on you again....
>
> I am not so simple to suppose, but that there be some of the Lower House whom these grievances never touched; and for them, I think they spake out of zeal to their countries, and not out of spleen or malevolent

affection as being parties grieved; and I take it exceedingly gratefully from them, because it gives us to know that no respects or interest had moved them, other than the minds they had to suffer no dissimulation of our honour and our subjects' love for us. The zeal of which affection, tending to ease my people and knit their hearts unto me, I embrace with a princely care. . . .

I have ever used to set the Last-Judgment Day before mine eyes, and so to rule as I shall be judged to answer before a higher Judge, to whose judgment seat I do appeal, that never thought was cherished in my heart that tended not to my people's good.

Then, having done her best to make evident her good intentions, Queen Elizabeth came to her conclusion, in which she pleaded for sympathy and understanding—a far different tone than the "we require you" mode she had felt it proper to use seventeen years earlier.

To be a King and wear a crown is a thing more glorious to them that see it, than it is pleasant to them that bear it. . . .

There will never Queen sit in my seat with more zeal to my country, care for my subjects, and that will sooner with willingness venture her life for your good and safety, than myself. For it is my desire to live nor reign no longer than my life and reign shall be for your good. And though you have had and may have many more princes more mighty and wise sitting in this seat, yet you never had nor shall have any that will be more careful and loving.

Her concluding words, however, were not to beg for their forbearance but to request their submissive obedience.

And so I commit you all to your best fortunes and further counsels. And I pray you, Mr. Comptroller, Mr. Secretary, and you of my Council, that before these gentlemen go into their countries, you bring them all to kiss my hand.

So it ended.[11] During not only the next decade but also on through the following centuries, this Golden Speech was reprinted many times, inspiring many readers (or so Neale believes) to "look back nostalgically to the spacious days of Gloriana." G. W. O. Woodward found, in this speech and in her reign, the essential meaning that "Elizabeth I had of necessity a profound respect for her Parliaments. They had found their strength, and were learning to make use of it. The Queen never openly flouted their wishes."[12]

The parliamentary debates of the time reveal the uncertain and shifting yet progressive development during the Tudor dynasty of a growth toward representative government—sometimes advancing, sometimes retreating; at times boldly assertive, at times submissive. At the end of Elizabeth's reign the monarchy remained supreme, but no longer beyond question and challenge. Its authority remained, but hedged by the necessary recognition that the welfare and the will of the subjects must be accorded full respect. It was left to the following century to test how the authority of the Crown and the restraining power of the Parliament might be defined.

Notes

1. Waldo Frank, *The Re-Discovery of America* (New York: Scribners, 1926), pp. 49–50.
2. See, for example, Wingfield-Stratford, *British Civilization*, pp. 293–406.
3. A. L. Rowse, *The English Spirit* (New York: Macmillan, 1945), pp. 89, 90. For a confirmatory view, and for multiple instances of the brutality of the time, see G. R. Elton, *Reform and Reformation: England, 1509–1558* (Cambridge: Harvard University Press, 1977).
4. Perhaps this brave little speech is no more than legendary. It was first recorded by John Foxe, in the third edition of his *Acts and Monuments of These Later and Perilous Days*, three decades after it was supposed to have been spoken. At least it is true to the spirit of many who went with dignity and courage to the flames or to the block for their outspoken advocacy of their beliefs.
5. Cited by Catherine Gavin, *The Great Tudors* (London: Eyre and Spottiswoode, 1956), p. 15.
6. For further consideration of the problem, see Conrad Russell, *The Crisis of Parliaments: English History, 1509–1660* (Oxford University Press, 1971), particularly pp. 38–45.
7. See Allan G. Chester, *Selected Sermons of Hugh Latimer* (Charlottesville: University of Virginia Press, 1968).
8. Legouis and Cazamian, *History of English Literature*, p. 258.
9. See George Kennedy, "Antony's Speech at Caesar's Funeral," *Quarterly Journal of Speech* 54 (April 1968): 99–106.
10. For Wentworth's influence, see Faith Thompson, *A Short History of Parliament, 1295–1642* (Minneapolis: University of Minnesota Press, 1953), pp. 182–86.
11. Neale's "Parliament of 1601," from which this account is compounded, is from his second volume, *Elizabeth I and Her Parliaments* (New York: St. Martin's Press, 1958), which was largely dependent upon a journal kept by Harry Townsend, a young lawyer who represented Shropshire in the Commons.
12. G. W. O. Woodward, *Reformation and Resurgence: England in the Sixteenth Century* (London: Blandford Press, 1963), p. 59.

5
Crisis and Confrontation—Determining the Mastery

The two great verbal confrontations of the seventeenth century were the trials of Thomas Wentworth, the Earl of Strafford, and of the king, Charles I. These were part of the great Civil War, which in its military phases was notable for heroism, sieges, and bloodshed. The vital struggles, however, were the trials, which exhibited stratagems and ambuscades, cruelties and heroism of their own kind. The climax was shattering: The English killed their king. High-handed as the proceedings were, they presented the usual pattern of prosecution and defense—in a strange and unfamiliar guise.

The monarchy was soundly rooted in the affections of the people, regardless of whether they liked a particular monarch. What held their loyalty was institutional, not personal. After 1066 few of their kings were native. They were Normans from France, Tudors from Wales, Stuarts from Scotland—just as, afterward, they were to be a Hollander from Nassau and Germans from Hanover. The bonds that united the masses of the people, the nobility, and the throne were the outgrowth of centuries. Now in this century there arose a new class—the nouveau riche—with its own interests, which did not fit naturally into the traditional hierarchy. It is understandable that a struggle developed to determine the mastery within the government. A new kind of national consensus was demanded. And, as it had to be, it was talked into being.

The fundamental struggle of the Civil War was less military than rhetorical. The rhetorical circumstances took shape as the first Stuart was followed by the second. The situation was a mélange of religious dissention intermingled with political resentments and ambitions. Parliament rudely insisted upon having a voice. Amid the turmoil, not only was the range of discussable topics greatly enlarged; discussion itself became vastly more vital. Through it the new consensus was forged. This was the real nature of the English Civil War.

"Nothing Is Heard but Cries, Shouts, and Confusion"

The reign of James I commenced with a quietness that had not been expected. As Queen Elizabeth's anticipated death drew closer, the national mood was tinged with dread. She had no heir. She refused to designate her choice of successor. Who would succeed to the throne? Would there be another period of uncertainty and of struggle? Then came the proclamation that ended the doubt. In her last hours, Elizabeth finally revealed her decision: James VI of Scotland was to become the new English king. He was little known in England, and for the English to be ruled by a Scot was nothing to cheer about. But the choice was made, and no one arose to contest it. Whatever else, there was to be no civil war.

"The proclamation was heard with great expectation and silent joy," we are told, "but no great shouting. To the astonishment of all men, there was no tumult, nor contradiction, nor disorder in the City; every man was going about his business as readily and securely as though there had been no change, nor news ever heard of competitors, so that the people, finding the just fears of forty years for want of a known succession to be dissolved in a minute, do so rejoice as few wish the Queen alive again."[1]

The reign of Elizabeth ended about 2:00 A.M. on 24 March 1603, while cold winds blew through London's near-deserted streets. The Great Council met. Then, at 10:00 of that same morning, in accordance with ancient custom, its members knocked at the gate of the City to announce to the lord mayor the person of the new king.

Historians, always plagued by the distortions of hindsight, have portrayed James I unfavorably. The deeply Whiggish Macaulay derided his "awkward figure, his rolling eye, his rickety walk, his nervous tremblings, his slobbering mouth, his broad Scotch accent." To the more objective Wallace Notestein (in his *Winning of the Initiative by the House of Commons*), James was stigmatized as being "fitted for opposition"—because of his mental and emotional weaknesses, his Presbyterian associations, his Catholic sympathies, and his being a Scot. Conrad Russell emphasizes personal factors that handicapped the incoming king: "He had a poor head for drink, and frequently failed to make sufficient allowance for it. He showed an undignified curiosity on unsuitable occasions. For example, the day after his daughter's marriage, the couple was not allowed to get up until the king had visited them and heard a detailed description of the night from the bridegroom. In business, he was lazy and frequently absent at crucial times, and yet was not good at delegating responsibility to the ministers who were doing the work.[2] His speeches, which were too frequent, were verbose, plaintive, and pompous. . . . He was continually talking about his kingly dignity and yet was not dignified. . . . Moreover, he was often so vacillating in his decisions that it was hard to know how to avoid opposing him."[3] Despite his fathering of several children, he was widely reputed to be homosexual. A kingly figure he was not.

James made no secret of his dislike for Parliament, and despite his need for funds he called it into session only four times during his twenty-one year reign.[4] To the Spanish ambassador he frankly revealed his feelings: "The House of Commons is a body without a head. The Members give their opinions in a disorderly manner. At their meetings nothing is heard but cries, shouts, and confusion. I am surprised that my ancestors should ever have permitted such an institution to come into existence. I am a stranger, and found it here when I arrived, so that I am obliged to put up with what I cannot get rid of."[5] Despite this, James I got along reasonably well with Parliament, primarily by not asking much from it. He was right in his observation that it was growing stronger, and he was sufficiently prescient to warn his son that he could expect to have "his belly full of grievances and impeachments."

One of the puzzlements of the early Stuart period is that James I, who was by many measurements both a bad king and an unattractive man, should have not only survived but actually gained a good measure of popularity, whereas his son, who came to reign as Charles I, was manifestly superior to him as a person and devoted greater talents with more assiduity to being a good ruler—yet lost popularity, allowed the kingdom to be rent by civil war, was brought to trial, impeached, and executed. The tangle of circumstances may, perhaps, best be understood when viewed in rhetorical terms, for a variety of alternative social, religious, and political solutions were emerging into sufficiently clear definition that they demanded discussion and debate. The governing concerns were no longer being taken for granted; they had to be threshed out.

Like his predecessors, James I claimed to have absolute power based upon divine right to rule. But he was ill fitted to solve the problems that beset the kingdom. Both Puritans and Presbyterians were becoming stridently assertive. The Established Church was far from being firmly established. The Catholics were looking to the new reign to restore their right to worship without political restraints. Members of Parliament were reaching for broader powers, and they became restless and resentful, especially when, immediately after his accession, James insisted that it was his prerogative to validate local elections. In broad terms, it may justly be said that two vitally different conceptions of the nature of society merged into confrontational dispute.

> One was a view of society as functional, according to which the various groups and individuals in the population performed their own special functions for the good of the whole. . . . The other conception . . . was of a society composed of individuals who had no functions to perform but who had only rights which the State existed to protect.[6]

Caught between these two emergent views, James I chose to assert his own royal authority to make the final determinations. His incapacity to do so became quickly evident.

James's first Parliament met for four sessions, each lasting about one hundred days. In the first of them, a series of angry debates was concluded with the drawing up of a stern warning—"Let your Majesty be pleased to receive public information from your Commons as to the civil estate and the government"—and a demand for his acknowledgment that "the voice of the people, in the things of their knowledge, is said to be the voice of God." Even more testily, this strangely termed *Apology* that the Commons adopted added that "the prerogatives of princes may easily and do daily grow; the privileges of the subjects are for the most part an everlasting stand." And to stand for them everlastingly was precisely what the Commons meant to do.

James I's own favorite project was the highly unpopular one of cementing a union of England and Scotland. Loftily describing himself as the New Arthur, he demanded from Parliament an Act of Union that would pronounce the two peoples to be one, "under one allegiance and loyal subjection, in me and my person, to my person and my posterity for ever." Appealing to both morality and loyalty, he told the Commons that any Englishman who "doth not love a Scotsman as his brother, or a Scotsman that loves not an Englishman as his brother, is a traitor to God and to the King." To accomplish this union was the first Stuart's most persistent aim. But his mode of demanding it, rather than of developing a conciliatory atmosphere in which it might naturally evolve, aroused such opposition that it was not accomplished for a full century.[7]

Before the second parliamentary session convened, Catholic disillusionment with the new reign led to the notorious Gunpowder Plot, which aimed to blow up the Parliament while the king and his chief ministers were meeting with it. In one of the strange convolutions of history, James I managed to convert this threat to his advantage; in dealing with it, he showed his best qualities. He found the wit to brush off the failed plot with a deft comment. Had it succeeded, he jested, he would have ended his life amid the best company in England, rather than in an alehouse or a brothel. The resulting public acclaim for the king's wit and courage induced such a spasm of goodwill in the Commons that it gave passing thought to granting his wish for the Union. But the goodwill that he won, he quickly lost. During its next two sessions, the Commons engaged frequently in sharp and ill-natured debate that was peppered with complaints about taxes and with protests against James's practice of granting control over trade to his Scottish favorites. The king's fiscal problems persisted until 1618, when he finally solved them by securing the customs revenues for the royal treasury.

Despite deep and far-reaching discord, the early Stuart period glowed with a continuance of the greatness of the age of Elizabeth. Shakespeare did not die until 1616, and it was during the reign of James I that the Globe Theatre produced his *Othello, Lear, Macbeth, Timon of Athens*, and such bitter comedies as *Measure for Measure* and *Troilus and Cressida*. Despite the popularity of his plays, this was for Shakespeare a time of personal distress, as indicated by his sonnets, and of a gloomy pessimism that contrasted with the cheer of his earlier plays—doubtless reflective of disappointment and disgust with the political situation. A similar darkness of spirit is evidenced in Webster's *Dutchess of Malfi*, Ford's *'Tis Pity She's a Whore*, and Ben Jonson's plays. The gloom was enhanced by the execution of the popular Sir Walter Raleigh, who had allowed himself to become enmeshed in the plot to elevate a Catholic to the throne and was imprisoned in the Tower for thirteen years, where, as he said, he was "oppressed with many miseries." When, finally, he was beheaded on 28 October 1618, he made a moving speech from the scaffold that heightened the contrast between his virtues and the authoritarian petulance of James I. Still other great speaking in that time was by John Donne, in his sermons in Saint Paul's, and by Francis Bacon, whose speeches won him higher repute among his contemporaries than did his essays or his philosophy. Still another effective persuasive speaker of the period was John Preston, who is now remembered only by specialist historians but who was held in high regard both as a parliamentarian and as a preacher.

Still, it is not the glory but the disagreements that left the most lasting effects. It was, nevertheless, a period pregnant with a growing inclination toward democracy. The roots of such faith had been long nurtured, as has been seen, by men of insight and great personal courage. But it was during the early Stuart period that the view became influential that "men of reasonable intelligence and normal good will could communicate . . . and could reach by negotiation as much understanding and agreement as was needed to serve the purposes of a limited public authority."[8]

The general discussion of this new concept centered around two related questions: First, what should be the nature of the State? And second, how should its governing decisions be made? Was it the function and purpose of government to enforce discipline and maintain orderly stability, or did it have a greater duty of preserving the rights and advancing the well-being of its citizens? If discipline was the essential function, then a strong and centralized authority seemed best, but if the promulgation of privileges and benefits for all was the aim, the governance would best be broadly representative. Such questioning was directed not only to the political structure but also to religion and to economic arrangements. The distinction that had to be made, as Francis Bacon put it in *Of the Interpretation of Nature*, lay between "two ends of tradition of knowledge, the one to teach and instruct for use and practice, the other to impart or intimate for reexamination and progression." What Bacon made clear was that the problem was dynamic. It could neither lie in abeyance nor solve itself. It was a problem in a state of animation. It was precisely the kind of social issue that demands discussion. The answer had to be sought by examination and reexamination. It had to be dealt with in rhetorical terms: by teaching or inspiring, by imparting or intimating. Different minds had to be engaged, either to find a consensus or to clarify the differences of opinion. Proponents of both views—of looking back to maintain, and of looking ahead to adapt—engaged freely in public discussions that exercised far more influence than discourse had attained in the more static prior times.

Those who were reaching toward democracy conceived the barrier that lay in the way to be the authority of the throne. A natural means for curbing it was to win a larger role for Parliament. But, from the other, the conservative, point of view, the chief threat to stabilized government came from unbridled individualism. The prevalent practice of dueling, which was becoming endemic, was a form of individual assertiveness that could be dealt with. Against this practice Bacon delivered a speech that won a wide audience by being repeatedly published. And against dueling James I took a strong hand. The issue was important primarily because dueling was an open flouting of the disciplinary function of social organization. To curb it was something the king could undertake as a way to symbolize his right and his duty to maintain public order. On this issue James won popular support.

He was less fortunate in dealing with the religious disputes that continued throughout his reign, that mounted in intensity, and that were finally, to contribute substantially to the undoing of his successor, Charles I. As had been true in the past, religion and politics were so tightly intertwined as to be virtually inseparable.

The theologians divided into two major groups, known as Covenanters and Arminians, with views about the nature of religion and how it was to be practiced that closely paralleled the secular issue concerning the nature and function of the State. The Calvinist Covenant, which became the foundation of Protestantism, portrays God as having entered into a covenant to assure salvation to all who believe in the redemptive function of Christ and follow his virtuous example—a bargain fully as binding upon God himself as upon his creatures. The Arminian view, in contrast, held that salvation must be found through the church, as the chosen mediator between God and man. The Arminians were not only Roman Catholics but also the Anglicans. They tended to be internationally minded, linked in their beliefs with the Catholics on the Continent. The Covenanters, on the other hand, were both more individualistic and more nationalistic, with the great bulk of them being Puritans and Presbyterians. The differences between Arminians and Covenanters were basic and irreconcilable. But almost as virulent were internal disagreements: between Catholics and Anglicans and between Puritans and Presbyterians.

Thus, in effect, there were not two but four distinct religious groups, each so devoutly certain that it was right that conflict was inevitable. On such a matter, involving the will of God and prospects for eternal salvation, compromise was out of the question. The issues could be debated but not discussed. There was no available common ground. Truth had to oppose Error.

This distinction between debate and discussion merits close consideration, for it characterized the rhetorical changes that were taking place. Debate connotes confrontation. Its analogy is battle, with contestants aligned on opposing sides, seeking to defeat one another. Discussion depends upon acceptance of a common purpose and agreement concerning values and methods. It presupposes a state of mind in which participants say to one another in effect, "We all know that something must be done—let us explore together to determine what." Another difference is that debate typically concerns a duality of viewpoints, discussion a plurality. The debaters say "no" or "yes," the discussants, "maybe," "perhaps," or "let us see." It is not fanciful to view this early Stuart period as the time when Englishmen turned, in a general sense at least, from debate to discussion. This is what is implied in titling this chapter a search for mastery and the next a seeking for balance.

"A Better Man but Even Less Suited for the Role"

James I was lucky. He died before the disputes raging among the people broke out into direct confrontations. His second son and accidental heir, Charles, inherited the whirlwind. Since James's first son, Henry, was the designated successor, Charles was educated not for duties but for pleasures. The interests that engaged him were scholarly. He read theological treatises, studied mathematics and music, and learned some Greek and Latin. He became proficient in French and Italian and spoke a little Spanish. He was passionately fond of art, especially of the great Italian and Dutch paintings. He was also a loyal son, a faithful husband, and a father whom his children idolized. He was physically so frail that he could not walk until his seventh year; like Theodore Roosevelt, however, he undertook a pursuit of exercise and sports that strengthened his physique. Likewise, his speech was so impeded that he could scarcely speak understandably until about the age of ten, and through all his life he could avoid stammering only by speaking slowly. Another of his burdens was the rumor spread through the public that he had somehow caused his older brother's death. For all these various reasons, he avoided the social life of the Court and withdrew into a self-contained solitude. This surely contributed to his tragedy, for the great failure of his reign was his inability to comprehend the feelings that animated the public and the Parliament. He not only adopted his father's inflexible insistence upon the absolute supremacy of the Crown, but he committed the error of marrying and of remaining devoted to a French princess who was both a devout Roman Catholic and an uncompromising believer in monarchal absolutism. He was a better man than his father but was even less suited for the role he had to play.

The storm that broke upon Charles derived both from the politico-religious divisiveness among the people and from the high-handed manner in which he sought to control them. He compounded his problems by appointing as archbishop of Canterbury an arch-Arminian, William Laud, who hated Catholicism but also despised Puritanism and Presbyterianism and was determined to bring English religious practice back under the firm control of the Established Church. The political challenges that confronted the king were enormous, including the commencement of a war with Spain that had been started by James I with the eager support of the predominantly Protestant Parliament. As his chief minister, Charles kept the inept and tactless Duke of Buckingham, whom James had appointed to the post. The House of Lords, with one hundred members, was overshadowed by the five hundred men who were elected to the Commons, three-fourths of whom were Puritans, and who overmatched the Lords in wealth and local popularity. This Parliament, much more concerned with the defense of its own mercantile interests and with the limitation of taxation than with the international contest against Continental Catholicism, refused to vote the funds essential for conduct of the war. Charles angrily dissolved the session, declaring, "Remember that Parliaments are altogether in my power for their calling, sitting, and dissolution. Therefore, as I find the fruits of them good or evil, they are to continue or not to be."

The outstanding leader in the Commons was Thomas Wentworth, who attempted to mediate the constitutional dispute by championing the prerogatives of the Crown while insisting that taxation was solely the right of Parliament. King Charles, suffering defeats in the war because of inadequate funding, had Wentworth arrested. He called a new Parliament, which proved as uncompromising as its predecessor. Then the Duke of Buckingham was assassinated, and Charles turned to Wentworth for support. Wentworth abandoned his ties with the Commons, in what was called the Great Apostasy. Wentworth explained his own views—which were eventually to lead him to the scaffold—that while Parliament had the sole power to make laws, the king could either enforce or ignore them, depending on his judgment as to whether they served the true interests of the realm. What he sought to cement was a mixed government, within which the power to veto would be held by the king, the Commons, and the Lords. The difficulty in such a concept was that it resulted in governmental impotence, for the Parliament could refuse to vote taxes and the king would administer only such laws as he approved. Wentworth was rewarded by the king by being named Earl of Strafford and appointed as head of the Council of the North and later as lord lieutenant of Ireland. The Commons adopted a Petition of Rights, and Charles responded by dismissing it and by attempting to rule for the next eleven years without a parliamentary session, raising funds meanwhile by forced loans and other arbitrary devices.

"Not Our Woodden Walls That Will Guard Us"

Meanwhile, the feelings of the great masses of the people were more meaningfully involved in religious than in political concerns. As H. N. Brailsford reminds us, "the church was the one social centre the scattered population possessed"; and to it the "yeoman and labourer, pedlar and squire, resort gladly." It was in church meetings that opinions were shaped, and it was from them that influence spread. "Then as now, but more then than now, the spoken word with the drama of human contact and the mass emotion of an assenting congregation was more powerful than the printed page; only from the pulpit could the preacher, in the robe that marked him off from the common run of men, claim some measure of divine inspiration."[9]

The power of the pulpit derived from the fact that both the preachers and their congregations believed that words spoken from the pulpit were directly inspired by God. The preachers spoke boldly, convinced that as ordained messengers of divinity they could speak only truth. They also generally felt a sense of responsibility to address the secular problems of their parishioners, as well as dwelling upon the need for subjection to the will of God. No topic lay outside their purview, for God's governance was all-inclusive. Holding such faith, they could see no distinction between the secular and religious realms. As Charles I wryly noted, "People are governed by pulpits more than the sword in times of peace." And the pulpits that mattered most were Puritan in most of England and Presbyterian in Scotland. In major ways, they spoke with similar messages.

Presbyterianism was shaped in Geneva and implanted in Scotland by John Knox. It was carefully organized, as a covenant between God and man, with methods and discipline maintained by its own established clergy. Puritanism was less formalized in its system of beliefs and was far from being well organized. The Puritan preachers were priests of the Church of England, and their congregations were episcopal, but they were orthodox in their own way. Their clergy formed an informal brotherhood of ecclesiastics who turned away from ritual to emphasize preaching; who stressed their close connection with their parishioners; who scorned luxury and display while stressing plainness of manner in living and in worshiping; who extolled the virtues of hard work and sobriety; and who taught that the acquisition of wealth was a sign of God's favor. As Brailsford said, "Wealth . . . afforded a presumption, though not an infallible proof, that those so blessed were among the elect."[10] As mercantilism expanded, so did Puritanism. Its clergy became increasingly rebellious against church discipline. Many advocated the abolition of bishops, with parishes to be autonomous members of independent assemblies. Like the Lollards, many of them favored the undisciplined, free-speaking, itinerant preachers. Presbyterians and Puritans alike resisted the authority of Canterbury and thereby came under duress from Archbishop Laud.

A third body of independent country preachers, somewhat akin to the Puritans, were the Anabaptists, who poured into the country from the Netherlands. These zealots drew their beliefs largely from the New Testament, in which respect they differed from both Presbyterians and Puritans, whose concern was more with the God of wrath portrayed in the Old Testament. For the Anabaptists, Jesus represented pacifism, the common ownership of property, and abolition of capital punishment. They rejected infant baptism, holding that conversion is a result of mature judgment, and they scorned church ritual. They also resisted the leadership of paid professional clergy, insisting that laymen should worship together in full confidence that God's will is revealed to all who sincerely accept Christ. In their meetings, the sermon was subordinate to congregational discussions, and they made small distinction between the lay teachers who led the discussions and the members of the congregations. From their example, and from that of the Seekers who followed similar practices, there emerged in the latter years of the century yet other powerful and influential sects—the Quakers (or Society of Friends) and the Baptists.

The religious discussions, with significant political implications, led to the emergence of a wide range of powerful preachers, both orthodox Arminians and independent Covenanters. Through their preaching they did much to crystallize sentiments of both loyalty to the Established Church and to the Crown, on the one hand, or to individualistic rebelliousness, on the other. Their rhetorical significance was that they heightened the divisiveness within the population that erupted in the Civil War.

A leading Covenanter was John Preston, a brilliant commoner who graduated from Cambridge University with a burning ambition for fame. In 1611 he was converted to Puritanism by a sermon preached by the learned and eloquent John Cotton—who was driven by the persecution of Archbishop Laud to emigrate to Massachusetts, where he earned lasting renown. Because of Preston's brilliance in disputation, in 1615 King James appointed him to be chaplain to Prince Charles. Seven years later Preston accepted the post of preacher in the highly influential Church of Lincoln's Inn, where his congregation included members of Parliament and other leading men. In that same year he was also named master of Emmanuel

College, a Puritan stronghold, and worked skillfully to make Puritanism dominant in the Court. After Charles became king, he turned against Preston, appointing Laud and Wentworth with the express charge to bring the dissidents under royal and Canterburian control.

Preston responded to the challenge in a series of great sermons delivered during 1626, in which he directly and sternly warned Charles I to abandon his Arminian policies. His last sermon, which Laud prevented him from delivering, was distributed widely in print, and "was more talked of at Court, and in the City, than any sermon he had ever preached before."[11] Preston's persuasive strategy was one of direct frontal attack. Having been the spiritual mentor of the king during the latter's youth, Preston had no fear of him nor did he hold him in awe. His central message was a demand for moral reform in the government. After warning King Charles both against entering into an alliance with Catholic Spain and against abusing his royal power in domestic affairs, Preston continued as though speaking directly to the king.

> It is not our Armies by Land, nor our Navie at Sea, that shall secure us at home, or prevaile abroad, though it bee well that these things be done. . . . It is not our woodden walls that will guard us, it is not the Sea wherewith you are invironed, nor our policy, counsell and strength that will secure and defend us, but it is a turning to the Lord, and cleansing the Land from the sinners wherewith He is provoked that will do the deed.

It is difficult to fault Charles I and his archbishop for brushing aside such counsel, delivered in so petulant a tone. After all, what had Preston to offer? Keep up your armament, he urged the king, but do not expect any good from it. Clean up your government and trust in the Lord. Charles had to be exasperated with the man who for seven years had been his personal chaplain. After all, "cleansing the land from sinners" was precisely what Canterbury was trying to do. The difficulty is the old one—charges of guilt were being freely made in all directions except inward, toward themselves. It was a time of intense convictions, fueled by strong feelings, made all the more virulent by the freedom of speech that was demanded and vigorously exercised. A spirit of rebelliousness was astir.

Revolutionary sentiments were affecting not only politics and religion but also the literary mode of the time. In literature the leader of the rebels was John Donne. The change of mood and of style that he instigated are both well illustrated by comparison of a representative couplet from Edmund Spenser's *Faerie Queene*, in which a lovelorn knight woos his lady in such extravagantly romantic terms as

> He wept, he wail'd, he swoon'd, he perdy died,
> He threw himself on ground his love beside

with the poem by Donne in which he had his lover exclaim to his reluctant mistress,

> For godsake, hold your tongue and let me love.

But the forthrightness of speech that Donne employed in poetry, he curiously avoided in his sermons. The revolution he started in literature contrasts with the conservatism he defended from his influential pulpit of Saint Paul's. The distinction reflects the rhetorical circumstances of the time: Literature was a safe haven, but topics that intermixed religion and politics presented turmoil and danger. Some topics were safely discussable, but others threatened not only the safety of individuals but the stability of the State. Donne stood for individualism in the literature but for conformity in religious and civic affairs. He is a prime exemplar of the "vexed and troubled Englishmen" of his time.

Born into a prosperous Catholic family, Donne spent his youth in amorously libertine pursuits. After his family's properties were confiscated during the Protestant uprising against Catholicism, he spent a brief period in prison. Then he was converted to Anglicanism and became an effective champion of Arminian doctrines of subjection to the authority of the State. With outstanding abilities, he quickly rose to respectability and to high renown, first as a diplomat and then as a preacher of the Established Church. A typical sermon is one he preached on Easter Day 1625, to a packed audience in Saint Paul's. In it he agreed with the Covenanters' insistence upon personal morality, but he reinterpreted it in terms of strict conformity. Like many Englishmen, Donne was a common-sense realist. Rebelliousness, he realized, costs more than it is likely to gain.

The intricately stylized pattern in which he praised James I's "constancie in the true reformed religion" was so convoluted that, as one of his listeners believed, "he spake as if himself were not so well satisfied."[12] Whether satisfied or not, he presented what the king wanted the people to hear. Trying to allay the religious ferment that was troubling the country, Donne set forth his theme in the opening sentence of his sermon.

> As the sun works diversely, according to the diverse disposition of the subject (for the sun melts wax and hardens clay) so do the good actions of good men: upon good men they work a virtuous emulation, a noble and holy desire to imitate, upon bad men they work a vicious and impotent envy, a desire to disgrace, and calumniate.

The sermon was rich in scholarship and intricate in its reasoning. Through the sacrifice of Christ, God assures us of the possibility of bodily resurrection, but this must be preceded by a prior resurrection of the soul from licentious to virtuous living. Marriage, he said by way of illustration, serves a useful purpose in saving men from licentiousness, but it fulfills

God's will only if it produces children. Sternly he warned against birth controls and abortions. As a guide for all forms of behavior, he advised:

> Never presume upon any other disposition in God, than such as thou findest in thine own heart, that thou art bound to have in thyself: for we find in our hearts, a bond of conformity and assimilation to God, that is to be as like God as we can.

Meanwhile, "there are no other means to be hereafter instituted for the attainment of a happy resurrection, than those that are now established in the Church." Do not be misled, he warned, by heretical preachers, for "Let the man be . . . a son of thunder, never so powerful a speaker, yet no thunder is heard over all the world." Those who follow their own will, rather than submitting to the will of God, will be condemned to endless suffering, "as a man condemned to be half hanged, and then quartered, hath a fearful addition in his quartering after, and yet had no ease in his hanging before, so [are] they that hath done ill, when they have had their hanging, when they have suffered in soul, the torments of hell, from the day of their death."[13]

Donne's ornate and contrived style went well with the courtiers who listened to him in London. It was far different from that which was heard in the country parishes, where the style was vigorous and direct, and where the subject matter tended not to conformity but to dissent. Among the best of the country preachers was the brilliant and forthright Thomas Hooker, who denounced the ritualism of the Established Church, telling his congregation: "I have sometimes admired at this: why a company of Gentlemen, Yeomen, and poore women, that are scarcely able to know the A. B. C. Yet they have a minister to Speake Latine, Greeke, and Hebrew, and to use the Fathers, when it is certaine they know nothing at all. The reason is, because *all this stings not*, they may sit and sleepe in their sinnes, and *goe to hell hood-winckt*." Similarly rebellious was the learned John Cotton, who (like Hooker) was forced to leave for Massachusetts; while still in England, he conducted sermon-discussions lasting for periods of four hours, to arouse the people to self-assertion. As John Selden sententiously observed, these and like "Lecturers doe in a parish what the Fryars did heretofore."[14]

The defense of the Established Church against the Dissenters was conducted with greater skill than Hooker indicated. Two Anglican bishops who were as much admired among the well-educated as was John Donne, like Donne preached in an elaborate style marked by conceits, convoluted sentences, and scholastic wit. One of them, Lancelot Andrewes, was so highly esteemed that he was called the Star of Preachers and the Angel of the Pulpit. Despite his own stylistic intricacies, he often reviled rhetoric as being beneath the dignity of a spokesman for divinity. Nonetheless, he strove mightily for rhetorical effects and was outspokenly proud of the precision of his diction. It was his mastery of fifteen languages that led to his being appointed by James I to supervise the translation of the Bible that came to be known as the King James Version.

It was one of the most unlikely literary triumphs ever produced. The consistency, as well as the beauty, of its style is remarkable in view of the fact that it was the work of an extensive committee. Bishop Andrewes assembled a body of forty-seven theologians, over whom he presided as chairman. Each of them worked on a designated portion of the Bible, drawing upon all available texts in Hebrew, Greek, Latin, and any other languages into which earlier translations had been made. Periodically the group sat together to listen as a newly translated book was read aloud, to criticize the rendition and to offer improvements. The sole aim that was supposed to guide them was to be unfailingly accurate in their English rendition from the best sources. What they produced by this cumbersome method was a work that has had tremendous literary as well as religious influence. Its rhetorical effects were far deeper and far more widespread than flowed from any of Andrewes's preaching. Since many of its passages (notably the Book of Revelation) are obscure, its general usage resulted in continuing discussions and disputes concerning divergent interpretations. For some two centuries this translation served for many millions of English Protestants as the most dependable revelation of divine purpose and wisdom, until "revised" editions multiplied.

The other great Anglican preacher of the midyears of this century was Jeremy Taylor, who from the start of his ministry in 1634 represented such heights of eloquence that he was variously called the Spenser or the Shakespeare of the pulpit, or the English Chrysostom. During the Civil War he was deprived of his benefice and exiled to Wales, but after the Restoration he was named bishop of the Irish see of Dromore. In reaction to the persecution of the Anglicans during the period of the Commonwealth, Taylor, like his fellow Churchmen, became a champion of religious toleration. Like Andrewes and Donne, Taylor delighted in using analogies and metaphors. Unlike them, his speech was forthright and his diction simple. His sentence structure, however, was elaborate. The simplicity of his diction, amid the complexity of his imagery, may be illustrated by a single sentence from his sermon on the value of prayer.

> For so have I seen a lark rising from his bed of grass, and soaring upwards, singing as he rises, and hoping to get to heaven and climb above the clouds; but the poor bird was beaten back with the loud sighings of an eastern wind, and his motions made irregular and inconstant, descending more at every breath of the tempest than it could recover by the irregular and frequent weighing of his wings, till the little creature was forced to sit down and pant and stay till the storm was over; and then it made a prosperous flight, and did rise and sing as if it had

learned music and motion from an angel, as he passed sometimes through the air, about his ministries here below; so is the prayer of a good man.

What Taylor apparently was trying to convey was "the beauty of holiness"; and what his listeners gleaned from such sermonizing was not intellectual stimulation but a feeling that his words were "their kind of talk" and that religion was "good for them." There was nothing in it to arouse questioning, surely nothing to stimulate resentment that their own problems were being ignored. A serene acceptance that "all was right" was the underlying aim of such preaching. This it was that chiefly distinguished the Anglicans from the Dissenters. It also marked the distance they sought to maintain from the political disputes and squabbles that were disrupting the society.

"Not to Be Believed How Great the Malice Is"

The widespread disaffection of the people found both support and incitement not only from the country preaching but also from the contentiousness that stirred the successive parliamentary sessions. In 1625, 1626, and 1628 Charles I convened Parliaments, in an effort to get the funds needed, and dissolved them in quick order. He supplemented the royal income through a system of forced loans from the wealthy. The House of Commons that convened in 1628 included no fewer than twenty-seven resentful members who had been jailed for refusing to make such loans. Among them were such notables as Sir John Eliot, Sir Edward Coke, John Pym, and Thomas Wentworth. They were reputable citizens, not members of any special or rebellious groups. But they came bristling with resentments. Their anger burned all the hotter when King Charles warned them that if they refused his demand for funds he would "use those other means, which God hath put in my hands, to save that which the follies of particular men may hazard to lose." This challenge met a quick response.

Sir John Eliot rose on 3 June 1628 to reject the king's demands. According to his biographer, Eliot was inspired equally by hatred and by love—"hatred of a fellow man and his policies, and love of his country." This mix of feelings led him into an "oratorical denunciation of the English Government such as never before had been heard in the House of Commons."[15] The most stunning aspect was his consideration of the king as no more than "a fellow man." He left no doubt that he considered the people to be sovereign and Parliament to be their voice. It is revealing that his listeners were not only willing to listen to such sentiments but were actually determined to support them. Eliot minced no words as he detailed wrongs that had to be righted.

The exchequer, you know, is empty, and the reputation thereof gone.... What perfect English heart is not almost dissolved into sorrow for this truth?

For the oppression of the subject, which, as I remember is the next particular I proposed, it needs no demonstration. The whole kingdom is proof....

These are the things, Sir, I shall desire to have taken into consideration; that as we are the Great Council of the Kingdom, and have the apprehension of these dangers, we may truly represent them to the King, which I conceive we are bound to by a triple obligation—of duty to God, of duty to His Majesty, and of duty to our country.

Since King Charles was wholly unable to control this Parliament, he grimly told the members four days later that "it will be as you wish"—whereupon he adjourned the session. A year later, when he was obliged by necessity to convene Parliament again, the mood was still so rebellious that members forcibly held the Speaker in his chair to prevent adjournment, while they adopted resolutions condemning Arminianism and refusing taxes. Eliot and others who led the tumult were arrested. Eliot, the most outspoken among them, died in the Tower of London in 1632. In this confrontation was the start of the Great Rebellion.[16] The dramatic conflict between the king and the Parliament continued for a quarter of a century, but henceforth the issue between them could neither be avoided nor resolved.

In a book by James I, *The True Law of Free Monarchies,* Charles found his guiding star: "A good King will frame his actions to be according to the law, yet he is not bound thereto but of his own good will." For his coronation, Charles amended the oath so that he swore only to maintain such laws and liberties as did not clash with his own royal prerogatives. In his dealing with protesting members of Parliament, he showed his faith in an aphorism he had written on the margin of one of his books: "Good talkers are not doers." His mistake was that he did not realize how fully the parliamentarians meant what they said. After his dismissal of the Parliament, he tried for years to get along without calling another, but his desperate need for funds required him to convene another session in April 1640.

On the second day of this short parliamentary session Charles learned of the mood of the members from a long speech given by the leader of the Commons, a prosperous businessman, John Pym.[17] Pym itemized three areas in which basic reforms were demanded: religion, the just enforcement of laws, and the protection of the power and privileges of Parliament—"and if we do not preserve this, we cannot long hope to enjoy either of the others." The speech was crammed with unsparing denunciation of multiple abuses of all three of these fundamental necessities by the king and his ministers. But in his conclusion Pym offered cooperation, and asked for it in return. There was, he said, an unused resource of "wisdom and justice in His Majesty. . . . And when we shall be blessed in the enjoying of it, we shall thereby be incited to return His Majesty such thanks as may make it shine more clearly in the world, to his own glory, and in the hearts of the people, to their joy and contentment."

By the calmness of his style and mode of speaking, and by the moderation of his appeal to the king, Pym strengthened the adherence of Parliament to his leadership. He was truly representative of the determination of the majority to insist upon, rather than merely to request, a redress of the grievances that he described. But instead of adopting a revolutionary tone, he paid due respect to the central position of the throne. His language was not that of a blunt countryman from the west, from which he came, but was marked by the courtly wit and labored conceits that were popular in London. His whole manner emphasized his intent to identify himself with the majority rather than to try to dominate either it or the Crown. Charles I, however, responded by angrily dissolving the session, thereby giving it the label of the Short Parliament.

For the next twelve years the king tried to rule without Parliament. To secure funds, he continued to demand forced loans and impounded the customs receipts. But his troubles were intensified by uprisings against him in both Ireland and Scotland. He sought to gain additional revenues by grants authorized by his Counsel of Peers. But none of these devices sufficed. In October 1640, he was forced to call new elections for what turned out to be the Long Parliament. In an effort to control the intransigence of the members, Charles called for Wentworth, now the Earl of Strafford, to come back to London from Ireland, where he was both lord lieutenant and commander in chief of the armies. Strafford reluctantly accepted the call to confront the parliamentarians, remarking gloomily that "it is not to be believed how great the malice is, and how intent they are about it." Even with this realization, he made the major strategic mistake of advising the king not to yield his prerogatives but to enforce them by calling the army home from Ireland. The result was that he had only six months longer to live.

The situation was desperate. A Scottish army invaded England, and when Parliament convened on 3 November, the Scots were in virtual control of London. Nothing but hard alternatives were available to the policymakers. The king and the Parliament might have united against the Scots; or the king and the Scots might have joined to oppose the Parliament; or the Parliament and the Scots might have united against the king. What the Scots were demanding was a grant of £300,000 in restitution for damages they had suffered, along with a demand that the institution of bishops be abolished in England. What Charles considered to be indispensable was acknowledgment of his right to rule by divine right. What Parliament insisted upon was a new basis for taxation, recognition of its sole right to raise funds, abolition of the Star Chamber, a guarantee of triennial

Parliaments, an end to the centralized authority of the church, and a share in policymaking. The issue was brought to a quick head by adoption of a bill that not only authorized triennial Parliaments but that also declared they would meet whether or not the king chose to convene them.

King Charles at first protested that he would abrogate the new law, then agreed to accept it, thereby compounding the two basic faults of intransigence and irresolution. He next sought to break the impasse by appointing leading members of Parliament to key offices, but he denied them any share in formulating policies. Abruptly, the Parliament decided to enforce its rights by impeaching the Earl of Strafford for treason.

"I Suffer and Must Be Content"

As Strafford's trial commenced, the rhetorical circumstances were confused. In supporting the king's policies, Strafford was operating in accordance with law. His crime was that he was alleged to have advised Charles that the power of the Crown extended above and beyond the laws. Charles might have saved Strafford from being tried by accepting full personal responsibility and by yielding to at least some of the parliamentary demands. But this he refused to do. The legality of the trial was so dubious that many members opposed holding it. But Pym was determined to proceed. He secured from a notable jurist, Oliver St. John (later, under Cromwell, to be named chief justice) a judgment that "we give laws to hares and deer, because they are beasts of chase, but it never was accounted foul play to knock wolves and foxes on the head, because they be beasts of prey."[18] The implication was clear: King Charles was the wolf and the Earl of Strafford the fox. In effect, a verdict of guilt was assured before the trial commenced.

The impeachment proceedings were in Westminster Hall, in a joint meeting of the Lords and Commons, with King Charles in daily attendance. Strafford, who was accounted "possibly the most powerful orator in one of the greatest trials in English history," chose to conduct his own defense. He was a man of powerful intellect and great knowledge, along with a remarkable memory that enabled him to respond to all the charges in great detail without reference to notes. He came to his trial dressed all in black, and he comported himself with decorum and dignity. The seven prosecutors, including the best lawyers from the Commons, were led by John Pym. Each session lasted for about five hours, with Strafford under the continuous pressure of having to respond to specific charges. His conduct was so exemplary that one of the prosecutors, Bulstrode Whitelocke, conceded, "Never any man acted such a part, on such a theatre, with more wisdom, constancy, and eloquence, with greater reason, judgment, and temper, and with better grace in all his words and actions than did this great and excellent person; and he moved the hearts of all his auditors—some few excepted—to remorse and pity." Despite such feelings, the verdict was inevitable—based less on the evidence than upon the solidly developed determination of Parliament to assert its predominance.

In his closing speech, on 13 April 1641, Strafford reviewed the charges against him and refuted them all. But he, no less than the auditors, understood the true nature of the case, and he stated it well.

> All the strings of this government and monarchy have been so perfectly tuned through the skill and attention of our forefathers, that if you wind any of them any thing higher, or let them lower, you shall infallibly interrupt the sweet accord that ought to be entertained of King and people. . . .
> Therefore, I beseech you, prejudice not the deputy, to the disabling him from serving the Crown hereafter, by beating down me, who am this day to answer to you; for if you take away the power of the deputy, you shall not have the Kingdom long depend upon this Crown. . . .
> And when it comes to the point, here is no proof, nor any part of the charge made good. . . . But, in the meantime, I suffer and must be content.

Strafford's defense was sufficiently convincing to persuade one of the prosecutors to make a sudden and dramatic shift. George Digby, a young man of twenty-eight, and only the previous year elected to the Commons, had quickly proved himself to be both exceptionally eloquent and boldly energetic in denouncing monarchal power. He had been an admiring follower of John Pym and a dependable advocate of parliamentary rights. He did believe Strafford to be guilty of high crimes, but as the trial continued, he came to believe that the conduct of it by Parliament was illegal. This conclusion he stated with both clarity and power.

Digby's rhetorical problem was one that politicians try to avoid—that is, to confess that he had been in error, and to try to undo what he had been trying to accomplish. Under such circumstances, a major problem is credibility. Should those believe him now who are told by him that they should not believe what he had urged upon them earlier? Digby undertook to solve this problem in three steps: first, that in his prosecution of Strafford he had been not only sincere but also right, for he agreed wholly with the general conviction that Strafford was "a man worthy to die" for his crimes against the State; second, that he had found that the chief witness against Strafford, on the charge of advising King Charles to bring the army home from Ireland to intimidate the Parliament, was uncertain and contradictory in his testimony; and third, that the acts for which Strafford was charged were not specifically defined by law as being treasonable. He concluded with an emotional appeal to the members to do what was right rather than what was expedient.

> Away with personal animosities! Away with all flatteries to the people, in being the sharper to him because he is odious to them! Away with all fears, lest by sparing his blood they may be incensed! Away with all such considerations, as that it is not fit for a Parliament that one accused by it of treason should escape with his life! Let not former vehemence of any against him, nor fear from thence, that he cannot be safe while that man lives, be an ingredient to the sentence of any one of us.

Having in such terms shifted from defense of his own inconsistency to warn the members against voting for guilt merely from the fear of becoming unpopular if they did not, Digby urged that they join with him in the sincere upholding of justice.

> Of all these corruptives of judgment, Mr. Speaker, I do before God discharge myself to the utmost of my power; and do now, with a clear conscience, wash myself of this man's blood by this solemn protestation, *that my vote goes not to the taking of the Earl of Strafford's life.*

Digby sat down amid stunned murmurs of disapproval. His was a brave speech; it was also soundly reasoned and eloquently phrased. It failed to win votes because the members were committed not to legality but to revolution. The verdict was inevitable.[19]

"Expect What Justice Other People Will Have"

Charles I reacted to the verdict with a series of clumsy mistakes. He first threatened to dissolve the Parliament, then dared not do so. He asserted that he would veto the bill of attainder, then accepted it. He attempted to have Pym and other leaders of the prosecution arrested, but the House of Commons averted it. Then Charles set off for Scotland, where he negotiated an inconclusive truce with the Scottish rebels. Rebellion again broke out in Ireland. Civil discontent mounted in England, leading to rioting in London. Charles fled from the city and never afterward met with Parliament until he himself was brought to trial before it.

In the fall of 1642 war broke out between the Royalists and the Puritans. Parliament was caught in the middle, for what it wanted was not an end to the monarchy but a recognition of its own right to share fully in the government as the true voice of the people. But the people found a new voice that was more extremist than the Parliament was ready to be.

A considerable number of fiery agitators calling themselves Levellers began to exhort the public. They were far from being an organized party, but they rallied around the most vocal among them, John Lilburne, who has been accounted "a figure as gallant and vital as ever strode through English history."[20] Lilburne poured out a succession of radical pamphlets and speeches, all highly inflammable, for which he was several times arrested. In 1646 he was brought to trial for treason by the Lords. In defending himself, Lilburne directed his burning wrath not only against the king but also against Parliament, for its failure to represent the revolutionary temper of the people:

> All you intended when you set us fighting was merely to unhorse and dismount our old riders and tyrants, that so you might get up and ride in their stead. And therefore, my Lords . . . if you shall be so unworthy as to persevere . . . in destruction of fundamental laws and liberties of England . . . I will venture my life and heart's blood against you with as much zeal and courage as ever I did against the king's party.

What Lilburne demanded was not reform but a complete revolution, whereby "no Parliament, council, synod, emperor, king, or magistrate hath any authority or jurisdiction." Instead, government should reside only "in the souls and consciences" of men who dedicated their lives to Christ. His avowed aim was to arouse public resistance to any and all acts of injustice, on the grounds that "what is done to anyone may be done to everyone." Brailsford believed him to be "easily the most popular man in England in his day." The record shows him to have been extraordinarily determined. Many times during his short life he was arrested and imprisoned. On his first arrest, King Charles ordered that he be flogged on his naked back while being dragged at the tail of a cart all the way from Fleet Street to Westminster, and that he then be shackled and kept in a dank cell for three months, sustained only by bread and water. But Lilburne was not subdued. From his jail cell he sent out word to the people that he rejoiced to have been singled out by God as an exemplar for the people. He was indeed representative of widespread feelings.

Among his chief lasting contributions was his insistence that no man be compelled to testify against himself, thereby curbing the common practice of using torture to exact confessions. More broadly, he denied that kings could rule by divine right. He insisted that legislative power be fixed in the Commons, as the best representative of the people. This was the view that came to prevail, but Lilburne reaped no reward from the triumph. Cromwell found him fully as troublesome as had the king and the Parliament. He also had Lilburne arrested repeatedly. Finally, Cromwell exiled him for life to the Isle of Jersey, where after two years he died.

The extremism that Lilburne represented led to an ever-deepening divisiveness, both within the Parliament and among the people. A breach developed between the Puritans and Presbyterians over the issue of centralized versus local church controls. The Parliament split into peace members and a war party, with John Pym striving unsuccessfully to hold them together. In the civil strife that ensued, the rebels prevailed, for the king lacked funds with which to maintain the army. Charles I scorned a compromise settlement, asserting that "God will not suffer rebels and traitors to prosper." Even as his forces were defeated, he insisted, "I cannot flatter myself with expectation of good success, more than this, to end my days with honour and a good conscience." His expedient was to yield himself to the Scots, in the hope that they would rally to defend their own Stuarts.

Cromwell, leading the Puritan rebels, was beset with problems for which there seemed to be no available solutions: how to get the Scottish army back into Scotland; how to subdue the rebellious Irish; how to disband his own army, with its own assertive leaders; and how to reach a settlement with the king that would be dependable. The last of these problems was the most troublesome. Even during the course of the war there was no widespread sentiment for ending the monarchy. But the problem was that Charles could not be trusted to abide by any agreement he might make. The Puritan majority in Parliament sought to end the impasse by presenting the king with a set of demands known as the Propositions of Newcastle. The terms were harsh. The king was asked to abolish the Church of England; to surrender command over the armed forces for a period of twenty years; and to consent to the punishment of all his principal supporters. Naturally the king refused; thereupon the Parliament offered the Scots a large cash settlement as the price for their turning the king over to its control. The religious problems were submitted to a Westminster Assembly, which lacked both the wisdom and the power to solve them. Cromwell undertook to cut the Gordian knot by having his Model Army seize the person of the king. Amid the confusion that ensued, King Charles escaped to the Isle of Wight. The Royalists in the north who rose to support Charles were soon dispersed by Cromwell's forces. One of Cromwell's agents, Colonel Pride, "purged" the Commons of its Royalist members, numbering 140, and left it with only a "Rump" of some 50 or 60. It was this Rump Parliament that voted on 1 January 1649 to bring Charles I to trial for treason.

The Lords refused their assent to this trial; nevertheless, a court of 135 commissioners was created to hear the charges. Charles denied the authority of the court and refused to testify before it. "The king," he declared staunchly, "cannot be tried by any superior jurisdiction on earth." Fully half of the commissioners agreed with him and refused to serve. After the prosecutors presented their case, Charles changed his mind and attempted to be heard, but permission was not granted. The king managed to have the last word, exclaiming: "I am not suffered to speak. Expect what justice other people will have." The result of the trial was preordained. Cries of "Execution!" rang out, and the verdict was proclaimed. The rule of force prevailed. At the end of the month Charles was found guilty and executed.

But rhetoric had the major role to play before, during, and after the trial. On 4 January, what was left of the House of Commons voted that "the

Commons of England . . . have the supreme power in this nation." A week later, another vote declared that "the House of Peers in parliament is useless and dangerous, and ought to be abolished." On the following day, yet another resolution asserted that "the office of a king," was "unnecessary, burdensome, and dangerous." On 17 and 19 March, the monarchy and the House of Lords were terminated. To replace them, a Council of State was created to administer the laws. Oliver Cromwell was dispatched to Ireland, where his soldiers cruelly massacred the inhabitants of Drogheda and Wexford, to "prevent the effusion of blood in the future." Cromwell then hurried to Scotland, where the king's son had been proclaimed Charles II. After the Scots were defeated, both Ireland and Scotland were declared to be united with England and were allotted members in Parliament. Cromwell then undertook to formulate arrangements for the Commonwealth in a series of speeches to Parliament.

It was these speeches, more than the execution of Charles I, that defined the transition to the new era. What Cromwell tried to do was to affirm what he was convinced the generality of the people had come to believe and to feel. The public sentiment, however, was far from being unanimous. Richard Baxter, in his book *The Holy Commonwealth*, published in 1659, interpreted it in Puritan terms: "It will never be a good world while knights and gentlemen make us laws, that are chosen for fear and do but oppress us, and who do not know the people's sores. It will never be well with us till we have Parliaments of countrymen like ourselves, that know our wants." This appears to have been the majority view, much like that held by the Levellers. An anonymous pamphlet entitled *Tyranipocrit Discovered* repeated what Lilburne had earlier said: "The new tyrants which have driven out the old are in all things as bad or worse than the old tyrants were, only they have, or pretend to have, a better faith and a new form of tyranny."

"Everyman's Hand Almost Was against His Brother"

How could Cromwell deal with such divisions of sentiment? He was aware of how badly affairs were being managed. In the first Parliament to meet under his Protectorate, he was confronted by members who presented many complaints. One pressing need was to find a remedy for the religious differences that flourished under the new rule of toleration. Another was to establish an acceptable mode of government. The monarchy had been cast off, but democracy was not yet conceived, and there were no forms by which it could develop. As Cromwell confronted his parliamentary audience, he was troubled by the limitations that bound his administration. The disturbance that he felt was amply evidenced by the frequent and cumbersome disclaimers and qualifications in his speech.

Opening the new parliamentary session on 4 September 1654, his first words acknowledged the uncertainties with which he had to deal: "I should let you know, as far as I have cognizance of it, the occasion of your assembling together at this time." He meant to sound like a leader, even though he wrestled with doubts as to which way to lead. "In the way and manner of my speaking to you I shall study plainness, and to speak to you what is truth, and what is upon my heart, and what will in some measure reach to these concernments."

Such sentiments, expressed in so tentative a manner, illuminate the vast change that came about as the monarchy was replaced by the Protectorate. Englishmen had never experienced anything like it before. The Civil War had brought them to what Cromwell termed "this day of hope." But as Cromwell surveyed the problems with which he had to deal, his mood was somber. Somehow the Parliament had to be brought to acceptance of the heavy responsibilities that were to be borne. Measures were urgently needed, he said, for "healing and settling." For years the Parliament had struggled against the uncontrolled executive power in the government. Cromwell's task was now to convert the members to constructive cooperation with himself as the new executive. He spoke less as "one having authority" than as one who stood in their midst, sharing their sorrows, their perplexities, and their sense of duty.

> What was our condition? Everyman's hand almost was against his brother. . . . Was not everything almost grown arbitrary? Who knew where, or how, to have right without some obstruction or other intervening? Indeed we were almost grown arbitrary in everything. . . . The magistracy of the nation, was it not almost trampled under foot, under despite and contempt, by men of levelling principles?
> Indeed, in spiritual things the case was more sad and deplorable. . . .
> What hath the magistrate to do with these things? He is to look to the outward man, but not to meddle with the inward. . . .
> Whilst these things were in the midst of us, and the nation rent and torn, in spirit and principle, from one end to another, after this sort and manner I have now told you: family against family; husband against wife; parents against children; and nothing in the hearts of men but "Overturn, Overturn, Overturn," . . . the common adversary sleeps not.

Having reminded them of the disruption of society that they all had combined to bring about, and of the mischievous activity of the devil, "the common adversary," in whose evil functioning they all believed, he turned their attention to the need that they all shared to devise remedies suitable to the ills that existed.

> It is one of the great ends of calling this parliament, that this ship of the Commonwealth may be brought into safe harbor; which, I assure you, it will not well be, without your counsel and advice. You have great works

upon your hands. . . . I do therefore persuade you to a sweet, gracious, and holy understanding of one another; and of your business, concerning which you had so much counsel this day. . . .

Having said this, and perhaps omitted many other material things through the frailty of my memory, I shall exercise plainness and freeness with you, in telling you that I have not spoken these things as one that assumes to himself dominion over you, to the interest of these great affairs, and of the people of these nations. I shall therefore trouble you no longer, but desire you to repair to your house, and to exercise your own liberty in the choice of a Speaker, that so you may lose no time in carrying out your work.

The striking contrast in content and in tone between this speech and the communications of preceding English kings with "their" Parliaments emphasizes the revolutionary changes that came upon England when the early Stuart dynasty was overthrown. Representative Englishmen were now to speak for themselves. They now had their own problems in their own hands, to deal with them as best they could. The center of government was no longer dogmatic and authoritarian. The new spirit was well summarized when Cromwell said to one of his lieutenants, "I pray you, by the bowels of Christ, to consider the possibility that you may be wrong." Problem solving had become the charge that was laid upon them. If they failed, they knew where the fault had to lie.

This was the new rhetorical circumstance the Civil War had brought about. The members of Parliament and to some extent the people knew now where the mastery lay—with them. And as the weight of their new responsibilities pressed upon them, they felt the pain that was expressed by Shakespeare, "Uneasy lies the head that wears a crown." The unease was far from being diminished by the fact that the heads were now many rather than one.

Notes

1. G. B. Harrison, *A Jacobean Journal, Being a Record of Things Most Talked about during the Years 1603–1606* (New York: Macmillan, 1941), p. 2.

2. J. Vernon Jensen, "The Staff of the Jacobean Privy Council," *Huntington Library Quarterly* 9 (November 1976): 11–44.

3. C. Russell, *Crisis of Parliaments*, p. 259.

4. David Wilson, *The Privy Councillors in the House of Commons, 1604–1629* (Minneapolis: University of Minnesota Press, 1940), p. 127; and Clayton Roberts, *The Growth of Responsible Government in Stuart England* (Cambridge: Cambridge University Press, 1966), chap. 1.

5. Cited by John H. Timmis III, *Thine Is the Kingdom: The Trial for Treason of Thomas Wentworth, Earl of Strafford* (University: University of Alabama Press, 1974), p. 5.

6. Wilson H. Coates, "An Analysis of Major Conflicts in Seventeenth-Century England," in *Conflict in Stuart England*, edited by William Appleton Aiken and Basil Duke Henning (Hamden, Conn.: Shoe String Press, Archon Books, 1970), p. 19.

7. David Harris Wilson, "King James I and Anglo-Scottish Unity," in ibid., pp. 46 and passim.

8. George H. Sabine, *A History of Political Theory*, rev. ed. (New York: Holt, 1950), p. 907.

9. H. N. Brailsford, *The Levellers and the English Revolution* (Stanford: Stanford University Press, 1961), pp. 26–34.

10. This theme of the holiness of work, which is rewarded with prosperity, has been explored in detail in the classic works by Ernst Troeltsch, *Die Soziallehren der christlichen Kirchen und Gruppen*, 1912 (*The Social Teaching of the Christian Churches*, 1931), and by Richard Henry Tawney, *The Acquisitive Society* (1920) and *Religion and the Rise of Capitalism* (1926).

11. T. Ball, *Life of the Renowned Dr. Preston* (1885), p. 161.

12. Cited by Carl Bridenbaugh, *Vexed and Troubled Englishmen, 1590–1642* (New York: Oxford University Press, 1968), p. 299.

13. *Sermons of John Donne*, edited by Evelyn M. Simpson and George R. Potter, 10 vols. (Berkeley and Los Angeles: University of California Press, 1953–62, reprinted 1984). For helpful analyses, see Evelyn M. Simpson, *A Study of the Prose Works of John Donne* (Oxford: Oxford University Press, 1924).

14. This and the quotation from Hooker are cited by Bridenbaugh, *Vexed and Troubled Englishmen*, pp. 219, 305.

15. Harold Hulme, *The Life of Sir John Eliot, 1592–1632: Struggle for Parliamentary Freedom* (London: Allen and Unwin, 1957).

16. C. V. Wedgewood, *The King's Peace, 1637–1641* (New York: Macmillan, 1956).

17. For careful analyses of this speech, see Goodwin F. Berquist, Jr., "Revolution through Persuasion: John Pym's Appeal to the Moderates in 1640," *Quarterly Journal of Speech* 49 (February 1963): 23–30; and Laura Crowell, "The Speaking of John Pym, English Parliamentarian," *Speech Monographs* 33 (June 1966): 77–101.

18. This and the following two quotations are from C. Russell, *Crisis of Parliaments*, pp. 329–41.

19. The best analysis of the trial is that by Timmis, *Thine is the Kingdom*, in which he reaches the right conclusion: "It was unfortunate for Strafford that he came before the Lords just at the time that monarchical and aristocratic government in England was entering the climax of its breakdown" (p. 173).

20. H. N. Brailsford, *Levellers and the English Revolution*, p. 73.

6
Muddling Through—Royalty Restrained

One of the things for which the British are often praised, a little backhandedly, is their ability to "muddle through" when times are tough. Just what this means is less than crystal clear. As a trait it is contrasted with the "rationality" of the French and the "practicality" of Americans. According to a standard dictionary, when the term *muddle* is applied to Britons, it means finding a way through a maze of confusion. Perhaps the term's guiding principle is that the best way to see ahead is by looking back. Somewhere in the depths of tradition there has to be a guide to the future. When figuring out what to do now, it pays to think back to what has been done before. This is why Winston Churchill appealed to pride in the past while summoning the people to "their finest hour." And this is the kind of decisions the English made when they turned away from their brief experiment with quasi democracy in order to restore the Crown.

Both politics and religion were confused. A new note of skepticism crept into philosophy. The problems that had been fought over in the Civil War remained to be talked out, in search for proper solutions. Institutions had to be reshaped. Minds and feelings were deeply disturbed. Adjustments were needed and were passionately discussed. Opinions were paraded and defended. New ideas were spewed forth so freely as to cause concern. Bunyan's *Pilgrim's Progress* came to the point. When Faithful encountered Talkative, he exclaimed scornfully: "How bravely doth he speak! How he presumes to drive all before him!" Then, to shut off Talkative's effluence of assertiveness, he said to him, "The proverb is true of you which is said of a whore, to wit, that she is a shame to all women; so are you a shame to all professions." To this Talkative could only make the lame reply, "You are some peevish or melancholy man, not fit to be discoursed with; and so adieu."[1] Too much talk, then as now, risks being scorned.

The English were forced to adjust themselves to a whirl of changes as the trials of Strafford and Charles I were succeeded by the Commonwealth, then the Restoration of the Stuarts in 1660, the Glorious Revolution of 1688 that again drove the reigning king from his throne, the importation of William and Mary, and the accession of Queen Anne. Underlying these shifts in government were basic issues that were remolding English society in ways that were decisive without being clearly understood. Historians dealing with the period find the formative influences too tangled and confused to permit simple explanation. Articulate spokesmen were urging so many different solutions that it was difficult to know where to turn. In the process the monarchy was shorn of many of its traditional powers, and parliamentary discussion entered a new phase of partisan division, with the emergence of Whig and Tory political parties. In politics, in religion, and in intellectual developments, the tendency was to dash off in all directions without quite knowing where or how.

"God He Bids Us to Preach, and Men Bid Us Not to Preach"

Looking back at the period with the benefit of hindsight, it is clear that this troubled period was the womb of the future—that it nurtured new attitudes and new ideas that are fundamental to modernity. To those who lived amid the challenges, it was a time of confusion. Society resembled a choppy sea, beset by contrary winds that tossed the waves first one way and then another. But in the hidden depths basic currents were altering their courses so decisively that human affairs underwent a profound alteration. The rhetorical circumstance was that old ideas were brought under searching question. New directions were sought. The realm of the discussable was enormously expanded.

Those who lived through the period needed spokesmen who could clarify their understanding, interpret their feelings, and redirect their modes of thought and of action. And spokesmen did step forth to undertake the task. Those who dared to be leaders accepted the responsibility that Sir John Eliot had affirmed in the opening sentence of his speech to Parliament, discussed in the last chapter.

> We sit here as the Great Council of the King; and in that capacity it is our duty to take into consideration the state of affairs of the kingdom; and, when there is occasion, to give a true representation of them by way of counsel and advice, with what we conceive necessary and expedient to be done.

A major function of leadership is to hold society together in a tolerable stability while only partially comprehended transitions are taking form. Social guidance there has to be; the more troubled the times, the greater is the need. What the political leaders perceived, and what they communicated, may aptly be described in the terms that Cardinal Newman much later stated to be his guiding star: "I do not ask to see the whole way; one step enough for me." In religion, on the contrary, the years spanning the close of the seventeenth century and the opening of the eighteenth, far from being a time of uncertainty, comprised a period of sharp and confident assertiveness.

In consequence, the articulate leadership presents two contrasting types. The political speakers were mostly jobbers, who were seeking advantages for themselves and for their groups as they fumbled amid circumstances they did not even pretend to comprehend fully. In religious affairs, on the contrary, outstanding preachers did know what they believed, and they pointed boldly and clearly the directions in which their visions led. In their differing ways, both groups made their own contributions: the one, to hold society together; the other, to reshape the individuals who composed it.

The currents of fundamental change are what are most apparent as one looks back at that period. In science, there was the founding of the Royal Society, along with Sir Isaac Newton's discovery of the law of gravity, which required a reshaping of physics. In philosophy, new emphasis was placed on human reason as the best means for exploring God's governance of the universe. In economics, the rise of mercantilism enlarged the middle class and stimulated a world-shaking era of colonialism. In political theory, a new vision of egalitarianism challenged the age-old hierarchal structure of society. Literature brought forth the savage ironies of Jonathan Swift, the hardheaded practicalities of Daniel Defoe (well-spiced with religion), the expedient accommodations of John Dryden, and the calming quietism of Joseph Addison. Rhetoricians sought for better ways by which words might be used to draw people together while circumstances were splitting them apart. Society was changing, and so was the self-concept of individuals.

In political terms, the seventeenth century extended from 1603 to 1714 and divides into neat compartments: first, the early Stuarts; next, the Commonwealth; then, the Restoration; later, the Glorious Revolution; and afterward, the reigns of William and Mary and of Queen Anne. In religion, the latter part of the century presents a curious mélange of strange alliances and of extremist-versus-conservative views that diverted attention away from the underlying trend toward humanistic and latitudinarian tolerance. Anglicans opted for stability and traditionalism, aiming to hold fast to their waning prerogatives. Puritans struggled to avert their own decline. Presbyterians, too, were on the defensive. Catholics tried to regain their lost rights. New-fangled "Fanatics," chiefly Baptists and Quakers, engaged in unrestrainedly emotional evangelism. For a time all these divergent Protestants found common cause with Catholics in a common advocacy of "toleration" within which to nurture their sharply antagonistic convictions. There was much to dispute, much to debate, and some common concerns to discuss.

Rhetorical occasions—wherein the available solutions are best sought through talk, not action—were multiple. It was a talkative time, more so than ever before. Much of the speaking was characterized by wisdom masquerading as wit. To be graceful was safer than to be bold, and (except by the deeply committed religious spokesmen) safety was the desired goal. Two popular minor poems of the time are illustrative. In one, the Earl of Rochester capsulized the widespread belittlement of Charles II, in a verse that he pinned on the monarch's bedroom door:

> Here lies our sovereign lord the King
> Whose word no man relies on;
> He never says a foolish thing,
> Nor ever does a wise one.

The other, by the sprightly Sir John Suckling, indicated the widely felt approval of witty and graceful conversation:

> Why so dull and mute, young sinner?
>   Prithee, why so mute?
> Will, when speaking well can't win her,
>   Saying nothing do't?
> Prithee, why so mute?

The upper-class social scene is well portrayed in the diary kept by Samuel Pepys during the decade from 1659 to 1669. It is replete with accounts of his twice- and even thrice-weekly attendance at sermons, which he usually found to be "poor, dry stuff." It also records many exceedingly lively and revealing conversations in which he was an avid and able participant.

Among the early entries, on 19 March 1660, when Pepys was just twenty-eight years old and already an influential public official, he noted that "all the discourse now-a-days is that the King will come again; and for all I can see, it is the wish of all." The Restoration, however, disappointed more than it pleased, for "people of all sides are very much discontented; some thinking themselves used contrary to expectations, too hardly; and the other, that they are not rewarded as much as they expected by the King." Pepys frequently referred to "Fanatiques" who complained that "the King do take away their liberty of conscience." In his 17 July 1661 entry, he quotes a Parson Herring's observation that "God he bids us to preach, and men bid us not to preach; and if we do, we are to be imprisoned and further punished." Yet preach they did, many of them with great fervor and variety of views, as is instanced in Pepy's entry of 25 November of that same year: "Great talk among people how some of the Fanatiques do say that the end of the world is at hand, and that next Tuesday is to be the day. Against which, whenever it shall be, good God fit us all."

It was a time of social disorder, with Pepys himself escaping arrest on one occasion only by fleeing over the next-door housetop. Near the end of the decade, on 8 September 1667, Pepys reported a conversation concerning a not unusual courtroom scene. In Salisbury, in the courtroom of Sir Thomas Richardson, a man who was convicted "for a small matter . . . flung a great stone at the Judge, that missed him, but broke through a wainscot. Upon this, he had his hand cut off, and was hanged presently."

In 1665 there came a great plague upon London, in which some 70,000 people died and were buried hastily in mass graves. Pepys's friend and neighbor, William Penn, recorded that the plague gave him "a deep sense of the Vanity of this World, of the Irreligiousness of the Religions in it." Penn also noted that the disaster led some to seek only for their own safety (among them Penn's own father, who hastily took his family off to Ireland) and he began to be drawn to the Quakers, who, he noted, fearlessly entered the homes of the sick to bring them food and care. Shortly, thereafter, in the following year, the lesson was reinforced by the Great Fire that consumed much of London and again distinguished the self-seekers from the humanitarians.

Pepys, during this time, was doing well. He rose to be Secretary of the Admiralty and as such was often called upon to speak to committees of Parliament. On 9 March 1667, he happily recorded a conversation with a man who "tells me with great joy, how the world upon the 'Change talks of me; and how several Parliament-men . . . do say how bravely I did speak, and that the House was ready to give me thanks for it; but that, I think, is a vanity." After failing eyesight forced him to leave off keeping his diary, Pepys was elected to Parliament, where (as was asserted in the contemporary *Collier's Dictionary*) "he feared no one, courted no one," and was esteemed for his sound judgment, and "great elocution" in both conversation and public speaking. In the conclusion of his diary, on 28 May 1669, Pepys gave an account of a revealing conversation he had with King Charles and his brother, the Duke of York, who was to become James II: "But Lord! what a deal of sorry discourse did I hear between the King and several Lords about him here! but very mean, methought."

"The One Arts and Sciences, the Other Speech and Arguments"

Mean the time must have seemed to those who lived in it, and great was the need for speakers who could rationalize what was happening and find meaning in the midst of the confusion. This need was strongly felt by the three great philosophers of the century: Francis Bacon, Thomas Hobbes, and John Locke. All of them devoted considerable attention to rhetoric. The faculty of speech, they agreed, is of fundamental importance in the shaping of the individual personality, as well as in the guidance of the society.

Bacon was the only one of the three who was also notable as a public speaker. Of him Ben Jonson wrote (in his *Timber*) that his eloquence was so great that "his hearers could not cough or look aside from him without loss. He commanded where he spoke . . . [and] the fear of every man who heard him was lest he should make an end."

Bacon viewed speech as the cutting edge of human relations. In his essay, "Of Studies," he pointed out that "reading maketh a full man, conference [or speech] a ready man, and writing an exact man." It is through skill in speaking that people are enabled to deal with one another. But he was also deeply concerned about the observable fact that what is said often misrepresents what is true. In his *Novum Organum* he pointed out that "Invention is of two kinds, much differing: the one of Arts and Sciences, and the other of Speech and Arguments." Consequently, "understanding" is one thing, and the "transmission" of it to others is something quite different. Among the reasons are the kinds of relationships that exist between a speaker and his listeners. In our ordinary conversation, he pointed out, "if a man should speak of the same thing to several persons, he should nevertheless use different words to each of them." This is a sensible practice, and he advised "the greatest orators" to observe it. But it also risks diverging into misinterpretations.

One of Bacon's principal concerns was how true understanding may first be attained and then how it may be communicated. For both processes, the imagination is essential. On the one hand, it is the faculty that enables us to generalize from specific instances so that the whole meaning may be comprehended. Beyond this, "when by arts of speech men's minds are soothed, informed, and carried hither and thither, it is all done by stimulating the imagination." In his *Colours of Good and Evil* he explained more fully his view that imaginative [or emotive] terms "quicken and strengthen . . . opinions and persuasions," whereas, "reasons plainly followed . . . enter [the minds of listeners] but heavily and dully." The lesson he sought to impress was that leadership consists not only of formulating policies but also of winning their acceptance. It was a concept reflecting the fact that government was coming more and more to be effective only by winning the consent of the governed.

Both Thomas Hobbes and John Locke, in the generation after Bacon, indorsed this same point, though their thinking evolved from sharply contrasting views of the nature of both man and society. Hobbes's philosophy centered on his belief, set forth in *Leviathan,* that the life of man is "solitary, poor, nasty, brutish and short." So poor a creature has no way of knowing anything except what comes to us from our senses. Somehow, however, we do attain to generalized understandings. He agreed with Bacon that imagination is the unifying and organizing function of the mind, calling it "the conception remaining, and little by little decaying, from and after the act of sense." The "faculty of imagining" permits us to conceive generalized meanings, and it is by using general terms (such as *love, hate, fame, sympathy,* et cetera) that we accomplish "transition from one imagination to another." It is this process that makes society possible. As he pointed out in his book, *The Whole Art of Rhetorick*, "In sum, the discourse of the mind, when it is governed by design, is nothing but *seeking*, or the faculty of invention." The damage occurs when "the train of our thoughts" is transmuted into "a train of words." The reason is that "true and false are attributes of speech, not of things." Consequently, "where speech is not, there is neither truth nor falsehood. But since society is possible only as we do communicate with one another, both errors and falsehoods are certain to abound, and this compounds the original difficulty that our basic nature is itself "nasty and brutish." With such a dreary conception, Hobbes is associated both with the traditional, and with the emergent Tory, view that man must be tightly governed, for his own good as well as for the good of society.

John Locke, in contrast, became the Father of Democracy through his endorsement of the belief that everyone is basically equal—each of us being at birth a tabula rasa, or blank tablet, with later differences being the result of divergent social privileges and restrictions. Many of the ills that afflict society, he believed, arise from the fact that what people *say* may be quite different from what *is*. Basically, our minds seek naturally for "truth and knowledge." Consequently, "the art of speaking well consists chiefly of two things, viz, perspicuity and right reasoning." The first requires that the speaker use "proper terms for the ideas and thoughts" that he seeks to "pass from his own mind into that of another man." If what the speaker says is indeed clear but does not arise from "right reasoning," then "perspicuity serves but to expose the speaker." With his favorable estimation of basic human nature, Locke believed that truth is in fact discernible and that individuals tend naturally to aim to convey it. Why then does communication so often prove to be erroneous? One reason may be that either the speaker or his listeners are diverted from truth by a prejudiced adherence to some particular cause or party. Another reason may be simply "laziness, impatience, custom, and want of use and attention." All these faults are correctable, and consequently social improvements and reforms are possible. All that is required is to follow our natural bent toward knowing and doing what is right.[2]

The failure of speakers to communicate truth, for whatever reason, was a cause of considerable dissention and turmoil during this period. Old certainties were being undermined. The changes that were taking place were only partially understood. Some speakers and many listeners were less concerned to discern what was true than to support particular causes or policies. Perhaps this tendency was no stronger then than it is in human affairs generally, but the discussion was sharpened by the nature of the political and religious issues that were being debated.

"So Complicated and Mysterious That No One Knew the Answer"

In every period there are both continuity and change. Sometimes traditionalism is the stronger, sometimes innovation. During this time it was innovation that was most marked, but it was the sense of continuity that held the society together. Consequently, the changes were evolutionary rather than revolutionary. For the first time in English history (and the last time, as well), a king was beheaded as a result of legal processes. A commonwealth, presumably based on parliamentary democracy (though in fact more of a dictatorship), was implanted. Then the monarchy was restored. After this, another king was dethroned. With no direct line of succession available, an unprecedented dual monarchy was brought in from abroad. Following William and Mary, another indirect heir, Queen Anne, was installed on the throne. Finally, since she left no heir, the nation again brought in another foreign monarch, George of Hanover. Meanwhile, religion underwent convulsive controversies. The relation of Parliament to the throne and the relationships of parliamentary members with one another underwent decisive revision.

All these momentous changes, except for the establishment of the Commonwealth, were accomplished without civil warfare. They were accomplished instead by deals, discussions and persuasive maneuverings, and (particularly on the religious front) by fervently emotional discourses. This was the new emergence: a settling of great issues without recourse to military power. The warfare, instead, was verbal.

Complexity bedevils any attempt to depict a straight line of historical development—such as Arnold Toynbee sought valiantly to establish for his interpretation of world history. One of the evils that historiography constantly battles with is the temptation to oversimplification. Yet some kind of generalization is inevitably demanded. To Lord Macaulay, one of the great simplifiers, "the authority of law and the security of property were to be found to be compatible with a liberty of discussion and of individual action never before known."[3] Essentially, Macaulay was right. There was more of democracy—more "liberty of discussion" and more freedom of "individual action" in this period than were to be evident again in English history until well into the nineteenth century. Yet within a lifetime, it dimmed before it increased.

The generalization underlying the rhetorical review of English history is that in the long run social solutions are found only through discussion; no more than temporary and partial are the solutions that are imposed by force. This thesis requires especially careful consideration for the latter part of the seventeenth century. One of the curious characteristics of the time is that discussion was in fact accorded great leeway, yet its operations were sharply bifurcated. In politics, controversial discussion was much more evident in private than in public, whereas in religious forums controversies raged openly. The shaping influence continued to be persuasive discourse of two very divergent types: in politics, ambiguity, for the sake of personal safety; in religion, vigorous assertiveness, to propagate what the speakers believed to be essential truth. Politicians developed the art of muddling through, with the consequence that the solutions they supported proved to be transitory. Preachers, speaking far more decisively, pointed the way to the future. Both modes of discourse were responsive to the rhetorical circumstances of the time.

The virtual breakdown of government under Cromwell's son Richard led to widespread consent to the return of the monarchy. From his exile in France, Charles sent home two promises: to leave important decisions to Parliament, and to grant full liberty of conscience in religious observances. Consequently, in May 1660 he returned to England, meeting little opposition to his accession to the throne. As king, Charles II respected his second promise even less than his first. An anti-Puritan Parliament accepted his request for a Corporation Act that restricted municipal offices to members of the Anglican Church, and it enacted a Bill of Uniformity that required use of the Anglican Book of Common Prayer in all church services. Nonconformists were too dispirited and disorganized to make their resistance effective. Charles meanwhile attempted to reduce his dependence upon Parliament by selling Dunkerque to the French and by acceptance of an annual subsidy from France. Despite this failure to adhere fully to his pledges, the king's luxurious living and enjoyment of his mistresses won him popularity as the Merry Monarch. On the whole, the populace welcomed their relief from the moralistic restrictions and from the military disorder of the preceding decades.

Charles was succeeded by his brother, James II, whose brief reign (of only three years) was troubled by his effort to restore Catholicism to at least a state of equality with the dissenting sects. When this forced him from the throne, William of Orange and his wife Mary, nephew and niece respectively of Charles II, were forced by their deep involvement in European wars to permit domestic policies to be settled largely through debates and deals. Historians are in general agreement concerning the pattern of the time.

> The facts of the growing independence of Parliament—and the classes represented in parliament—and the increasing grip of Protestantism and nonconformity upon the minds of the English people are writ large in the history of the seventeenth century. So too are a distaste for autocracy, for militarism, and for the dragooning of the human mind. Finally, in an age which witnessed the beginnings of scientific thinking and of rational humanism, men were becoming more realistic and more tolerant. A spirit of expansion, adventure, and discovery was fed by a vigorous nationalism.[4]

But democracy, far from being strengthened, was in retreat. Members of Parliament continued to be only vaguely and very selectively representative of the people. Even so, the parliamentary debates not only influenced public opinion but also, to an increasing degree, were influenced by it. Within the Parliament, individual preferences were giving way to party organization. Modern scholarship finds that "this period created the very names of Whig and Tory, linked the development of party strife to the older principles of Civil War, and in the fierce orgy of debate, pamphleteering, and propaganda, fixed the traditional lines of division for another generation."[5]

Macaulay, taking the Whiggish view, declared that the Glorious Revolution of 1688 "brought the Crown into harmony with Parliament," but that it was the much later Reform Bill of 1832 that "brought Parliament into harmony with the nation." The "harmony" he meant, however, was only that the king necessarily accepted the fact that Parliament acquired an independence the throne could no longer deny. In a later passage in his history Macaulay clarified what he meant: "The government was no longer a limited monarchy after the fashion of the middle ages. It had not yet become a limited monarchy after the modern fashion. With the vices of two different systems it had the strength of neither. . . . All was transition, conflict, and disorder."[6]

The two great milestones often cited as marking the development of democracy are the *Magna Carta* of 1212 and the Bill of Rights of 1688. Neither of them, however, intended more than to adjust relations between the Crown and the landed gentry. The people were not to govern but to be governed. The question was, How? After the power of Parliament was assured the question was, How should it be exercised?

The Whigs were organized in an attempt to exclude James II from the throne. The Tories accomplished their unity largely through efforts to restore the throne to the Stuart heirs. Under the leadership of the Earl of Sunderland and the Marquis of Halifax, the Tories maneuvered first to use and thereafter to weaken the influence of the country gentlemen. Public opinion was wooed by the Tories by blaming the Whigs for the alleged plots against the life of Charles II: the Popish Plot in 1678 and, a few years later, the Rye House plot. These efforts were so successful that the founder of the Whigs, Lord Shaftesbury, was forced to take refuge in Holland, and two other Whig leaders, Lord John Russell and Algernon Sidney, were declared guilty in a rigged trial and were executed. Liberty of discussion and freedom of action were far from having become assured. The issues with which Parliament dealt were far less subject to open debate than to "closet discussions" and intrigue. As Maurice Ashley summed up, "The intrigues of that time are so complicated and so mysterious that no one knew the answer." Macaulay found them not only mysterious but also so debilitating to governmental processes that England was reduced to "a blank in the map of Europe."

The situation of William III and Mary II was one of the oddities of the time. Never before or since has the throne been divided. Even then, the division was only formal, for Mary pledged full obedience to the authority of her husband. But this helped matters only slightly, for William was far from suited for the kingship. He was personally ugly and partially crippled. He spoke only a little English and was wholly unable to understand it when it was spoken to him. Few Englishmen, even in his intimate circle, could speak Dutch. William had little respect for the members of Parliament, objecting particularly to their quarrelsomeness among themselves. Nor did they like him. As he told Halifax, his favorite advisor, "the Commons use him like a dog" to the extent that "their coarse usage boiled so upon his stomach that he could not hinder himself from breaking out sometimes against them." Halifax, who accurately described himself as the "Trimmer," wisely urged him to pretend at least to grant them respect, for "the world is a beast that must be cozened before it be tamed." When King William did condescend to speak conciliatorily to the Parliament, the members insultingly refrained from applause.[7] For a time the distinction between Whigs and Tories lost meaning, as the landed gentry banded together to oppose the royal demands for the funds William needed for the carrying on of his unpopular Continental wars.

"The General Entertainment of All Companies"

While the politicians were pursuing their personal vendettas, the influential public speaking was that by churchmen. But they, also, were dealing with problems that were difficult to untangle.

The Anglicans resented and resisted the increasing influence of dissenting sects that were rapidly gaining converts. Bishops Burnet and Tillotson, who were in general supporters of the authority of the throne, sought primarily to enlarge the power of the Established Church. Richard Baxter was doing his best to avert the decay of Puritanism, which had fallen into disfavor in England because of its excesses during the Commonwealth, even while it was dominant in the New England colonies. Baptists and Quakers were aggressively assertive. Latitudinarian spokesmen were fostering the new spirit of rational humanism. One of them, Henry More, a Cambridge Platonist, aptly summarized the emerging challenge to traditional religion—a challenge that had not seriously been raised since the coming of Augustine.

> The times we are in and are coming on are times wherein Divine Providence is more universally loosening the minds of men from the awe

and tyranny of mere customary superstition and permitting a freer perusal of matters of religion than in former ages.[8]

Among the religious spokesmen of the time, Bishop John Tillotson was the most prominent. Coming from a Presbyterian family, as a young student at Cambridge, when only seventeen years of age, he embraced the revolt against "superstition." But as he matured, he turned against the religious Dissenters. When the Stuarts were restored to the throne, he converted to Anglicanism. In quick succession he was rewarded with appointment as chaplain to Charles II, then as dean of Saint Paul's, and shortly thereafter as archbishop of Canterbury. With a mind that was basically liberal and open to new ideas, he so eloquently advocated the universal applicability of natural law that he was elected to membership in the new Royal Society. In such great speeches as his "Sermon at the Yorkshire Feast" and "The Wisdom of Being Religious," he insisted that a proper interpretation of the Scriptures showed them to be wholly in accord with both human experience and reason. In the view of sound rhetorical critics, "he made Christianity so reasonable that it seemed immoral not to accept it."[9] As a student of philosophical language, and as a pioneer lexicographer, Tillotson was determined to preach "what men might understand, and what they ought to believe and practice, in a plain and unaffected and convincing manner." As a consequence, in the judgment of these same critics, his popularity was so great that he "secured once and for all the triumph of the plain style in preaching."

It was not, however, as a liberal but as a conservative that he exercised his great influence. His role as a defender of the status quo is well represented in a sermon he preached on 25 February 1694, before William and Mary at Whitehall, "Against Evil Speaking." His aim was not to change the thinking or the behavior of his highly respectable listeners, but rather to support his adherence to "things as they are." The disturbed feelings of the time, he argued, were not at all due to bad government, but rather to irresponsible critics. "Right thinking" would solve all the problems. What the public most needed was to be soothed and calmed. The fault lay with troublemakers, whom, for the most part, he carefully avoided identifying. His tone was admonitory, but on safe grounds.

> To speak evil of others is almost become the general entertainment of all companies, and the great and serious business of most meetings and visits, after the necessary ceremonies and compliments are over, is to sit down and backbite all the world. It is the sauce of conversation, and all discourse is counted but flat and dull which hath not something of piquancy and sharpness against somebody.

The topic he chose was gratifying to the listening monarchs and their loyal retainers. No less pleasing was Tillotson's prompt violation of his own precept against speaking ill of others when, to support the anti-Catholic sentiments of the ruling circle, he asserted: "But of all sorts of people, I have observed the priests and bigots of the Church of Rome to be the ablest in this way, and to have the strongest faith for a lusty falsehood and calumny. Others will bandy a false report, and toss it from one hand to another, but I never knew any that would so hug a lie, and be ever so fond of it." The audience could safely relax; the preacher was on their side.

The general public, Tillotson went on, was fully as malicious as were the irresponsible gossips, for "we easily forget the good that is said of others . . . but the contrary sticks with us." The real problem is that "when men are bad in themselves, they are glad to have any opportunity to censure others." What was inciting dissatisfaction among the populace was "an itch for talking and meddling in the affairs of other men, which do no wise concern them." And what should be the remedy? Not governmental reform, rather "let us accustom ourselves to pity the faults of men, and to be truly sorry for them, for then we shall take no pleasure in publishing them." What he recommended was "a resolute silence." No one except the Catholics, whom alone he targeted for his own abuse, could object to such counsel. The sermon was well designed to please the king and queen and all others who had more to gain from stability than from change.

Similarly, Tillotson's good friend Richard Burnet, bishop of Salisbury, another counselor of the Court, was equally staunch in his defense of the establishment. Unlike Tillotson, Burnett was disliked by the general public, who suspected him of being more loyal to the throne than supportive of the needs of the people. His popularity among the elite was earned by such flattering encomiums as that which he pronounced at the funeral of Queen Mary, in which he praised "her understanding, her piety, and her virtue, without discovering the least defect or fault in her." His conclusion was that "the purity and sublimity of her mind was the perfectest thing I ever saw." How could her subjects, then, be otherwise than content?

In contrast with these spokesmen for Anglicanism, Richard Baxter spoke out boldly to defend Puritanism as an ideal, even while he also condemned its excesses during the Commonwealth. In his *Reliquiae Baxteriana*, he related how, as a young man, he had preached before Cromwell a sermon in which he brashly demanded that the monarchy be restored. His experience well illustrates the strange admixture of tolerance and autocracy that marked Cromwell's rule.

> A while after, Cromwell sent to speak with me, and when I came, in the presence only of three of his principal men, he began a long and tedious speech to me of God's providence in the change of government, and what great things had been done at home and abroad. When he had wearied us all with speaking thus slowly about an hour, I told him, it was too great condescension to acquaint me fully with all these matters that were above me, but I told him that we took our ancient monarchy to be a

blessing and not an evil to the land, and humbly craved his patience, that I might ask him how ever England had forfeited that blessing, and unto whom the forfeiture had been made. Upon that question he was awakened into some passion . . . and then he let fly at the Parliament . . . and I presumed to defend them against his passion; and thus four or five hours were spent.

Despite this audacity, Baxter was allowed to continue his preaching. For another fourteen years he continued to address meetings, many of them in private homes, with great effectiveness. As he relates:

One advantage was that I came to a people that never had any awakening ministry before (but a few formal, cold sermons of the curate) . . .
Another advantage was that at first I was in the vigor of my spirits, and had a naturally familiar, moving voice (which is a great matter with the common hearers) . . . for drowsy formality and customariness doth but stupify the hearers, and rock them to sleep. It must be serious preaching, which must make men serious in hearing and obeying it.

Baxter's success won for him so large a congregation that five galleries had to be erected in his church to accommodate those who flocked to hear him. Partly his popularity derived from his adaptability to circumstances. As did the generality of Puritans, he remained within the Anglican church. His general tenor was conservative. Like Tillotson and Burnet, he sought to allay discontent, while stressing the need to live ethically. His preaching exemplified "the spirit of reform that conformed,"[10] thus appealing to the general desire to find relief from the prior period of conflict.

The radical Dissenters were of a very different stripe. What they advocated was a change of direction, into a new way of life. Chief among them were the Baptists and the Quakers, who not only belabored the Catholics and the Anglicans but also vigorously denounced one another. A leading spokesman for the Baptists was John Bunyan; for the Quakers, George Fox. Both were uneducated, and neither of them was ordained. They both scorned general learning and drew their guidance principally from the Bible. Each of them was utterly convinced that he spoke out of direct inspiration from God and therefore could not be wrong. Both were well characterized by what Fox wrote of himself in his *Journal:* "I used in my dealings the word *verily*, and it was a common saying among people that knew me if George says *verily*, there is no altering him."

John Bunyan, the son of a tinker or tinsmith of Bedford, was a zealot who delighted in self-condemnation. Since he called himself "the chief of sinners," his enemies invented tales of his alleged licentiousness, all of which he indignantly denied. The sinfulness he steadfastly insisted upon was his inability to live fully in accordance with the high standard set by Christ. It is not baptism, he insisted, but Christ-like living that opens the door to salvation. This view he presented with an arrogance that derived from humility. As the appointed voice of God, he could not be wrong. Since he had only a small congregation in a remote rural parish, his influence flowed not from his speaking but from his writing. His *Grace Abounding to the Chief of Sinners* won him immediate popularity.

Because of his freely expressed contempt for the ineffectualness of the Established Church, he was frequently imprisoned. Even so, the religious tolerance of the time was such that local authorities were always ready to release him whenever he would promise to end his attacks against other religious sects. But even though his family was impoverished, and his love for them was great, he felt unable to abandon the role that was assigned to him by God. It was during a twelve-year period in jail that he commenced his greatest work, *Pilgrim's Progress*. The book was ridiculed by intellectuals but soon became popular. During the following years he continued to write in a similar vein and also continued to preach. During these latter years of his life, the Baptist Church commenced the divisiveness into contending sects that has ever since characterized its history. Baptism by immersion was its unifying theme, and the Baptists continued to be more tolerant of other denominations than of their own divergent sects. Bunyan's rhetorical influence was to entrench the practice of speaking to individuals about problems that they felt to be real in terms of their personal need for salvation.

George Fox, the founder of Quakerism, the son of a poor weaver in Leicestershire, commenced his ministry in his fifteenth year. He had no intention of founding a new denomination. Like Bunyan, he was appalled by the empty formalism of the post-Restoration churches and set out to emphasize the importance of repentance and dependence on the inward revelation of God's will. From the beginning of his ministry he attracted large crowds, whom he addressed in barns, in open fields, at crossroads, and occasionally in churches. He refused to occupy a pulpit—partly from his feeling of unworthiness but largely because he denied the special functions of an ordained clergy.

It was Fox's followers who organized the Society of Friends—including such aristocrats as Margaret Fell of Lancaster and William Dewsbury. But it was Fox who drew up the rules that came to govern the movement. Organization was the least of their concerns. The stress of them all was on the "Inner Light" upon which alone individuals should wholly depend. Few among the rapidly expanding group of adherents to this new revelation quoted either from Fox or from one another. The only guidance they valued was direct personal revelation. Consequently, they saw no need for preachers to expound the truth to them. Instead, they gathered in groups to sit silently awaiting the inspiration that would move first one then another to speak of the vision of truth that came to them. Far from rushing into speech, they evolved what may be called a "rhetoric of silence,"[11] seeking the moment of divine revelation. Their persuasiveness derived largely from the evident sincerity of their quiet quest for dependably divine guidance. They stressed neither the Bible nor the example of Christ; rather, they searched for the "Christ within." Their intensity of introspection led to such physical manifestations as jerking and spasmodic movements. Unless they were quaking, they were not receiving messages from God. For this reason, they soon came to be known as Quakers.

Like other sects, they developed contradictory modes and practices. Very soon, leading members among them came to be distinguished as teachers or preachers who were especially open to spiritual inspiration. Individualism began to give way to their own brand of orthodoxy, which defined the kinds of messages that were indubitably divine—including the refusal to take oaths, the possibility of obtaining in this life a full victory over sin, a commitment to pacifism, and the equal right of women to receive and reveal truth. Neither the Sabbath nor a particular place for worship was important to them. These heresies led them to be sharply condemned by all other religious denominations. Their "mass hysteria" brought them not only contempt but also persecutions. Such martyrdom they welcomed, as offering a solid test of the strength of their beliefs.

Their success was immediate and sensational. "From Fox's encounters with small separatist groups in the far Northwest developed a regional movement that emptied the few churches and drew thousands to their outdoor meetings. . . . The momentum they gathered freed them from being merely one more Puritan sect among others, and drove them out across England and the New World as an independent, world-changing movement."[12] What motivated them and drew converts from other faiths was the intensity of their conviction that they had a direct and personal relationship with God. As they sat together seeking insight, "the Light searched out sin and brought into sight all of a man's inward motives and outward acts." The intensity of their emotionalism "risked sending the neurotic into insanity; and the same overwhelming emotional release, joy, and spontaneity followed their various processes for reuniting the self that ought to be and the self that he knows he is."

Since their entire emphasis was upon individual introspection, and since they scorned the usual ecclesiastical organization that led to the building of churches and the recruitment and training of ministers, what was it that drew them together? Perhaps it was mere herd instinct. More likely, it was a shared understanding of the reality underlying group therapy—namely, that the inner self is released for outward expression in the midst of kindred fellows. Yet a third factor was the need for protection and mutual support in view of the community enmity aroused by their renunciation of the customary religious forms. In any event, they soon realized that individualistic spontaneity was not enough. They needed leadership as much as they needed their shared agreement concerning their own new orthodoxy.

Dominant individuals among them were recognized as being especially receptive to the divine light and as being especially effective in providing guidance. Thus preaching developed—"aimed to break men open, driving them to despair about the bright, tight image they had of themselves by which they tried to live." Although the goal they sought—to live by the "light within" rather than biblical precepts—was different from that of Bunyan's Baptists, they shared to the full Bunyan's concern about their own self-centered sinfulness and the need to reach out toward God.

The growth of their influence was hastened by the conversion to their cause of various prestigious citizens, notably of William Penn. Penn was favored by James II, who strongly advocated tolerance as a means by which he might win restoration of the civil rights for Catholics. Moreover, certain of their beliefs—notably their emphasis upon the work ethic and the accumulation of wealth as a sign of God's favor—also contributed to their growing respectability. The Act of Toleration adopted in 1689 relieved them partially from persecution, although they continued to suffer imprisonment because of their refusal to pay tithes to the Anglican Church. Their extreme individualism was diverted into a new unity by the establishment at Prendle Hill of an organizational center. The grant from James II to William Penn of a charter for the colony of Pennsylvania was a signal achievement. Less spectacular, but equally significant, was the spread of their influence beyond the confines of their own groups, facilitating the later emergence of Universalism and Unitarianism and the general liberalization of social attitudes. The Society of Friends never became one of the larger denominations, but its effects have been considerable. The dissatisfaction with social conditions which they represented was felt not only in religious concerns but also in politics.

"The Subtlest and Most Salutary Statesman of the Day"

As H. C. Foxcroft makes abundantly clear in his biography of Halifax, "long and bitter debates" marked the sessions of both the Commons and the Lords.[13] The political speakers of greatest influence were Anthony Ashley Cooper, the earl of Salisbury, who founded the Whig party; and George Savile, marquis of Halifax, "the subtlest and most salutary statesman of the day . . . who stood aloof from all parties."[14] The issues that they debated were fundamental and crucial—including a Test Act by which Charles II attempted to divert or to control reforms, and an Exclusion Act, by which the Whigs sought to bar the Catholic James II from the throne. Unfortunately, the debates concerning these acts were neither reported nor recorded. Since they were not published, their effects upon either policymaking or the shaping of public opinion were less than that of private deals and maneuvers within the Court circle. Not even James II's most serious mistake—which was to bring to trial seven Anglican bishops who rejected his indulgence of Catholicism—resulted in public discussion, for James rectified this mistake by quickly dropping the charges. Even the arrangement that brought William and Mary to the throne was accomplished sub rosa. The "bitter political rancour which was the political curse of the time," as Foxcroft illustrates, was expressed in private quarrels and in closet counsels rather than in public discourse.

Rhetorical occasions were in fact numerous, since crucial decisions had to be made, and the political leaders who shaped them were skilled in persuasion. Shaftesbury credits Halifax, who was his principal opponent, "with that quickness, learning, and elegance that are inseparable from all his discourse." The persuasive abilities of Shaftesbury himself, and of John Russell, his most effective associate, were no less highly praised by contemporaries who heard them. Nevertheless, "set speeches" had little influence over the course of events. The leaders reflected rather than guided the agitated feelings of the public. Neither the Bill of Rights, adopted as part of the deal that brought in William of Orange, nor the Act of Settlement, designating George of Hanover as Anne's successor, resulted in any notable parliamentary debates. During the reign of Queen Anne, the most critical political influence was exercised by John Churchill, the duke of Marlborough, and his wife Sarah, and by Robert Harley, the earl of Oxford; their effectiveness, however, was in "closet dialogues" with the queen and other political leaders rather than through public speeches.

The muddling method that was developed consisted chiefly in avoidance techniques. Principal among these was the art of allegory, which reached a height that has not since been surpassed. Bunyan made it the framework for his *Pilgrim's Progress*. Defoe utilized it in his narrative of Robinson Crusoe, the typical Englishman, who surmounted enormous difficulties through ingenuity, hard work, self-reliance, and religious faith. Jonathan Swift employed allegory in depicting how Gulliver, in his visits to strange lands, found that human nature is vicious everywhere and that human ingenuity is sadly misdirected.

What is rhetorically significant is that the allegorical method fitted the circumstances of the time, which were a tangle of religious enthusiasm, of philosophical skepticism, and of rational and humanistic latitudinarianism. Also significant is the fact that allegory was utilized by writers rather than by speakers. It was "timely" in that it enabled urgent discussion of the issues of the time with an indirectness that safeguarded such discussion from political restrictions and punishment. It best served writers rather than speakers since it required an elaboration of detail than can better be comprehended by readers than by listeners. It took advantage of the idealistic and skeptical philosophy of the Irish bishop, George Berkeley, who insisted that reality is not what the five senses directly experience but the conceptions of the mind.

The nature of the rhetorical circumstances is well illustrated in the contrasting rhetorical techniques of Joseph Addison and of the Marquis of Halifax. Addison won high fame as a conversationalist and essayist. Despite his social and political prominence, he was no public speaker. As he explained the reason, "I can draw for a thousand pounds, but I have only sixpence in my pocket." He lacked the readiness that Francis Bacon had identified as the chief characteristic of speech. It is significant that his essays appeared under the titles of the *Tatler* and the *Spectator*. What he depicted were scenes of quiet and noncontroversial talk in country homes and coffeehouses. His prevalent theme was that "good nature is more agreeable in conversation than wit, and gives a certain air to the countenance which is more agreeable than beauty." Like Bishop Tillotson, Addison advised that "a true Critick ought to dwell rather upon excellencies than imperfections . . . and communicate to the world such things as are worthy of their observation."

Safety and stability were also the aims that guided the Marquis of Halifax and made him the Trimmer. He knew well what he was about, and he was successful in influencing the course of affairs. But at the end of his life he regretted that his course had been too largely to avoid controversies. In one of his last letters to his son, written on 4 July 1693, he advised, "You have tools to work with, therefore do not let them gather rust for want of their being employ'd."

This counsel from Halifax marks well the transition from the uncertainties of politics in the late seventeenth century to the more decisive eighteenth century, which was to be a time of confrontation. Muddling through was useful in the period of transition. Afterward, as the issues were sharpened, it gave way to face-to-face discussion and to public debate.

Notes

1. John Bunyan, *Pilgrim's Progress* (New York: Pocket Books, 1957), pp. 78–83.
2. Fuller, and in some respects different, analyses of the rhetorical ideas of these three philosophers are presented in Donald G. Douglas, ed., *Philosophers on Rhetoric: Traditional and Emerging Views* (Skokie, Ill.: National Textbook Publishing Company, 1973), containing essays on Bacon, by Karl R. Wallace (pp. 25–50); on Hobbes, by Lester Thonssen (pp. 50–55); and on Locke, by Wilbur Samuel Howell (pp. 77–95).
3. In the introduction of the history he wrote to "prove" that the Whigs were the defenders of the rights of the people.
4. Maurice Ashley, *Great Britain to 1688* (Ann Arbor: University of Michigan Press, 1961), p. 420.
5. Keith Feiling, *British Foreign Policy, 1660–1672* (London: Cass, 1930); and Basil Williams, *The Whig Supremacy, 1714–1760* (Oxford: Clarendon Press, 1939).
6. Thomas Babington Macaulay, *The History of England*, abridged by Hugh Trevor-Roper (Harmondsworth: Penguin, 1980), pp. 20, 85.
7. Elizabeth Hamilton, *William's Mary* (New York: Taplinger, 1972), describes the rela-

tionship of the two monarchs with one another, and William's relations with the Parliament. See specifically pp. 216, 304–5.

8. Cited by Edward Augustus George, *Seventeenth Century Men of Latitude: Forerunners of the New Theology* (New York: Scribners, 1908), p. 121.

9. Donald C. Bryant, et al., *An Historical Anthology of Select British Speeches* (New York: Ronald Press, 1967), p. 156. The sermon from which passages will be quoted is included in this volume, pp. 157–72.

10. George, *Men of Latitude*.

11. See Richard Bauman, *Let Your Words Be Few: Symbolism of Speaking and Silence among Seventeenth Century Quakers* (New York: Cambridge University Press, 1983).

12. This and the subsequent quotations are from Hugh Barbour and Arthur O. Roberts, *Early Quaker Writing, 1650–1700* (Grand Rapids, Mich.: Erdmans, 1973), pp. 16–46.

13. H. C. Foxcroft, *A Character of the Trimmer: Being a Short Life of the First Marquis of Halifax* (Cambridge: Cambridge University Press, 1946).

14. Winston Churchill, *A History of the English Speaking Peoples*, 4 vols. (New York: Dodd, Mead, 1956–58), 3:8, 10.

7
Elitism—The Rhetoric of Privilege

In sharp contrast with the disagreements in interpretation of the seventeenth century, historians find little to dispute about concerning the major characteristics of British government in the period that followed. Royalty had been restrained. Parliament had gained much greater power. Only the people were the losers.

Such gains as democracy had won were considerably diminished. "Power became gradually concentrated in the hands of a small minority."[1] In parliamentary elections, "111 patrons influenced or determined 205 of the borough seats."[2] Corruption became institutionalized, with parliamentary votes freely and openly bought with bribes, pensions, and appointments to office.[3] The persuasive appeals that mattered were less to patriotism or the rights of the people than to defense of the privileges of the ruling oligarchy.

The result, in the harsh judgment of Wingfield-Stratford, was "to depress the common people to a state of impotence and degradation scarcely precedented since the 'devils and wicked men' of King Stephen's days."[4] It was distinctly an age of political bossism. Politics had become a profitable business. Men sought to win parliamentary seats not to serve the people but to get rich.

What all this meant rhetorically was not that debate and discussion were reduced in importance. On the contrary, they rose to even greater heights as fundamental instruments of government. Agreement is general that "the debates in both lords and commons rose to an importance and created an interest in the cultivated world rarely equalled in our history."[5] The whole period of the eighteenth century proved to be one of the world's greatest ages of oratory. In the latter part the speaking dealt with great issues; in the opening years it was largely a contentious defense of privileges of classes and individuals.

"Enjoyment of Their Properties in Peace and Safety"

Parliamentarians who represented primarily their self-interest and the demands of local leaders who had appointed them were far from quiescent. They were too alert to what might be gained to be readily disciplined. Not even the largess that poured out from the Crown through its ministry could insure a controllable majority. What was given to some members merely whetted the appetites of the rest. "It is impossible to gratify all; and all that are not gratified are disobliged. Whoever, therefore, is Head of a Party has but an uneasy station. Whatever Blaze he may take and however absolute he may seem, his Disappointments often equal his Triumphs."[6] Robert Walpole, "the Minister of the King in the House of Commons," was more dominant than any minister ever had been before him. Yet he was toppled from power after his twenty years of dominance, and he well understood why. As he said in the 1741 debates that led to his ouster, "Men easily admit the force of an Argument which tends to support Notions that it is their interest to diffuse . . . but When their Passions have subsided and their Interest is disunited from the Question, those Arguments appear only loud Assertions or empty Sophistry."

The problem inherent in boss control was that there never were emoluments enough to go around. During Walpole's long ministry, "the proportion of placemen went up from less than a quarter to about a third of the house."[7] This left a substantial majority of members whose votes were unbought. At least after 1734, "Walpole found himself confronted by an ever-increasing array of Opposition talent whose rhetorical outbursts could frequently sway those independent members on whose support Sir Robert in the last resort had to depend." As a result, "no other period in our history can show such keen and well-informed debates or such masters of parliamentary craft and eloquence as the reigns of the first two Georges." This judgment was only partially right. By all means, the time must be extended to include the reign of the third George as well.

"The important fact about the corruption of the century is that it produced so small a result after such intense application."[8] Discussion, far from being squelched, was intensified. The rhetorical circumstances not only permitted it but demanded it. Society was undergoing fundamental changes. The traditional unifying slogan of Church and King! had lost its magic. Religion no longer maintained its centuries-long coherence—rationalistic deism was eating away at its base; new evangelical faiths were challenging the Anglican centralism. Self-seeking was undermining the spirit of nationalism. Preservation of property was becoming the dominant theme. John Locke, in *An Essay concerning the True Original Extent and End of Civil Government*, stated what many believed: "The great end of Men's entering into Society being enjoyment of their Properties in Peace and Safety."

The political complexities were unusually intricate. Tory doctrine favored both the Stuarts and the Established Church; yet since both James II and his grandson, Bonnie Prince Charlie, refused to abjure their Catholic faith, these two loyalties were inescapably antagonistic. The Whig party was similarly unstable. After the adoption of the Act of Settlement, the Whigs scrambled to align themselves with the House of Hanover, and they held the allegiance of the rising commercial class. But as Continental war was waged less for English than for Hanoverian advantages, and as taxation to support the war became increasingly burdensome, these two allegiances became sharply divergent.

Still further instability was caused by compromises that were inserted in the Act of Settlement, which assured the throne to George I. Among its dozens of qualifying conditions was the requirement that the king must always be Anglican, to which both parties agreed. Unmanageable requirements were that the king could never leave the country (to visit his Hanover domain) without the explicit consent of Parliament and that he must depend upon parliamentary guidance rather than counsel from his Germanic friends. The aim and the consequence of such provisions were to strengthen the role of Parliament. But how its power would be exercised remained ambiguous.

Parliamentary debate became increasingly important for three major reasons. The first was the nature of governmental organization, which was administered by a diverse group of ministers who were not united coherently into a cabinet. The second reason was that many members of Parliament were well above the average in intelligence. Third, they were dependent for their positions on local interests. For such reasons, they resisted control by the king's ministers. As Laprade has shown, localism was of far more consequence in the shaping of affairs than was nationalism.

The sentiment of patriotism was reduced by the coronation of a foreign king. The Hanoverians had small hereditary claim of divine right to the throne. George I did not have, nor did he court, popularity. As a stolid German burgher, already in his mid-fifties when he became king, neither in person nor in personality was he attractive. Only reluctantly did he quit the comfortable security of his small Continental demesne to accept the kingship of the island nation that he had only once visited very briefly and for which he did not disguise his dislike. He could neither speak nor understand English, and since Walpole did not understand German, their conversations had to be conducted awkwardly in their inadequate command of Latin. George knew little of English customs and felt no real kinship with the English people. In the first year after his accession, an attempt was made to replace him with the Jacobite Pretender—an effort that quickly collapsed, chiefly because it was ineptly managed. But a considerable anti-Hanover sentiment remained.[9]

Six parliamentarians who exercised the greatest rhetorical influence during this period were Bolingbroke, Walpole, Chesterfield, Wyndham, Pulteney, and (at its close) the greatest of them all, the Elder William Pitt. The rhetorical problems that they confronted, and their means of dealing with them, constituted the political framework within which significant changes were taking place. All of them except the last were elitist spokesmen who were more representative of privileged groups than of the nation at large. What they sought to attain was government by the best, rather than by the people. It was an idea so deeply entrenched that not even Pitt, when he emerged as the "Great Commoner," seriously questioned it. The age of democracy lay yet far ahead.

The record of the parliamentary debates is only fragmentary. It was forbidden to record the speeches, and journalists were debarred from the galleries, the aim being to protect the independence of the members from the disruptive influence of public opinion. Samuel Johnson in his young manhood earned a meager living by fabricating the debates for *The Gentleman's Magazine*, and although his reports were afterward reprinted as the actual parliamentary journal, they were (in his words) no more than "the mere coinage of his own imagination." All he had to work from were notes secretively made for him. When he was complimented for his fairness in balancing the arguments of the two factions, he replied, "I saved appearances tolerably well; but I took care that the WHIG DOGS should not have the best of it."[10]

What is known for sure is that eloquence mattered. Because government was loosely organized and without a strong central power, politics was more than usually personalized: Influence derived more from persons than from parties. Great speaking there surely was, and its effectiveness was demonstrated. Charismatic individuals won influence by their wit, brilliance of both mind and diction, and impressiveness of bearing. Their speaking, however, did not provide much support for Quintilian's ideal—that "the orator of our quest is a good man who is skilled in the arts of speech." The most influential leaders exhibited more skill in speech than goodness. Their effectiveness flowed more from expediency than from undeviating adherence to high moral principles or from advocacy of inherently sound policies. The moving power of their words was enforced by the prestige of their positions. One of their skills was to tell their listeners what they most wanted to hear. Their speeches scintillated with wit and shone with vivid imagery. Self-interest and class-interest were strong motivations. They had little sympathy with the needs of the masses. Their speeches had less of the common touch than of aristocratic elegance.

In short, it was a time of elitist eloquence, with little of the shirt-sleeve spirit of "Come, let us reason together," and more of the assured tone of "Listen, and I will show the way to success." It was the kind of speaking that fitted the tenor of the times. And it worked—it produced results.

"Our Throats Would Be Cut"

No orator in the history of Great Britain more exemplifies this characteristic than did Henry St John, Lord Bolingbroke. Bolingbroke spoke as though posterity was listening. He spoke with the authority of superior abilities, but not from a foundation of sound character. His unchallenged position among England's most admired and influential speakers is an anomaly for two reasons. The first is that no text of his speeches, even in fragmentary form, was published. They simply were not recorded. His reputation rests upon the responses he won from his listeners and upon their testimony. And the second reason is that his influence over his auditors was not because of but in spite of their opinion of his character.

Few politicians in the long history of the islands have been more controversial. No other won such acclaim for effectiveness, combined with such harsh condemnation as was heaped upon him for immorality, lack of intellectual integrity, and sheer opportunism. The amazing fact is that without winning respect he nevertheless exercised a well-high irresistible appeal. His own close followers condemned his character and resented the ineptness of his political management. Yet they clung to his leadership. He prevailed over them, and he did it not by buying or forcing but by winning their support.

Winston Churchill's condemnation of him was biased because Bolingbroke led in undermining the military victories of Churchill's personal hero, the Duke of Marlborough. Yet his harshness was akin to what many of Bolingbroke's contemporaries also felt and asserted: "By personal vices of heart and mind, by deeds of basest treachery, by violation of law and public faith this man St John—unpurposed, unprincipled miscreant adventurer—had brought his native land to the edge of the abyss, and in this horrid juncture he could not even clothe his crime with coherency." Even Bolingbroke's generally admiring biographer capsulized his career as a "ruthless pursuit of power."[11]

The fact that Bolingbroke was notoriously promiscuous was not in itself unusual among the aristocrats of his time. What many found abhorrent was the embarrassing frankness of his avowal that he married his wife only for her money and that he vilely mistreated her and and deliberately humiliated her over a long span of years. Even worse, politically, was his crass betrayal of his closest associates and his cowardly retreat in their time of crisis. Throughout his career he was viewed as being even more an opportunist than his predecessor, Halifax the Trimmer.

He could not, of course, have been so persuasive over so long a period had he not also possessed qualities of genuine greatness. It is noteworthy that he won not only admiration and respect but also affection from such intellectuals as Alexander Pope, Jonathan Swift, and Voltaire. It is also significant that he remained through the years the guiding spirit of the choice Society of Brothers, who, among all his contemporaries, knew him best. The highest testimony to his power is that even during his latter years, while he was publicly disgraced and officially debarred from office, he nevertheless maintained the leadership of his party and strongly influenced the course of legislation. And he proved his acuity by writing a book, *The Patriot King,* which accurately predicted and helped to shape the future development of the British constitution.

How is it possible to assess such a mishmash of contrarities? The only tenable answer is to be found in Bolingbroke's power of eloquence. Jonathan Swift put it well in a letter to Stella, written in 1711, while Bolingbroke's career was at its zenith. "I think Mr. St John is the greatest young man I ever knew: wit, capacity, beauty, quickness of apprehension, good learning, and an excellent taste; the best orator in the House of Commons, admirable conversation, good nature and good manners, [though] what truth and sincerity he may have I know not."[12]

The failure to preserve the texts of his speeches was much regretted in the following generation, which, based on reports they had heard, considered them to be "more priceless than the lost fragments of antiquity."[13] The testimonials from those who heard him were impressive. Wrote Lord Chesterfield: "I am old enough to have heard him speak in Parliament, and I remember that, although prejudiced against him by party, I felt all the force and charm of eloquence. . . . All the internal and external advantages and talent of an orator are undoubtedly his: figure, voice, knowledge, and, above all, the purest and most florid diction, with the justest metaphors and happiest images."[14] What metaphors mean to public speaking has been well analyzed by J. Vernon Jensen.

> Metaphors do many things, both good and bad. They clarify, vivify, simplify, make the abstract concrete, give strength to a point, heighten emotions, and make a subject more interesting. But sometimes these "good" functions can become unfortunate ones. For instance, a complex, abstract, fluid reality may be made inappropriately into a simple, concrete, and static "reality" through the metaphor. A rigid format is created. Vision narrows, positions harden, options are reduced, and the rhetoricians are trapped by their own image making. "As we speak, so we think," operates with powerful force. The participants are forced to fit everything, every new fact, into that prefabricated mold. Roles are assigned, good intentions and good ends are proclaimed for oneself; evil intentions and evil ends for the antagonist. The metaphor pushes the antagonists into their respective corners, from which escape is difficult.[15]

What this analysis does not point out, perhaps taking it for granted, is that the "ills" resulting from metaphorical compression are philosophical rather than rhetorical. We may hope that speakers will evaluate their chosen theme from all relevant points of view, and form their own judgments soundly. When they come to the task of influencing their listeners, what they aim to do is precisely to "reduce options," to fit facts into their "prefabricated mold," and to differentiate their own "good ends" from the purposes of their antagonists. It is this in which Bolingbroke excelled, and he succeeded in winning the approval of his peers. William Pitt, for example, attested that among all the "lost works" of the past, the most to be regretted were the speeches of Bolingbroke. Alexander Pope, describing his persuasive power, explained that, "he would fix upon that point which was the most material, would place it in the strongest possible light, and manage it so as to make it serviceable for his purpose." Lord Brougham judged from Bolingbroke's published writings that he must have been "the greatest of modern orators."[16] F. S. Oliver, who argued that in general oratory has little to do with statesmanship, nevertheless made an exception for Bolingbroke, concluding that his "greatest superiority over his accusers and judges lay in his own powers. He was a consummate debater; the greatest orator before Chatham." He also noted his weaknesses: "The only thing that really mattered to him was the verdict of public opinion." And, in sum, "he was incomparably the best parliamentarian of his time."[17]

What Bolingbroke left in print were not his speeches but a series of philosophical treatises. His *Patriot Prince* is a portrait of a scheming but enlightened leader, who knows how to dominate and to guide the legislature; in short, a strong monarch who uses his central authority with skill. In his *Spirit of Patriotism*, he summed up what he had learned of politics, concluding that "eloquence has charms to lead mankind, and gives a nobler superiority than power, that every dunce may use, or fraud, that every knave may employ." Yet, despite the power of his own persuasiveness, he knew better than to depend upon it alone. When more votes were needed in the Lords to win approval of the Peace of Utrecht, he had Queen Anne create twelve new peers who would support it. In a "shameless anticipation of Tammany," Bolingbroke frankly confessed his motivation: "I am afraid that we came to court in the same disposition as all parties have done: that the principal spring of our actions was to have the government of the State in our hands; that our principal views were the conservation of this power, great employments to ourselves, and great opportunities of rewarding those who had helped to raise us, and of hurting those who had stood in opposition to us."[18]

Unhappily, Bolingbroke's lack of intellectual integrity was illustrated again and again. He was a deist who strongly disdained oranized religion, yet he supported the Anglican claim to supremacy. He first wooed the favor of Queen Anne, then of the French court. He joined the circle around the Stuart pretender, who called himself James III, until the Act of Succession settled the choice upon the Elector of Hanover, whom he thereupon began to court. On his behalf it should be noted that such shifts were not uncommon. What made them uncommonly evident in Bolingbroke was his prominence—as secretary of state for foreign affairs and as leader of the Tory party. Moreover, in times of crisis he proved to be woefully indecisive.

The crisis that triggered the collapse of his career came on the day of Queen Anne's death. Bolingbroke had shared in shaping an inept plan—

little more really than a wistful hope—that aimed to block the Hanoverian succession and to bring the claimant James over from Paris. The principal plotters were the Duke of Ormonde, commanding the armed forces; Francis Atterbury, bishop of Rochester, representing the Anglicans; and Bolingbroke and William Wyndham, leading the Tories. When word came of Anne's death, these men and a few others assembled. Atterbury spoke passionately, urging the need for quick action. He himself, he said, would stand in the Royal Exchange and read a proclamation announcing that James III was the new king. France would lend support, if necessary with arms. Ormonde expressed his readiness to rally the army to the cause. Basil Williams reports what happened next. "Bolingbroke said that all our throats would be cut. To which the Bishop reply'd that if a speedy resolution be not taken, by God all would be lost. Lord Bolingbroke harangued upon this subject, and the Bishop fell into a great passion and said that this pusillanimous fellow will ruin our country; and so he quitted them."[19] Bolingbroke's sober assessment of the mood of the public was undoubtedly right: "England would as soon have a Turk as a Roman Catholic for King."

After that meeting, Bolingbroke lost the confidence of his closest associates. In a sudden panic of being tried for treason, he secretly fled to France. Thus his career, which had risen to greatness in his mid-thirties, quickly fell into what appeared to be irretrievable ruin. Yet such were his abilities that he surmounted this disaster. Within a decade he was back in England, having won a pardon for his part in the plot. But he was debarred from returning to the Parliament. What is most remarkable is that even after his desertion, and while he had to operate as a mere counselor from outside, such was his personal magnetism that he was able again to command the adherence of the Tories in Parliament.

"Let Us Suppose a Man Abandoned to Virtue and Honor"

In 1721, while Bolingbroke was still exiled in France, there emerged into parliamentary leadership the most skilled political strategist of his time and perhaps in all English history—Sir Robert Walpole, who was to maintain a tight control over English political processes for the next two decades. In the previous year England was shaken by the "bursting of the South Sea Bubble," an investment scheme in which many were ruined in an elaborate program of bribery and corruption. Walpole won the confidence of George I and of the aristocracy by preventing prosecution of the guilty, on the ground that it was better to let sleeping dogs lie. In consequence, he was named chancellor of the Exchequer, with a wealth of patronage to dispense. Even so, the country gentlemen on the back benches had to be convinced in order to win their votes, and Walpole was a master convincer.

It was in terms of his persuasive abilities that his career was summed up:

"He was above all a house of commons man . . . he always paid it the compliment of luminous explanations of his policy and was influenced by good speeches even from his opponents."[20] His accomplishments were monumental. Not the least of them was that he guided the process of change quietly and soothingly. Under his leadership the nature of the English government was fundamentally altered. The power of the monarch was restricted both by public opinion and by a growth of legislative authority. Supremacy in the Parliament was shifted from the Lords to the Commons. A cabinet system of administrative responsibility was evolved. All this was accomplished during a time of involvement in unpopular wars and under the continuing threat of rebellion in behalf of first the Old Pretender and then the Young Pretender. Moreover, the Opposition with which he had to contend was both determined and verbally adept.

While Bolingbroke was abroad, leadership of the Tories devolved on his lieutenant, William Wyndham, who had remained at home to be imprisoned in the Tower and then forgiven in a general act of amnesty. Wyndham joined with Walpole in a discreet declaration by the Commons, which was formulated as a statement of loyalty to the Anglican church and a reproach to the Dissenters, the Catholics, and the Pretender. Wyndham had himself lost large sums by investing in the inflated bonds of the South Sea Company, and thereby was absolved of responsibility for its misdeeds. During a period of "watchful waiting" to recover from that debacle, Walpole arranged for funding the national debt through the East India Company and the Bank of England; Wyndham supported him to a degree but objected to parts of the plan. In 1727, after the accession of George II, Wyndham spearheaded attacks on the foreign policies that seemed to favor Hanover at the expense of English interests.

The conflict came to a head in an explosion of eloquence by both men on 13 March 1734. The debate was on a motion, instigated by Bolingbroke and introduced in the commons by Wyndham, to require triennial parliamentary elections—fueled by their expectation that their party would win a majority. Wyndham gave an impassioned speech that rose to a crescendo of attack on Walpole, in which he skillfully interwove the deep dissatisfactions felt by different segments of the House membership.

> Let us then suppose, Sir, a man abandoned to all notions of virtue or honor, of no great family, and of but a mean fortune, raised to be chief minister of state by the concurrence of many whimsical events; afraid or unwilling to trust any but creatures of his own making; and most of them equally abandoned to all notions of virtue or honor; ignorant of the true interests of his country, and consulting nothing but that of enriching and aggrandizing himself and his favorites; in foreign affairs trusting none but those whose education makes it impossible for them to have such knowledge or such qualifications, as can either be of service to their country, or give any weight or credit to their negotiations. Let us suppose

the true interest of the nation, by such means, neglected or misunderstood; her honor and credit lost; her trade insulted; her merchants plundered; and her sailors murdered; and all these things overlooked, only for fear his administration should be endangered. Suppose him next, possessed of great wealth, the plunder of the nation, with a Parliament of his own choosing, most of their seats purchased, and their votes bought at the expense of the public treasury.

In such a Parliament, let us suppose attempts made to inquire into his conduct, or to relieve the nation from the distress he has brought upon it . . . suppose . . . these reasonable requests rejected by a corrupt majority of his creatures. . . . Upon this scandalous victory, let us suppose this chief minister pluming himself in defiance, because he finds he has got a Parliament, like a packed jury, ready to acquit him at all adventures. Let us further suppose him arrived to that degree of insolence and arrogance, as to domineer over all the men of ancient families, all the men of sense, figure, and fortune in the nation, and as he has no virtue of his own, ridiculing it in others, and endeavoring to destroy or corrupt it in all.[21]

The listening members could not but admire the shrewdness with which Wyndham avoided being ruled out of order by merely "supposing" there could be such a miscreant minister. Neither would they miss the point that "men of ancient families" and of "sense, figure, and fortune" had been excluded by Walpole not only from office but also from any share in the public plunder. This was a source of resentment always available to be inflamed. And the wit of the speaker amused while it also aroused them.

Walpole well realized that he had to make an effective reply. Experience taught him that his majority had to be held "above all by his own consummate skill in debate and use of practical arguments most fitted to the understanding of the rough country squires and hard-headed business men who thronged the benches behind him."[22] Knowing well the receptivity of the members to abusive wit, he artfully adopted the pattern used against him—all the more effective in his speech since the members knew that he had to extemporize, in contrast to Wyndham's prior preparation. The members also appreciated the acuteness with which Walpole virtually ignored Wyndham and, instead, directed his response at Bolingbroke, who was well known to be the real leader of the Opposition, although restricted to the privacy of his estate at Battersea. With the equanimity of assured superiority, Walpole introduced his riposte.

I do assure you, I did not intend to have troubled you on this occasion. . . . When gentlemen talk of ministers abandoned to all sense of virtue and honor, other gentlemen may, I am sure, with equal justice, and, I think, more justly, speak of anti-ministers and mock patriots. . . .

But now, sir, let me suppose. . . . Let us suppose in this, or in some other unfortunate country, an anti-minister, who thinks himself a person of so great and extensive parts, and of so many eminent qualifications, that he looks upon himself as the only person in the kingdom capable to conduct the public affairs of the nation; and therefore christening every other gentleman who has the honor to be employed in this administration by the name of Blunderer. Suppose this fine gentleman lucky enough to have gained over to his party some persons of really fine parts, of ancient families, and of great fortunes, and others of desperate views, arising from disappointed and malicious hearts; all these gentlemen, with respect to their political behavior, moved by him, and by him solely; all they say, either in private or in public, being only a repetition of the words he has put into their mouths, and a spitting out of that venom which he has infused into them. And yet we may suppose this leader not really liked by any, even of those who so blindly follow him, and hated by all the rest of mankind. We will suppose this anti-minister to be in a country where he really ought not to be, and where he could not have been but by an effect of too much goodness and mercy, yet endeavoring with all his art to destroy the fountain from whence that mercy flowed. . . . Let us suppose this anti-minister . . . making it his trade to betray the secrets of every court where he had been before; void of all faith, of honor, and betraying every master he ever served. . . . If we can suppose such a one, can there ever be imagined a greater disgrace to human nature than such a wretch as this?

This reply proved to be devastating. The satirical wit, which was at least the equal of the premeditated image contrived by Wyndham, was so effective that Bolingbroke felt impelled once again to leave England for his safe refuge in France. The remainder of Walpole's speech was in a loftier vein of objective statesmanship. A triennial election of Parliaments would, he warned, place the members precariously under the influence of a public opinion that was necessarily uninformed and unstable. "It is certain," he said, "that ours is a mixed government; and the perfection of our constitution consists in this, that the monarchical, aristocratical, and democratical forms of government are mixed and inter-woven." Triennial elections would mean that ministers "would always be obliged to change their measures as often as the people changed their minds." In contrast, with elections held only at seven-year intervals, the administration could proceed to carry out sound policies even when they were unpopular. This posed no danger, for if in the long run policies proved to be wrong, the next election would provide a correction. When government is too closely dependent on public opinion, ambitious office seekers "have too many opportunities for working upon and corrupting the minds of the people."

Even though the speech won for Walpole the votes he needed, nevertheless the kinds of dissatisfaction to which Wyndham had appealed were real, and they persisted. The Opposition found its best opportunity in a long-continuing debate over the maintenance of a standing army. Ever since the Civil War, the English public had remained fearful of a large army that might be used to support governmental tyranny. This fear was not lessened but was actually heightened by the virtual perpetuity of wars. From 1739, when war broke out with Spain, until 1815, when Napoleon was defeated at Waterloo, England enjoyed only a few and always brief intervals of peace. Against the patriotic urge to support the country in time of war was the unquenched fear that the liberties of the people were endangered by the existence of a large armed force. Partly this fear arose from the lack of an organized national police, which meant that the army had to be used to prevent or to control public disorders. The unpopularity of the army was increased by the custom of selling commissions, which resulted in poor leadership, and by the practice of billeting troops in private homes, because of public uneasiness at the prospect of having them assembled in barracks. So deep-seated was the antimilitarist sentiment that England was forced to depend upon the employment of Hessians and other Continental mercenaries to fill its ranks for land battles. Walpole felt the necessity for a larger army, and it was upon this issue that he finally was driven from office.

The most persistent anti-army speaker in the Commons was William Shippen, but the most effective was William Pulteney, a Whig who fell out with Walpole and aligned himself with Bolingbroke. He spoke often in Parliament but almost none of his speeches have been preserved. As he himself said in a debate in 1738, "to print or publish the speeches of gentlemen in the House looks very much like making them accountable without doors for what they say within." He worked hard at developing a conversational extempore style, which was direct, vigorous, and addressed unostentatiously to the feelings of the members. Late in January 1742, Pulteney marshaled the Opposition for a massive effort to drive Walpole from office. The specific ground on which he chose to launch his attack was on a motion for reducing the army. "I have always been, sir, and shall always be, against a standing army of any kind. To me it is a terrible thing, whether under that of Parliamentary or any other designation. A standing army is still a standing army, whatever name it be called by. They are a body of men distinct from the body of the people; they are governed by different laws; and blind obedience, and an entire submission to the orders of their commanding officer, is their only principle."

In the remainder of his speech, which remains rather paraphrased than recorded, he set forth his objections to the bill in the form of three extended examples, which were drawn from contemporary Europe, from ancient Rome, and from England's own history of the prior century.

> The nations around us, sir, are already enslaved, and have been enslaved by these very means: by means of their standing armies they have lost every one of their liberties. . . . No, sir . . . from their misfortunes we ought to learn to avoid those rocks upon which they have split.
> It signifies nothing to tell me, that our army is commanded by such gentlemen as cannot be supposed to join in any measure for enslaving

their country. . . . Where was there a braver army than that under Julius Caesar? Where was there ever an army that had served their country more faithfully? That army was commanded generally by the best citizens of Rome—by men of great fortune and figure in their country; yet *that* army enslaved their country. The affections of the soldiers toward their country, the honor and integrity of the under officers, are not to be depended on. . . . If an officer were commanded to pull his own father out of this House, he would do it; he dares not disobey; immediate death would be the sure consequence of the least grumbling. . . .

Sir, I talk not of imaginary things. I talk of what *has* happened to the English House of Commons, and from an English army; and not only from an English army, but an army that was raised by that very House of Commons, an army that was paid by them, and an army that was commanded by generals appointed by them. If an army be so numerous as to have it in their power to overawe the Parliament, they will be submissive so long as the Parliament does nothing to disoblige their favorite general; but when that case happens, I am afraid that, in place of Parliament's dismissing the army, the army will dismiss the Parliament, as they have done heretofore.

There is no extant record of specific responses to this speech. It could not have failed to be effective. Without pretension, with no array of facts that the members did not already know, and with no battery of logic, it simply set forth a set of precedents that could not be ignored. Walpole was voted out of office, and on Walpole's advice, King George offered the chief ministry to Pulteney. This burden Pulteney was disinclined to accept; in its place, he accepted a peerage, as earl of Bath, and went, along with Walpole, into the House of Lords. There Walpole greeted him in a spirit of mingled pleasantry and bitterness: "Here we are, my Lord, the two most insignificant fellows in England."[23]

"People Have Ears but Few Have Judgments"

Another of the great parliamentary speakers of the period was Philip Dormer Stanhope, the fourth earl of Chesterfield, who was born in 1694 and lived for seventy-nine years. His career can be divided into two periods. From 1728, when he was appointed ambassador to Holland, on to 1746 (when he accepted his last appointment, as Secretary of State) he served in various public offices with high distinction. Then he retired, for the rest of his life, to leisure, literature, and a final end in illness and despondency—only to emerge once more (in 1751) for a final and valedictory service with a great speech on reform of the calendar.

Best remembered for his essays, and even more for his letters to his illegitimate son, he was notable in his own time as a skilled debater and orator. In part he is remembered for a scathingly bitter and unfair letter written to him by Samuel Johnson to repudiate his patronage of the Great Cham's *Dictionary*. He is commonly depicted as an urbane aristocrat who valued good manners above morals. He deserves better. He was also a masterly public speaker who through his speeches helped to guide the events of his age; he was also a discerning critic of the persuasive stratagems of his associates.

How Chesterfield perceived the nature of public speaking is described in a letter of 9 December 1749 to his son. This son was an awkward fellow, and many of Chesterfield's letters to him were aimed at inducing him to develop social graces. Hence this letter emphasized a theme he often raised—the value of diction.

> I, like all the rest of the world, will willingly exchange and give up some degree of rough sense, for a good degree of pleasing sound. . . . The vulgar, who are always mistaken, look upon a speaker and a comet with the same astonishment and admiration, taking them both for preternatural phenomena. . . . But let you and I analyze and simplify this good speaker; let us strip him of those adventitious plumes with which his own pride and the ignorance of others have decked him; and we shall find the true definition of him to be no more than this: a man of good common sense, who reasons justly, and expresses himself elegantly, on that subject upon which he speaks. . . .
>
> Most people have ears, but few have judgment; tickle those ears, and, depend upon it, you will catch their judgments, such as they are.
>
> . . . I call that man an orator who reasons justly, and expresses himself elegantly, upon whatever subjects he treats. . . . The subjects of all parliamentary debates are subjects of common sense singly.

Common sense expressed elegantly was not only Chesterfield's ideal for parliamentary speaking; it was also his practice. To it he added a lively and felicitous wit, along with a depth of conviction that elevated him above the personalized bickering of many of his associates. His reputation has suffered in part because of Dr. Johnson's continued disparagement of him. Often quoted is Dr. Johnson's indictment of him as having "the morals of a whore and the manners of a dancing master." When Chesterfield's *Miscellaneous Works* was published, Johnson magisterially claimed, "Here now are two speeches ascribed to him, both of which were written by me: and the best of it is, they have found out that the one is like Demosthenes, and the other like Cicero." In all of Boswell's recurrent notations of Johnsonian comments on Chesterfield, the best he said of him was that he was dignified—quickly qualified by the amendment that he was also insolent. On all these counts, Johnson's opinions must be discounted, with the recollection that he was notoriously careless of facts and that, in his conversation, as

Goldsmith observed, "If his pistol misses fire, he knocks you down with the butt end of it."[24]

Aside from the highly quotable belittlements of Chesterfield by Johnson, there has also been a general tendency to interpret the letters to his son as indicative of a supercilious and cynical mind. Underlying them, however, is the devotion of a parent to shaping his son for success. Repeatedly, he advised against sexual promiscuity, gambling, idleness, and gossip, as impediments to social effectiveness. Chesterfield's own life was far more devoted to public service than to private pleasures. His most careful biographer, and editor of his letters, shows clearly that he was highly reputed as an "honest patriot," and that "as an orator . . . he was undoubtedly, on occasion, the greatest of his time."[25] This judgment he supported with a cogent summary of Chesterfield's persuasive methods, in part as Chesterfield himself described them:

> He had not the fiery dramatic quality of Pitt, with "the strength of thunder and the splendour of lightning," whom tragic actors used to go to hear to learn their craft; nor would that style have been effective in his sphere. He had the House of Lords manner, though he was probably not so gifted as "silver-tongued Murray" [the Earl of Mansfield], whose art he extolled to his son. His speeches were carefully prepared, chiefly by soaking his mind in the matter under debate; he probably arranged it roughly, and relied on practice for the actual phrasing and gesture: and he always held his audience; his friends by delight in, his enemies by fear of, his wit. His method is best illustrated by his letters to his son, many years later than this period, where he explained his success in speaking on the reform of the calendar. "I consulted the best lawyers," he wrote on 18th March, 1751, "and the most skillful astronomers, and we cooked up a Bill for that purpose. But then my difficulty began; I was to bring in this Bill, which was necesarily composed of law jargon and astronomical calculations, to both of which I am an utter stranger. However, it was absolutely necessary to make the House of Lords think that I knew something of the matter, and also to make them believe that they knew something of it themselves, which they do not. For my own part, I could just as soon have talked Celtic or Sclavonian to them as astronomy, and they would have understood me full as well; so I resolved to do better than to speak to the purpose, and to please instead of informing them. I gave them, therefore, only an historical account of calendars, from the Egyptian down to the Gregorian, amusing them now and then with little episodes, but I was particularly attentive to the choice of my words, the harmony and roundness of my periods, to my elocution, to my action. This succeeded and ever will succeed; they thought I informed them because I pleased them; and many of them said that I made the whole very clear to them, when God knows, I had not even attempted it." He goes on to say in this letter, and one of 7th April, that Lord Macclesfield's speech was far better than his as to matter, but had less effect because it pleased less.

In this brief passage is comprised an entire volume of insight concerning the role of public speaking in the conduct of government. The speaker must keep clearly in mind his always dominant purpose—to win the requisite votes. To accomplish this, he must understand precisely what will be most effective for influencing his listeners. The factual substance of the speech is purely a secondary concern. What is "absolutely necessary" is to make the hearers believe that the speaker knows what he is talking about and to make them further believe that he conveys to them their own genuine understanding. What the speech undertakes is to bring them to the conclusion that the proposed measure merits their votes. On different subjects and under different circumstances, the mode of speaking might be very different. The political function is served if the speaker knows what will work—and then if he makes it work.

The early stage of Chesterfield's career—when he was a member of the House of Commons—was undistinguished. He neither knew how to talk to the country squires nor cared to do so. Consequently, he spoke seldom and never well. It was not until after the accession of George II, and his own elevation to the family title brought him into the Lords, that his effectiveness developed. Even then—and despite the reputation he earned as an effective ambassador to Holland—his decision to support the Whig rebels who opposed Walpole kept him out of the ministry. What he did do was to demonstrate that Opposition can make momentous contributions to government. His most notable participation in the parliamentary debates (prior to his late speech on the calendar) came in the discussions on the Theatre Licensing Bill in 1737, and his speeches on the Gin Act in February 1743.

His speech against the Licensing Bill, which came to the Lords in May 1737, after it had already been approved in the Commons, was neither well reasoned nor effective in winning votes. The evils of censorship, against which he warned, proved to be far less onerous than he depicted them. Nevertheless, this speech won for him a personal reputation for liberalism, and a popularity with the public that greatly enhanced his parliamentary influence.

As always, his pattern of motivation was carefully contrived to conform to what he knew to be the basic feelings of the audience he sought to reach—not the members but the general public. "One of the greatest blessings we enjoy," he reminded them, "one of the greatest blessings a people, my Lords, can enjoy, is liberty." The licentiousness of the stage, he admitted, was evident. But, "it is a speck upon the eye of the political body, which I can never touch but with a gentle, with a trembling hand, lest I destroy the body." There was no urgency, no crisis, that demanded the restraints called for in the Bill. "I hope it will not be pretended that our Government may, before next winter, be overturned by such licentiousness." The real target at which the ministers aimed, he warned, was not the theatre but the flood of pamphlets and other antigovernment publications. "It is an arrow that does but glance upon the stage; the mortal wound seems to be designed against the liberty of the press." For his conclusion he shifted to the motive having the strongest appeal. "Nay, my Lords, it is not only an encroachment upon liberty, but it is likewise an encroachment upon property. Wit, my Lords, is a sort of property; it is the property of those who have it, and too often the only property they have to depend on. It is indeed but a precarious dependence. Thank God! we, my Lords, have a dependence of another kind; we have a much less precarious support, and therefore cannot feel the inconvenience of the bill before us; but it is our duty to encourage and protect wit, whosoever's property it may be." The appeal failed for reasons that Chesterfield well understood, as his adjurations to his son repeatedly affirm: Listeners are far more responsive to their own needs than to their duty. Since the Lords were not themselves threatened, they felt no need to oppose the ministry. The appeal launched by Chesterfield was far more effective out of doors than within. Its effect, therefore, was primarily to build more popular support for the Tory opposition and more partisan leadership for Chesterfield—two results worthy of his efforts.

Six years later—in February 1743, after Walpole had been deposed and his successor not yet selected—Chesterfield spoke twice during the debate on a proposed revision of the tax on gin. The circumstances were complex. What the government proposed was a substantial lowering of the tax, but what it sought was a considerable increase in the revenues to be derived from it—an increase to be used for the war that was highly unpopular because it was widely supposed to be for the benefit not of England but of the Hanover Electorate. The existing tax on gin shops was so high—fifty pounds annually—that it had proved to be unenforceable, with the number of illegal, unlicensed gin shops in London alone surpassing six thousand. What the new bill proposed was to lower the tax all the way down to one pound—a levy low enough to be collectable. The challenge Chesterfield faced was to make the Lords believe that less actually meant more, and that adoption of the bill would have the two undesirable effects of encouraging already prevalent drunkenness and of paying mercenaries to fight on behalf of Hanover. In pursuit of this difficult aim, Chesterfield spoke twice.

His first speech was devoted almost wholly to the theme that what the lower tax would do was to encourage the vice of drunkenness—"which almost necessarily produces a breach in every one of the ten commandments." He suggested satirically a preamble for the bill, to read: "Whereas, the designs of the present ministry, whatever they are, can not be executed without a great number of mercenaries . . . and whereas the present disposition of the nation to drunkenness inclines us to believe that they will pay more cheerfully for the undisturbed enjoyment of distilled liquors than for any other concession . . . be it enacted, by the King's most excellent Majesty, that no man shall hereafter be denied the right of being drunk."

His second speech discussed the reasons that made the existing high tax ineffective. "The magistrates may be vicious, and forbear to enforce that law by which themselves are condemned; they may be indolent and inclined rather to connive at wickedness, by which they are not injured themselves, than to suppress it by a laborious exertion of their authority; or they may be timorous, and, instead of awing the vicious, be awed by them." Ministers had pointed out that the present tax was uncollectable; but "I never heard that a law against theft was repealed or delayed because thieves were numerous." As for the new tax, "it appears to me that it will only enrich the government without reforming the people." He shifted then to an attack on the war. New revenue, he said, should be "withheld till it is known in what expeditions it was to be employed. Parliament ought not to approve of wars on the Continent, while our plantations [in America] are insulted and our trade obstructed; they may think the house of Austria of more importance than our own defense; and may perhaps so far differ from their fathers, as to imagine the treasures of Britain very properly employed in supporting the troops, and increasing the splendor, of a foreign Electorate." The Lords applauded but did not vote down the new tax.

Chesterfield's biographer, reporting on the debate, missed the point. "His wit flashed, his sarcasm stung, his reasoning powers and his oratory drew forth the admiration of both sides; but his speeches never seemed to have the least effect." It is true that sense and eloquence do not always prevail in the parliamentary forum—as Fox, Sheridan, Burke, Grattan, Flood, O'Connell, and on down through the decades to Disraeli and Churchill were also made to know. But there is another audience—the public—that was becoming of ever greater importance as gradually a spirit of democracy arose to counter the elitist control. And even within the two Houses, Opposition was coming to have its own enlarged sphere. This was a time of transition, and the speaking by Lord Chesterfield helped in its own degree to pave the way for change.

When, in 1751, the need to revise the English calendar became acute, Chesterfield again took the lead in defense of the new system of dating; and this time his persuasiveness made the difference in winning the necessary votes.

The circumstances required the utmost of rhetorical skill. The English calendar (Old Style) had become so far out of joint that it was a full eleven days short of correctness. Worse, it was also that far removed from conformity with the calendar used in almost all of Europe. The difficulties of international communication were consequently exceedingly troublesome. Nevertheless, the English public was strongly committed to the customary calendar on which their lives were based. For many centuries the beginning of the New Year had been 21 March, which, as the commencement of spring, seemed far more natural than the arbitrary date of 1 January. The date for Easter, too, was to shift. Family, community, and religious sentiments were all affected. Moreover, the new dating system that was proposed aroused a clamor to "give us back our lost eleven days." The due date for payment of debts was affected. But most of all, personal feelings were deeply disturbed. All of this argued against change. Against this traditionalism was the simple fact that the English calendar was astronomically wrong. Both logic and practicality combined to favor the change. But how was it to be brought about?

Lord Chesterfield was fully retired—elderly, physically weak, largely deaf, and already threatened with blindness. From reappearing in the public arena, especially to support an unpopular cause, he had nothing personally to gain. All he could expect was severe public condemnation. Yet his sense of patriotism prevailed. He returned to the House of Lords, made his wholly effective speech, and won the necessary votes. It was a splendid climax for his career, and it was also a signal demonstration that in politics the skillful use of persuasive speaking does indeed make a difference.

He explained how he did it in the letter of 18 March to his son, which has been quoted. He depended entirely upon rationalization rather than reason. He pleased his listeners while making them believe he was informing them. Without himself understanding the astronomical complexities, he made them think that he was clarifying their own comprehension. Through this speech he won both admiration and votes.

As a still further political contribution, he helped to bring into office the towering personality of William Pitt. The time was half a decade after the calendar debate. George II was old, infirm, beset by the difficulties of the Seven Years' War, and unable to find ministers able to master the political turmoil. "We have in truth no minister," Chesterfield wrote on 17 June 1756 to a friend, "but the administration is a mere republic, and carried on by the Cabinet Council, the individuals of which think only how to get the better of each other." Chesterfield did not like Pitt, considering that his "ruling passion was an unbounded ambition," but he realized that no administration could operate without him. In a whirl of negotiations, Chesterfield persuaded the king, Lord Newcastle, Pitt, and their principal supporters that a coalition cabinet was the only available solution. On 29 June, 1757, the coalition was established, with Newcastle nominally in charge and with Pitt the real power.[26]

"It was a ministry in which Pitt was absolute master; the rest were ciphers. . . . He had the sole control. . . . The King was checkmated, Parliament became obsequious and silent; and Pitt, freed from the solicitations of obscure place-hunters and the worry of a strong opposition, was able to devote his whole soul to the nation. This ministry, for now it was virtually Pitt's ministry, in four years won more temporary glory and effected more permanent results than any English ministry within the same time."[27]

A new era had come in: the era of empire building. It was also an era in which public opinion became the chief foundation for government. The mixed government was becoming democratic in effect, if not yet in form. The elitist period was ushered out. A new kind of politics and a new kind of public speaking became dominant. Bolingboke was long gone; Walpole faded to a mere memory; Wyndham and Pulteney were forgotten; and Chesterfield, for all his contributions, sank in general esteem. The new age belonged chiefly to William Pitt.

Notes

1. Wingfield-Stratford, *British Civilization*, p. 627.
2. J. Steven Watson, *The Reign of King George III, 1760–1815* (Oxford: Clarendon Press, 1960), summarizing the prior period, p. 52.
3. William Thomas Laprade, *Public Opinion and Politics in Eighteenth Century England: To the Fall of Walpole* (New York: Macmillan, 1936).
4. Wingfield-Stratford, *British Civilization*, p. 627. King Stephen reigned from 1133 to 1154.
5. Williams, *Whig Supremacy*, p. 2.
6. Thomas Gordon, writing in the *British Journal*, 30 November 1723.
7. W. A. Speck, *Stability and Strife: England, 1714–1760* (Cambridge: Harvard University Press, 1979), p. 212.
8. See Watson, *King George III*, pp. 8–9, for these quotations.
9. This traditional view of George I has been only partially qualified by his most recent biographer, Ragnhild Hatton, *George I: Elector and King* (Cambridge: Harvard University Press, 1978), who proved that he did on occassion utter short English phrases (p. 130), and who summed him up as "the most competent and politically imaginative of the Hanoverians" (p. 297). If true, he was only the best of an incompetent lot.
10. Joseph Wood Krutch, *Samuel Johnson* (New York: Holt, 1944), pp. 48–49.
11. Douglas Harkness, *Bolingboke: The Man and His Career* (London: Staples Press, 1957), quoting Churchill (p. 116); summing up (p. 137). For a study of Bolingbroke's contributions to political theory, see H. C. Mansfield, *Statesmanship and Party Government: A Study of Burke and Bolingbroke* (Chicago: University of Chicago Press, 1963); and Jeffrey Hart, *Viscount Bolingbroke* (London: Routledge & Kegan Paul, 1965).
12. Ibid., p. 79.
13. Quoted by Arthur Hassall, *Life of Viscount Bolingbroke* (Oxford: R. H. Blackwell, 1915), p. 101.
14. Harkness, *Bolingbroke*, from chap. 8, which compiles various testimonies.
15. J. Vernon Jensen, "British Voices on the Eve of the American Revolution: Trapped by the Family Metaphor," Quarterly Journal of Speech 63 (February 1977) p. 43.
16. Harkness, *Bolingbroke*.
17. F. S. Oliver, *Endless Adventure*, pp. 186, 180.
18. Wingfield-Stratford, *British Civilization*, p. 624. "The politics of Anne's reign form a sordid prelude to a sordid epoch. . . . Bolingbroke was about right when he said, in effect, that private and party interest came first. . . . The whole atmosphere of politics was low and base" (p. 646).
19. Williams, *Whig Supremacy*, p. 144.

20. Ibid., p. 201.

21. The text of these remarks, and also of Walpole's reply, is from Chauncey A. Goodrich, *Select British Eloquence*, rev. ed. (Indianapolis: Bobbs-Merrill, 1963), pp. 31–32, 32–35.

22. Williams, *Whig Supremacy*, p. 195.

23. See Goodrich, *Select British Eloquence*, pp. 43–44, for this comment and the summarized text of Pulteney's speech.

24. These comments are from *Boswell's Life of Johnson*, 2 vols. (London: Oxford University Press, 1927), 1:70–71, 2:226, 291, 464; 1:398.

25. Boname Dobrée, *The Life of Philip Dormer Stanhope, Fourth Earl of Chesterfield*, vol. 1 of *The Letters of Chesterfield* (New York: AMS, 1932), pp. 82–83.

26. Ibid., pp. 186–87.

27. Frederick Harrison, *Chatham* (London and New York: Macmillan, 1925), p. 92.

8
The People Find a Voice—The Elder William Pitt

Above all his other attributes, the Elder William Pitt, the Earl of Chatham, was an orator incarnate. In his career and in his personality he invites comparison with Sir Winston Churchill. Each was a linchpin of history, uniting and strengthening loyalties through personal leadership in a time of crisis. Neither one was suited to the usual means of political leadership, through deals, compromises, and adaptability. Each endured the frustrations and humiliations of defeat before attaining dominant, even domineering, power. Together they represent the force of a great vision that they were able to imprint into the emotions and minds of the public. What they accomplished they won through persuasive speech, each in his own way.

"A Singularly Radiant Man"

Both the career and the personality of Pitt illustrate what rhetoric means: its good and its bad, its strength and its weakness, its effects and its limitations. It is impossible to consider Pitt in other than oratorical terms: standing on his feet, glowering at his hearers, stating his terms, improvising, extemporizing, hot with conviction, cold only to compromise. He was the antithesis of Halifax the Trimmer and of Walpole the Strategist. What he cared about was the grand design. What he believed was undimmed by doubt or qualifications. What he uttered was Truth. By choice he stood alone, yet he became the lodestar of his party and won the trust of the people to a degree only Churchill came to match. He whirled through the English sky like a meteor, pursuing a sometimes erratic course toward a single goal while glowing with a brilliant light. In what he was and what he did the influence of rhetoric may be judged—what it can do and what it cannot. His charisma was both his weapon and his shield, overwhelming except for its cracks.

His career was by no means an unbroken whole. Like a volcano, he had his quiescent times, when flow became sputter. For a time, in midcareer, his fire seemed quenched. The eruption ceased. Uncharacteristically, he tried his best to compromise, to plead for what he could not demand, to conciliate those whom he could not control. But this was an art he neither understood nor could learn to wield. His energy was like fire that requires fuel and a favorable draft. Like fire, his flame flickered when its fuel was consumed. Throughout his life he was plagued by ill health, suffering acutely from a most painful gout that time and again forced him to withdraw from the combat and to yield ground that he had gained. The antagonisms he aroused proved stronger than even he could master. If his greatest virtue was the centrality of his unshakable convictions, this also was his principal political flaw. His nature was to rule or ruin. Like the heroes of the ancient Greek tragedies, his fate emanated from within himself. What he did was incomparably great. Where he failed, the reasons were much like those that accounted for his success.

Mostly in Opposition, and sometimes in the ministry, he served his country as its surest guide through the most crucial half-century since the time of King Alfred. It was largely his leadership that elevated England from being just one among the contentious states of Europe to becoming head of a dominion on which the sun never set. He found it a nation and left it an empire. Finally, near the close of his life, when through mismanagement that empire was losing its richest part, even though he was old and severely ill, he rose valiantly on the floor of the Lords to demand changes that even at that late date might have repaired the breach. Nor was empire building by any means the sum of his contributions. It was also his influence that steered the government from its ancient aristocratic base toward the eventual evolution of democracy. His was both a dynamic and a decisive role. But his flaws limited what he was able to achieve.

To a singular degree, Pitt's influence flowed from his persuasive eloquence: from right words rightly spoken at critical points of time. This is the clearest thread amid the complexities of his career.

On the great issues he sometimes held contradictory views. He did not always lead his followers along a consistent course. His parliamentary auditors, whom he had sometimes to persuade and sometimes to cow into submission, included able and determined opponents. His followers also had minds of their own, with beliefs not always in consonance with his. He did not act and could not have acted alone. The drama in which he played his part—as vast and complicated as Ibsen's *Peer Gynt* and Shaw's *Man and Superman*—was woven of many strands, evolving through many scenes that were essentially but not always clearly connected, and that were crowded with many actors. To shift the analogy, he was like a superb athlete in a game of rugby. His role was central and vital, yet what he could do was always subject to shifts in the play and was intertwined with the actions of his teammates and his opponents. It was not always he who scored the goals. The strategies and the maneuvers of the game were only in part of his devising. There was also the role of chance, along with the conduct of others in the fray. No one doubted, however, that he was the star. Had he not lived, or had he been early removed from the scene, the history of the time would have taken different turns. His rhetoric was crucially effective.

Historians agree that "the great issue which absorbed the whole of his career was the formation of a transatlantic dominion; the problem of whether the North American seaboard and commerce should be under British or French or Spanish control."[1] It was essentially his guidance that transformed the long, inconclusive, and lingering wars over the relative roles and influence of Austria, France, and Spain into a decisive struggle for dominance across the world. Nor was this all. So nearly did he serve as the voice of the people that they claimed him as their own, as the "Great Commoner." He was, in the apt phrase of Thomas Carlyle, discussing him in his essay on Frederick the Great, in his *Heroes and Hero-Worship*, "a singularly radiant man." And it was Carlyle who pinpointed an essential fact—that his speeches impressed his hearers as "things which with his whole soul he meant to *do*."

In considering William Pitt, the mind turns naturally to analogies with great natural forces: to volcanoes, meteors, lodestars, fires, and to complicated dramas and games. In discussing him, style tends to become elevated, even grandiose. Read the biographies and the histories; their terms are much alike: "He lavished on England all the passion of which his mighty nature was capable"; "to Chatham the Constitution was a priceless heritage of ancestral wisdom, whose very soul was liberty"; "He did things which no human being but himself would have attempted"; "He could not cooperate, he could only dominate"; "England has long been in labour but at last she has brought forth a man."[2] England "had need for the rise of a great orator, and the greatest orator who ever trod the floors of Parliament had now appeared on the scene."[3]

The impression he made upon those who listened to him was well described by a Catholic lawyer who heard many of his speeches.

> In his look and gesture grace and dignity were combined, but dignity presided; the "terrors of his beak, the lightnings of his eye" were insufferable. His voice was both full and clear; his lowest whisper was distinctly heard; his middle tones were sweet, rich, and beautifully varied; when he elevated his voice to its highest pitch, the House was completely filled with the volume of the sound.
>
> The effect was awful, except when he wished to cheer and animate; he then had the spirit-stirring notes, which were perfectly irresistible. He frequently rose, on a sudden, from a very low to a very high key, but it seemed to be without effort. His diction was remarkably simple, but words were never spoken with more care. . . . The terrible was his peculiar power. Then the whole House sank before him,—still he was

dignified; and wonderful as was his eloquence, it was attended with this most important effect, *that it impressed every hearer with a conviction that there was something in him even finer than his words; that the man was infinitely greater than the orator.*[4]

What mattered more than his voice and his bearing, or his words, or his platform skills was the power of his personality. With a sublime confidence, he spoke as one having authority. Most importantly of all, on the great issues he was generally right. His insight was bolstered by a depth of historical knowledge and was directed by his clarity of vision as to what England was, and his faith in what it might become. Many of the issues with which he dealt were confused, even obscure. It was his great strength that he perceived solutions that could work, and he urged measures to be taken by methods that were within reach. Whatever the opposition, he swept objections aside and proposed goals and methods that even the doubters felt impelled to accept.

It was not that he was a giant among pygmies, for he lived with great contemporaries, both as teammates and as opponents. They included those already discussed—Bolingbroke, Walpole, Chesterfield, Pulteney, and Wyndham. They also numbered such able politicans as Henry Fox, William Murray, the Earl of Granville, Henry Pelham, and his brother, the incapable but amply supported Duke of Newcastle. And opposing him were such power wielders as George II and George III, along with Lord Bute and Lord North. The issues that had to be dealt with were so slippery that from time to time Pitt found himself on contrary sides of them. None of this diminished his prominence and only partially limited his success.

A major difficulty in analyzing his effectiveness is that none of his speeches was reported in full. Many of them, particularly during his principal prime ministry, were not recorded at all. What remains are his accomplishments, the nature of his character and personality, and the unanimous agreement among his contemporaries that his eloquence was a torrent against which it was well nigh impossible to stand. In the splendid image used by Chauncey Goodrich in his essay on Chatham, he was like a great cliff that overshadowed all around him. "He carried through triumphantly what would have covered any other man with ridicule and disgrace." And the reason, as Goodrich believed, was that he was "the most powerful orator of modern times."

The dominating power of Pitt's speaking had to be the key that explains his political successes. This is not to claim more for his speeches than they deserve. No one could quarrel with the judgment stated by Lord Chesterfield, in his speech on the Gin Act, that the motives by which parliamentary debates are influenced are by far too complicated to be governed by a particular speech, regardless of how overwhelming it may be. The sway of Pitt over the government by no means depended upon specific speeches. What mattered most was the continuous effect of his personality—both in

Westminster and across the nation. The eloquent Irishman, Henry Grattan, assessed it as irresistible: "There was in this man something that could create, subvert, or reform; an understanding, a spirit, and an eloquence to summon mankind to society, or to break the bonds of slavery asunder, and rule the wildness of free minds with unbounded authority." Benjamin Franklin, representing the mid-Atlantic American colonies in London, observed of him, "I have sometimes seen eloquence without wisdom, and often wisdom without eloquence; but in him I have seen them united in the highest possible degree." Being right was doubtless his great source of strength; but being able to manifest that rightness with lightning-like clarity brought that strength to bear where and when it counted most. The effect he produced was well noted by King George II, who feared, disliked, and opposed him, and yet was forced to appoint him as the chief minister, with the comment that "his conduct does honor to human nature."[5]

"When Trade Is at Stake, Defend It or Perish"

During Pitt's career in Parliament, elitism was pushed aside by the stirring of democracy, even though electoral reform lay a full two generations in the future. The transformation is dramatized in a letter that Lord Chesterfield wrote to his son on 1 August 1766. In it he expressed dismay and astonishment that Pitt should have been "duped by low cunning" to allow himself to "fall upstairs" from the Commons into that "hospital for incurables, the House of Lords." It is true that the Lords had by then sunk into secondary significance. It is untrue that by accepting a peerage Pitt, having become Lord Chatham, lost effectiveness. Despite Chesterfield's belief that "all his enemies, without exception, rejoice; and all his friends are stupefied and dumbfounded," Pitt's leadership was far from ended. Even after the severity of his illness forced Chatham into virtual retirement, he (like Bolingbroke) emerged again—on the issue of how to deal with the American revolt—as the dominant voice that called upon government to heed the sense of the people.

It should not have surprised Chesterfield, a prime elitist, that Pitt accepted the king's offer of a peerage. All of Pitt's life was a struggle to rise through the ranks. He was the younger son in what was known as "a very new family." His grandfather had won great wealth through trade with India, and his father had enlarged the family fortune by a favorable marriage. The family estate in Cornwall, however, was inherited by his elder brother, Thomas. Pitt's connections were with the wealthy class, but he had to make his own way. His early plan was to make a career in the army, which he began with such zeal that, as he said, he read every book ever written on military affairs. But from early youth he suffered so acutely from gout that ill health inhibited an army career. Consequently, he accepted a seat in Parliament from the family-controlled rotten borough of Old Sarum. The date was 1 February 1735, during the latter years of the ministry of Robert Walpole. He dismayed his older brother by associating himself with the "Patriots," who formed the core of the Bolingbroke-Pulteney Old Whigs, to constitute the government's Opposition.

During his first year in the House, Pitt did no speaking. Instead, he prepared himself for oratory by hard study of the speeches of Demosthenes and Cicero. When he felt himself ready to venture into the debates, his initial speaking was florid and fiercely dramatic. With utter fearlessness, he arose without restraint to lash and to denounce the spokesmen. His charges againt them were unrealistically exaggerated, yet his solid marshaling of facts, heightened by his stinging sarcasm, was so overpowering that, as a fellow parliamentarian observed, "he could convince any man of anything."

The issues he addressed were of the highest consequence. The foreign affairs of the kingdom were, as the public and as many in Parliament felt, being badly mismanaged. Pitt set himself to force a revision. On 8 March 1739, in a thunderous series of invectives, he attacked Walpole's plan to form an alliance with Spain. In these speeches he stressed what was to be his lifelong theme: *"When trade is at stake, it is your last entrenchment; you must defend it or perish."* Spanish power was enlarged by galleons bringing back treasures from the New World, and Pitt demanded that these galleons be captured. When an English sailor, Jenkins, a man of dubious veracity, complained that one of his ears had been shorn off by the cruel Spaniards, Pitt led the public clamor that demanded war with Spain. And he got it.

But Pitt was no more pleased with the conduct of the War of Jenkins' Ear than he had been with the appeasement policies that preceded it. In October 1739 he demanded an official inquiry into the measures of the ministry. "We are now to examine," he told an intent House, "whether it is probable that we shall preserve our commerce and our independence, or whether we are sinking into subjection to a foreign power." Walpole was forced to enlarge the navy, and he undertook to do it by the unpopular measure of authorizing the search of private homes to seek out deserters. This offered an opportunity for Opposition that Pitt was quick to seize.

The rhetorical problem he had to solve was delicate: to favor, as he always had, the enlargement of the navy but to demolish what appeared to be a sound method for obtaining it. His solution was astute. "For God's sake, Sir, let us not put our seamen into such a condition as to make them worse than the cowardly slaves of France or Spain." He pinpointed the single decision by Walpole that was most vulnerable, and he lunged to exploit it.

> I say, and I do not exaggerate, that we are laying a trap for the lives of all the men of spirit in the nation. Would any of you, gentlemen, allow this law to be executed to its full extent? If, at midnight, a petty constable with a press-gang should come thundering at the gate of your house in

the country, would you, at that time of night, allow your gates to be opened? I protest, I would not. Would any of you submit to such an indignity? Would you not fire upon him, if he attempted to break open your gates? I declare I would, let the consequences be never so fatal; and if you happened to be in the bad graces of a Minister, the consequences would be, either your being killed in the fray, or hanged for killing the constable or some of his gang.

The means by which Pitt mastered the House through his speaking becomes clear as this single paragraph is considered. The great national issue of enlarging the navy, which Walpole proposed, is simply yet vividly converted into an equally patriotic and much more personal issue of protecting the traditional heritage of liberty by which every man's house is his castle. Patriotism becomes the major resource not for Walpole but for Pitt. A pitch of emotionalism is reached, but it is accomplished wholly without flamboyance. The tone of the speech is utterly reasonable. Who could resist—let alone deny—the personalized resistance to tyranny that Pitt proposed? The conclusion of the paragraph approached, if it did not indeed cross the line into, sedition. But so artfully was it linked with defense of freedom that Walpole did not call upon the Speaker to rebuke it. Instead, he tried to brush aside the appeal to rebellion as a mere youthful outburst. To this Pitt responded with an even higher pitch of passion.

> If any man shall, by charging me with theatrical behavior, imply that I utter any sentiments but my own, I shall treat him as a calumniator and a villain; nor shall any protection shelter him from the treatment which he deserves. I shall, on such an occasion, without scruple, trample upon all those forms with which wealth and dignity entrench themselves. . . .
> I will not sit unconcerned while our liberty is invaded, nor look in silence upon public robbery. I will, at whatever hazard, repel the aggressor, and drag the thief to justice, whatever may protect them in their villainy, and whoever may partake of their plunder.

Against this kind of rhetoric, Walpole was all but helpless. He could not but be confused, even stunned. What he had proposed was precisely what Pitt, and his Opposition following, had demanded: that the navy be enlarged. Walpole had undertaken to accomplish this without such a budgetary enlargement as would require an unacceptable increase in taxation. But now, in the course of the debate, Pitt had converted his patriotic proposal into tyranny, robbery, aggression, villainy, and plunder. And all this was accomplished so simply and so clearly that it could not be brushed aside. For the listeners, it was no matter that Pitt's grammar slipped from the singular into the plural, or that he revised his imagery from invasion into robbery. Such flaws were no more than incidental. They were mere slips of a kind to be expected in the conversational, extempore mode. The members knew that Pitt's speeches were not prepared in advance. He spoke with the full force of immediacy, out of the depths of his mind and his feelings. His sincerity shone through the very abandon with which he left himself open to the charge of recklessness. And all the time he made his listeners his allies by peppering his assertions with questions, by demanding their response, and by making them feel that their emotions and their convictions were the same as his own.

This manner of speaking was effective because it fit precisely the nature of the Parliament as it then was. "If any man were to measure the Parliament of the eighteenth century by the standards of the democratic assembly of the twentieth, one would meet nothing but anomalies and absurdities at every turn."[6] Members of the Commons, as well as the Lords, shared a sense of their natural and rightful aristocracy. They felt strongly their traditional rights, as well as their dignity and their responsibility. They were a select (which is to say, selected) body. They had an absolute right to speak their minds, and to respond as they felt inclined. No party discipline restricted them. No cabinet directed their votes. The king himself was no longer sacrosanct. Moreover, they also felt the need for leadership. The issues were in flux and were so complicated as to require guidance for their understanding. The Continental wars had worn down the spirits of the people who increasingly felt them to be as futile as they were endless. What should patriotic Englishmen think? What should they do? Across the seas, a New World was beckoning. It was intolerable to see its riches garnered by Spain and France, while the resources of England were being diverted to the defense of a mere Germanic Electorate, or while their nation was haplessly involved in European rivalries that demanded their sacrifices without providing for them equivalent rewards. This was the issue that was clear to Pitt and which he made clear to them.

William Pitt had the self-confidence, the clarity of understanding, and also the brazen effrontery with which to point the nation's way. What he called for was a realistic patriotism that would serve the real needs of the nation and of the people of England instead of serving their foreign allies. The twin prizes that he held out before them were *national greatness* of a kind that would procure for them *personal profits*. Both patriotism and self-interest could be served by launching England into a new era of empire building. Through such appeals Pitt not only mastered his legislative audience but simultaneously captured the admiration and the affection of the people. It was by such means that he won the cognomen of the Great Commoner, as one upon whom they could depend confidently to serve their own best interests.

"This Absurd, Ungrateful, and Perfidious Partiality"

A politician, in the mode of either Bolingbroke or Walpole, Pitt was not. The processes of administrative organization bored him—with the notable exception of the interval in which he was granted responsibility for the intricate strategic conduct of making war. He was temperamentally unsuited for the compromises and contrivances required for the knitting together of a party—although even to these he tried awkwardly enough to adjust himself during the coalition ministry he shared briefly with Newcastle. In his impetuosity, he resembled Bolingbroke, but with a patent sincerity and reckless courage that placed him in a different light. He was not like a reed that preserves itself by bending before the wind, but like a towering oak that is strong enough to withstand and to survive the gales. Like an oak, he suffered damage from the winds of change; nevertheless, he stood tall and stately as both a beacon and a shelter amid the storms.

The career of Pitt was not always steady, and was far from static. It can be divided into five periods, each with its own challenges, each requiring different methods. The first lasted for a decade, from his entrance into Parliament on to the close of 1744, during which period he rose rapidly to leadership of the Opposition. The second period lasted for another decade, down to 1754, during which time he held subsidiary offices in the administration headed by Henry Pelham. It was then that he astonished and aroused the admiration of both his foes and his friends by refusing the customary under-the-table rewards of office. And it was then, too, that he showed an unexpectedly conciliatory spirit toward the officials who were his nominal superiors.

It was in the third period, during the mismanaged three-year ministry of the Duke of Newcastle, while Pitt was debarred from the ministry by the petulant dislike of George II, that he burst into torrential attacks—against the weak direction of the war with France, and against Henry Fox and William Murray, who were appointed by Newcastle to be his principal spokesmen in the House of Commons. Then afterward, from December 1756 to October 1761 came Pitt's great opportunity, to serve as prime minister. This was his chance to do what he had been advocating, and he performed magnificently. During this period he possessed the authority that precluded his need for speeches, or at least, such as he made were not recorded.

His final, fifth period, lasting for some sixteen years until his death in 1778, found him largely forced into retirement by his illness, though interrupted by another brief tenure as prime minister, except by occasional appearances in the House of Lords to thunder support for the Opposition against Lord Bute and Lord North. Had his health permitted, it is conceivable that he might have prevented the disastrous policies that led to the breaking away of the American colonies; and it was, finally, a last desperate effort in this cause that precipitated his death. Discussion of this period must be postponed to the chapter on the American war.

Different as his status was in each of these differing periods, his oratory always had a shaping influence—both when he was storming against governmental policies and during the brief but critical periods while he was in a position to direct them.

His effectiveness derived from four factors that distinguished the whole of his career. The first, as has been said, was his oratory—a veritable drumbeat of invectives, sarcasm, and assertiveness—all expressed with such vigor of diction, such personalized directness, such acute adaptation to the issues and to the interests of his listeners, and delivered with such majestic dignity and assurance of superiority that his associates were heartened and his targeted opponents were cowed by the unrestrained torrent of his speech. The second factor was his self-confidence, which enabled him to speak with authority whether he was in office or not. The third source of his influence was his personal integrity, unusual among the politicians of his day, which gave to his words those qualities of ethos which were identified by Aristotle as the essential wellsprings of effective persuasion. But transcending all these characteristics was the overriding fact that he saw clearly, and advocated persistently, policies that were fruitful both for national greatness and for the personal needs, pride, and self-satisfaction of the people. Such a combination of qualities made him not only a commanding but virtually an overwhelming personality. When he spoke there was little doubt in the minds of his listeners that they should properly follow where he led.

After Walpole had been driven from office and King George had appointed the Earl of Granville to replace him, out of the depths of his disgust and disappointment, Pitt directed his rage against royalty itself.

> This great, this mighty nation, Sir, is considered only as a province to a despicable Electorate. . . . Every year shows this absurd, ungrateful, and perfidious partiality toward the German interest, yearly visits [by the King] to that *delightful* country, sums spent to aggrandize and enrich it. Let us perform our duty as representatives of the people: and if ministers prefer the interests of Hanover, Parliament regards only the interests of England.

After this attack on the king, he poured his scorn upon the ministry. "From one extreme, our administration have run to the very verge of another. Our former minister betrayed the interests of his country by his cowardice; our present minister would sacrifice them to his quixotism. Our former minister was for negotiating with all the world; our present minister is for fighting with all the world. Our former minister was for agreeing to every treaty, however dishonorable; our present minister will give ear to none, although the most reasonable that can be desired. Both are extravagent. The only difference is that the wild system of the one must subject the nation to much heavier expenditures than ever did the pusillanimity of the other." Against such attacks, the ministry could not stand; Granville, like Walpole, was driven from office.

The new ministry, headed by Henry Pelham, a competent bureaucrat, sufficiently pleased Pitt that he accepted office in it, though the post he was given—paymaster of the forces—had no policymaking power. In that same year—1745—the Scots and some of the Whigs joined in a rebellion designed to bring Bonnie Prince Charlie to the throne. Concurrently, the Whigs renewed a plan they long had nurtured of having parliamentary members elected every three years, by which means they hoped to increase their numbers in the Commons. As a member of the administration, Pitt opposed the electoral reform bill, all the more so since a Scottish army was threatening London. As Pitt coolly told the House, this was no time "to sit contriving bills to guard our liberty from corruption, when that very liberty, when everything else dear to us, are in danger of being wrested from us by arms. When thieves have burst into the mansion, the fool only would plan out methods to prevent the fraud of his servants." The Jacobite rising was subdued, and the reform bill was defeated. Pitt gave to the country a model of how best to accomplish reform when he refused to accept the indirect emoluments that customarily belonged to the paymaster. His own finances were wholly inadequate to support his luxurious mode of living, but the problem was solved in part by a gift to him of ten thousand pounds by an admirer, Lady Marlborough. Only half a dozen years later did he attain the income his life-style required, through another gift of thirty thousand pounds, plus an annuity of two thousand five hundred pounds and, when he accepted the peerage, still another annuity from the government of another two thousand pounds.

During the Pelham ministry, and then for another brief period after Pelham was succeeded as chief minister by his brother, the Duke of Newcastle, Pitt showed an embarrassing and wholly untypical subserviency, partly from disappointed ambitions, and partly because his gout had become so painful that he was forced into semiretirement to take the waters at Bath. Pitt sought to please Newcastle by supporting the ministerial proposal of a subsidy for the Electorate of Bavaria. He also wrote from Bath a succession of abject letters that were entirely out of character: to Newcastle, signing himself, "Your unalterable humble servant"; to Lord Hardwicke, complaining that "the weight of irremovable royal displeasure is a load too great to move under; it must crush any man; it has sunk and broke me"; to Granville, to Lyttleton, to Temple, urging them all to use any tactic, "to talk modestly, to fish in troubled waters," in order to get a suitable appointment for him. Nothing availed. Pitt's spirits sank even lower when Henry Fox, instead of himself, was appointed to be leader of the House of Commons. Newcastle did make some offers to Pitt but nothing that was attractive. Then, unaccountably, Pitt's spirits improved, and he broke out of retirement.

The occasion that brought him again into action was relatively trivial. A dispute over an inconsequential by-election was being discussed in the

Parliament in a spirit of levity marked by roars of laughter. Pitt at the time was sitting in the gallery, with his pain-wracked legs wrapped in flannel and propped up on a chair. Stirring with anger, he hobbled down onto the floor to make what Henry Fox declared to be "his finest speech." He excoriated the House for degenerating into a "mere French Parliament"; he denounced Newcastle in terms so harsh that they "spoiled his stomach." A few days later he was back again, this time to attack William Murray with "words like daggers." According to a listener, "this thunderbolt, thrown from a sky so long clear," confounded the members of the House. The great Pitt, whose fires had been quenched, was aflame again. Newcastle, feeling impelled to strengthen his ministry by including Henry Fox in it, drew more withering scorn from Pitt. Clapping his hand to his forehead as though struck by a sudden thought, Pitt exclaimed: "Now it strikes me. I remember at Lyons to have been carried to see the conflux of the Rhone and Saône—the one a feeble, languid stream, and, though languid, of no great depth; the other a boisterous and impetuous torrent. But different as they are, *they meet at last;* and long, *long* may they continue united, to the comfort of each other, and to the *glory, honor,* and *security* of this nation." The sarcasm cost him his position as paymaster. Pitt's spell of apologetic subservience was ended, and he rushed back into leadership of the Opposition. Very quickly he regained the power of his eloquence. In his speeches of this period, Horace Walpole found "more humor, wit, vivacity, fine language, more boldness, in short more astonishing perfection" than had ever appeared anywhere before, even in the orations of Demosthenes and Cicero.[7] Such testimony is all the more convincing, coming from the admiring and devoted son of the Walpole who had been so severely dealt with by Pitt. A member of the Commons who attended the sessions of 1755–56 also noted that "Mr. Pitt found occasion, in every debate, to confound the ministerial orators."[8]

"I Will Go On No Longer"

The significant question is what Pitt made of his persuasive power, beyond astounding and entertaining his hearers. The answer is that he used his speeches as weapons with which to drive Newcastle from office; he also used them to build such a foundation of national popularity that the king, however reluctantly, was forced to hand over the ministerial leadership to a man he regarded with a mingling of dislike and dread. And Pitt did it by clarifying the issues and by stating them in such terms that the rightness of his own views became irresistibly clear. He was no mere verbal magician; he was also a statesman with superior insight.

There were great issues to be decided; and once Pitt managed to shake off his depression, he proved his capacity to master them. Under three successive ministries the overseas affairs of England had been marred by defeats and retreats. The French entrenched themselves strongly in India and were advancing into control over the entire southern area of that key country. In dealing with Europe, England had bolstered a series of weak alliances by paying annual subsidies to such inconsequential cities and dukedoms as Cologne, Bavaria, and Saxony. The compromise peace terms negotiated at Aix-la-Chapelle had opened the way for French advances in Canada and then southward into Trans-Appalachia from Pittsburgh through Ohio to Detroit. When, in 1754, General Braddock attempted to repel them, despite his numerical superiority his army was all but annihilated. Even at sea, where the English had clearly the means of superiority, their ships were unable to master the French navy. These were the failures that Pitt denounced.

And he did it so vividly that they could not be ignored. The climax came in November 1755, with a withering attack on Newcastle so impressive that, in the words of Horace Walpole, "his eloquence, like a torrent long obstructed, burst forth with more commanding impetuosity—haughty, defiant, conscious of injury, and of supreme abilities."[9] The attacks mounted until it became evident to all that Pitt must be brought in to head the government. "The King grumbled, but the voice of the people called for Pitt." In the oft-cited words of Samuel Johnson, "Walpole was a minister given by the King to the Parliament; Pitt was a minister given by the people to the King." On 15 November 1756, the die was cast. Pitt had at last the office he so long had sought. Then, just six months later, the prize seemed to slip away from him, when George III peremptorily dismissed him and recalled Newcastle once more to head the government. Even then, Pitt could not be brushed aside. He was given the portfolio of Ministry for War, with full authority to conduct the military operations. In effect, it was still Pitt who was in control.

One of his first decisions was to wage major warfare in Europe—where, as he proudly claimed, "America was conquered in Germany." His primary efforts were directed to the rebuilding of the navy. Another step he took was to change the policy that had so far denigrated the colonial forces that George Washington, as a colonel, had been inferior in rank to a mere lieutenant in the British army. Such revisions of strategy, and the inspiring influence of Pitt's leadership, proved so effective that in 1757 English armies won decisive victories both in Europe and in Canada. The successes continued to their climax in the annus mirabilis of 1759, during which the power of France was shattered. The British flag rose unchallenged all over the New World, from Quebec and Detroit on down through the Caribbean island of Guadeloupe. And no one questioned that this was owing to the magnificent leadership of William Pitt.

But the monarchy remained the stumbling block. On 25 October 1760, George II died and was succeeded by his grandson, George III, who came to the throne "determined to be King." He appointed Lord Bute, his friend and favorite, to be his secretary, and the prime ministry sank into secondary significance. Pitt was required to enter into peace negotiations that surrendered basic English advantages. Among them, Guadeloupe was given back to the French, in return for their abandonment of their claims to Canada. When, still further, Pitt was ordered also to make peace with Spain, he angrily refused. To a meeting of the cabinet on 3 October 1760, he said imperiously, "I was called by my sovereign and by the Voice of the People to assist the State when others had abdicated the service of it. That being so, none can be surprised that I will go on no longer since my advice is not taken." Peremptorily, he surrendered his seals of office. Then to the astonishment of all, he accepted the king's offer of the barony of Chatham for his wife and of a grant of an annual pension from the king. Again it appeared that Pitt was defeated, both politically and morally.

It also quickly became evident that the peace King George had demanded was not yet practical. The war dragged on, to be finally concluded, on terms to which Pitt stoutly objected, in the Peace of Paris, which was signed on 10 February 1763. In some ways the peace settlement greatly pleased the public. For one thing, the long war was ended; for another, British supremacy in India was confirmed. Another apparent advantage was that the French were barred from Canada, except for fishing rights off the Atlantic coast, and they gave up any claim to the American territories east of Louisiana. In return, the French got Guadeloupe, and with it virtual control over the rich trade with the West Indies. The more significant, though indirect, effect was that elimination of the French threat freed the American colonies from incursions by the Indians and enhanced their growing spirit of independence. Even more basically, it resulted in the strengthening of the throne as the central authority in government. In sum, "Europe sank into peace in 1763, a merciful peace following a merciless war. . . . Put in terms of men, the peace was the handiwork of Lord Bute and the still lesser men who had forced Pitt from office . . . sacrificing their country's prestige and surrendering those paramount imperial interests which Pitt had so unreservedly pursued . . . thus gaining for George III the prestige and popularity without which he could not hope to end the humiliating 'elevated nullification of the Crown.' "[10]

Pitt's biographer put it in terms less favorable to Pitt than to King George. "At the bar of humanity and civilization it must be judged that the Peace was salutary and just. But we can understand the feelings of Pitt and those whom he inspired, that much which had been won by lavish sacrifices of blood and treasure was being flung away in the glorious haste of the King and his creatures to obtain a free hand at home."[11] In Pitt's own view, the peace spelled abject defeat. In the long run, it marked the beginning of the train of events that split the English-speaking peoples apart. In personal terms, it appeared to be the end of Pitt's career. He was rendered miserable by his gout and was again depressed by the unappeasable hostility of the king. There seemed to be no longer any opportunity for him to wield political influence. Once more he retired to his home in Bath, doomed, as it seemed, to virtual obscurity.

George III, with Lord Bute as his principal advisor, was firmly in control of the government. The throne was restored to more authority than it had had since the last days of the Stuarts. The results, both in India and in America, were to be momentous. And Opposition withered, as Pitt appeared to have given up the struggle. In 1766 he was rewarded by being named Earl of Chatham.

With his new title as Lord Chatham, he lived on for another sixteen years. Once more, very briefly, he was brought in as prime minister, but for the most part he lived in retirement. Only near the end of his life did he emerge once more into greatness, to make one last eloquent plea in his country's behalf. But this reappearance came too late, under very different circumstances, when key policy decisions had already been made. No longer was he the central character in the national drama, but only an ailing and incidental participant. The speaking he then did, and the effects flowing from it, must be left for consideration of the new problems of a new age.

Like a meteor Pitt had risen to shine boldly in the English sky, and like a meteor he faded away, trailing clouds of glory but no longer dominating the view. His name and his fame remained bright in the public mind, but his leadership in shaping affairs had dwindled. The future was to unfold the results. Whether they were to be lamented or worthy of being celebrated has been assessed differently on the two sides of the Atlantic.

One effect at least is clear. The great empire that was carved into being by the leadership of the Elder Pitt fell apart when his guidance was rejected. Perhaps it may be said of the English-speaking peoples of the world what was said by Benjamin Franklin to the assembled delegates of the American colonies: "We must all hang together, or assuredly we shall all hang separately." The date of this statement was 4 July 1776, when the American Declaration of Independence was signed. Since then, in these later years, new enemies confront both parts of the dissevered peoples. Instead of independence, *inter*dependence has become a vital theme. But all of this lay far beyond the lifespan of William Pitt, when new generations had new problems to confront. From the perspective of the twentieth century, Chatham remains indubitably great.

Democracy has come to rule. Pitt saw its weaknesses but not its strength. The throne has lost its power, as he believed it should. His rhetoric had accomplished what rhetoric can do—it had pointed a viable way. But it was not eloquence but power that came to dominate affairs. George III became, as he meant to be, veritably the king. It was a shift of governmental authority that could not last; and the price for it had to be paid.

Notes

1. F. Harrison, *Chatham*, p. 25.
2. Cited from Wingfield-Stratford, Goodrich, Donald Bryant, and "Frederick the Great."
3. F. Harrison, *Chatham*, p. 25.
4. Ibid., pp. 18–19.
5. These three judgments are cited by Goodrich, *Select British Eloquence*, pp. 75, 72, 57.
6. Erich Eyck, *Pitt versus Fox: Father and Son, 1735–1806* (London: G. Bell and Sons, 1950), p. 20.
7. *The Letters of Horace Walpole,* edited by Peter Cunningham, 9 vols. (London: Richard Bentley, 1891), 2:67.
8. Goodrich, *Select British Eloquence*, pp. 58–59.
9. *Letters of Walpole,* 2:68–69.
10. Leo Gershoy, *From Despotism to Revolution, 1763–1789* (New York: Harper, 1944), pp. 1–2.
11. F. Harrison, *Chatham*, p. 138.

9
Concern for the Little Man—Religion and Reform

What people talk about is largely governed by the fundamental convictions of the time in which they live. John Locke gave to eighteenth-century England a new idea that stimulated discussion and directed it into new dimensions—the idea that all individuals at birth are equal. This was a challenging new idea for minds to nibble at and it stimulated discussions reaching into every aspect of society. Locke had other ideas that were scarcely less influential. His belief in the sanctity of property, which it was government's chief responsibility to defend, was only a reaffirmation of what was generally taken for granted. Lord Chatham made it the basis for empire building. Another idea of Locke—set forth in his treatise, *The Reasonableness of Christianity*, that the sanction on which religion depends is not revelation but reason—led to a substantial growth of deism—by which the image of a Father God, a Sacrificed Son, and an Ever-present Spirit was converted into an abstraction of divine purposiveness.

New basic premises were emergent. In France they led to the great Revolution. In England they also had revolutionary effects, which were stimulated and guided by talk, and which started a chain of changes that determined the shape of things to come.

Politics is only one perspective from which to view the affairs of a nation. During the generations politically dominated by Walpole and Chatham, there were other strong currents changing the attitudes and the feelings of the people of England. One was a new trend of enthusiasm and individualism in religion—differing not only in degree but also in kind from that exemplified by the Baptists and Quakers. Another was a rising demand for social changes that would lead toward equality of justice and a broadening of opportunities for economic and social advancement. Both trends were fought by defenders of conservatism. But both proved strong enough to burst through such constraints.

Conclusions that for many centuries had seemed obvious were becoming ambiguous. The changing attitudes came into clear focus in the eighteenth century—though the first change of direction had commenced as early as the Renaissance (see Chapter 4, above), and the fruition was to be delayed until well into the nineteenth and twentieth centuries.

A question that was becoming discussable was whether humanity really is God's special concern. From this questioning, other doubts emerged. Should the interpretation of God's will be the special function of the Established Church, or was it in the province of individual reason? Is it proper for God's mercy to find expression only in an afterlife, or should his superintendence also assure better living conditions on earth? These were issues to be discussed, and eloquent speakers proposed and advocated their own answers.

"A Most Disturbing Turbulent Time"

The speakers whose influence was most strongly felt in the areas of religion and of social reform were a strangely diverse lot: Henry Sacheverell, a radically conservative Anglican; the Wesley brothers, founders of Methodism; George Whitefield, a hypnotically eloquent Presbyterian; John Wilkes, a disreputable libertarian; and William Wilberforce, an evangelical parliamentarian who led the crusade for abolition of the trade in slaves. All were urgently persuasive—each in his own way—but they differed widely from one another in their convictions, in their personalities, and in their rhetorical strategies and manner of speech.

The greatest among them, undoubtedly, was John Wesley. His influence has been estimated in extreme but scarcely exaggerated terms. "When it comes to the nice calculation of greatness by its influence on mankind, what can discount the fame of one who transformed the religion of a race? . . . Wesley's influence is as wide and enduring as Napoleon's, and more permanant than Bismarck's."[1] He was poor, without social status, and held no public office. The revolution he accomplished was a triumph for the spoken word.

John Hutchinson, a theologian and a philosopher (and in his mind these two kinds of inquiry are not competitive but complementary) defines *religious language* as "symbolic or expressive language used for the purpose of total life orientation." The theme he develops is that "religious language consists, then, of powerful and luminous symbols by which men delineate their path through the mortal woods."[2] "Total life orientation" was indeed the high goal set by these leading eighteenth-century spokesmen for religious and social guidance "through the mortal woods." Their concerns were with the whole person, the whole society, the whole meaning of life. We should not just *do*, we should *be* what they proclaimed to be everlastingly true and right. Theirs was not the political art of compromise but the assured certainty of prophets.

Such conviction was held not only by the innovators but also by the most fervent of the traditionalists. As the century opened, the most widely influential religious spokesman was Henry Sacheverell, an inconspicuous Anglican priest who leapt into national notoriety through two sermons in which he viciously attacked the policies of religious toleration that had been enacted by the Whigs. In retrospect, the storm he aroused might be dismissed as no more than a tempest in a teacup. But in his three-year span of fame, the feelings he aroused were so strong and so widespread that, as Daniel Defoe wrote in the *Review*, "It looks as if the nation had lost its senses." All this was effected by a man virtually unknown even within his own church, by the two sermons that he delivered as a guest preacher in two famous pulpits. The first, entitled "The Communication of Sin," was preached at Derby, on 15 August 1709. It aroused such national attention that he was invited to speak on the following 5 November at Saint Paul's in London. For this latter sermon he had a congregation of the nation's notables, and to them he delivered a scathing denunciation of the government, entitled "The Perils of False Brethren, Both in Church and State." So violent was his language, and so tremendous was its effect upon public opinion, that the House of Commons brought him to trial for fomenting public disorder. Defoe, for the March 1710 issue of the *Review*, wrote of the "fatal consequence" that the government feared.

> We have had a most disturbing turbulent time . . . occasioned by the prosecution and defence of a high-flying churchman. . . . which has made them seem very formidable to the world—rabbles, tumults, plundering houses, demolishing meeting houses, insulting gentlemen in the streets and honest men in their dwellings . . . not without most fatal consequences over the whole nation, as it has revived the heats, feuds, and animosities among us.

The instigator of this furor was a demagogic zealot who undertook on his own authority and solely through his own speaking to reverse the tide of humanistic tolerance that followed the excesses of the Civil War. Sacheverell felt himself equal to the task he undertook. A contemporary described his appearance in Saint Paul's: "I was surpriz'd by the Fiery red that overspread his Face (which I have since seen fair and effeminate enough) and the goggling wildness of his Eyes. And I may truly say, He was (if ever Man was) transported with an Hellish Fury."[3]

His "hellish fury" was evident not only in his appearance but in his views and the language in which he set them forth. In the first of his guest sermons he was content merely to charge that "the principles and interests of our Church and Constitution are shamelessly betrayed and run down" by the "undermining treachery" of those who promoted religious tolerance. The great outburst of public support for his views, which led to his invitation to occupy London's most prestigious pulpit, encouraged him to stronger language as he directed his attack against both religious Dissenters and government officials who tolerated their heresies.

> What a vast scandal and offense must it give to all persons of piety and integrity, to see men of characters and stations thus shift and prevaricate with their principles. . . . To see men's opinions set as loose about them as their garments, to be put on or off for convenience?
>
> What can unwary persons conclude from such pergiversations [sic] and hypocrisy, but that all religion is statecraft and imposture? That all godliness is gain; and that the Doctrines of the Church lie not so much in her Articles, as her honours and revenues? Without doubt, this modern latitude, and infamous double-dealing, as it can proceed from nothing but the rankest atheism, so it must prosecute it wherever it goes.

So much for religious tolerance! Sacheverell's demagoguery might have been ignored by the authorities except for the nationwide attention and wide public support that he won. When he was brought to trial by the House of Lords, with the prosecution managed by a House of Commons committee headed by Robert Walpole, Sacheverell defended himself in a "studied, artful, and pathetic speech" in which he persisted in his denunciation of the protection afforded to heresies, while representing himself this time as being both reasonable and humble.

> I submit myself to your Lordships' judgment, be it what it will. One thing I am sure it can never take from me: the power of wishing and praying . . . most earnestly beseeching Almighty God to preserve all orders and degrees of men amongst us from all false doctrines, heresies, and schisms, from hardness of heart, from contempt for His word.

When the trial ended, the verdict was for guilt, by the narrow margin of 62 votes to 59. Sacheverell was debarred from preaching for three years and his sermons were publicly burned. But in the broad court of public opinion the verdict went strongly for him. For more than two years afterward he rode around England, from town to town, on a white horse, accompanied by crowds of attendants, to be greeted with acclaim in massed public meetings. Then a reaction set in, and he was burned in effigy. After this he retired to live quietly until his death in 1723. His speeches would be entirely without significance except for the public support given to him. It was obvious that religious tolerance rested upon very shaky grounds.

"Nothing Less than All Mankind"

The great test of freedom of conscience came in a much quieter way and with far different and vastly greater effect from the remarkable family of Wesleys, who were as respectable as Sacheverell was wildly unrestrained.

In the Epworth rectory near Lincoln there lived a poor and inconspicuous minister of the Church of England named Samuel Wesley, whose loyal devotion to his ministerial duties was surpassed only by his desperate ambition to be a poet. All through his long life he poured out an endless stream of religious verse, some of it good enough to win kind words from the great Alexander Pope. He and his wife, Susanna, produced eighteen children, which kept them impoverished to the extent that Samuel was for a time committed to a debtors prison. Two years after his release, at Christmas time in 1707, his wife gave birth to another baby boy—born prematurely and condemned to lifelong ill health. He was given his grandfather's name of Charles, and joined two other older surviving sons, Samuel and John. Susanna taught them to "cry softly" so as not to disturb their father's writing of poetry; and in her view, "never were children better disposed to piety, nor more in subjection to their parents."[4] Especially the younger two, John and Charles, were destined to exercise a religious influence that has not often been overmatched.

Despite the poverty of the family, such were the generous provisions for the education of promising young ecclesiastics that all three were able with scholarship grants to earn degrees from Oxford. Samuel, the eldest, won appointment to a small parish. From his meager income he made frequent small but essential grants to his brothers, and he undertook the paternalistic responsibility for shaping their minds and characters through a constant flow of well-meant advice. His counsel was that they be loyal and obedient to the church while devoting themselves to piety and prayer. This guidance suited their temperaments, which were inclined toward monastic seclusion.

Oxford, in their time, resembled a country club devoted to hard drinking, hunting, and cockfighting. Edward Gibbon, in his *Autobiography*, complained that students "had absolved their consciences from the toil of reading, thinking or writing." The Wesley brothers, on the contrary, studied hard and remained aloof from campus society. In 1729, the year in which Charles took his A.B., he joined with three other pietistic students in sessions of daylong meditation and prayer, which won for them the derisive designation of the "Holy Club." Soon he persuaded his brother John to join with them. This was a rare reversal of roles, for as Charles later truly observed, John "always had the ascendance over me."

Their thinking was decisively influenced by a book published in 1728 and already widely popular, *A Serious Call to a Devout and Holy Life*, written by William Law, a retired dissenting minister. Law set out to demonstrate that Christianity becomes effective "not by ceremonial devotion but by a new principle of life, a change of temper and aspiration." One of Law's principles was, "If we are to follow Christ, it must be in our common way of spending every day." The whole book, and most specifically this comment, made a deep impression upon the Wesley brothers and their schoolmate George Whitefield.

This early, John Wesley concluded that "the common way of spending every day" was indeed essential to the truly religious life. As he told his brother, "He that has begun to live by rule has gone a great way toward the perfection of his life."

Here was the seed that grew into Methodism. Even before their reading of Law's book, the two brothers had made almost a fetish of "system." The program for every day was planned: sessions of prayer, of quiet thought, of reading, of talk together about their devotion to God. This was a far cry from the Sabbath formalism that characterized the Anglican church; it was a complete, an orderly, and a methodical devotion of their whole lives to religious observation. Both brothers were devoted members of the Established Church and remained so all their lives, but theirs was Anglicanism with a difference. They left nothing to chance. They lived day by day and hour by hour according to plan. The ritualism and formality of the Anglican service came to be repugnant to them, and they rejected the division of the week into six days for work and one for worship. They had no intention of being rebels. They valued respectability and believed themselves to be soundly orthodox. As John Wesley asserted, "I have been all my life (until very lately) so tenacious of every point relating to decency and order that I should have thought the saving of souls almost a sin if it had not been done in church."

The mission to save souls, however, came later and was undertaken very reluctantly. John and Charles, in Oxford, devoted themselves solely to the goal of personal perfection in the completeness of their own faith. They did not plan on being ordained preachers. What dominated their thoughts was their own personalized search for salvation. Almost by accident, and against their own wishes, they were impelled into missionary work even before they attained certainty that they would be saved. The field into which they were taken was not England but the new American colony of Georgia.

What led them to this decision was the patronage of a humane member of Parliament, General James Edward Oglethorpe, whose feelings were deeply stirred by the dismal sufferings of inmates of English prisons. Under the prevailing penal system, prisoners were completely dependent for their survival upon the contributions by outside relatives or friends for food, fuel, and money with which to bribe their jailers. Oglethorpe had no thought of reforming the system, but only of rescuing as many of the inmates as he could. To this end he secured a charter to found the colony of Georgia, to which prisoners could be shipped in order to relieve the unmanageable congestion of the jails. On his second voyage to the new colony he took with him the two Wesley brothers, who later persuaded Whitefield to join them.

The Wesleys could scarcely have been worse suited for their mission. Neither had been ordained, and they accepted ordination only on the eve of their departure, and then with great reluctance. Both felt wholly unequal to the challenge to convert unbelievers. What they intended, as John noted in his journal, was simply to live lives of such holiness that others might be inspired by their example. Their feeling of inadequacy was quickly justified. On shipboard they were harshly condemned by ex-convict passengers for their insistence upon compulsory attendance at four sermons every day, the first scheduled for 5 A.M. Their spirits, especially John's, were lighted only by the staunch faith they found among other passengers who were devout Moravians.

Their failure in Georgia was devastating and quickly evident. Charles had been selected by Oglethorpe to be his secretary and hated the work so much that he shortly resigned and returned to England. John remained for what proved to be two years of misery. During this time he quarreled with his patron and made himself ridiculous by wooing—but refusing to marry—the daughter of the colony's storekeeper. Marriage for both brothers was to come later and only after anguished self-searching. As John wrote of himself, "I still hanker after creature happiness." It was a barrier to piety that they felt impelled most strongly to resist. Nor had they yet found the certainty of an inner faith. Both brothers considered themselves to be "seekers" for salvation, far from having faith enough with which they might guide others. As John recorded after his return home: "I went to America to convert the Indians; but Oh! who shall convert me?"[5] He had abundant reason for self-doubt, for throughout his mission he was "intolerant and autocratic. . . . He soon set a whole congregation by the ears. And perhaps worst of all he was extraordinarily silly, tiresome, and uncharitable."[6]

Upon his return, he visited his mother, who encouraged him with her satisfaction that he had come to believe in the mercy of God. Three days later he preached a sermon at Oxford, "The Nature and Necessity of Our New Birth in Christ Jesus, in Order to Salvation." This has been called his Great Manifesto. But it remained insufficient. Still he felt primarily the yearning solely for his own salvation. Seeking help from the Moravians, he went to Helmond, in Holland, and spent three months among them. There he would have stayed except that "my Master called me to serve in another part of the vineyard." Together with Charles, he joined with a small band of religious seekers in London's Fetter Lane Society. There he was urged by a devout evangelist, Lady Huntingdon to "attempt nothing less than all mankind." Still he was unready.

The decisive conversion of the two Wesley brothers occurred separately but almost at the same time. On Sunday, 21 May 1739 Charles, alone in his room at Oxford, was suffering one of his lifelong bouts of illness and depression when suddenly, as he noted in his journal, "I saw that by Faith I stood." Just three days afterward, while John was listening to the preaching of one John Bray, "a poor ignorant mechanic," there came similarly to him the conviction of his own salvation. He bounded joyously upstairs to

Charles's room exclaiming, "I believe!" Neither of them, however, felt a call to save others.

"Proclaimed in the Highways the Glad Tidings"

It was George Whitefield who led them out into evangelism. Unlike the Wesleys, he found his true vocation while in Georgia. During his eight-month stay he preached with great effectiveness and won hundreds of converts to his insistence upon utter submission to the "predestined" will of God. Upon his return to England, he went to Bristol to conduct a massive campaign. He wrote to John Wesley, urging him to leave Fetter Lane to take over the London pulpit he had left. The year was 1739. The train of circumstances was commenced that laid the foundation for Methodism.

In Bristol, on a Sunday in February, Whitefield preached to a crowded congregation, while some thousand who wished to hear him stood outside, unable to get in. "This," Whitefield attested, "put me first upon thinking of preaching without doors." On 17 February, in a field near Bristol, he gave the first of his open-air sermons. Such out-of-doors preaching had not been uncommon before and during the Reformation, but for a century or more it had been infrequent. John Wesley was at first scandalized by Whitefield's heretical example. But soon, as he recorded, "I submitted myself to be more vile and proclaimed in the highways the glad tidings of salvation, speaking from a little eminence in a ground adjoining to the city to about three thousand people."[7]

George Whitefield's preaching was by far more dramatic than the quietly serious conversational mode of the Wesleys. As a speaker, he was positively hypnotic. Benjamin Franklin, as he attests in his *Autobiography*, went to hear him, intending to scoff but was so moved that he emptied his pockets into the collection plate. The equally skeptical Lord Chesterfield was similarly affected. Much of Whitefield's speaking was done in America, which he traversed from south to north. In this sense, he belongs to the history not of English but of American preaching.[8] But he made thirteen transatlantic voyages and preached incessantly, wherever he went. As Eugene White found in his doctoral study of Whitefield's ministry in America, he preached for at least forty hours of every week. Many of his sermons lasted for some two hours. Fervently he called upon sinners to repent and to yield themselves wholly to God's will. Whether they had been predestined for salvation was merely incidental. Their duty was submission, whatever their fate might prove to be. To this hard doctrine he converted scores of thousands.

Whitefield seemed made for oratory. His musical voice was so strong that it could be heard by thousands. His rhythmic tones were so overwhelming that the great actor David Garrick exclaimed, "I would give one hundred guineas if I could say 'O' like Mr. Whitefield."[9] His language was simple, direct, and highly personalized. He called upon his hearers not to question or to study or to think but to accede willingly to the sovereignty of God. The effects were indeed hypnotic. So was his method. In one sermon he commenced fourteen successive short sentences with the exclamation "Oh!"—and by such ritualistic repetition he beat down all resistance. In his sermons, pathos intermingled with humor. His theme was obedient submission to the inexorable justice of an implacable God. Truth is truth; any efforts to evade it are futile. The one ray of hope that he held out was that God, in his great wisdom, had ordained that those whom he intended to save would be marked by their acceptance of his overlordship. You cannot "win" salvation, he taught, but you can become worthy of it. In this crusade he spent his life until his death in 1770.

"They Shall Never by My Consent Call Me Bishop"

The Wesleys were no less orthodox but their interpretation of the Scriptures was basically different. They believed implicitly in the doctrine of original sin. No one deserves the mercy of God. As John noted in his journal, "If every man among us got his just deserts, who would escape hanging?" Since all are equally undeserving, none should be especially scorned or rejected. All stand alike in their need of redemption. Happily, as they perceived, salvation is available through acceptance of the sacrifice of Christ. No one who accepted Christ as his savior would be denied. Their preaching, consequently, dealt less with justice than with hope. What they stressed was not the sternness of God but the compassion of Jesus. What they offered to their hearers was not the mere satisfaction of submission but the promise of eternal bliss.

John, who was always the leader, was also exceedingly practical. He knew how to build an organization. Even while resisting the urgency of his followers to form a new denomination, he established local churches and appointed pastors for them. This was the strategy that separated him most definitively from the Anglican church. He issued "tickets of membership" to his followers and called them not only to Sunday services but also to midweek confessionals and to quarterly "Love Feasts." He traveled methodically, always by horseback, for the staggering total of some 250,000 miles. The number of sermons he delivered averaged fifteen each week. He allowed himself neither rest nor recreation. The High Church Tory Samuel Johnson admired and liked him but wryly protested that "John Wesley's conversation is good, but he is never at leisure; he is always obliged to go at a certain hour. This is very disagreeable to a man who loves to fold his legs and have out his talk, as I do."[10] Such labors culminated, in 1744, in establishment of Wesley's own centralized conference, which he kept tightly under his own control. He refused to break away from the Church of England, yet maintained a separate entity within it.

Charles preached with equal assiduity. But instead of being an organizer, he persisted in his ambition to be a poet. He wrote poetic hymns so prodigiously that he published some three thousand of them—including many that became the most beloved in the language. This was his rhetorical contribution, more influential than preaching.

The development of a separate denomination, which was far from the Wesleys' intent, came about inevitably. Robert Southey, in his *Life of John Wesley* (1820) explains how:

> One step drew on another. Because he preached an enthusiastic and dangerous doctrine [that salvation does not depend on church ritual], which threw his followers into convulsions, he was properly, by most clergymen, refused the use of their pulpits. This drove him to field-preaching; but field-preaching is not for all weathers, in a climate like ours. Prayer-meetings were also a part of his plan: and thus it became expedient to build meeting-houses. Meeting-houses required funds; they required ministers, too, while he was itinerating. Few clergymen could be found to cooperate with him; and though at first he abhorred the thought of admitting uneducated laymen to the ministry, lay preachers were soon forced upon him, by their own zeal, which was too strong to be restrained, and by the plain necessity of the case.

The independence of Wesley from the Anglican church derived in part from his own dominant personality, and in part from disappointment with the preaching he found in it. In his journal he recorded, on Sunday, 10 May 1772, "I attended the Church of England service in the morning" and found it to be insufferably "dull and dry." Four years later, in another jotting, he expressed his disgust that many communicants of the church, "with all their orthodoxy . . . had no religion still." In this same entry he told of talking with a teenaged girl who was a regular church member. "But to my surprise, I found her as ignorant of the nature of religion as a Hottentot." Still he persisted in his loyalty. "I see clearer and clearer none will keep to us, unless they keep to the Church. Whoever separates from the Church will separate from the Methodists." Nevertheless, on 8 February, 1784, Wesley took the decisive step of registering a "deed of declaration" in the Court of Chancery, giving his societies a fixed constitution. The Anglican church refused to sanction the ordination of Wesley's uneducated ministers, and he was urged to formalize the new group of societies under his own authority. This he stoutly refused, saying (in 1788) that "men may call me a knave or a fool, a rascal, a scoundrel, and I am content, but they shall never by my consent call me a bishop."[11]

On 1 January 1790, he wrote in his journal:

> I am now an old man, decayed from head to foot. My eyes are dim; my right hand shakes much; my mouth is hot and dry every morning; I have a lingering fever almost every day; my motion is weak and slow. However, blessed be God, I do not slack my labor. I can preach and write still.

The following morning, as was his custom, he arose at 4 A.M., to preach again. On 2 March 1791, at the age of eighty-eight, he died. His brother Charles had preceded him in death three years earlier, at the age of eighty.

As a preacher John Wesley was far from being physically impressive. His height was only five feet five inches. His mind was capacious and well filled. He read voraciously, often on horseback, not only the Bible but from a wide range of English literature. He learned enough Greek and Hebrew so that he could study early biblical texts, and he also knew enough Spanish, French, and German to translate from and into those languages with freedom. In a letter he wrote in November 1774, he described his own convictions about how to preach.

> In public preaching speak not one word against opinions of any kind. We are not to fight against notions, but sin. Least of all should I advise you once to open your lips against *Predestination*. It would do more mischief than you are aware of. Keep to your one point, present inward salvation by faith, by the divine evidence of sins forgiven.

His sermons came from his heart as well as from his head. His greatest source of strength lay in his identification with the great mass of the people. For them his sympathy was boundless. In his journal, for 5 November 1766, is this revealing entry:

> I have thought much on the huge encomiums which have been for many ages bestowed on a *country life*. . . . But, after all, what a flat contradiction is this to universal experience! See that little house, under the wood, by the riverside! There is rural life in perfection. How happy, then, is the farmer who lives there! Let us take a detail of his happiness. He rises with, or before the sun, calls his servants, looks to his swine and cows, then to his stables and barns. He sees to the plowing and sowing his ground, in winter or in spring. In summer and autumn he hurries and sweats among his mowers and reapers. And where is his happiness in the meantime? Which of these employments do we envy?

The texts of his sermons are rhetorically unimpressive. He made no effort to be impressive. His sermons made small use of figures of speech. He did not strive for rhythmic flow, for pleasing alliteration, or for the triphammer emphasis of repetition. Quite to the contrary, his speaking style was effortlessly simple. He did not mean for his sermons to be admired, nor did he expect or desire to have them read. What he did mean was to speak seriously and directly, aiming solely to break through the shield of indifference seeking to penetrate into the inmost consciousness of his listeners, where he could confront them with his message that salvation is their real concern and that belief in Christ would insure it for them. What he said he believed. And his earnest and thoughtful manner carried belief to his listeners. He spoke less as their mentor than as their representative. "Come," he seemed to say, "let us be serious about this. Let us see what is truly important. And let us respond as we must to what is both universally true and personally right." One of his biographers summed up his appeal in the following terms:

> Wesley combined in his own person the two essential aspects of the eighteenth century. He was a Man of Feeling, full of the new Humanitarianism, but he was also a man of clear and even dry intelligence whose appeal was always to Reason. Even his preaching was as remote as possible from the perfervid methods of a Whitefield. He had no tricks of oratory, no perorations, no dramatic pauses or histrionic gestures. He stood perfectly still, save for a characteristic raising of his hand as if to enjoin silence; he spoke in a clear, level, unemotional voice; and his matter was as plain as his manner.[12]

E. J. Hobsbawn, in his penetrating study of the spirit of revolution that swept across the Western world toward the end of this century, credits John Wesley with preserving England from its destabilizing effects. As he pointed out, the views of Wesley were apolitical and "strongly conservative, for they turned away from the evil outside world to personal salvation or to the life of the self-contained group, which often meant that they rejected the possibility of any collective alteration of the secular arrangements."[13] In short, Wesley was no social reformer. He saw no need for it. Since our life span is only a preparation for eternity, his interest lay in what must be done to insure entry into heaven.[14]

"The Cloudy Phrases in Which Weaker Men Sought Safety"

What the Wesleys accomplished was a long-term, broad-ranging spiritual renovation that during succeeding generations spread across the world. Its immediate effects were considerable but were not adequate to satisfy the needs of the largely disenfranchised masses. In desperation, huge mobs demonstrated and rioted to protest fuel scarcity, high prices, unemployment, poor living conditions, and taxation without representation.

Fanning these fires of discontent were two radicals who differed as much from one another as their goals differed from those of the churchmen. One was the "rascally" John Wilkes; the other the "saintly" William Wilberforce. Neither was a frequent public speaker, yet both proved to have charismatic appeal that aroused public feelings to fever pitch and that led to positive effects in the form of parliamentary decisions. Like the two Wesley brothers, Wilkes at least was assuredly no great orator. Yet his speaking, like that of the Wesleys, was enormously effective. He helped significantly to nurture the innovative belief that secular life can and must be systematically and institutionally improved.

In basic respects, John Wilkes appeared to be peculiarly unsuited for the role of reformer. He was a man of weak character and of self-centered ambitions. Yet he proved to exercise great persuasive charm, and his influence was decisive. A biographer of George III (who bitterly detested Wilkes) admirably sums up his combination of contrarieties.

> Wilkes first appears in history as a martyr for the cause of freedom of the press, next for the right of electors to choose freely their Members of Parliament, and lastly as a successful agitator for the liberty to publish reports of parliamentary proceedings. Yet no man was less disposed to suffer martyrdom and no martyr cared so little for the cause for which he suffered. Wilkes was a jolly blackguard, fond of his bottle and his whore, with a taste for good scholarship and good conversation, and out for what he could get.[15]

Wilkes has been depicted by historians as "no demagogue"[16] (for his parliamentary speeches were carefully prepared, restrained in tone, and far from being inflammatory), and also as "a reckless demagogue" who "scorned the decent concealment, the hypocrisy, the cloudy phrases in which weaker men sought safety."[17] He was both. In his speaking in the House of Commons, his infrequent speeches were carefully molded as argumentative statements. In his journalism and in his speeches to his constituents, he indulged in gross exaggerations and flamboyant attacks on the government.

The son of a wealthy London distiller, the youthful Wilkes was a poor scholar and an arrant pleasure seeker. While Wilkes was still in his teens, his father married him to a much older woman of some considerable wealth, whom he cozened out of her fortune (which he lost in gambling) then divorced and left in poverty. His father also purchased for him a seat in Parliament, representing the rotten borough of Aylesbury, and a colonelcy in the militia. Wilkes associated himself with the radicals in the Hellfire Club and with Pitt's Opposition group in Parliament. Then in 1762, he founded a weekly periodical, *The North Briton,* in which he belittled the Scots and scurrilously attacked the Scottish Lord Bute, whom he helped Pitt to drive from office. When Bute was replaced by Grenville, Wilkes's attacks on the government became even more venomous. "How far," his friend madame de Pompadour asked him, "does freedom of the press extend in England?" "That," said Wilkes, "is what I am trying to find out."

The Peace of Paris, which was negotiated by Bute and supported by George III, aroused widespread resentment among the English public, since it surrendered many of the gains that had been won by Pitt. Wilkes's furious attack upon this treaty, published in *The North Briton* on 23 April 1763, caused his hitherto undistinguished career suddenly to explode—when he was thirty-six years of age—into national prominence. He had already aroused the wrath of George III by implying in an earlier article that Lord Bute's influence at Court rested largely upon an adulterous relationship with the Princess Dowager. In issue number 45, he described the treaty as "the most abandoned instance of ministerial effrontery ever attempted to be imposed upon mankind." Then he went even further, to blast as a deliberate lie the assertion in the king's address to the Parliament that the peace was "honourable to my Crown and beneficial to my people."

In an ill-judged fury of response, the government issued a general warrant for the search of Wilkes's home and editorial offices and for his arrest. Wilkes's writ of habeas corpus was ignored. The Court of Common Pleas brought him to trial on 3 and 6 May 1763. In this trial Wilkes spoke in his own defense in measured terms. Seeking the broadest possible support, Wilkes argued that general warrants were illegal, that the secretary of state (who had issued it) lacked such authority, and that as a member of Parliament he was immune from arrest. There was no question of his guilt of seditious libel; but the public was deeply aroused by the illegality of the proceeding against him. When he was briefly freed on a writ of habeas corpus, he fled for safety to France, whereupon the House of Commons expelled him, with only one dissenting vote. This action, however, inflamed rather than quieted resentments. The following February, when the House debated the legality of the trial, the ministry was upheld by only fourteen votes.

Five years later, in February 1768, Wilkes returned to England to accept imprisonment as an outlaw. His money had run out and his only resource was the enormous popularity won for him by his prosecution. The government forbore to arrest him, and in the general election held that spring he was again elected to Parliament, this time from the prestigious county of Middlesex. Benjamin Franklin, who was then posted as a colonial representative in London, wrote, "It is really an extraordinary event to see an outlaw and exile, of bad personal character, and not worth a farthing . . . immediately carrying it for the principal county."[18] London rang with slogans of Wilkes and Liberty!" and rioting became widespread, after Wilkes was arrested, fined, and imprisoned. When the new Parliament met on 10 May, riotous crowds assailed the prison in which he was held and threatened the House of Lords. King George demanded that Wilkes be expelled from Parliament, a measure "whereupon almost my Crown depends." The motion for expulsion carried. Two weeks later Wilkes was again elected from Middlesex and again he was expelled. Once more Middlesex elected him with a four-to-one majority and again the House refused him his seat.

The issue was clearly understood both in Parliament and without: Was the Commons representative of the people or did it have its own authority to govern as it saw fit? The people stood for representation, but they were far from having achieved it. In a population of about 8,000,000 there were only 160,000 voters. Moreover, fully half the members of the Commons had been chosen by only 5,723 voters; 364 voters elected one-ninth of the members. The 558 members of the Commons and the 268 peers in the Lords felt bound by no duty to represent their constituents. As Edmund Burke insisted to the voters of Bristol in his successful bid for their votes in 1774, "Your representative owes you, not his industry only, but his judgment; and he betrays, instead of serving you, if he sacrifices it to your opinion." Six years later, in his unsuccessful appeal for reelection, he was still maintaining stoutly: "I did not obey your instructions: No. I conformed to the instructions of truth and nature." In acknowledging his defeat, he recognized the reason for it: "I confided perhaps too much in my intentions." The demand for representation had prevailed. Electoral reform was yet to come, but the groundwork for it had been laid. The stubborn stand maintained by John Wilkes deserves considerable credit for it.

In a bitter speech to a London crowd, on 24 June 1776, after he had failed to win the lucrative post of city chamberlain, Wilkes gave his own interpretation of the independence of mind that Burke had praised. Elected officials he branded as "mercenaries of corruption and despotism." He went on venting his spleen.

> No longer worthy of the name of freemen, they are sunk into tame, mean vassals, ignominiously courting, and bowing their necks to the ministerial yoke. . . . All public spirit in the capital is visibly decaying. . . . A dissolution of the empire, ruin, and slavery are, I fear, advancing with giant strides upon us. We are ripe for destruction.[19]

The sentiments fitted the recipe for demagoguery, but the style limped in awkward phrasing and was utterly lacking in exclamatory strength. It is obvious that far from being a great orator, John Wilkes attained importance by being a great symbol. The roiling discontent of the public needed a personality around which to rally. Through bravado and boldness, Wilkes provided the rallying point they sought. The fastidious and aristocratic Horace Walpole had many reasons for heartily disliking Wilkes, but he was probably right in his judgment that the successive expulsions of Wilkes from his elected seat in Parliament constituted a major ministerial mistake. "In my own opinion," he wrote to his friend Sir Horace Mann, "the House of Commons is the place where he can do the least hurt, for he is a wretched speaker, and will sink into contempt."[20]

When Wilkes was grudgingly granted the membership he had won in four successive elections, he made no effort to bully the House. His sentiments were strongly antiministerial, particularly in his opposition to the conduct of the war with the American colonies. But his language was mild and his manner restrained. Neither did he have the gift of a Chatham to turn words into daggers, nor the comprehensive mind of a Burke to put the issues in a philosophical context. Instead of scintillating with wit, ridicule, and sarcasm, his speaking style was bland and trite. Typical of it was his speech on 25 November 1781, protesting against a bill to enlarge the naval forces. According to the summary provided in the *New Annual Register*, Wilkes declared,

> He would not give thanks for victories, which only tended to protract a destructive war. Peace with America could only save this sinking state, and give us permanent prosperity. There was more matter of grief than of triumph, of bewailing than thanksgiving, in this civil contest.

After the war ended and the Younger Pitt was named prime minister, Wilkes spoke to his London constituency in an ooze of bland satisfaction.

> The city of London, sir, with pride and satisfaction, now beholds revived in the son those solid virtues, shining talents, and powerful eloquence which they long admired in the father. . . .
> Much is to be done [he went on, addressing his remarks to Pitt]; but you have youth, capacity, and firmness. It is the characteristic of a true patriot never to despair, and we have a well-grounded hope of your making us again a great, powerful, happy, and united people.[21]

In these latter years Wilkes even deviated into such respectability that he was offered by King George a grant of £2,000, which he happily accepted.[22]

How could it be that an indifferent speaker of low character could have exercised so great an influence in the bringing about of "the new sort of politics"?[23] It was not how he spoke but what he represented that mattered. The "old politics" was well illustrated in Edmund Burke's *Thoughts on the Present Discontents* (1770), in which he described "the wise people" who formed "the natural strength of the kingdom" as comprised of "the great peers, the leading landed gentlemen, the opulent merchants and manufacturers, the substantial yeomanry."[24] A new strength was coming to be asserted by the masses of the laboring poor. In Wilkes they found an early voice. In the generation that was to come they were to find others who were better.

"Not Yet Ready for Freedom"

A vastly different instigator of the new era of reform was William Wilberforce, best remembered for his long campaign to abolish the slave trade, although in the breadth of his sympathies he was virtually a "complete reformer." His popularity with the public exceeded even that of Wilkes and, quite unlike Wilkes, he also was held in the highest of esteem by his fellow members of Parliament. The great jurist Henry Lord Brougham, who knew him well, wrote of "one . . . among the greatest benefactors of the human race," and "one whose genius was elevated by his virtues, and exalted by his piety," then added that it was not necessary to identify whom he meant, for it was "impossible that what has been said could apply to any but Mr. Wilberforce."[25]

In the opinion of Brougham, "his eloquence was of the highest order. It was persuasive and pathetic in an eminent degree; but it was occasionally bold and impassioned, animated with the inspiration which deep feeling alone can breathe into spoken thought, chastened by pure taste, varied by extensive information, enriched by classical allusion, sometimes elevated by the more sublime topics of holy writ"—all making him appear to Brougham to resemble the Prophet Isaiah. Brougham went on to describe the "singular kindness, the extreme gentleness of his disposition, wholly free from gall, from vanity, or any selfish feeling, [which qualities] kept him from indulging in any of the vituperative branches of rhetoric." Brougham cited just one instance of an uncharacteristic outburst of sarcastic rejoinder to a member of the Commons who referred slightingly to his "religious character." This was regarded as having "greatly outmatched Pitt himself, the great master of sarcasm," but it was also "a more singular proof of Wilberforce's virtue than of his genius, for who but he ever was possessed of such a formidable weapon, and never used it?"[26]

Leslie Stephen concurred with this judgment. Discussing Wilberforce's unquestioned leadership of the campaign to abolish slavery, Stephen judged that "his true praise is not that he was the independent originator of the agitation, but that he was admirably fitted to represent and stimulate the national conscience. His independent position, his high principles, and the singular charm of character which made him popular even with his antagonists, marked him out as an ideal leader of the cause."[27]

This singular character, whom it was impossible to dislike and difficult to oppose because of the manifest purity of his later life and motives, spent his early days in the pursuit of fashionable pleasures. Born into a family of moderate wealth in Hull, Yorkshire, in 1759, he attended Saint John's College in Cambridge, where he was an indifferent student but learned to love the classics. He also learned to spend his time in idleness, except for his passion for gambling. This practice, however, he abruptly abandoned on an evening in which he won £600 from an associate who could not afford so great a loss. One of his other skills was mimicry, in which he indulged freely at the expense of Lord North, until he was warned that a reputation for ridicule would bar him from influence. The love for sociability and the habit of exercising lavish hospitality, which he had acquired as a youth, persisted and grew throughout his life.

In 1780 his father procured for him a seat in Parliament from Hull, and he promptly associated himself with the Chathamite Whigs. He also accepted as his London home a room in Chatham's house at Wimbledon, and developed a wide and friendly acquaintance with London's liberals. The great change in his life came in 1785, when he was converted and, like the Wesleys, devoted himself centrally to living as best he could a religious life. Through the remainder of his seventy-two years, he became the principal symbol and guiding influence in reform.

His first reform measure was a bill to reform the treatment of prisoners, which he introduced and carried to an affirmative vote in the Commons, only to see it defeated in the Lords. The following year he introduced, with similar results, a bill to register voters in county elections, as a safeguard for electoral purity. More importantly, he undertook to organize a following (through the Proclamation Society) with the broad aims of improving social manners, combating vice, and restraining pornographic and obscene publications. By this time his generous spirit and social attractiveness, buttressed by his sincerity of dedication to promoting goodness, was making him a public figure of increasing influence.

The great aim to which he chiefly devoted himself was to eradicate the evil of slavery. This aim, which became the guiding passion of his career, came into focus for him through the work of an abolitionist writer, Thomas Clarkson, who in 1785 (the year of Wilberforce's conversion), persuaded him to become the leading spokesman for the then-unpopular cause in the House of Commons. Thenceforth, year after year, he introduced and ardently supported in the Parliament a succession of bills, designed to eliminate or at least to control the profitable and extensive slave trade. On 12 May 1789, he made his most notable speech in their support, lasting for three and a half hours, which elevated him in both public and parliamentary opinion to leadership in this movement.

In 1791 he carried his campaign outside of Parliament by commencing what proved to be a long series of massive out-of-doors meetings. This was the year of a great uprising of slaves in the plantations of Santo Domingo, which so frightened the public that the abolitionist fervor was diverted. Wilberforce himself expressed his conviction that the Negroes were not yet ready for freedom. Neither, he felt convinced, were Englishmen fitted to be their masters. The outbreak of the French Revolution still further induced a general fear in England of the excesses of radicalism. Against these feelings, Wilberforce's gentleness of spirit and quietness of manner made him an effective persuader. During England's war with France (and particularly after the fall of Robespierre) Wilberforce spoke often and fervently in favor of making peace. Meanwhile, his annually introduced bills against the slave trade were generally carried in the Commons and defeated in the Lords. In 1807, finally, his great aim was accomplished; on 25 March the English trade in slavery was abolished.

As Lord Brougham summed up the long campaign, the public was virtually unanimous in demanding an end to the evil that was "confessedly, from beginning to end, not a commerce but a crime." It was an "enormous evil" and a "disgrace to the country," upon which "no two men, endowed with reason, could possibly differ." Burke and Fox joined in denouncing it. Pitt, as prime minister, also spoke against it but forbore to exercise his authority to end the trade. The opposition to the reform was also formidable. King George opposed the abolition from fear that it might encourage the demand for general reforms. Men of property, who dominated the Parliament, feared that it might lead to attacks on other forms of property. Against these powerful forces, Wilberforce finally prevailed.[28]

The fear that antislavery sentiment was only one manifestation of the demand for generalized reform was wholly justified. Revolution was in the air. Wilberforce himself devoted his great talents also to such other movements as political emancipation for Catholics, and in 1796 he organized a Society for Bettering the Condition of the Poor. In that same year he also established a missionary society and a bible society, and wrote a book on practical Christianity that became widely popular. In 1813 he undertook yet another crusade, "to introduce the light of Christianity into India." Then he fell victim to ill health and spent his last two decades largely in retirement.

By this time the invention of the spindle, "probably the most important event in world history, at any rate since the invention of agriculture and cities,"[29] had launched the industrial revolution. This renovation, "whose only law was to buy in the cheapest market and sell without restriction in the dearest, was transforming the world."[30] But before its effects came to be recognized, there were other great political questions to be dealt with—among them the American and French revolutions and the English governance of India. It was with these issues that the greatest political speakers of the time—and of almost any other time—were chiefly concerned.

Notes

1. William Holden Hutton, *John Wesley* (London: MacMillan, 1927), pp. vii, 3.
2. John A. Hutchison, *Language and Faith: Studies in Sign, Symbol and Meaning* (Philadelphia: Westminster Press, 1963), pp. 13, 14.
3. Laprade, *Public Opinion and Politics*, pp. 51–52, 61–65. The capitalization of the quoted passages has been modernized.
4. Mabel R. Brailsford, *A Tale of Two Brothers: John and Charles Wesley* (New York: Oxford University Press, 1954), pp. 18, 19.
5. Hutton, *John Wesley*, p. 49.
6. Ibid., pp. 45–46.
7. Ibid., p. 46.
8. See Robert T. Oliver, *History of Public Speaking in America* (Boston: Allyn and Bacon, 1965); reprint, Westport, Conn.: Greenwood Press, 1977), pp. 37–39.
9. Stuart C. Henry, *George Whitefield: Wayfaring Witness* (New York: Abingdon Press, 1957), p. 61.

10. *Boswell's Life of Johnson*, 2:176.
11. Hutton, *John Wesley*, p. 113.
12. John Laver, *Wesley* (New York: D. Appleton, 1933), pp. 87–88.
13. E. J. Hobsbawn, *The Age of Revolution: Europe, 1789–1848* (London: Weidenfeld and Nicolson, 1962), p. 227.
14. Though not a reformer, Wesley was a convinced philanthropist. As John Telford wrote for the Encyclopaedia Britannica: "He provided work for the deserving poor, supplied them with clothes and food in seasons of special distress. . . . He established a lending stock to help struggling businessmen and did much to relieve debtors who had been thrown into prison."
15. John Brooke, *King George III* (New York: McGraw-Hill, 1972), pp. 144–45.
16. *Dictionary of National Biography*, s.v. "Wilkes, John."
17. Watson, *George III*, p. 98.
18. Brooke, *King George III*, p. 152. See Charles Chenevix Trench, *Portrait of a Patriot* (Edinburgh: Blackwood, 1962); R. W. Postgate, *That Devil Wilkes* (New York: Vanguard, 1929); Horace Bleakley, *Life of John Wilkes* (London: Bodley Head, 1917); Percy Fitzgerald, *The Life and Times of John Wilkes*, 2 vols. (London: Ward and Downey, 1888).
19. Quoted by S. Maccoby, *English Radicalism, 1762–1785* (London: George Allen and Unwin, 1955), p. 234.
20. Letter of 31 March 1768, *The Selected Letters of Horace Walpole*, edited by W. S. Lewis, 15 vols. (New Haven: Yale University Press, 1973).
21. Maccoby, *English Radicalism*, p. 409.
22. Brooke, *King George III*, p. 258.
23. Ronald Butt, *The Power of Parliament* (New York: Walker, 1967), p. 57.
24. *The Works of the Right Honorable Edmund Burke*, 6 vols. (London: Oxford University Press, World Classics Series, n.d.), 2:38.
25. Henry Brougham, *Historical Sketches of Statesmen Who Flourished in the Time of George III*, 2 vols. (Philadelphia: Lea and Blanchard, 1842), 1:232.
26. Ibid., pp. 232–33.
27. *Dictionary of National Biography*, s. v. "Wilberforce, William."
28. Brougham, *Sketches of Statesmen*, pp. 325–36.
29. Hobsbawn, *Age of Revolution*, p. 29.
30. Ibid., p. 52.

10
The Rights of Englishmen—Debating the American War

The American Revolution was part of a broader struggle by deprived and discontented Englishmen to gain the rights of full citizenship. What they sought to overthrow was a deeply entrenched notion of superiority of the few over the many. How England was viewed from the upper levels of society was indicated in the smug observation included in a *History of English Poetry*, written during the early 1770s by Thomas Warton, professor of poetry at Oxford University: "We look back on the savage condition of our ancestors with the triumph of superiority; we are pleased to mark the steps by which we have been raised from rudeness to elegance." Warton represented the squirearchy—the wealthy and the content. He neither knew about nor cared about the resentments that seethed among the many who were determined to secure advantages that had long been denied them by their self-proclaimed betters.

Benjamin Franklin, who was sent to London by rebellious-minded colonials, wrote to his patrons that England boiled with resentments similar to their own. What he reported was: "Mobs patrolling the streets at noonday . . . coal heavers and porters pulling down the houses of coal merchants who refuse to give them more wages; sawyers destroying saw mills; sailors unrigging all the outward-bound ships . . . soldiers firing among mobs and killing men, women, and children." To Samuel Adams, the shooting down of five rowdies who harassed a British sentry post seemed to be a "Boston Massacre." It was petty in comparison with the slaying of 450 mobsters in Parliament Square in London a decade later when, as part of a mob of 70,000 anti-Catholic fanatics, they threatened the Houses of Parliament.

What was wrong in the treatment of British citizens was brought to question not only in the American colonies but also in the British Isles. On the domestic scene it was confronted and dealt with by discussion rather than by war.

"More Easy, Happy, and Satisfied"

On both sides of the Atlantic resentments were aflame against poverty (which to the poor did not seem quaint) and injustice (which to its victims did not seem to be divinely ordained). Widespread discontent is always a fertile field for public speaking. In England sentiments aimed at expressing or correcting it were sharpening. An anonymous critic who styled himself "Junius"—and whose identity became subject to a great guessing game among the gossips of London—blistered the government with savage satire in articles for the *Public Advertiser*. Public meetings of protest were held in the cities, especially during the winter of 1769–70, with as many as seven thousand in attendance. Clubs with reformist themes sprang up like thistles in a field: the Society for the Supporters of the Bill of Rights, the Constitutional Society, the Whig Club, the Friends of the People, the London Corresponding Society. The political memorialist Sir Nathaniel William Wraxall, writing in 1787, declared: "There is still a tribunal in this country, superior to and independent of the vote of the Commons, or a sentence of the Lords. It is the Tribunal of the People of England, and of Public Opinion." In the assessment by the historian Freemantle of the effect upon Parliament, "every member's vote was weighed in the estimation of his colleagues by the degree in which he represented a popular interest." Far more than ever before, the people, even without direct representation, were making their influence felt.

And they did have voices in Parliament, notably those of the Elder William Pitt, returning to the forum in his latter but scarcely declining years; of Edmund Burke, who contributed to literature and political philosophy as well as to decision making in Parliament; of Charles James Fox, whose advocacy of popular rights overshadowed even his pursuit of pleasure; of Richard Brinsley Sheridan, whose dramatic talents shone even more brightly in his speeches than in his celebrated plays; and of the Younger William Pitt, the coldly eloquent son of his hotly eloquent father.

Across the Channel, Maximilien Robespierre, dominating the early stages of the French Revolution from his minor post as chairman of a subcommittee of the Assembly, posited that "he who can phrase it can lead it." In England this proposition did not seem to be strictly true, for the great speakers were mostly in Opposition. Still, their leadership counted. They did have influence, and England would have been better served had their views been more quickly adopted. They pointed a way that came to be followed a generation too late.

The audience they had most immediately to influence was intransigent. Public opinion supported them, but the forces that had to be dislodged were the king and his bought following in the House of Commons and in the Lords. "The only sources of political power in Great Britain were the Crown and the House of Commons, and the man who commanded the greatest power was he who enjoyed the confidence of both."[1] Lord Chatham, surveying the problem, stated the cardinal fact: "If any noble Lord challenge me to assert that there is much corruption in both Houses, I would laugh in his face, and tell him he knows it as well as I." What it signified was illustrated in the letter written by Lord North to his father on Christmas Day 1769, just after George III appointed him to head the government: "Notwithstanding the untoward political events of the last year, I never felt more perfectly easy, happy, and self-satisfied than I do at present; I think I have done what I ought, and what every reasonable and honest man will approve. I feel myself totally disencumbered from all connections, obligations and engagements, and entirely free to chuse the path that my conscience and opinion dictates. A very handsome feel it is!"[2] There was no one, really, whom he had to please except King George.[3]

George III, coming to the throne in 1760, was better as a person than as a king. He was firm in his determination to regain the power that the throne had lost. His sense of duty was strong and he tried to be a good ruler. But he was fonder of and better suited for gardening than for politics. When he was crowned, he was only twenty-two. He was not only inexperienced, he was also uncommonly shy. His education was scanty. While he was in his early teens his tutor reported that "a right system of education was impractical . . . the best which could be hoped for was to give him true notions of common things; to instruct him by conversation rather than by books; and sometimes, under the guize of amusement, to entice him to more laborious studies." He longed for popularity, and through much of his reign he enjoyed it. His first address from the throne contains a paragraph, apparently written by himself, in which he wistfully set forth his hopes and his aims to please and to improve his subjects:

> Born and educated in this country, I glory in the name of Briton; and the peculiar happiness of my life will ever consist in promoting the welfare of a people whose loyalty and warm affection to me I consider as the greatest and most permanent security of my throne; and I doubt not but their steadiness in those resolutions will equal the firmness of my invariable resolution to adhere to and strengthen this excellent constitution in church and state; and to maintain the toleration inviolable. The civil and religious rights of my loving subjects are equally dear to me with the most valuable prerogatives of my crown.

George III, it appears, born not very bright, was destined for misfortune. Part of it he brought upon himself. As his first formal speech to his subjects frankly attests, he valued "the prerogatives of my crown" fully as highly as the "civil and religious rights" of the people. As the first of the Hanoverians to be truly English, he meant also to be the one to regain the royal powers the first two Georges had lost. Unwisely he placed his confidence in blundering advisers, first Lord Bute then Lord North; and when he found a better one in the Younger Pitt he refused to support him on the most critical issues. Unfortunately, he was handicapped by a mysterious illness that plagued him throughout his reign, presumably a manic-depressive psychosis that afflicted him most severely in 1766, 1788–89, 1801, 1804, and then finally in 1811, by which time it proved irremediable, and his son was named to be regent. It is unfortunate that the fate of the nation rested so largely in his hands during the generation in which the struggle over the rights of the people came to its critical climax.

The Parliament, which was the second half of the essential audience that political speakers had to address, was as difficult in its own way as was George III. It is worth taking a good look at it, as it was described by a young German visitor, who viewed it with eager curiousity in 1782.

> I now for the first time saw the whole British nation assembled in its representatives, in a rather mean-looking building, that not a little resembles a chapel. The Speaker, an elderly man with an enormous wig, with two knotted kinds of tresses or curls behind, in a black cloak, his hat on his head, sat opposite to me on a lofty chair, which was not unlike a small pulpit, save only that there was not in front of it a reading desk. . . .
> All round on the sides of the house under the gallery are benches for the members, covered with green cloth, always one above the other, like our choirs in churches, in order that he who is speaking may see over those who sit before him. The seats in the gallery are on the same plan. The Members of Parliament keep their hats on, but the spectators in the gallery are uncovered.
> The Members of the House of Commons have nothing particular in their dress; they even come into the house in their great coats, and with boots and spurs. It is not at all uncommon to see a member lying stretched out on one of the benches, while others are debating. Some crack nuts, others eat oranges, or whatever else is in season. There is no end to their going in and out. . . .
> Those who speak seem to deliver themselves with but little, perhaps not always with even a decorous, gravity. . . . If it happens that a member rises who is but a bad speaker, or if what he says is generally deemed not sufficiently interesting, so much noise is made and such bursts of laughter are raised that the member who is speaking can scarcely distinguish his own words. . . . On the contrary, when a favourite member, and one who speaks well and to the purpose, rises, the most perfect silence reigns; [until] his friends and admirers, one after another, make their approbation known by calling out *hear him*, which is often repeated by the whole house at once, and in this way so much noise is often made that the speaker is frequently interrupted by this same emphatic *hear him*.[4]

Since neither the king nor Parliament (which he and his prime minister largely controlled) offered an audience that was receptive to persuasion, why did so much eloquence flourish—and did it in fact have influence? This question, which is central for a history of public speaking, was no less crucial for the speakers themselves. Edmund Burke undertook to answer it in a session of Dr. Johnson's informal club:

> I should say, in general, that it is very well worth while for a man to take pains to speak well in parliament. A man who has vanity speaks to display his talents; and if a man speaks well he gradually establishes a certain reputation and consequence in the general opinion, which sooner or later will have its political reward. Besides, though not one vote is gained, a good speech has its effect. Though an Act of Parliament which has been ably opposed passes into a law, yet in its progress it is modelled and softened in such a manner that we see plainly the Minister has been told that the members attached to him are so sensible of its injustice or absurdity from what they have heard that it must be altered.[5]

Burke well knew whereof he spoke. By the date of his comment—3 April 1778—Lord North's methods for dealing with the colonies had clearly proved to be disastrous and he, along with members of the parliamentary Opposition, was trying to think of what changes were feasible. Burke himself, after a long struggle to emerge from relative unimportance even within his own party, had won a great reputation as the most impressively brilliant speaker among a varied array of eloquent peers. For him, for many of his associates, and for the good of the nation, rhetorical excellence had been productive.

Burke's friend Charles James Fox pointed to yet a different reason to justify the value of persuasive speeches—namely, the effects upon public opinion when the speeches were published. "It must be from movements out of doors," he said, "and not in Parliament that opposition can ever gain any strength."[6] Trevelyan explains why Burke, Fox, and the other Whigs were unable to shift votes: "The late comers were full of wine; and those who remained on duty through the dinner hour were impatient for their suppers. It was a terrible audience for an ambitious orator."[7] Richard Brinsley Sheridan agreed with Fox that the real audience that they sought to move was out of doors: "The whole world knows that never was there a period when fine speeches more powerfully affected the public."[8] Macaulay, with his broadened perspective as both orator and historian, had no doubt that the nature of the constitution required effective persuasive speech: "In such a government," he wrote, "the power of speaking is the most highly prized of all the qualities which a politician may possess."[9]

Public opinion was becoming a genuine force—because the people were interested; their feelings were strongly aroused; they wanted to be informed; and they wanted their interests to be served. Both the king and his majorities in the two Houses of Parliament were forced to recognize that the Opposition speakers had strong support from the people. They realized, too, that what their opponents were saying proved often to be justified by events. They were too often right to be safely or wisely ignored.

The issues that demanded attention were momentous: revolt by the American colonies, English conduct in India, emergence of a new spirit of nationalism in Ireland, a new assertiveness in Scotland, and underlying all these others the effects in England of the shatteringly disruptive influences from France.[10] These issues were all interwoven, but each in itself had such significance that separate chapters must be devoted to their consideration.

When George III came to the throne in 1760, "the basic fact in politics," in the judgment of J. Stevens Watson, was instability caused by distrust. The young king, whom Watson pointed out was destitute of "the old fashioned virtues of tact and conciliation," sought to impose his will upon a Parliament that was disunified by partisan squabbling. During the first decade of his reign King George sought vainly for a minister able to carry out his policies, shifting from Newcastle, to Bute, to Grenville, to Rockingham, to Chatham, to Grafton, and finally, in January 1770 to Lord North, whose twelve-year tenure proved to be as ruinous as it was stable. During all this time the Opposition speakers bombarded the government with persuasion aimed to point a better way.[11]

"Never Lay Down My Arms"

The American question became central during 1764 and 1765, when the Grenville ministry imposed a stamp tax upon imports of the colonies as a means of securing from them their share of the expenses of defending them. The rage of resentment that resulted, not only from the colonials but also from the English merchants who dealt with them, caught the ministry by surprise. What the merchants resented was the diminishing of their trade. What the colonials angrily rejected was not only the tax but the right of the Parliament in which they were not represented to impose it. The Grenville ministry fell, and the successor ministries were no more successful in seeking to impose the king's demands upon both the rebellious colonies and the commercial interests injured by them at home. A common spirit of resentment and resistance was rooted on both sides of the Atlantic.

It was this spirit that brought the invalided Elder Pitt hobbling back to the Parliament from his retreat in Bath to deliver a savage blast against the Grenville taxation policies, on 14 January 1766. His position was clear: to keep the Americans in the empire by granting their just demands. "I will only speak to one point, a point which seems not to have been generally understood. I mean, to the *right*. It is my opinion that this kingdom has no right to lay a tax upon the colonies."[12] In a burst of fury, he exclaimed, "I rejoice that America has resisted. Three millions of people, so dead to all feelings of liberty as to voluntarily submit to be slaves, would have been fit instruments to make slaves of the rest." This outburst brought such cries of protest that he paused to explain.

> I am no courier of America. I stand for the kingdom. I maintain that the Parliament has a right to bind, to restrain America. Our legislative power over the colonies is sovereign and supreme. . . . The greater must rule the less. But she must so rule it as *not to contradict the fundamental principles that are common to both*.

He pinpointed the problem as he saw it: "There is an idea in some that the colonies are *virtually* represented in the House. I would fain to know by whom an American is represented here. . . . The idea of a virtual representation of America in this House is the most contemptible idea that ever entered into the head of a man. It does not deserve a serious refutation."

There was, however, another kind of right, the right to govern, and this he insisted not only should but could be maintained.

> A great deal has been said without doors of the power, of the strength of America. It is a topic that ought to be cautiously meddled with. In a good cause, on a sound bottom, the force of this country can crush America to atoms. I know the valor of your troops. I know the skill of your officers. There is not a company of foot that has served in America out of which you may not pick a man of sufficient knowledge and experience to make a governor of a colony there. But on this ground, on the Stamp Act, which so many here will think a crying injustice, I am one who will lift up my hands against it.

The speech represented too well the interests of the English commercial class for it to be ignored. The Stamp Tax was repealed. But in its place a Declaratory Act affirmed the right of Parliament to impose such new taxes as the ministry might propose. Such turmoil resulted that, as King George confessed to Lord Bute, "I can neither eat nor sleep." In his distress he asked the Elder Pitt to form a coalition government, but Pitt was so distraught by his illness that the "ministry of incompatibles" he put together was not well directed. After the War of American Independence broke out, Pitt again returned to London to urge a change of policies. In a speech in the Lords on 18 November 1777, he expressed his dismay: "My Lords, *you cannot conquer America*. . . . If I were an American, as I am an Englishman, while a foreign troop was landed in my country, I would never lay down my arms—never—never—never." As an observer reported, this repetition sounded like the tolling of a death knell. Lord Chatham hesitated for a few moments, then resumed.

> My Lords, no man wishes for the dependence of America on this country more than I do. To preserve it, and not confirm that state of indepen-

dence into which *your measures* hitherto have *driven them*, is the object which we ought to unite in attaining.

Then, saying he was "old and weak, and at present being unable to say more," he sank back into his seat. Three weeks later, on 11 December, he was on his feet again to urge that the government grant to the Americans everything, except independence, that they were demanding. The reason for such concessions, as he was ready to admit, is that "we have not nor can procure any force sufficient to subdue America. It is monstrous to think of it."

Again his illness forced him to withdraw, back to Bath. But early in April he came again to the Parliament to tell the Lords, "I rejoice that the grave has not closed over me, that I am still alive to lift up my voice against the dismemberment of this ancient and most noble monarchy." In a last desperate appeal for a compromise that might save the empire, he pleaded, "Let us at least make one effort, and, if we must fall, let us fall like men." His health was so frail that at this point he sank back into his seat with exhaustion; when he sought to rise again, his body shook with convulsions. His son William, then a youth of seventeen, sprang forward to assist him from the House. A month later, on 11 May 1778, at the age of seventy, Chatham died. The changes of policy he had urged the ministry to accept might have diverted the American Revolution if they had been put into effect four or five years earlier. By 1778 any such compromises were futile. For one thing, the king would not accept them. But then, neither would the colonies. Chatham's last speeches were among the most eloquent that he ever delivered, but they came too late.

"A Great Empire and Little Minds"

By general agreement, the greatest opponent of the ministry's colonial policies was Edmund Burke. But *greatest* does not mean "most effective." Both by his contemporaries and among later critics and historians, the judgments concerning Burke have intermingled admiration close to awe with cautiously phrased comments that he lacked a sense of realism. Typical of much that was said about Burke both in his own time and since is the conclusion that Sir Leslie Stephen reached in the second volume of his prestigious *History of English Thought in the Eighteenth Century*.

> Considered simply as a master of English prose, Burke has not, in my judgment, been surpassed in any period of our literature. Critics may point to certain faults of taste; the evolution of his thought is sometimes too slow; his majestic march is trammelled by the sweep of his gorgeous rhetoric; or his imagination takes fire, and he explodes into fierce denunciations which shock the reader when the shock which excited them has

become unintelligible. But, whatever blemishes may be detected, Burke's magnificent speeches stand alone in the language. They are the only English speeches which may still be read with more than a historical interest when the hearer and the speaker have long been turned to dust. His pamphlets, which are written speeches, are marked by a fervour, a richness, and a flexibility of style which is but a worthy incarnation of the wisdom embodied in them.

Then, as though but in afterthought, Stephen concluded somewhat apologetically, "His political strategy was a little too complex for the rough give-and-take of ordinary partisans."

It was Edmund Burke who, along with Chatham and after him, stood in the forefront of the courageous and able parliamentarians who recognized and who argued that the rights demanded by the Americans were owed not only to them but equally to the great mass of the English public at home.

Like Chatham, Burke demanded for the colonials the basic civil and human rights to which all Englishmen were entitled, and of which they were unnaturally deprived. But in persuasive methods, Burke and Chatham were in different realms. Whereas Chatham demanded submission to his views, barraging his listeners with withering sarcasm and exclamatory assertiveness, Burke always appealed to the understanding, supplying an enlarged philosophical examination of whatever question he discussed. His mind was impressively comprehensive and his opinions were supported by a vast depth of knowledge that was thoughtfully integrated. His imagination reveled in imagery. He sought, and too well succeeded, to say the last word on the problems under consideration.

Burke's manifest superiority derived rather from the qualities of his mind than from physical or social graces. He came into the Parliament an Irishman without status, from an inconspicuous family, and therefore an outsider. He was not personally attractive. His articulation was slurred, his voice was nasalized by frequent colds, and his brogue advertised his origin. Moreover, he wore eyeglasses, which in his day were an oddity and an admission of a physical handicap. His features were thin, and his nose was long. This appearance, together with his recurrent demands for "inquiries" into ministerial programs, won for him the derisive nickname of Peter Pry.

How could such a man be a great speaker? The reactions of his hearers were mixed. They felt compelled to call him "the greatest of English orators," but they qualified this encomium by calling him also "the dinner bell of the House." The behavior of Thomas Erskine, among the most erudite and thoughtful of Burke's listeners, was revealing. When Burke delivered his magnificent four-hour speech on conciliation with the colonies, Erskine sneaked out of the Commons to avoid listening to it; yet when it was published he wore his copy of the text to tatters by frequent rereadings.

William Wordsworth, in *The Prelude*, lines 512–25, epitomized this view of Burke:

> Silence! hush!
> This is no trifler, no short-flighted wit,
> No stammerer of a minute, painfully
> Delivered. No! the Orator hath yoked
> The Hours, like young Aurora, to his car:
> Thrice-welcome Presence! how can patience e'er
> Grow weary of attending on a track
> That kindles with such glory! All are charmed,
> Astonished, like a hero in romance,
> He winds away his never-ending horn;
> Words follow words, sense seems to follow sense;
> What memory and what logic! till the strain
> Transcendent, superhuman as it seemed,
> Grows tedious even in a young man's ear.

There was general agreement that Burke's speeches read better than they sounded. Adolphous, a contemporary historian, said of Burke's American speeches that "his exertions were sufficient to influence, in considerable degree, the politics of his time; but great and admired as they were, the effect they produced was not to be compared with that which resulted from the efforts of the honourable Charles James Fox."[13] The popular novelist, Fanny Burney, who became Burke's good friend, wrote of his speeches in the trial of Warren Hastings: "All that I had heard of his eloquence, all that I had conceived of his great abilities, was more than answered by his performance. Nervous, clear, and striking was almost all that he uttered. . . . When he narrated, he was easy, flowing, and natural; when he declaimed, energetic, warm, and brilliant. The sentiments he interspersed were as nobly conceived as they were highly coloured . . . and the wild and sudden flights of his fancy bursting forth . . . in language fluent, forcible, and varied, had a charm for my ear and attention wholly new and perfectly irresistible." And then, as Burke went on, and on, and on, she confessed, "I was aware of the declension of Burke's power over my feelings, I found myself a spectator in a public place, and looking all around with my opera glass in my hand."[14]

Burke was far from being unaware of such reactions. Lecky, in his history of the time, noted that Burke was "constantly interrupted by cries of 'Order' and derisive laughter."[15] Cunningham relates an incident wherein a county member interrupted Burke "to inquire if the honourable member meant to read his large bundle of papers, and to bore the house with one of his long speeches." Upon this, "bursting with rage, yet incapable of uttering a word, Burke strode across the floor, and positively rushed out of the house."[16] A similar instance is cited by Moritz, who sat in the gallery listening to Burke amid "much talking and many murmurs," causing Burke to exclaim, "This is not treatment for an old Member of Parliament as I am!" and "I will be heard!"[17]

Burke's personality was a handicap rather than an aid to his persuasion. He was overly aware of his intellectual superiority, and when he tried to mask his feelings about it he did so awkwardly—as when he commented, during a speech in 1771, "Conscious as I am of my own natural imbecility, I endeavor to get knowledge wherever I can." His most detrimental personal trait was arrogance. When Lord Shelburne was asked why Burke was excluded from the Rockingham cabinet, he exclaimed: "Burke! he was so violent, so over-bearing, so arrogant, so intractable, that to have got on with him in a cabinet would have been utterly and absolutely impossible."[18]

Despite such negatives, Burke's principal defect as a political speaker was simply his profligacy of genius. His Irish colleague, Henry Flood, put it well: "He is always brilliant to an uncommon degree, and yet I believe it would be better if he were less so. . . . I sincerely think that it interrupts him so much in argument that the House is never sensible that he argues as well as he does."[19] Lord Brougham amplified this same criticism, saying: "In fact, he was deficient in judgment; he regarded not the degree of interest felt by his audience in the topics which deeply occupied himself; and seldom knew when he had said enough."[20] The astute Samuel Johnson, who knew Burke well, who liked him enormously, and who admired him greatly, summed up the good and the bad in Burke with two comments. For one, "If a man were to go by chance at the same time with Burke under a shed to shun a shower, he would say—'This is an extraordinary man!'" And for the other, "I can live very well with Burke: I love his knowledge, his genius, his diffusion, and affluence of conversation; but I would not talk to him of the Rockingham party."[21]

In attempting to change the ministerial policies toward the American colonies, Burke illustrated both his limitations and his virtues. In the first of his major speeches on the problem, "On American Taxation," delivered on 19 April 1774, he rose to speak extemporaneously in the midst of a heated debate over the motion to tax the tea the colonials imported.[22] He denounced the "disgusting argument" offered in defense of the tax, then proceeded to a pitiless, sarcastic, and contemptuous review of what he termed the cowardly, contradictory, and undiplomatic conduct of the ministry's dealings with America. With little heed for winning votes, he poured his scorn upon the ministers.

> They never had any kind of system, right or wrong; but only invented occasionally some miserable tale for the day, in order meanly to sneak out of difficulties, into which they had proudly strutted. . . . By such management, by the irresistible operation of feeble counsels, so paltry a

sum as three-pence in the eyes of a financier, so insignificant an article as tea in the eyes of a philosopher, have shaken the pillars of a commercial empire that circled the whole globe.

The second of these speeches, "On Conciliation with the Colonies," presented on 22 March 1775, was a result of careful preparation. His approach was as conciliatory as was his title. "I do not know the method of drawing up an indictment against a whole people," he said. Consequently, "No way is open but . . . to comply with the American spirit as necessary." It was natural for the ministers to feel reluctant to admit the failure of their policies, he acknowledged, but it must be done.

The question with me is, not whether you have the right to render your people miserable; but whether it is not your interest to make them happy. It is not what a lawyer tells me I *may* do; but what humanity, reason, and justice tell me I ought to do. Is a politic act the worse for being a generous one? Is no concession proper, but that which is made from your want of right to keep what you grant?

His conclusion was an appeal for votes, and it was based upon an appeal to the all-encompassing English respect for justice.

All this, I know well enough, will sound wild and chimerical to the profane herd of those vulgar and mechanical politicians, who have not a place among us; a sort of people who thinks that nothing exists but what is gross and material; and who, therefore, far from being qualified to be directors of the great movement of empire, are not fit to turn a wheel in the machine. But to men truly initiated and rightly taught, these ruling and master principles, which, in the opinion of such men as I have mentioned, have no substantial existence, are in truth everything, and all in all. *Magnanimity in politics is not seldom the truest wisdom; and a great empire and little minds go ill together.* [Italics added.] If we are conscious of our situation, and glow with zeal to fill our places as becomes our station and ourselves, we ought to supplicate all our public proceedings on America with the old warning of the Church, *Sursum Corda!* We ought to elevate our minds to the greatness of that trust to which the order of Providence has called us. By adverting to the dignity of this high calling, our ancestors have turned a savage wilderness into a glorious empire; and have made the most extensive, and the only honourable conquests, not by destroying, but by promoting the wealth, the number, the happiness of the human race. Let us get an American revenue as we have got an American empire. English privileges have made it all that it is; English privileges alone will make it all that it can be.

Circumstances were favorable for the kind of appeal Burke made. Lord North was searching for a conciliatory course, and English merchants were demanding reforms that would restore their trade. Lord Chatham was urging the withdrawal of English troops from the colonies in order to create an atmosphere favorable to compromise. It was the colonials, now, who were unwilling to consider concessions. Volunteers at Lexington had attacked British troops. In Virginia, a fiery young orator named Patrick Henry was declaiming that war had already commenced. Neither Chatham nor Burke quite understood that, while they were asking more than their government would grant, they were also asking for less than the Americans felt they had to have. The ground for a compromise solution was difficult to reach from either side.

Burke's concern about the treatment of the colonies was actually subsidiary to his much broader humanitarian feelings, which stretched to include also India, Ireland, and England's own poor. His devotion to the ideal of justice, however, did not lead him to favor extention of the franchise as a step toward democracy, nor welfare provisions for the needy. "The poor," he asserted, "are not poor but men." What served them best was independence, not dependence. His basic conceptions were hierarchal, not egalitarian. Society, in his view, is and by right ought to be so structured that governing decisions are made by the "best" not by the "most." But for this system to serve the general interests required that those who held power must be just rather than greedy, and responsible rather than self-serving. These feelings impelled him, in February 1780, to one of his major rhetorical efforts, his speech "On Economic Reform."

What he proposed was that members of Parliament and other officials should voluntarily restrict the huge rewards by which they were enriched. If he could succeed, the people would be pleased, since it would lower their taxes, and the Parliament would become much more independent of the patronage power of the throne. He prepared a speech to support his reform bill "with a fervid assiduity that has not often been exampled, and has never been surpassed."[23] As an example of persuasive discourse, it is masterful. He interwove facts and fancy so skillfully that he held the close attention of his auditors for some four hours; moreover, while he amused, he also persuaded them. He understood full well the enormity of his task, which was to ask his listeners to surrender emoluments that traditionally were theirs. As he said in his introduction, "I advance to it with a tremor that shakes me to the inmost fiber of my frame. . . . I risk odium if I succeed and contempt if I fail." Then came his basic appeal: "My excuse must rest in my own and your conviction of the absolute, urgent necessity there is, that something of the kind should be done." The only question before them was to determine "the best time and manner of yielding what it is impossible to keep." His mode was conciliatory: "Our ministers are far from being wholly to blame for the present ill order which prevails."

He proceeded to describe the offices he wanted to abolish, with a gentle humor that exposed their ridiculousness without wounding the sensibilities of the placeholders. When he described "the perpetual sitting adjournment, and the unbroken sitting vacation" of the Board of Trade, not even his patent exaggeration kept the members of the board from laughing at themselves. As one of them, Edward Gibbon, confessed in his *Autobiography*, "it must be allowed that our duty was not intolerably severe," and "the Lords of Trade blushed at their insignificancy." In a subsequent vote, the Board of Trade was abolished, by a vote of 207 to 199.

What Burke proposed was limited. There must be great rewards for great services. "There is a time when the weather-beaten vessels of state ought to come into harbor." But the system could work only if it were restrained. "What the law respects shall be sacred to me"; "individuals pass like shadows, but the commonwealth is fixed and stable."

Burke's bill was not immediately approved, But Lord North did not feel able to oppose it, and it remained under consideration for several months. When in 1782 Burke was named to the most profitable sinecure of all, paymaster of the forces, he surrendered the profits customarily attached to that office. When his reforms were adopted, credit was owing less to his speech than to the strength of public demand; nevertheless, it was his rhetoric that provided the rationale for it.

"Opinions Are Open . . . Innocent and Harmless"

Burke's friend and longtime associate, Charles James Fox, was vastly different from his philosophic mentor—in intellectual qualities, in temperament, in social behavior, in appearance, and in his mode of speaking. Unlike the Irish outsider, Fox was a member of the establishment, the son of a prominent father, with wealth enough to enable him to indulge his fashionable love for gambling. Fox was overweight, slovenly in dress, a lover of good company, of drink, and of convivial conversation. He was enormously energetic and ambitious. Unlike Burke, he was careless of style in his speeches, commenting rather that if a speech read well it was not a good speech. But he was superior as a debater, skilled at making points sharply, directly, and well adapted to the feelings of his listeners.

Far from being a political philosopher, Fox must be assessed in terms of his tangible accomplishments. His success was considerable but short of being complete. He became the leader of the Whigs and for two decades conducted the most influential Opposition prior to the advent of Churchill. He helped to create sentiment against the American war. He survived Pitt's personal attack upon him for the illegalities attending his election to Parliament from Westminster County. He prevented the implementation of Pitt's inadequate plan for Ireland. He diverted England from an ill-considered war with Russia. He contributed to freedom of the press by winning adoption of his Libel Act. He won respect for his diplomatic ability during his brief tenure as Secretary of State. Moreover, he held together the Whig minority during the reactionary period of the French Revolution, when English liberties reached their lowest ebb since the time of the Stuarts. And he contributed substantially to ending the atrocious slave trade. In sum, he paved the way for the Liberal Party that was to renovate English politics in the next century.[24] Nevertheless, he devoted his life to politics without becoming the directing force in government. His great abilities were not fully utilized. In a twenty-five year contest, the Younger Pitt succeeded in keeping him from office. What Fox did accomplish was owing to his superiority in debate.

Lord John Russell explained why Fox rather than Burke emerged as leader of the Whigs: "While Burke was the greater philosopher, the more profound reasoner on general principles of government, Mr. Fox had far more readiness in debate, a more popular style of eloquence, and more judgment in the practical conduct of affairs."[25] As Lecky assessed Fox: "That great master of persuasive reasoning never failed to make every sentence tell upon his hearers, to employ precisely and invariably the kind of arguments that were most level with their understandings, to subordinate every consideration to the single end of convincing and impressing those who were before him."[26] What made Fox effective was "that peculiar quality which inspires both confidence and obedience, the quality which makes a leader, who towers above his fellows," as Lascelles, one of his biographers, concluded. Moreover, as Lascelles pointed out, he used his leadership to good effect: "If in the panic of revolution and war no statesman of Fox's eminence had continued to profess his faith in liberty and justice and his hatred of tyranny and oppression, the claims of democracy might have been drawn from constitutional into revolutionary methods, and the reforms of the next century might not have been achieved without bloodshed."[27]

Loren Reid, Fox's other recent biographer, selected three statements by Fox as indicative of both his political principles and his methods. First: "Public discussion is the best security for public welfare, and for the safety of every good government." Second: "In proportion as opinions are open, they are innocent and harmless. Opinions become dangerous only when prosecution makes it necessary for the people to communicate their ideals under the bond of secrecy." And third: "It is the energy, the boldness of a man's mind, which prompts him to speak, not in private, but in large popular assemblies, that constitutes . . . the spirit of freedom."[28] In short, full and free discussion is what makes government tolerable.

On the American question, Fox's stance was much like that of Chatham and Burke, but as failures mounted he used them for the utmost of partisan advantage. On 19 April 1774, he assured the ministry that "the Americans will become useful subjects, if you use them with that temper of lenity which you ought to do." After the war had begun, on 26 October 1775, he blasted Lord North as "the blundering pilot who has brought the nation into its present difficulties." In another speech, on 8 December, he said: "I have always given it as my opinion, that the war now carrying on against the Americans is unjust; but, admitting it to be a just war, admitting that it is practicable, I insist that the means made use of are not such as will obtain the end." He ridiculed the ministerial mode of conducting the war "by Acts of Parliament."

> If they complain of one law, your answer is to pass another more rigorous that the former. . . . Show them that your laws are mild, just, and equitable, and that they therefore are in the wrong, and deserve the punishment they meet with. The very contrary of this has been your wretched policy. . . . If you are forced to punish the innocent to come at the guilty, your government there is, and deserves to be, at the end.

As leader of the Opposition, Fox guided the attacks on the conduct of the war. On 24 April 1776, he charged that the war had been "commenced unjustly," and said that its aim was "the extirpation of freedom." On 31 October he denounced the employment of Hessian mercenaries, saying that "if we are reduced to that, I am for abandoning America." By 18 November of the following year he was asserting that "the idea of conquering America is absurd." The employment of Indians he condemned as "the most violent, scalping, tomahawk measures." When Lord North finally agreed to grant to the colonies everything they demanded except independence, Fox attacked him with heavy sarcasm in a speech on 17 February 1778:

> The noble Lord hoped and was disappointed. He expected a great deal, and found little to answer his expectations. He thought America would have submitted to his laws, and they resisted them. He thought they would have submitted to his armies, and they were beaten by inferior numbers. He made conciliatory propositions, and he thought they would succeed, but they were rejected. He appointed commissioners to make peace, and he thought they had powers, but he found they could not make peace, and nobody believed they had any powers.

If this barrage against his own government in time of war were not enough, after France entered into alliance with America, Fox expressed his rage against the king himself: "How will it sear the eyeballs of the prince to see the decline of his empire dated from his accession, and its fall completed within a single reign!" He urged the withdrawal of all forces from America so that they might be employed on the Continent, for "America must be conquered in France; France never can be conquered in America." On 30 May 1781, he audaciously charged that the majority was supporting the war solely from self-interest: "The American war begot extraordinaries; extraordinaries begot loans; loans begot douceurs; douceurs begot members of Parliament; and members of Parliament begot all these things." When Lord North complained reasonably enough that the Foxite Whigs were encouraging the Americans to persist in their struggle, Fox replied with a crescendo of ridicule.

> O miserable and unfortunate ministry! O blind and incapable man! whose measures are framed with so little foresight, and executed with so little firmness, that they not only crumble to pieces, but bring on the ruin of their country, merely because one rash, or wicked man in the House of Commons makes a speech against them!

Then, after the surrender of Cornwallis at Yorktown, King George, in an effort to make the defeat palatable to the public, offered to bring Fox into the government in a coalition with Lord North—and to the astonishment of his friends, Fox accepted. In justification, Fox asserted, "My friendships are perpetual, my enmities are not so." There were, naturally, policy differences, but they could be bridged. "The American war was the cause of the enmity between the noble Lord and myself. . . . But it is now no more; and it is wise and candid to put an end also to the ill will." As the charges continued that he had let ambition overcome his integrity, Fox replied with unaccustomed gentleness, in a speech on 21 February 1783, "I trust the consequences of the coalition will be the salvation of the country." Actually the coalition lasted for less than a year, and its only substantial effect was to win confirmation of the Peace of Paris, which acknowledged the independence of the United States. For the remainder of his life, except for a few months in 1806, Fox was back again in Opposition.

This freedom from the responsibilities of office suited his temperament and his style. He could hurl charges against the ministry without having to prove that he could do better. All that was needed was that his complaints sound plausible. Every mistake by the government, he could attack. Any misjudgments by himself were soon forgotten since they were not put into operation. He was free to pour ridicule, sarcasm, and denunciations on unpopular policies and taxes, and equally free to stand as champion for whatever the public seemed to want. Like a buzz fly attacking a horse, he could shift and veer without regard to consistency. The wonder is that his statesmanship was so substantially constructive that what he stood for were such liberal programs as an end to slavery, political emancipation for Catholics, complete freedom of the press and of public discussion, and the maintenance of basic human rights—even for the rebels of America, the distant people of India, and the English populace during the conservative reaction against the French Revolution.

Whether beneficial or not, one of his contributions was to strengthen the idea of party solidarity. In forming policies, he generally followed the guidance of Burke—that is, until their split over the question of how England should react to the Revolution in France. In devising strategies, he did not impose his will upon his associates but freely consulted with them. Even during the unpatriotic opposition to the American war, and despite his own inconsistency in veering first toward and then away from democracy, he held the loyalty of his followers to such an extent that they were known as "Fox's Martyrs." Like Chatham and Wilkes, he was viewed by the people as their champion, yet he was too much an aristocrat to believe in democracy. In the debate held on 8 February 1780, he declared staunchly that "it is the duty of members of Parliament to conform to the sentiments, and in some degree even to the prejudices of the people." But nearly a decade later, on 16 December 1788, he asserted that he "had no great trust in majorities." On 1 March 1791 he told the Commons that "the worst of all tyranny was that of the many over the few." On 7 May 1793 he declared that he had "always disliked universal representation." In general, he opposed "the monstrous influence of the Crown"; yet he vigorously insisted on the inherent right of his friend, the Prince of Wales, to exercise full authority when he was named as regent during the last illness of the king.

He was accounted to be typically English in his convictions, in his sympathies, and no less in his faults. If impetuosity often overruled his judgment, he defended this tendency, in his speech on 17 December 1783, with the claim that "delicacy and reserve are criminals where the rights of Englishmen are at hazard." Above all, he had a winning personality. Even his enemies loved him. He wore his heart on his sleeve and followed his sentiments to the point of indiscretion. His personal conduct was often criticized, but his sincerity was seldom questioned. In English history, he stands with a small group of outstanding enthusiasts, including Henry VIII, Chatham, Disraeli, and Churchill. When he was right, he was very, very right; even when he was wrong, he was dashingly attractive.

"The Effect He Desired, and Never Commit Himself"

The Younger William Pitt was an absolute contrast to Fox: cool, collected, and carefully self-controlled. For nearly twenty of his twenty-five years in public life, he served as prime minister. His lightest public utterance was an official pronouncement of government. In a literal sense, whatever he said could be used against him. Neither could he avoid trouble by refusing to speak. He held office primarily because of his courage and skill in defending the king's policies against the continuous and determined opposition of the great Whigs who stood against him. He also had the tremendous advantage of a majority entrenched in support of him by self-interest. Even so, it was his masterly skill in debate that was his chief resource, for he had to provide justifications for the votes he had to have.

Whether he was successful is open to dispute. The sheer fact that he held the highest civil office longer than any other except Walpole has to be accounted a signal success. But underlying this fact is a foundation of failure. He entered public life with the liberal sympathies that won for his father the title of the Great Commoner, yet his position forced him to oppose the rising clamor for reforms and to stand, instead, as the proponent for monarchal and aristocratic privileges. The aims he chiefly cherished were to balance the budget and to make England economically secure; yet, plagued by the French war, his government piled up both taxes and deficits. Had England been able to remain at peace he would assuredly have been the greatest of prime ministers; as a war leader, he won out, but the costs were great.

His failure consisted of the completeness and apparent ease with which he sacrificed his Whig principles. He entered Parliament in 1781 as an opponent of Lord North's management of the American war, but he cautiously avoided arousing the resentment of the king. When the North-Fox Coalition fell, it was the Younger Pitt, just twenty-three, whom the king chose to carry out his policies. As head of a majority that was cemented by grants and pensions, Pitt found himself the spokesman for the most reactionary members of the Parliament. The limitations imposed upon him precluded almost all that he most wanted to achieve. He could not carry out the electoral reform that his father had considered to be essential. He was forced to curtail the liberties of the people. He could not even bring into effect his heartfelt aim to abolish the slave trade. He was required (to his shame) by King George to break an explicit agreement he had made with the Irish Catholics to grant them emancipation in return for their votes for the union of Ireland with Great Britain. He had to sanction forms of bribery that he detested as fully as had his father. His economic principles had to be abandoned to finance the war against Napoleon. He gave up his liberalism to become the founder of the modern Tory Party.

Charles Robertson summed up his career in severe if sentimental terms:

> The tears of human beings, of pathos and tragedy, haunt the career of this solitary man, dwelling apart on the heights of great affairs; who never knew the love of wife or child; who worked so hard in the golden promise of his political apprenticeship for peace, retrenchment, and reform; who in the maturity of his powers constituted himself the champion of a cause that linked continuous war abroad with repression and reaction at home, with swollen debt and bloated armaments; who died in the bitter knowledge that popular liberties had been suspended, the National Debt more than doubled, taxation strained to the breaking point, a quarter of a million human lives sacrificed, and that peace and reform were further out of sight than ever.[29]

In the view of Fox, furiously excoriating Pitt for his war measures in the debate in the Commons on 1 March 1792, Pitt's failings were unforgiveable: "Let him but keep his place, he cares not what else he loses. With other men, reputation and glory are objects of ambition. . . . For the minister, power and place are sufficient of themselves. With them he is content."

Of course this unsparingly negative view of Pitt is unfair. Above all, he was a patriot. What his country was committed to, he undertook to do as well as he could. The kind of speaking that his position required of him was necessarily less exciting than that of his Opposition critics, and his personality fitted his role. He had none of the impetuosity, or indiscretion, or indecisiveness that is commonly associated with youthful inexperience. He had a serene self-confidence that kept him aloof from companionability. Wraxall noted that upon Pitt's appointment as prime minister, he strode into the House looking to neither right nor left, with no smiles for his followers and no sign of amiability, so that he "seemed made to command, even more than to persuade or convince."[30] Moritz, listening to him in 1782, "was astonished that a man so youthful in appearance should stand up at all. But I was still more astonished to see how, while he spoke, he engaged universal attention."[31] Even his opponents found his "fluency of language" to be "almost preternatural," even if "it too much resembled the diction of a state-paper."[32] Pitt's rhetorical problem was that he had no choice except to speak only in official and carefully controlled terms.

Typical of the mildness of his tone is the reply he made on 8 December 1796 to one of the typically vitriolic attacks Fox made upon him.

> An imputation of the most serious kind has been advanced . . . but it is necessary that all which may be offered on both sides should be fairly heard. . . . It is requisite that gentlemen should be in full possession of every important fact. . . . The house should clearly know the principles on which it is to decide.[33]

Unquestionably the style was dull; the emotional tone was restrained; the reasoning was trite. It was these very factors that made Pitt's leadership reassuring. He was not rocking the boat, he was steering it through rocky passages, and his guidance inspired confidence by being steady and calm. When he needed to be, he was indeed eloquent; when he avoided eloquence he did so cannily, deliberately, and with skill. As one of his biographer's noted, "When one listens to Pitt's speech, one smiles at the skill, the evasion, the circumlocution, the sheer bluff, by which he emerges from a tight corner."[34] As the Opposition realized, it was this kind of ability that made him almost invulnerable: "Above all, he excelled in the use of both topics and language with a view to produce the effect he desired, and never commit himself . . . to balance his expressions so nicely, conceal or bring forward parts of his subject so artistically,—approach, and yet shun dangerous points so dexterously,—often seeming to say so much while he told so little."[35] In short, Pitt was a master of the art that comes close to being the very heart of rhetoric: the setting of the agenda of what must be talked about, and the defining of the approach and the methods to be followed in the discussion.

Of course, his position as head of the government gave him a vast initial advantage for doing this, but few other heads of state have used that advantage so well. Moreover, the necessity he was under to set the agenda and the tone of debate was far from being wholly advantageous. The policies he had to defend derived in part from the authority of George III, and in part were dictated by events. Whether he liked them or not, he had to defend them. As an acute observer pointed out, "Perhaps his greatest errors originated from his early and constant immersion in public business, and from his being always an actor, never a spectator of affairs."[36]

Pitt has often been praised for his unusual ability to make dull facts—such as details of the budget—interesting. He also could be truly eloquent when situations called for it. His eloquence emerged most tellingly when his humanitarian and patriotic sentiments were most deeply aroused. As William Wilberforce noted in his journal, Pitt's speech of 2 April 1792 in which he urged abolition of the slave trade, was regarded even by his opponents as "one of the most extraordinary displays of eloquence they had ever heard." In this speech appears the real Pitt, who might have been a great libertarian if he were not constrained by his official position to defense in general to the status quo. In a succession of passionate passages he most surely reveals the qualities inherited from his father:

> Think of eighty thousand persons carried out of their country by *we know not what means;* for crimes imputed; for light or inconsiderable faults; for debt, perhaps; for the crime of witchcraft; or a thousand other weak and scandalous pretexts! . . .
>
> Africa is known to you only in its skirts. Yet even there you are able to infuse a poison that spreads its contagious effects from one end of it to the other; which penetrates to its very center, corrupting every part to which it reaches. You there subvert the whole order of nature; you aggravate every natural barbarity; and furnish to every man living on that continent motives for committing, under the name and pretext of commerce, acts of personal violence and perfidy against his neighbor. . . .
>
> Let me remark, too, that there is no nation in Europe that has, on the one hand, plunged so deeply into this guilt as Britain; or that is so likely, on the other, to be looked up to as an example, if she should have the manliness to be the first in decidedly renouncing it. . . .
>
> Grieved am I to think that there should be a single person in this country, much more that there should be a single member in the British Parliament, who can look on the present dark, uncultivated, and uncivilized state of that continent as a ground for continuing the slave trade. . . .
>
> We were once among the nations of the earth as obscure, as savage in our manners, as debased in our morals, as degraded in our understandings, as these unhappy Africans are at present. But in the lapse of a long

series of years, by a progression slow, and for a time almost imperceptible, we have become rich in a variety of acquirements, favored above measure in the gifts of Providence, unrivaled in commerce, pre-eminent in arts, foremost in the pursuit of philosophy and science, and established in all the blessings of society.

Here in this speech, one may say, the career of Pitt came full circle from his private feelings to his public position. Despite the sincerity of his humanitarianism, he did, in fact, fail to endorse the abolition of the slave trade when the Commons were ready for it—and the reason he gave was that the income from the trade was needed for support of the war against France; he utterly failed to realize that the government over which he presided was harsly restrictive of the rights of the great masses of the people.

"To Watch Over the Rights of the Subjects"

A summation of the worst that could be said of Pitt was veiled in an analogy spoken by his most vitriolic critic, the great dramatist Richard Brinsley Sheridan:

> I can suppose the case of a haughty and stiff-necked minister, who never mixed in a popular assembly, who had therefore no common feeling with the mass of the people, no knowledge of the mode in which their intercourse was conducted, who was not a month in the ranks of this house before he was raised to the first situation, and though on a footing of equality with every other member, elevated with the idea of fancied superiority; such a minister can have no communication with the people of England, except through the medium of spies and informers; he is unacquainted with the mode in which their sentiments are expressed, and cannot make allowance for the language of toasts and resolutions, adopted in an unguarded and convivial hour. Such a minister, if he lose their confidence, he will bribe their hate; if he disgust them by arbitrary measures, he will not leave them until they are completely bound and shackled; above all, he will gratify the vindictive resentment of apostasy, by prosecuting all those who dare to espouse the cause which he has betrayed.[37]

The attack was severe but not very effective. Pitt was able to shrug it off, tagging Sheridan as a member "in most of whose speeches there was much fancy, in many shining wit, in others very ingenious argument, in all great eloquence, and in some few truths and justice." Neither was being fair to the other. Sheridan was not a great parliamentarian—no significant legislation was even introduced by him, let alone carried to completion—and in the two brief periods during his career that his party was in power, he was not brought into the cabinet. His reputation was of high order—but it was first as a dramatist and second as an orator—never as a statesman. To the Tory majority, "his whole existence was a farce. . . . He was a mountebank of amazing talent."[38] In the hard judgment of Lord Brougham, "as a statesman, he is without a place in any class, or in any rank; it would be incorrect and flattering to call him a bad, or hurtful, or a short-sighted, or a middling statesman; he was no statesman at all."[39] One of his biographers, whose charge was to portray him as a dramatist, brushed off his role in Parliament, calling him "a light-hearted adventurer in politics as well as in life, with keen perceptions and a brilliant way of now and then hitting out a right suggestion, and finding often a fine and effective thing to say. It is impossible, however, to think of him as influencing public opinion in any great or lasting way."[40]

If these views are correct, Sheridan obviously would have no place in a study of rhetorical influences in British history. They are, however, partial and incomplete, rather than definitive. Their chief value is to remind us of the very great handicaps under which Sheridan labored in his efforts to be an effective persuader. He was handicapped by his family background, by his temperament, and by the tremendous popularity of his plays. Like Mark Twain, of a later period, he wanted very much to have a serious effect as a social critic but was not taken seriously because of his high repute as a comedian and a wit. Moreover, his relative poverty, his lavish life-style, and his lighthearted avoidance of paying his debts created an image of him as a hedonist without intellectual or moral substance. In general, he was also catalogued as a "mere" orator, partly because for a time he taught public speaking, and because his father enjoyed a great reputation as an elocutionist, who espoused public speaking as an art form based upon fine diction, a cultivated voice, and gracefully executed gestures. In addition, it was well known by his colleagues in the Commons that he was far from being studious, and it was believed that he practised the faults he charged against Lord Mornington in one of his major speeches, on 21 January 1794, that he invented his facts and borrowed his anecdotes. Despite these limitations, Sheridan was even more brilliant as a speaker than as a playwright and contributed fully as much to oratory as he did to literature. And there is truth in his estimate of himself that he was a self-appointed champion of "the poorest people in the kingdom . . . those who stood most in need of friends."

Impressive testimony is not lacking to the power of his persuasiveness and to the breadth and depth of its effects. Wraxall, in his *Memoirs* cited Sheridan's central role in many of the debates on crucial issues and compared him favorably with Chatham, Burke, Fox, and Pitt for his comprehensive mind, keenness of wit, argumentative skills, and such eloquence that "he won his way by a sort of fascination." His son and his wife also rendered significant judgments. Of course, they were prejudiced in his favor, but they also were especially sensitive to his faults. What his son attested was that "no man can listen to my father and retain a judgment of his own." And his wife, writing to her sister, reported that "it is impossible, my dear woman, to convey to you the delight, the astonishment, the adoration, he has excited in every class of people. Even party prejudice has been overcome by a display of genius, eloquence, and goodness, which no one with anything like a heart about them could have listened to without being the wiser and the better for the rest of their lives."[41] In the final judgment of an objective and careful historian, "In an age of oratory, and among a society of orators, his supremacy was almost universally acknowledged."[42]

Since it is true that Sheridan never successfully sponsored any significant legislation, what then did his influence amount to? His major biographer gave a fair answer.

> If to watch over the rights of the subject, and guard them against the encroachments of power, be, even in safe and ordinary times, a task full of usefulness and honour, how much more glorious to have stood sentinel over the same sacred trust, through a period so trying as that with which Sheridan had to struggle—when liberty itself had become suspect and unpopular—when authority had succeeded in identifying patriots with treason, and when the few remaining and deserted friends of freedom were reduced to take their stand on a narrow isthmus, between anarchy on one side and angry incursions of power on the other. How manfully he maintained his ground in a position so critical, the annals of England and of the champions of her constitution will long testify.[43]

In short, Sheridan was a "radical" who was not looking for innovations. He had no wish to introduce parliamentary bills with which to break new ground. His interest, rather like Burke's, was to preserve the best feature of England's historic progression toward the strengthening of civil and human rights, in which crusade he persevered when Burke turned back. With this as his personal conviction, Sheridan did not tickle his mind to produce new laws. What he fought for was the just application of old principles. In doing so, he often erred in speaking with such vehemence and extravagance that he sounded not like a conservator of values but like a threatening demagogue. Such qualities gave to his speaking enormous cutting power, but they also shaped his reputation for instability and irresponsibility, thereby reducing his influence for changing votes.

Sheridan seemed to be frivolous without actually being so. He had a deep understanding of poverty and sympathy with the friendless poor. He hated oppression. And he had a persistent will to do all he could to support reforms. Outside of Parliament he associated himself with such enlightened groups as the Society for Constitutional Information, the Corresponding Society, and the Society of Friends of the People. In the view of the Tories, his aim was "to stir the lesser ranks of the people even by the hope of plundering their betters."[44] When Pitt became prime minister he sought to brush aside Sheridan's bitter criticisms by advising him to stick to his trade in the theatre and to leave serious politics to serious people. Sheridan's retort won admiration for him as a skilled parliamentary debater:

> On the particular sort of personality which the right honourable gentleman has thought proper to make use of, I need not comment. The propriety, the taste, the *gentlemanly* point of it must be obvious to this House. . . . Nay, I will say more. Flattered and encouraged by the right honourable gentleman's panegyric on my talents, if I ever engage again in the composition he alludes to, I may be tempted to an act of presumption, and attempt improvement on one of Ben Jonson's best characters, that of the *Angry boy* in the Alchemist.[45]

The "Angry Boy" tag continued to plague Pitt for many years. Sheridan's success with this quip encouraged him in the following year to try again. Commenting on the nature of the entrenched majority, Sheridan told the House, "Mr. Speaker, this is not to be wondered at, when a member is employed to corrupt everybody in order to win votes." To the cries of, "Who is it? Name him! Name him!" Sheridan blandly replied, "Sir, I shall not name that person. It is an invidious and unpleasant thing to do . . . but don't suppose, Sir, that I abstain because there is any difficulty in naming him; I could do that, Sir, as soon as you could say Jack Robinson." It was a nice touch, which gave a lasting phrase to the language: John Robinson had been Lord North's designated dispenser of patronage in the preceding administration.

In similar vein, during the debate on 8 February 1785, Sheridan pounced upon the remark of a "learned member" who described himself as a "chicken lawyer" who had reluctantly voted against the ministry because on this occasion he found the Opposition to be "in the right" but quickly added that he never expected to vote against the government again. Sheridan leaped to take advantage of the remark. "He was sorry," the report of his speech reads, "to find the chicken was a bird of ill omen, and that its augury was so unpropitious to their future interests. Perhaps it would have been well, under the circumstances, that the chicken had not left the barn door of the treasury, but continued, side by side, with the old cock, to pick those crumbs of comfort which would, doubtless, be dealt out in due time, with a liberality proportioned to the identity of the feathered tribe." Such quips display the quickness and sharpness of Sheridan's wit, but they do not unveil the depth of his legislative consequence. Humor, wit, and sarcasm have always had genuine effect in the parliamentary discussions, but they depend too much upon tone of voice, gesture, timing, and immediacy of reference to admit them to the anthologies of eloquence, much less to the history of statesmanship.

Sheridan's truly great speaking did not develop until later in his career, during the discussion of England's role in India, and in response to the severe restrictions on civil rights that were imposed during the Napoleonic Wars. In the meantime, he did become known as a staunch advocate of the needs of the people and as an able defender of their constitutional privileges. He also established a reputation as an independent liberal who did not hesitate to speak boldly against the leadership of Fox when he disagreed with it, who occasionally supported Pitt when he believed him to be in the right, and who led the attack against his longtime mentor Edmund Burke after Burke launched his conservative reaction against the new ideas of Rousseau and Voltaire.

The whole tenor of English politics underwent a dramatic change after the end of the American war, when the Whigs commenced their sensational crusade to prosecute Warren Hastings and to change English policies and methods in governing India. This was a new period in which the eloquence of Burke and Fox rose to new heights, but as the drama unfolded, no one doubted that Sheridan was the great star.

Notes

1. Brooke, *King George III*, p. 161.
2. Charles Daniel Smith, *The Early Career of Lord North, the Prime Minister* (Rutherford, N.J.: Fairleigh University Press, 1979), p. 182.
3. The corrupt nature of Parliament is detailed by A. F. Freemantle, *England in the Nineteenth Century, 1801–1825* (London: George Allen and Unwin, 1929), pp. 111–12.
4. Carl Philip Moritz, *Travels in England in 1782* (London: Oxford University Press, 1924), pp. 52–55. Punctuation is modernized.
5. *Boswell's Life of Johnson*, 2:178.
6. Freemantle, *England in the Nineteenth Century*, p. 112.
7. George Otto Trevelyan, *George the Third and Charles James Fox*, 2 vols. (London: Longmans, 1912–14), 1:47.
8. From his speech in the Commons on 31 January 1799.
9. Thomas Babington Macaulay, "William Pitt," in *Miscellaneous Works*, 4 vols. (New York: Macmillan, n.d.), 4:118.
10. Hobsbawn, *Age of Revolution*, passim.
11. Watson, *King George III*, pp. 7–9 and passim.
12. Pitt's speeches on the American question are reprinted in Goodrich, *Select British Eloquence*, pp. 114–42.
13. John Adolphous, *History of England from the Accession of George the Third to the Conclusion of Peace, 1760–1783*, 8 vols. (London: Cadell and Davies, 1805), 2:172.
14. Constance Hill, *Fanny Burney at the Court of Queen Charlotte* (London: John Lane, 1912), p. 159.
15. William E. H. Lecky, *A History of England in the Eighteenth Century*, 8 vols. (New York: Appleton, 1887), 5:133.

16. G. G. Cunningham, *Lives of Eminent and Illustrious Englishmen*, 8 vols. (Glasgow: A. Fullerton, 1839), 6:391.
17. Moritz, *Travels*, p. 219.
18. Lecky, *History of England*, 3:203n, citing the Charlemont MSS.
19. John Morley, *Burke* (New York: Harper, 1879), p. 139.
20. Brougham, *Sketches of Statesmen*, 1:151.
21. *Boswell's Life of Johnson*, 2:537; 1:460.
22. The speeches by Burke are cited from *The Works of the Right Honourable Edmund Burke, with Introduction by Judge William Willis*, 6 vols. (London: Humphrey Milford, Oxford World Classics ed., n. d.). For a summation of Burke's role in American affairs, see Ross J. F. Hoffman, *Edmund Burke, New York Agent, with His Letters to the New York Assembly and Intimate Correspondence with Charles O'Hara, 1761–1766* (Philadelphia: University of Pennsylvania Press, 1956).
23. Morley, *Burke*, p. 128.
24. Charles G. Robertson, *England under the Hanoverians* (New York: Putnam, 1930), pp. 369–70.
25. John Russell, *The Life and Times of Charles James Fox*, 3 vols. (London: R. Bentley, 1859–66), 2:1–2.
26. Lecky, *History of England*, 3:203.
27. Edward Lascelles, *The Life of Charles James Fox* (New York: Octagon, 1970), p. 159.
28. Loren D. Reid, *Charles James Fox, A Man for the People* (Columbia: University of Missouri Press, 1969), pp. 444–45.
29. Robertson, *England under Hanoverians*, p. 308. Robertson further concluded that "but for Fox and his colleagues, liberalism as a living and growing political faith might have perished" (pp. 369–70).
30. Nathaniel William Wraxall, *Historical Memoirs of My Own Time* (rpt; London: Kegan, Paul, Trench, Trübner, 1904), p. 627.
31. Moritz, *Travels*, p. 220.
32. G. G. Cunningham, *Lives of Eminent and Illustrious Englishmen*, 8 vols. (Glasgow: A Fullerton, 1839), 3:53.
33. This and other quotations from Pitt's speeches are from *Speeches of the Right Honourable William Pitt in the House of Commons*, edited by W. S. Hathaway (London: Longman, Hurst, Reese, and Orme, 1806).
34. E. Keble Chatterton, *England's Greatest Statesman: William Pitt* (Indianapolis: Bobbs-Merrill, 1930), pp. 265–66.
35. Cited by Cunningham, *Illustrious Englishmen*, 7:52–53.
36. Mary Berry, *Extracts from the Journal and Correspondence of Miss Berry, 1783–1852*, edited by Theresa Lewis, 3 vols. (London: Longmans, Green, 1865).
37. This and other quotations from Sheridan's speeches are from *Speeches (Several Corrected by Himself)*, edited by a Constitutional Friend, 5 vols. (London: Patrick Martin, 1816). Strangely, no modern selection of Sheridan's speeches has been published, leaving an unfortunate gap in the rhetorical history of England.
38. George Gilfillan, "R. B. Sheridan," *Eclectic Review* 31 (January, 1854): 19–28.
39. Brougham, *Sketches of Statesmen*, 1:217.
40. Mrs. Oliphant, *Sheridan*, English Men of Letters Series (New York: Harper, 1902), p. 134.
41. Both comments are cited by Walter Sichel, *Sheridan*, 2 vols. (Boston: Houghton Mifflin, 1909), 1:56, 2:148–49.
42. Michael T. H. Sadler, *The Political Career of Richard Brinsley Sheridan* (Oxford: B. N. Blackwell, 1912), p. 43.
43. In the *Quarterly Review* 33, an article on Sheridan by Thomas Moore, p. 592.
44. Gilbert Eliot, as cited in Lascelles, *Life of Fox*, p. 198.
45. In his speech on 17 February 1783.

11
Imperialism on Trial—The Indictment of British Rule over India

When Edmund Burke was feeling the approach of death, on a July day in 1796, he wrote to a literary friend to urge him to write up the history of the prosecution of Warren Hastings, and most especially of his own part in it. "Let my endeavors to save the Nation from that shame and guilt be my monument; the only one I ever will have. Let everything I have done, said, or written be forgotten, but this. . . . If ever Europe recovers its civilization, that work will be useful. Remember! Remember! Remember!"[1]

His wish, basically, has been fulfilled, for the Hastings trial has received a tremendous amount of attention from historians, as it did even more so from the English public while it pursued its ten-year course through the House of Lords. In these accounts the judgments range all the way from the Whiggish fury of Macaulay in picturing Hastings as one of the blackest villains in history, to the conclusion of V. A. Smith in his *Oxford History of India* that Hastings was "the greatest of Anglo-Indian rulers," and the praise of him by Wingfield-Stratford for, among many other virtues, having "a sympathetic understanding of the Indian people rare in an Englishman of that time." Whatever else is disputed, the importance of the trial is established. "This famous impeachment marks a turning point in the history of the empire, the point at which it may be said that the conception of Empire first begins to develop into that of commonwealth."[2]

This much more may be said of its importance—it illuminates unmistakably the historical significance of public speaking. The facts of Hasting's conduct in India are such a tangle as to make almost any interpretation plausible. A contrived interpretation of those facts was presented in Westminster Hall with such eloquence that it captured the attention of the English, aroused the national conscience, and led to fundamental changes not only in the colonial administration but in the attitudes concerning the relations between the mother country and her colonies.

Hindsight may not support the claim that Burke made when he arose on 1 December 1783 in support of Fox's East India Bill that "I am happy to . . .

take my share, by one humble vote, in destroying a tyranny that exists to the disgrace of this nation, and the destruction of so large a part of the human species." But the broader results justify his sixteen years of arduous study in preparation for the trial (and the judgment of his editors in devoting five out of the total of twelve volumes of his published works, including the texts of seventeen speeches, to his discussion of the India question). Nor can one lightly dismiss Burke's conclusion concerning Charles James Fox, who risked and lost his chance of governing England by challenging George III to introduce his East India bill: "He may live long. He may do much. But here is the summit. He can never exceed what he does this day." Nor is there any question of the judgment stated by Burke concerning Sheridan's first speech about Hastings's treatmnent of the Begums of Oudh as "the most astonishing effort of eloquence, argument, and wit united, of which there is any record or tradition." In the course of this long-drawn controversy is exhibited what rhetoric can do and, perforce, what it cannot.

For the trial ended, eventually, with a unanimous vote by the Lords attesting the innocence of Hastings on the two major charges against him, and dismissing the remaining charges by huge majorities. Moreover, before the contest ended, the interest of the public dissipated into boredom, and the fundamental effects that it initiated were not consummated until a century afterward. *Sic transit gloria mundi!* But while it lasted it was uncontestably glorious in its heights as it was inglorious in its depths. Once more we confront the circumstance that gives rhetoric its power: Facts may be facts, but it is the impression concerning them that governs reactions.

"Eloquence Misdirected"

The East India Company, in its governing of India, faced an unsolvable dilemma. It was expected to govern in accordance with English laws and contradictory policies; it was also expected, as a commercial institution, to produce profits. In its efforts to balance these two aims, profit making generally prevailed, and the profits—for individuals and for the nation— were enormous. Meanwhile, its governmental functions were rendered especially difficult by the division of India into more than a hundred principalities and by the conquest of large portions of the subcontinent by France. "Hastings was from the first in an impossible position. . . . He was supposed to serve both God and Mammon, or at least George III and the general court of the Company. He had to use the mechanics of an investment house to serve both the high political purposes of England and the welfare of a humble Indian population."[3]

In many ways he did well. He allowed the Indians so far as he could to govern themselves. He controlled corruption so far as was feasible under conditions that saddled him with appointments of favorites sent to him from London to make fortunes for themselves in return for services or connections at home. If he reaped a small fortune for himself, he took less than was customary. He dealt sometimes humanely and sometimes harshly with unsettled conditions and with local rulers whose own motives and actions were often vile; after a long apprenticeship of rising through the ranks, he capped his career with a decade of service as governor-general. Then he retired to return home, expecting a hero's welcome for a job well done—only to find his reception resolved into a fury of attacks that blackened his reputation and cost him virtually everything he had gained.

What brought about this transformation was a series of brilliant speeches spiced with sensational and pathetic narratives concerning exotic Indian and villainous English characters, all depicted with such artistry and power that the audience, both in the Lords and across the nation, was overwhelmed.

For anyone seeking to bring together a library of eloquence, these speeches are a prime resource. They represent very nearly the apex of oratorical mastery. They are also models of argumentative development, with issues clarified, essential arguments emphasized, and with cogent reasoning amply supported with clearly established and relevant facts. They also are epics of sustained emotionalism, all artfully controlled and skillfully directed to enhance the significance of the principal assertions of the speakers. In addition, they constitute sophisticated appeals that derive from deeply held convictions and the strongest feelings of the listening and reading audience. Moreover, their delivery exemplified sincerity, directness, and a pragmatic adaptation to the minds and emotions of the English public.

Nevertheless, they failed to win the verdict of guilt that was their aim. As a group of rhetorical specimens, the speeches represent oratory par excellence. They did indeed have tremendous long-range and indirect effects. The chief reason for their failure to attain their stated goal was that their aim was wrong. They directed their fire against a man rather than a system, and it was the system that was at fault. During the course of ten years of consideration, this disparity became evident and finally determined the outcome of the trial.

The failure of the speakers was due to their political misjudgment rather than to lack of rhetorical skills. They started with the wrong premise, but only gradually and ultimately did this mistake become evident. The misdirection of their zeal was owing chiefly to the faith they misplaced in the prime witness whose testimony shaped their judgment and provided their main ammunition: the miscreant Sir Philip Francis, a man of strong intellect and weak morals, who was a member of Hastings's governing board and his bitter enemy. Francis accumulated a vast body of carefully selected damnatory evidence against Hastings and presented it to Burke and his friends, who were so impressed that they failed to fit it into context. Eventually, this basic weakness in their case led to their defeat.

Their defeat, it must be understood, was only partial. They did succeed in impelling a new direction in the English government of India. Even more importantly, they focused the attention of the English public upon the nature of their own home government, with such impact that they unleashed a surge of advancement toward the new concept of representative democracy. It remained for the following generation "to create a Constitution designed to facilitate the expression of the popular will."[4] But these Whig orators laid the groundwork for it: at first in their unsparing denunciation of the Tory policies toward the American colonies; subsequently in their excoriation of English policies toward India. This much their persuasion did accomplish—a fundamental victory with great effects.

"Traditional English Privileges"

The evolutionary course of this sentiment is clear. As the debate on Fox's East India Bill commenced in 1784, Lord North confidently asserted to the Parliament:

> These gentlemen who hold that the instruction of the constituents ought on all occasions to be complied with do not know the Constitution of their country. To surrender their own judgments, to abandon their own opinions, and to act as their constituents thought proper to instruct them, right or wrong, is to act unconstitutionally.

Lord North's assertion that government was not derived from the public will could be stated with confidence, for not even the liberals questioned it. Pitt, in the following year, did not hesitate to characterize aristocratic control as the "pattern of perfection." George III extolled the existing system of relations between the monarchy and the parliamentary aristocrats as "the most beautiful combination ever framed." Even the Whig critics of the system were not asking for anything like extending the franchise. Instead, what they urged was a return to the "magnanimous government" of the time of Alfred the Great, when the royal authority was administered "as it ought to be." The theme of the liberals was that "the primitive 'Anglo-Saxon' purity of the constitution" had become "debased" by political corruption and that the "inherent virtues" of England's early history should be restored. What they demanded was not that the people be represented, but that the aristocrats should be more responsible.

During the discussion of the American war, as has been seen, a new emphasis emerged: that traditional English privileges were being undermined and must be protected. The transition to a democratic view came during two lengthy periods of debate. The first was that over English conduct in India; the second over the danger or the value of incorporating Jacobin principles into the English society. The new goal of democracy was given its first momentous clarification in a 1789 sermon by the Unitarian minister Richard Price, in which he asserted, "I see the ardour for liberty catching and spreading, a general amendment beginning in human affairs; the dominion of kings changed for the dominion of laws, and the dominion of priests giving way to the dominion of reason and conscience." The very basis of discussion was changed.[5]

The debate over India commenced with insistence that government should be responsible in the administration of the laws, then shifted to the ground that the government was worse than irresponsible—that it fostered privileges for the few at the expense of the many. The point of view that the Whig spokesmen had to deal with was that the colonial administration was conceived in much the same terms as the modern conception of a multinational corporation. What mattered was that the bottom line should show a profit. The side effects were incidental. What this view meant in the operation of the East India Company in India became clear only in retrospect, after new standards of morality were brought to bear: "Never, not even in Ireland, had the materialism of the eighteenth century produced such odious results. The Company fastened upon Bengal like a malignant vampire, draining its life-blood without any thought of imperial responsibility or ordinary humanity. As was the Company, so were its servants. Wretchedly underpaid, their only thought was to get huge profits as quick as possible by any corrupt or cruel means."[6] Aside from what this meant in the suffering of the exploited Indian population, it also had the effect of still further corrupting the English Parliament. After making their fortunes, the nouveaux riches returned to purchase parliamentary seats from rotten boroughs and to constitute an India interest dedicated to maintaining the system in the Commons. Let the Indians suffer as they must. As King George frankly wrote to Pitt, "I own I do not think it possible in that country to carry on business with the same moderation that is suited to an European civilized nation."[7]

"Risk Everything That Is Most Dear"

These were the conditions that aroused first the interest and then the fury of the Whig minority. What they confronted was a system of exploitation that was virtually unquestioned. The East India Company had been chartered on the last day of 1599, fortified with a grant of a monopoly over East India trade and with authority to operate as an extraterritorial government, with its own laws interpreted in its own courts and supported by its own army. The problems it had to deal with invited severity. The old

Mogul Empire was dissolved during the 1760s, to be replaced by numerous principalities, which were grossly corrupt and were embroiled in their own warfare between Hindus and Mohammedans. In order to exercise its rule the company had to deal as best it could with them. It also contested with first Portuguese and Dutch settlements and afterward with a very considerable effort by France to establish its own dominion in India. The consolidation of English control was accomplished by Robert Clive; then, in 1775, Warren Hastings succeeded him. As Hastings's governorship neared its end, and after the American colonies won their independence, Burke and Fox turned their attention to India. Actually, Burke had commenced his own serious study of India much earlier. The formation of the brief Portland-Fox-North coalition offered an opportunity that led Fox to introduce a bill designed to make the East India Company more directly responsible to Parliament.

In introducing his bill, on 18 November 1783, Fox told the members, "I risk my all upon the excellence of this bill; I risk upon it everything that is most dear to me, whatever men most value, the character of integrity, of talents, of honour, of present reputation and future fame." With the aid of Burke, he was well prepared; even so, he committed several tactical errors. He failed to consult with the London officers of the company, whose support he might have won. He also seemed to be reversing his long opposition to royal influence over Parliament, since under his bill appointments to the lucrative Indian posts would be made by the ministry. Finally, against the advice of his colleague Lord North, he refrained from consulting with King George.

He was, nevertheless, right in his judgment that he would have great public support. Visitors crowded the galleries. As Wraxall recorded in his *Memoirs*, "I scarcely remember a day on which public expectation was wound to a higher pitch than when Fox opened his bill."

When Fox gave his interpretation of the treatment of the Hindu Cheyte Sing and the Moslem Begums of Oudh, and of the conduct of British troops in the Rohilla and Maharratta campaigns, a reporter judged that "his eloquence in this part of his speech was truly great and masterly." A few days later, in another speech, Fox claimed that his efforts were for "the British and India people, for many, many millions of souls." A London journalist called Fox's speech "one of the completest performances ever heard in Parliament, both for accuracy, in the parts dependent on arithmetical statement, as well as for the finest energy of thought and expression." Even so, when Pitt rose to oppose the bill, he felt it sufficient to ridicule Fox's speech as mere "volubility that rendered comprehension difficult." Burke's supporting speech, on 1 December, claimed that his judgment was based on "three years of laborious research," and he assured the members that "we are on a conspicuous stage and the world marks our demeanor."

In the course of his three-hour speech, Burke sought to prove that the immorality of the East India Company was habitual, systematic, and incorrigible. He portrayed its exploitative measures in terms the English conscience could not excuse:

> Our conquest there, after twenty years, is as crude as it was the first day. The natives scarcely know what it is to see the gray hair of an Englishman. Young men (boys almost) govern there, without society, without sympathy with the natives. They have no more social habits with the people than if they still resided in England; not, indeed, any species of intercourse but that which is necessary to making a sudden fortune, with a view to a remote settlement. Animated with all the avarice of age and all the impetuosity of youth, they roll in one after another, wave after wave, there is nothing before the eyes of the natives but an endless, hopeless prospect of new flights of birds of prey and passage, with appetites continually renewing for a food that is constantly wasting. Every rupee of profit that is made by an Englishman is lost forever to India. . . . England has erected no churches, no hospitals, no palaces, no schools; England has built no bridges, made no high roads, cut no navigations, dug out no reservoirs. Every other conqueror of every other description has left some monuments, either of state or beneficence, behind him. Were we to be driven out of India this day, nothing would remain to tell that it had been possessed, during the inglorious period of our domination, by anything better than the orangutan or the tiger.

Throughout his speech Burke appealed to the British principle of fair play. He swept aside with disdain the argument that England would suffer if its India revenues were reduced. "My sole question, on each clause of the bill, amounts to this,—Is the measure proposed required by the necessities of India?"

Since neither the Indian nor the English public had representation in the Parliament, it was impossible to win the votes required for adoption of the bill. Both Fox and Burke aimed beyond the membership, to arouse public opinion. Fox was proven correct in his statement that he was making a personal sacrifice, for the bill so enraged the king that the coalition was replaced with the prime ministry of Pitt. But public excitement was aroused to such a pitch that Pitt felt impelled to introduce an India bill of his own. The Whigs opposed this on the ground that it did not go far enough. This was only the opening scene for the long discussion. The crucial struggle lay yet ahead.

"Too Much Elaboration"

In 1785 Warren Hastings returned home. The Whigs immediately called for his impeachment. Pitt incautiously granted that "gifts" Hastings had received justified an inquiry. Hastings confidently agreed to have his conduct examined. In the session that commenced in January 1786, the great debate began. Nine years later, Hastings was acquited. By this time, the public was bored with talk of India, and the concern of Parliament shifted to the convulsion in France.

The persuasive problem for the Whigs was unusually difficult. As a biographer of Pitt justly observes, "India presents a particularly tricky problem." It was agreed that there had to be some governmental supervision over the East India Company, but the ministers were convinced that "it would be politically dangerous and administratively impossible to take over those operations altogether."[8] The influencing of public opinion on a question so remote from domestic concerns was also difficult. It was easy for government spokesmen to assert that the Whigs were less animated by moral zeal than by maneuvering for simple partisan advantage. Even on the moral issue, Hastings's conduct was mitigated by the fact that conditions in India would not be improved by returning the rule to the atrocious Mogul princes.

So much for the climate of opinion. On the explicit question of winning votes, King George and Pitt were firmly in control of their majority. The astute Dr. Johnson summarized the circumstances in two pithy comments: that it was a "struggle between George the Third's sceptre and Mr. Fox's tongue"; and that "Fox is my friend"—but "the King is my master."[9] With this summation the Tory membership was in fullest accord.

Such a rhetorical occasion severely limited the alternatives of persuasive strategy among which the Whigs had to choose. They had to lessen the suspicion that all they sought was partisan advantage. They had to focus attention on the depravity of the course Hastings had pursued. On the ground they chose, they did superbly well. They had studied the subject ardently, and the facts, as they interpreted them, were decisive. They possessed the ability to phrase their charges vividly. Undoubtedly they were sincerely aroused by the enormity of the crimes they discussed. And they were effective in arousing in their hearers similar feelings of revulsion.

Their major mistake was in failing to realize that enough is enough. Emotions cannot be sustained indefinitely. Both their immediate hearers and the outside public eventually tired of their repeated cries of shame and their multiple proofs of guilt. The chief defect in their strategy was their failure to bring the prosecution to a much quicker end. But this was far from being wholly their own fault. The ministry skillfully employed the tactic of delay.

Burke was the principal manager of the prosecution. Herbert Grierson judged that his India speeches exhibited even "greater passion" than his two great efforts to change the policies toward America, but, as in those speeches, Burke diluted his effect through too much elaboration. Simply by speaking too long, he aroused a "wish to hear the other side."[10] Hastings's defense was relatively muted, allowing the impression gradually to grow that he was assaulted by attackers who spoke for their own partisan advantage.

As the trial unfolded the excitement created by the speeches of the prosecutors was enormous. As a biographer of Burke testifies:

> For four days, from February 15 to 19, the thronging and splendid audience of Westminster Hall listened to the great oration of the leader of the Managers. The effects of it were such as have never been witnessed in any assemblage of staid and unimpulsive English men and women. The narrative of the condition of the people of India and of the general conduct of the East India Company excited lively curiosity and interest; but at the thrilling and harrowing details of the cruelties practiced by the agents of Hastings, ladies shrieked and swooned and were hurried from the scene. All men felt a dread and unwonted emotion, and even the courage of the undaunted prisoner gave way. "I felt a villain under the magic of the orator" was, many years afterwards, the confessed statement of Hastings; and all who heard it concurred in the effect which the great display of eloquence produced![11]

If a vote had been permitted at this stage, Hastings would have been acquitted by the controlled majority, but his condemnation by public opinion would have been devastating. But more, much more, was yet to be said.

"The Wonders of That Speech"

The most effective speaking of all was that by Richard Brinsley Sheridan. He had devoted himself with unaccustomed assiduity to mastering the information provided by the unscrupulous Sir Philip Francis. Especially in two great speeches about the treatment of the Begums, or princesses, of Oudh, he rose to the height of what oratory can achieve. In the opinion of a hearer, the first of these speeches at least equaled "the most argumentative and impassioned orations that had ever been addressed to the judgment and feelings of the British Parliament."[12] The worldy-wise and cynical Horace Walpole noted that "one heard everyone in the streets raving on the wonders of that speech."[13] A critic of oratory agreed, concluding that

> the theme was peculiarly adapted to display the best powers of eloquence; and never, perhaps, were they exerted with superior skill. For more than five hours he continued, without abatement, to fascinate, arouse, and inflame the feelings of his audience, and when he concluded there was a spontaneous and general burst of applause expressive of a greater degree of enthusiasm than probably was ever before kindled by the influence of eloquence in a deliberative assembly.[14]

Burke described the first of these Begum speeches as "the most astonishing effort of eloquence, argument, and wit united, of which there was any record or traditions."[15] For Fox, "all that he had ever heard, all that he had ever read, when compared to it dwindled into nothing, and vanished like vapour before the sun."[16] Even Pitt, on the opposing side, confessed that "it surpassed all the eloquence of ancient and modern times, and possessed everything that genius and art could furnish, to agitate and control the human mind."[17]

Sheridan's purpose, in the speech delivered on 7 February 1787, was to blacken the reputation of Hastings for his treatment of the two Begums after they combined to rebel against his authority and for his seizing of their possessions. These were "acts which no political necessity could warrant." They were "criminality of the blackest dye,—of tyranny the most vile and premeditated,—of corruption the most open and shameless,—of oppression the most severe and grinding,—of cruelty the most hard and unparalleled." What proof could he offer? "The witness . . . would be . . . Warren Hastings himself." It was not evidence, however, but emotional enhancement that provided the compelling power over the listeners. From this distance one can scarcely imagine the effects, for they derived in part from the intensity and artistry of his delivery. But even the mere printed text is suggestive.

> As well might the writhing obliquity of the serpent be compared to the swift directness of the arrow, as the duplicity of Mr. Hastings's ambition to the simple steadiness of genuine magnanimity. In his mind all was shuffling, ambiguous, dark, insidious, and little; nothing simple, nothing unmixed; all affected plainness and actual dissimulation;—a heterogeneous mass of contradictory qualities; with nothing great but his crimes; and even those contrasted with the littleness of his motives, which at once denoted both his baseness and his meanness, and marked him for both a traitor and a trickster. Nay, in his style and writing, there was the same mixture of vicious contrarities;—the most grovelling ideas were conveyed in the most inflated language; giving mock consequence to low cavils, and uttering quibbles in heroics; so that his compositions disgusted the mind's taste, as much as his actions excited the soul's abhorrence.

So, Hastings was not only a liar, a cheat, and a tyrant—he was also a poor writer! Not even this unfortunate anticlimax, however, checked the effect as the speech rushed on. Hastings's own chosen agents had "the meanness of a peddler and the profligacy of pirates." In their rapacity, they behaved like auctioneering ambassadors and trading generals. As for the claim that they were but putting down the resistance of the Begums, "was it a crime that they should crowd together in fluttering trepidation like a flock of resistless birds on seeing the felon kite?" Not the Begums but Hastings was the criminal; who among them could doubt it? "Let gentlemen lay their hands on their hearts, and with truth issuing in all its purity from their lips, solemnly declare whether they *were* or *were not* convinced that the *real* spring of the conduct of Mr. Hastings, far from being a desire to crush a rebellion (an ideal, fabulous rebellion!) was a malignantly rapacious determination to seize, with lawless hands, upon the treasures of devoted, miserable, yet unoffending victims." In this same vein, with the same emotional intensity, the speech went on and on and on, for five full hours.

If this speech were to be assessed as entertainment, it would merit all the praise its hearers lavished on it. The response by the listeners speaks for itself. It was high theatre, both an artistic and a popular triumph. And it was accomplished under truly remarkable circumstances. Sheridan did not commence speaking until after midnight. The members of the two houses and the fashionable visitors who were lucky enough to obtain tickets of entry (for which they paid the doormen as much as fifty guineas apiece) came to hear him following their late suppers that were washed down with a plenitude of liquor. They remained in their seats until he finished, around 6:00 A.M. They broke the rules of Parliament by rewarding him with thunderous applause. But to be entertaining was not Sheridan's goal. His earnest endeavor was to win votes.

The most difficult part of his persuasive problem was not to prove that crimes against Indians had been committed; it was not even to make those crimes so vividly compelling as to sear the consciences of his hearers. What he had further to do was to convince as many as he could that the Whigs were not playing the political game—that it was justice, not partisan advantage, that they sought. His evidence that Hastings and his agents were plundering India was not enough—for indirect enrichment from the emoluments of office was so customary as to be acceptable. Besides, India was far away and its people were so "barbaric" (as King George had avowed) that they could not be dealt with except by severity and deception. The moot question was What does all this have to do with the Parliament? Was it all to result finally in strengthening the position of the Whigs? It was to this question that Sheridan devoted his conclusion. Partisan loyalties, he said, did have their own value, but they became insignificant when the issue was basic morality. On this theme he subordinated emotionalism to reason, as he addressed himself directly to the members who were to cast their votes.

> There was scarcely a subject upon which they were not broken and divided into sects. The prerogatives of the Crown found its advocates among the representatives of the people. The privileges of the people found opponents even in the House of Commons itself. Habits, connections, parties, all led to diversities of opinion. But when inhumanity presented itself to their observations, it found no division among them;

they attacked it as their common enemy; and, as if the character of the land was involved in their zeal for its ruin, they left it not till it was completely overthrown.

So much for partisan advantage. It was not the Whigs but the Tory majority, he reminded them, that customarily voted a strict party line, selling their votes in return for bribes and pensions. It was their own corruption that made it difficult for them to attest to Hastings's guilt. Emotionalism again took command.

They could not behold the workings of the heart, the quivering lips, the trickling tears, and the loud and yet tremulous joy of the millions whom their vote of this night would forever save from the cruelty of corrupted power. But though they could not directly see the effect, was not the true enjoyment of their benevolence increased by the blessing being conferred unseen? Would not the omnipotence of Britain be demonstrated to the wonder of nations, by stretching its mighty arms across the deep and saving by its fiat distant millions from destruction? And would the blessings of the people thus saved, dissipate into empty air? No! if I dare to use the figure,—we shall constitute Heaven itself our proxy, to receive for us the blessings of their pious gratitude, and the prayers of their thanksgiving.

He paused dramatically and then made his closing appeal. "It is with confidence, therefore, Sir, that I move you this charge, 'That Warren Hastings be impeached.'" The Lords did not, however, justify his confidence with their votes.

Sheridan had done all that he could. No other member of either House could have done so well. But the ministry had the crucial advantage; it controlled the procedure and it delayed the vote. Eighteen months later Sheridan rose again to make yet another speech on this same charge of the abuse of the Begums. This speech was even longer, running through a series of sessions, from 8 June through 13 June 1788. Again both the floor and the galleries were crowded. Most of those present had heard the earlier speech. Much of this renewed oratory was a restatement of what Sheridan had said before. Even so, the excitement created by this second speech was scarcely if at all less than from the earlier one. Lord Byron, in his "Monody" celebrated it in extravagent terms:

> His was the thunder, his the avenging rod,
> The wrath, the delegated voice of God,
> Which shook the nations through his lips and blazed
> Till vanquished seraphs trembled as they praised.

Again the testimony to its effectiveness is overwhelming. Sir Gilbert Elliot esteemed it as better than Burke at his best, finding it "strewed very thick with more brilliant periods of eloquence and poetical imaginations, and more lively sallies of wit." Fox and Sheridan himself considered this second effort inferior to his first, but Cunningham attested that "it seems to have produced a more general satisfaction." As Lloyd C. Sanders, in his *Life of Richard Brinsley Sheridan,* summed it up: "No barrister could have marshalled the facts with more critical sense of their legal effect; no solicitor could have gotten up the case with a keener eye to discrepancies in dates." Yet once again the verdict was postponed.

It was six years later, with the long trial finally coming to its close, with the nation bored and with parliamentary concern shifted to foreign affairs, when once again Sheridan returned to the same theme, on 14 May 1794, reiterating the same facts, and restating them with a fine mixture of sarcastic scorn, withering contempt, and irresistible reasoning. No one could answer him with success. The defenders of Hastings did not even try to do so. They simply sat back, waited until the attack was concluded, and then gave to the ministry the vote that was demanded of them. "Hastings was acquitted of all charges," and it was the reputation of the prosecutors, "rather than his, that was in need of repair."[18] The general view of historians is that even though Hastings had indeed committed grievous crimes, his general conduct had tended to improve the policies and the practices of England's rule of India.

"The Force of Rhetoric"

What, then, must one conclude concerning the force of rhetoric as a guiding influence in history? The best of speaking had not changed the foreordained verdict. Is "mere rhetoric" little more than glitter and show? J. Steven Watson, in his evaluation of the trial, judged that the Whigs would have been better advised not to attempt to impeach Hastings, but rather to have attacked the colonial system itself. Their strategy, he felt, should have been to "saddle Pitt with the duty of defending every mistake made in India." Wingfield-Stratford, who interpreted the indictment as "a mere slander and abuse of an innocent man," even so concluded that the speeches "mark a definite break with eighteenth-century notions of empire. In the time of Walpole and the Pelhams it is inconceivable that they would have been uttered, and they show what power the revival of emotion and human feeling had gathered during those few decades." In his view, however, the Whig speakers allowed their emotionalism such rein that it aroused suspicion of their reasoned statesmanship. He also agreed that their partisanship overwhelmed their patriotism, and he cited as applying to all of them the disparagement Goldsmith applied to Burke—

> Who, born for the universe narrowed his mind,
> And to party gave up what was meant for mankind.[19]

Mistakes in tactics there may have been, even serious mistakes. And the prosecutors may, indeed, have submitted their judgment too much to the partial and bitterly personalized information supplied to them by Hastings's enemy, Philip Francis. Nevertheless, in this prolonged trial, public speaking did not fail; it proved its power. And it also demonstrated its limitations. Even at its best, it is only one factor among the many that shape attitudes and events.

In addition to losing the verdict, the Whig speakers were only in part successful in their more general aims—of reforming colonial policies, of reducing the corruption in the home government, and of arousing a public demand for broad democratizing reforms. But their successes also loom large. Their persuasion undoubtedly paved the way to the great Reform Bill of 1832. Their criticism laid a foundation for the (much later) evolution of the Commonwealth.

Personal and party rewards they did not obtain. All they received, except for the momentary and widespread admiration for the splendor of their eloquence, is the accolade of history for having championed transcultural morality. These results were delayed largely by the effects of the French Revolution. And it was to this that their attention, like that of the nation at large, was drawn. In the convulsive spirit of condemnation and dread that it aroused, all else faded and was ignored.

Notes

1. Russell Kirk, *Edmund Burke: A Genius Reconsidered*, Architects of Freedom Series (New Rochelle, N.Y.: Arlington House, 1967), pp. 126–27.
2. Wingfield-Stratford, *British Civilization*, p. 767.
3. Watson, *King George III*, pp. 306–7.
4. Asa Briggs, *The Age of Improvement* (London: Longmans, Green, 1959), p. 99.
5. The progression is reviewed by Albert Goodwin in *The Friends of Liberty: The English Democratic Movement in the Age of the French Revolution* (Cambridge: Harvard University Press), 1979.
6. Wingfield-Stratford, *British Civilization*, p. 762.
7. Quoted by Derek Jarrett, *Pitt the Younger* (London: Wiedenfeld and Nicolson, 1974), p. 119.
8. Jarrett, *Pitt the Younger*, p. 114.
9. *Boswell's Life of Johnson*, 2:551.
10. Herbert J. C. Grierson, in the *Eclectic Magazine*, 16:18–19.
11. Robert Murray, *Edmund Burke, A Biography* (London: Oxford University Press, 1931), p. 336.
12. *Public Characters of 1799–1800* (London: Richard Phillips, 1807), p. 42.
13. Quoted by William Matthews, *Oratory and Orators* (Chicago: Griggs, 1891), p. 276.
14. N. Chapman, *Select Speeches*, 4 vols. (Philadelphia: Hopkins and Earle, 1808), 1:384–85.
15. Quoted by Cunningham, *Illustrious Englishmen*, 7:171.
16. In his speech on 7 February 1787.
17. Quoted by Cunningham, *Illustrious Englishmen*, 7:171.
18. Watson, *King George III*, p. 322.
19. Wingfield-Stratford, *British Civilization*, pp. 763–72.

12
The Specter of Jacobinism—Effects on the Discussable

The storming of the Bastille on 14 July 1789 set off a torrent of sentiments comparable to the mixture of hope and dread in the wake of Lenin's dramatic arrival at the railway station in Petrograd in April 1917. Like bolshevism and communism, *Jacobinism* proved to be a trigger term that unleashed an international flood of emotions.

There are many similarities in what the terms meant. Both had philosophical precursors: Marx and Engels for the one, Rousseau and Diderot for the other. Both championed the exploited poor; both claimed to promote brotherhood, justice, and equality. Both aimed at universalism through the withering away of the state. Both scorned and rejected religion in the name of reason. Both preached peace and mercy while practicing violence and cruelty. And the reactions also proved to be similar. In both times good people were appalled by the bloodletting, but many among them explained or excused it as a repugnant but necessary preliminary to the promised reforms—like a painful operation to remove a cancer. Both movements were based in nations with records of brutal tyranny; and both soon launched into imperialist expansion in the name of liberation. The effects of both were similarly profound—upon governments, and social classes, and individuals.

As the violence in Paris became intolerably sordid, and the constructive and liberating ideas that formed a part of Jacobinism began to circulate in England, neighbors began to eye one another with a mingling of abhorrence and hope. The costs of revolution were tragically plain. The threat to their own establishment and traditions was real and imminent. But what of benefits? Could they be won for England? Could they be won without the cruelties, the turmoil, the cost in blood?

"Questions That Had to Be Discussed"

These were questions that had to be discussed, and the discussions aroused bitter antagonisms. What could be discussed properly came into sharp dispute. What it was safe to say was squeezed into narrower limits, even as what actually was being said often stretched far beyond accepted proprieties. Public feelings were sharply divided. Both patriotism and traditionalism were challenged and defended as they never had been before, even more than they were in the seventeenth century. The very survival of religion was challenged by the French proclamation of a new age of reason. The Established Church and the established ruling class had no doubt that they must resist with all the power they had. Many dissidents, on the other hand, both religious and political, saw new opportunities to demand freedom of conscience and long-suppressed natural rights. There was much to talk about, and talk once unleashed can have epidemic consequences.

Mental attitudes and deep emotions were fundamentally stirred. The French Revolution was far from being the sole cause or the sole effect. Concurrently, a romantic revolution, strongly influenced by Rousseau's eloquent claim for the virtues of primitivism, created a new spirit in literature and a new view of morality. There also developed economic changes that resulted in the industrial revolution. Flux replaced stability and a new vision of progress beckoned minds away from the past toward what would have to be a very different future. The closing decades of the century proved to be a divide in human history, with old certainties replaced by doubts, and with unquestioned acceptance challenged by heretofore unavailing hopes. Ambitions took new forms that spread across the population and erupted with urgency.

The very concept of authority was threatened by the emergent sense of individualism. The social fabric was battered. Frantic efforts were made to devise new ways, new relationships, a broadening of privileges. Politics, economics, religion, and literature all responded in their several ways. Virtually everything became discussable, with little remaining that could be taken for granted. The outreaching question, Where do we go from here? was countered by the conservative response, By all means, let us preserve what we have. There was urgent need for trusted leadership that could point the way.

Such leadership was hard to come by. Many must have felt what the rural poet William Cowper wrote as the first stirrings were being felt, in 1784: "It is comfortable to be of no consequence in a world where one cannot exercise any without disobliging somebody."[1] As the spreading tide of Jacobinism reached England, men whose positions made them spokesmen had to examine their alternatives. Should they remain safely silent, or should they shout louder? Should they retreat into mutterings of ambiguities? Or was it their duty to turn attention aside to noncontroversial issues? What solutions could they propose? For English leaders all these alternatives were dangerous.

Postponement was one possibility, for England was safeguarded from revolution by the facts that its government was less centralized and much less tyrannical than that of Bourbon France. Its society was less rigidly compartmentalized. Its common law protected more equitably. Nevertheless, the stability of its traditions was shaken by the loss of its American colonies and by the revelations that its conduct in India had been marked by greed and despotism. The people had gained a voice of their own through the multiplication of newspapers, pamphlets, and reformist societies. Parliament was far stronger than was the French Assembly before 1789, and in it the outspoken minority kept watch over the largely subservient majority. Parliament remained what it had become—the foundation of the government—despite the encroachments of King George. But increasingly, guiding influences were coming from outside of Westminster Hall.

The experiences of two brothers, Edmund and John Cartwright, illustrate the problems that were besetting the society and suggest how they were being dealt with. Edmund was a textile manufacturer who invented the power loom and a wool-combing machine, with which he was able greatly to increase production while reducing his labor costs. When he built a new factory in Manchester with 200 power looms, he neglected even to try to explain the potential benefits to his displaced workers who saw their means of livelihood swept away. His factory was burned, almost certainly by arsonists, and he retreated to his farm. His younger brother, John, went first into the army, where he refused to fight against the Americans, and then into politics, becoming a member of Parliament. In 1774 John published a sensational pamphlet entitled *American Independence the Glory and Interest of Great Britain*. In 1776 he commenced his long campaign for annual Parliaments based upon universal suffrage. To promote this idea, he organized the Society for Constitutional Information and the Correspondence Society, out of which grew numerous local discussion centers known as Hampden clubs. Edmund was rewarded for his inventiveness by the House of Commons, with a grant of ten thousand pounds. John was found guilty of conspiracy, but freedom of speech and of the press was so well established that he had only to pay a small fine of ten pounds. Both brothers were harbingers of change. Edmund's experience illustrates the commencement of the labor unrest that was to become widespread as industrialization expanded. John's rebelliousness illuminates the role of the individual conscience. Both society and government were to be fundamentally affected by what happens when unrest and conscience combine.

"A Sacrifice of Friendship"

As the Terror unfolded in France, with the royal family beheaded, aristocrats trundled to the guillotine like oxen to the slaughter pen after only farcical trials, with the church outlawed and religion reviled, with brotherly love preached in scenes of unrestrained hate, and with proud claims that it was all being done for the sake of the brotherhood of man, Edmund Burke rushed to denounce what was happening with a passion born of dread. To him it was beyond doubt that Jacobinism was a threat to all that he believed to be morally right, eternally true, and politically indispensable. "The abyss of Hell seems to yawn before me," he wrote to a friend in November 1793. Three years later he described the nature of the abyss in terms strikingly similar to many twentieth-century Western reactions to communism:

> It is a war between the partisans of the ancient, civil, moral, and political order of Europe against a set of fanatical and ambitious atheists which seems to change them all. It is not France extending a foreign empire over other nations; it is a sect aiming at universal empire and beginning with the conquest of France.[2]

With many sharing Burke's revulsion, government became more censorious, and restrictive measures, including suspension of the habeas corpus and the imposition of curfews, were adopted. Fox and Sheridan, in contrast to Burke, joined with those who abhorred the French excesses but pardoned them with the confidence that much-needed reforms would follow. When the Parliament of 1796 enacted a series of restrictions on civil liberties, Fox exclaimed in the course of the debate in October:

> Show me a Parliament since the year 1688, the era of our Revolution, that has diminished the best and dearest rights of the people, so shamelessly, so wickedly, as the last Parliament have done!
>
> Show me a Parliament since that period that has so uniformly sacrificed the liberty of the subject to increase the influence of government, as the last Parliament have done!

Old alliances and friendships could not stand the strain of the contrasting emotions that were aroused. The Old Whigs broke apart. Most notably, the long friendship of Burke, Fox, and Sheridan was sundered. Burke took his direction from the past, which he deeply believed offered the best guidance for the future. Sheridan seized the opening to champion peace and human rights. Fox, no less devoted to popular liberties than was Sheridan, nevertheless, as the leader of his party, looked also for such partisan advantages as he could perceive. Since Pitt, as prime minister, was the instigator of defensive restrictions, the parliamentary struggle revolved around these two party leaders. As a major modern historian sums it up: "It was Fox, not Pitt, who shaped the modern constitution. On the greatest questions of the age—the war against France and the suppression of English liberties—Fox . . . was absolutely right and Pitt was absolutely wrong."[3] An analysis of the debates that ensued brings this judgment at least partially into doubt. In any event, Fox was the activist and therefore had more marks to score.

The preliminary stage in the debates required a regrouping of forces. The circumstances must be viewed as they appeared to the participants. Sir Walter Scott, representing the conservative elite, expressed the admiration he felt for Burke's leadership, as having preserved the very essence of English values. Looking back from the objective stance of 1831, he wrote:

> About 1792, when I was entering life, the admiration of the god-like system of the French Revolution was so rife, that only a few old-fashioned . . . ventured to hint a preference for the land they lived in, or pretended to doubt that the new principles must be infused into our own worn-out constitution. Burke appeared, and all the gibberish about the superior legislation of the French dissolved like an enchanted castle when the destined knight blew his horn before it.[4]

Scott's recollection was not entirely correct. Sentiments favoring the new revolutionary ideas by no means "dissolved" when the militant knight blew his horn. One reason was that prominent leaders dared to speak out on the other side. Fox and Sheridan, like Burke, responded to the events in Paris in consonance with their basic convictions. Despite the long and close allegiance of these three, the French Revolution revealed how far apart they were in their fundamental principles. When the Bastille was attacked, Fox greeted the event with an exultant exclamation in a letter to a friend: "How much the greatest event it is that ever happened in the World!" Sheridan viewed even the Terror as a healthful repudiation of despotism. When the views of these three came into collision in the parliamentary debate in February 1790, Sheridan scornfully rejected Burke's attack on the French National Assembly. Burke, he said, missed the essential point that instead of "creating evils," it was rather only remedying injustices "which they had found existing in full deformity at the first hour of their meeting." To Burke, Sheridan's acceptance of the cruelties and this direct attack upon himself were intolerable. Sheridan, he retorted angrily, "had made a sacrifice of his friendship for the sake of catching some momentary popularity."

Their divergence of views was so complete and so deeply felt that a continuance of their friendship, much less of their alliance, was impossible. On 2 March Fox observed to the House that Burke's attacks against the revolutionists "had filled him with grief and shame." As the debate continued, on 12 April Fox went so far as to describe the new French constitution as "the most stupendous and glorious edifice of liberty, which had ever been erected on the foundation of human integrity in any time or country." The Old Whigs and the New Whigs were irreparably separating. On 6 May Burke exclaimed that if he were about to die his last words would be, "Fly from the French Constitution!" Fox, with tears in his eyes, leaned over to whisper that there was no lessening of their friendship. Burke shook his head. Then rising, he walked across the aisle to take his seat beside Pitt.

Pitt's policies pleased Burke only a little more than those of Fox and

Sheridan. As head of the government, what Pitt favored above all was stability. "He determinedly set himself, to use the phrase of Candide, to cultivate his own garden, and to ignore all others. Let France settle her internal affairs as she chooses, was his unvarying principle."[5] His overriding concern was to balance the budget, which had been beset by deficits during two generations of warfare. He also wanted to reduce the taxes, which had become oppressive; to do this, he had to reduce the military. Soothingly, he assured his parliamentary followers that "although we must not count with certainty on the continuance of our present prosperity during such an interval, yet unquestionably there never was a time in the history of this country when from the situation of Europe we might more reasonably expect fifteen years of peace than we have at the present moment."[6] So much for prescience—he could scarcely have been more wrong.

When Burke demanded from Pitt a war to restore the French monarchy, he found the prime minister "cold and dead" to undertaking such a crusade. Instead, on this issue, Pitt sided with his old adversary Fox, to oppose any intervention. "The present convulsions in France," he solemnly promised the Commons,

> must sooner or later terminate in general harmony and regular order, and though the fortunate arrangements of such a situation must make her more formidable, they may also render her less obnoxious as a neighbor. . . . Whenever the situation of France shall become restored, it will prove freedom rightly understood, freedoom resulting from good order and good government; and thus circumstanced France will stand forward as one of the most brilliant pioneers of Europe.

This sounded more like Sheridan, or like Pitt's own early tendencies, than like the official spokesman for the views of King George. But what Pitt was most truly representing was his own deep commitment to maintaining a sound economy.

"Exhausted in Argument"

The contrasting persuasive strategies of the principal spokesmen were derived from their differing interpretations of what would happen after the Terror abated. This was the unanswerable question upon which the formulation of policies must rest. In Pitt's view, the government, in his hands, was far too solidly based to be endangered. To Burke there appeared to be great danger that the domestic reformers would be so eagerly receptive to the principles professed by Jacobinism as to be insufficiently repelled by its vicious practices. What mostly occupied the minds of Sheridan and of Fox—and especially that of Fox, as the leader of the New Whigs—was the devising of strategies by which to build upon the sentiments of liberty being trumpeted in Paris to accomplish those reforms to which his party was dedicated.

"The first of these," he wrote to a party associate, "related to religious liberty . . . to putting an end to all penal laws and disqualifications upon Catholics and Dissenters." The second was to bring the slave trade to an end. The third was governmental reform, which, to him did not mean broadening the franchise but reuniting the Whigs to make them again into an effective Opposition. None of these goals could be easily accomplished. "The times are very bad for us," he admitted, "but perhaps we are of that sort which in bad times is most useful, and we may be in our proper place."[7]

As has been noted in a prior chapter, the slave trade was finally abolished. Religious freedom, the very first of Fox's priorities, was far from having the amount of popular support required to secure parliamentary approval. The most vocal among the Dissenters were Unitarians, who were widely considered to be blasphemous and profane. The official pronouncement of atheism as French policy had the effect in England of strengthening orthodox resentment and fears of all manner of heresies. In the face of this reactionary sentiment, Fox undertook to aid the Dissenters as best he could.

On 11 May 1791, he proposed the repeal of all laws that limited the civil rights of those who did not conform to the Anglican church. In a speech supporting his bill, he took the high road of reasonableness. "To call on man to give up his religious rights," he told the Commons, "was to call on him to do that which was impossible." What was it, he asked, that the laws required? With great earnestness, and with the persuasive skill that none among his colleagues could match, he defined what the restrictive laws meant: "Read the Scriptures, understand them, make them the guide and rule of your actions and opinions"—an interpretation to which the members of the House could only nod their heads in agreement. Then came Fox's restatement of what the laws really required: "But take care you interpret them as the professors of the Church of England do, or else you shall be deprived of all the enjoyment which belongs to man in a social state." Moderate and sound as Fox's argument was, it could not prevail. Circumstances were too disturbed for reason to curb fear. The House voted 142 to 63 against Fox's bill. The penal laws against Dissenters were not repealed for another quarter century—by which time the concern of the English was not with French ideology but with the need to unify their nation by adjusting to the rising democratic sentiments and demands.

As another of his aims, Fox launched a new effort to defend endangered English liberties. Public discussion was being threatened and curbed by widespread arrests and condemnations for seditious libel. The standing laws gave to juries merely the authority to decide whether indicted individuals had in fact "uttered or published" statements that the prosecutors deemed to be dangerous. Whether such statements were indeed libelous was left to determinations by judges. In October Fox introduced a bill entitled "An Act to Remove Doubts respecting the Functions of Juries in Cases of Libels," so phrased as to give to juries the right to decide whether statements were truly libelous. This, in his own view, as in the judgment also of later historians, was Fox's supreme legislative effort. In preparation for it, Fox laboriously researched the history of English law. The arguments that he developed and presented were so convincing that the ministry did not oppose his bill. Consequently, it readily passed in the Commons, and in the following year it was confirmed in the Lords. The results he sought, however, were not immediately realized, for under the prevailing public mood, convictions for libel actually increased. It was only in the course of time that Fox's bill proved to be a secure foundation for freedom of speech. As so often happened in the course of his career, Fox spoke more for the future than for the present. Where he most failed as a politician he best shone as a statesman.

His statesmanship soon met yet another test, in which he was less successful. The excesses of the Terror aroused the monarchs of Europe to unite against the French, and Pitt reluctantly retreated from his defense of the budget sufficiently to propose an increase in military expenditures. Fox opposed the rearmament and demanded an inquiry into the reasons for it. His speech was acclaimed by Sheridan with a crescendo of admiration, during the 2 June debate: "There was nothing to reply to, nothing to refute, a convincing proof that the motion . . . was unanswerable. All the puny efforts by the other side to resist the blows of that club served only to expose them more to the eye of the House in that unequal conflict—they were exhausted in argument. But his right honorable friend was not exhausted. His rich and fruitful mind had produced the new and irresistible arguments which had given conviction to every thinking mind." The majority may indeed have been convinced, for, as Sheridan exulted, "they sat in dejected silence, and left the field to their conquering enemy." Fox was superior in his rhetoric but not in his political management. The votes demanded by the ministry easily prevailed to defeat his attack, and the rearmament commenced.

Then Pitt made a serious mistake, which provided Fox with another opportunity. Pitt unwisely directed his wrath against Russia, which, under Catherine the Great, had defeated Sweden, occupied Poland and the Crimea, and commenced a campaign to seize control of the Dardanelles by defeating Turkey. Pitt viewed these events as threatening both English trade and the European balance of power. In a debate that lasted for nine days in March 1792, Fox successfully led an Opposition rejection of war with Russia.

On 1 March Fox made what some have characterized as his greatest speech. What, he demanded, did Pitt's proposal mean? "To save the Turks from being too much humbled? No; they are in a worse situation than they would have been if we had not armed at all." What Pitt intended, he argued, was a mishmash of contradictions. "We are now tied down by treaties, and fettered by stipulations! We have guaranteed to Russia what before we said would be unsafe for the Turks to yield, and dangerous for the peace of Europe for Russia to possess!" Pitt was forced to withdraw from his plan for war and would have been removed from office except that Fox, whom the king detested, was the only alternative for prime minister. Pitt's loss of this crucial vote was the result of his growing isolation, so that he "was not in touch with his colleagues, still less with the pulse of the people."[8] Fox spoke the language of peace, which was what the public and the Parliament most wanted to hear.

What, in this set of circumstances, did public speaking accomplish? Both much and little. An unwise war with Russia was diverted, but peace was preserved only temporarily. The turmoil in Europe rose to a higher pitch. In July, just four months later, Russia and Austria combined to invade France. The French reacted by invading the Netherlands, where English trade was of paramount importance. This new set of circumstances led the public to favor war, and the war against France began. Russia, instead of being the enemy, was now an ally. As generally happens during a war, the influence of debate in Parliament subsided.

Fox not only sensed this effect, but also he was exhausted. He married his mistress, Mrs. Armistead, and retreated from Parliament to his books, his leisure, and his pursuit of happiness. For a time he abandoned the forum of debate. The judgment of Burke seemed to be vindicated. What he expressed in his *Reflections on the Revolution in France* had become the general view: "On the scheme of this barbarous philosophy, which is the offspring of cold hearts and muddy understandings . . . our institutions can never be embodied. . . . There ought to be a system of manners in every nation, which a well-disposed mind would be disposed to relish. To make us love our country, our country ought to be lovely." What this loveliness demanded was to take up arms against the threat to civilization itself. Few now disagreed that "the French were a set of demons. They had murdered their king, and cast off religion; it was, therefore, the duty of surrounding nations to put them out of the pale of civilized society—to treat them as robbers and pirates; and whatever violence might have resulted from such treatment was to be charged to the revolutionary spirit of the French."[9]

What is rhetorically significant is that Burke, even earlier than Fox, sought to exert his influence not by speeches in Parliament but by aiming toward the larger audience available through print. Burke's reasons were in part that since he was separated from his old friends it was awkward for him to stand in their presence, and also in the presence of his longtime adversaries, to utter sentiments that politically operated against positions he had advocated in prior years. Another reason was that in order to combat French ideology he felt himself forced to treat the question with a degree of complexity that even he realized was better suited for readers than for auditors. Beyond this, Burke, like Fox, was weary of the concentration and combative readiness demanded by oral debate. Writing served his current needs much better. Sheltered by the distance between writer and readers, Burke avoided the instant rebuttals from longtime associates and also the embarrassment of being applauded by longtime opponents. His consistency was more real than was immediately observable. Now, as during the American Revolution, he was the champion of a distressed [English] population. But not now, as then, did he ridicule "the indictment of a whole [French] people." And not now, as then, was he supporting the love of liberty that required rebellion against governmental tyrannies. Basically however, his views were unchanged.

Aside from his foolish praise of the "age of chivalry," which he asserted the Terror had washed away in blood, his perception of the long-range effects of the Revolution was truly prophetic—as when he warned that a military dictatorship under "some popular general, who understands the art of conciliating the soldiery, and who possesses the spirit of command, shall draw all eyes upon himself."[10] Scholars of later generations have traced a consistency of conservatism throughout the whole of Burke's life. But political persuasion is constrained to deal with immediate rather than with retrospective perceptions. In the immediate excitement of the time, Burke appeared to have made a complete reversal in his political stance. As he himself saw it, it was not he but the Old Whigs who had made a virtual recantation of their fundamental principles. To the New Whigs, whom he sought to rally, he complained in a speech on 9 June 1791 that it was Fox who had "deserted old friends and had preferred a new set in the party."

In the debating forum of the Commons, Fox also felt obliged to defend himself against the facile charge of inconsistency. On 21 January 1794, in the midst of the war with France, Fox came back from his semiretirement to refute the claim of the Tory spokesman, Lord Mornington, "that while the present, or any other Jacobin government exists in France, no proposition for peace can be received by us." Fox, in reply, asserted that, "I clearly think war might have been avoided." Then he defended his consistency.

> Such was the opinion which I expressed last year, contrary to the sense of the majority of this House, contrary to the voice of the nation at large, and contrary to the sentiments of some of those friends whom I most highly valued. Such was the opinion which I supported at the price of any political weight which I might possess in this House; at the price of any little popularity which I might enjoy abroad; and of what was still more dear to me, the friendship of those with whom I was most closely connected. However painful the sacrifices which I was then obliged to make, I repent not of what I then did; on mature reflection, I find as

much solid satisfaction from the advice I then gave, and from the conduct I then pursued, as it is possible to derive from the consciousness that they were precisely what they ought to have been.

For a time Fox's vigor was restored. With remarkable courage in resisting the demand for patriotic support of a war being waged, Fox spoke again and again against the folly of trying to impose English standards upon the French people; he also warned against the reactionary restrictions being imposed upon the English. On 30 May 1794, he contemptuously dismissed as "elegant rubbish" the justifications made by the ministry "upon false pretenses." And he exclaimed, "Desperate therefore, indeed, must be that war in which each wound inflicted on our enemy would at the same time inflict one on ourselves." A year later, on 29 October 1795, he described the hardships of the English populace and cried out, "Oh, miserable England, to what state have you fallen . . . the heart of every manly Briton sheds tears of blood."

"Not Fighting, They Are Pausing"

The war continued through a series of bloody and futile battles, the principal result being that in December 1799, Napoleon named himself first consul of France, with complete control over the government. One of his first acts was to send a letter written in his own hand to Prime Minister Pitt, suggesting that the war was fruitless and had been waged too long. Pitt, seeing victory in prospect, summarily dismissed this overture. In a speech on 3 February 1800, he demanded that an inquiry should be made into the origins of the war, to show that throughout its eight years France was always the aggressor. He also denounced the atrocities of the French against other European nations. And he characterized the spirit of the French Revolution as being not a love of liberty but "an insatiable love of aggrandizement, and an implacable spirit of destruction against all the civil and religious institutions of every country."

The issues were clear. Burke had died in 1797, but his views of the French Revolution could not have been better summarized. Fox, contrarily, persisted in his own conviction that the Revolution and its aftermath were solid—however unpalatable—steps toward a vastly better future in which egalitarianism, justice, and international peace would become feasible.

When Pitt concluded his speech rejecting the peace overture, Fox rose instantly to reply. The night was far advanced, and Fox apologized for holding the House longer in session. "Exhausted as the attention of the House must be," he said, "nothing but a deep sense of my duty could have induced me to trouble you at all, and particularly to request your indulgence at such an hour." His preparation was general rather than specific, for during the past decade the relations of England with France had been his main preoccupation.

As for the origin of the war, he pointed out that it was begun not by France but by Austria and Prussia. As for French atrocities, they had been no worse than those committed by England's allies. He pointed out that Pitt himself had sought to make peace in 1796 and 1797. "When is this war to end?" he demanded. Pitt's answer, he declared, was "Not till we establish the house of Bourbon—or at least, not until we have further experience with Napoleon in order better to understand the scope of his ambitions." This reasoning Fox blistered with scorn: "So that we are called upon to go on merely as a *speculation* . . . to keep Buonaparte some time longer at war, as a state of *probation* . . . to try an *experiment*, if he will not behave himself better than heretofore!" Then he turned to what for many of his listeners was the chief reason for fighting the revolutionists—their crusade against religion. Slyly, he sought to turn this argument against its adherents:

> Sir, if I understand the true precepts of the Christian religion as set forth in the New Testament, I must be permitted to say that there is no such thing as a rule or doctrine by which we are directed, or can be justified, in waging a war for religion. The idea is subversive of the very foundations upon which it stands, which are those of peace and goodwill among men. Religion never was and never can be, a justifiable cause of war; but it has been too often grossly used as a pretext and the apology for the most unprincipled wars.

Another major reason for fighting the French was that they invaded and sought to conquer their neighboring nations—a conduct which, he admitted, "cannot be justified." However, "is this the moment for us to dwell upon these enormities—to waste our time, and inflame our passions, by recriminating upon each other?" To follow such a course was to use rhetoric not to accommodate differences but to aggravate them. "So, in this war of words, if we are to use only offensive weapons, if we are to indulge only in invective and abuse, the contest must be eternal. If this war of reproach and invective is to be countenanced, may not the French with equal reason complain of the outrages and horrors of the powers opposed to them? If we must not treat with the French on account of the iniquity of their former transactions, ought we not to be as scrupulous of connecting ourselves with other powers equally criminal?" From this he went on to itemize crimes by their allies in the name of "this war for religion, social order, and the rights of nations." England, too, he ventured to say, had committed grave crimes during the war. Therefore, "we have no right to refuse to treat with the French on this ground." This, he realized, was a dangerous argument, but it had to be considered. "It is impossible to deny the facts . . . It is a painful thing to me, Sir, to be obliged to go back to these unfortunate periods of this history of this war, and of the conduct of this country; but . . . I think I have said enough to prove that if the French have been guilty, we have not been innocent."

Instead of leaving this unpalatable subject, however, he went further, to denounce England's continuance in the slave trade, which had been justified with such rationalizations as "I am not guilty of the horrible crime of tearing that mother from her infants; that husband from his wife; of depopulating that village; of depriving that family of their sons, the support of their aged parents! No; thank Heaven! I am not guilty of this horror; I only bought them in the fair way of trade."

He was not defending France, he insisted. "No man regrets more than than I do the atrocities France has committed." But this was not the point. "Are we for ever to deprive ourselves of the benefits of peace because France has perpetrated acts of injustice?"

> Sir, what is the question this night? We are called upon to support ministers in refusing a frank, candid, and respectful offer of negotiation, and to countenance them in continuing the war. Now I would put the question in another way. Suppose the ministers . . . had breathed a spirit of peace, your benches would have resounded with rejoicings. . . . On the present occasion, then, I ask for the vote of none but of those who . . . would have cheerfully and heartily voted with the minister for an address directly the reverse of this. . . .
>
> But what is our present conduct founded on but a theory, and that a most wild and ridiculous theory? What are we fighting for? Not for a principle; not for security; not for conquest even; but merely . . . to discover whether a gentleman in Paris may not turn out a better man than we now take him to be.

He came to his conclusion with reasoning supported by emotional intensity. "Where then, Sir, is this war, which on every side is pregnant with such horrors, to be carried? Where is it to stop? . . . I see no end to human misery. And all this without an intelligible motive—all this because you may gain a better peace a year or two hence! . . . Gracious God, Sir, is war a state of probation? Is peace a rash system?"

He turned to ridicule of the ministerial argument that there should be a pause in which to improve their military position before accepting a peace treaty. His voice dripped with sarcasm. "But if a man were present now at a field of slaughter, and were to inquire for what they were fighting: 'Fighting!' would be the answer, 'They are not fighting, they are *pausing*.' 'Why is that man expiring? Why is that other writhing with agony? What means this implacable fury?' The answer must be: 'You are quite wrong, Sir, to deceive yourself.—They are not fighting.—Do not disturb them—they are merely *pausing!*'" Fox himself paused, to look around the House. "Sir, I have done. I have told you my opinion. . . . I have a right to expect the vote of every gentleman who would have voted with the ministers in an addresss to His Majesty diametrically opposite to the motion this night."

Powerful as his speech was, and truly as it represented the war weariness of the public, it could not prevail. Like those who 160 years later opposed the American war in Vietnam, Fox opened himself to the charge of being unpatriotic. Along with abuse, he also received high praise, such as that published in the *Morning Post:* "He stood against the Court—he stood against the Country—he stood against both united—he was the isthmus, lashed by the waves of democracy on the one side and the billows of despotism on the other, unmoved by either, superior to both." It was a nice tribute, and Fox enjoyed it, but the party he led was in disarray. It was small comfort that Pitt's majority was also split in disagreements over the budget, over Catholic emancipation, over Irish policies, and over what to do about the war. To make matters even worse, King George suffered another of his recurring mental illnesses. Pitt resigned the prime ministry to be replaced by his friend Addington. A peace treaty was signed on 27 March 1802. But it was no more than a patched-up truce, and the war began again, just a year later.

Leadership was in flux. On 21 January 1806, Pitt died, at only forty-seven years of age, with the bitterness of knowing that almost all he stood for, both personally and officially, had failed. On 13 September of that same year Fox also died, in his fifty-seventh year, asserting stoutly, "I die happy!"—even though his ambitions had been thwarted, and such victories as he had won were to bear fruit mostly in years yet to come. These two seasoned antagonists were buried with high honors in Westminster Abbey, just inches apart.

Burke, by this time, was almost forgotten. Only Sheridan from among these four remained. He briefly enjoyed the political reward of being brought into the Grenville ministry as secretary of the navy—a post for which he was peculiarly unfit. It proved to be a brief triumph. When the war with France was renewed, he resigned to take his place again in Opposition. Three years later he was ruined financially when his Drury Lane Theatre was burned. When he died in 1816, he, like his famous compeers, was buried in Westminster Abbey. His funeral was conducted with great pomp. But he was not honored as a statesman; his place was in Poets' Corner, apart from those who point the nation's political way.

"The Fury Which You Have Inspired"

Nevertheless, for Sheridan himself, it was politics, not the theatre, that was his greatest concern. His speeches were the productions he valued most. As the war continued, his denunciations of it were sharper even than those of Fox. Typical of both his views and his persuasive strategy—which amounted simply to direct attack—was the speech he made on 21 January 1794. In it he admitted the wickedness of the French but charged that England was an even worse culprit.

> We had unsettled their reason, and then reviled their insanity; we drove them to the extremities that produced the evils we arraigned; we baited them like wild beasts, until at length we made them so. . . . Such has been your conduct toward France, that you have created the passions which you prosecute; you make a nation to be cut off from the world; you covenant their extermination; you swear to hunt them in their inmost recesses; you load them with every species of execration; and you now come forth with whining declamations on the horror of their turning upon you with the fury which you have inspired.

Obviously, this was no way to win votes or to court popularity. What it amounted to was proof of his utter sincerity and depth of feeling. What is remarkable is that such utterances, by him and by Fox, were allowed to be made. Freedom of parliamentary discussion could not be further enlarged or more truly preserved. And it was the maintenance of freedom with which Sheridan was most fundamentally concerned. His war against war was waged basically in defense of the liberties of Englishmen, which were being whittled away.

In this same speech, Sheridan devoted himself primarily to his libertarian theme. "We are engaged in a contest, on the issue of which depend the maintenance of our constitution, laws, and religion; and the security of all civilized society." He had given up the quest for votes—"for never, surely, was the minority so small." But, he felt confident, the stand of the Whigs for human rights "would make us more formidable." He excoriated Pitt by paraphrasing what he interpreted as being Pitt's promises to his subservient majority. "Do I demand of you, wealthy citizens, to lend your hoards to the government without interest? On the contrary, when I come to propose a loan, there is not a man of you to whom I shall I shall not hold out at least a job in every part of the subscription, and a usurious profit upon every pound you devote to the necessities of your country. Do I demand of you, my fellow placemen and brother pensioners, that you should sacrifice any part of your stipends to the public exigency; on the contrary, am I not daily increasing your emoluments and your numbers?" He sought to shame them by demanding, "Can it be that people of high rank, and professing high principles, that *they* or *their families*, should seek to thrive on the spoils of misery and fatten on the meals wrested from industrious poverty? . . . Oh! Shame! Shame! Is this a time for selfish intrigues, and the dirty traffic for lucre and emoluments? . . . Is there nothing that whispers to that right honorable gentleman that the crisis is too big, that the times are too gigantic, to be ruled by the little hackneyed and everyday ordinary means of corruption?"

In the following year, on 5 January, Sheridan introduced a bill to restore the suspended habeas corpus, declaring that he "would not consent that the people of England should be fettered and shackled even for an hour." He argued that the character of a people is shaped by the conduct of their government. The way to stem the spread of Jacobinism was not by depriving the people of their freedom but by maintaining it.

As a statesman, Sheridan is yet to be given his due. No less than Fox was he the creator of the modern English constitution. As a political leader he was in the forefront of the movement to limit the powers of the Crown. In his sympathy with the poor, in his belief in taxation of the rich, and in his hatred of injustice in all its forms, he was far in advance of his age. His best epitaph is his earnest plea to the Parliament that "the poorest people in the kingdom were those who stood most in need of friends in that House." The spirit of reform that he did his best to animate was strengthened by his parliamentary career, even though it was not effectuated until after Waterloo.

All through the contentious eighteenth century, those who most truly pointed the way for the future were mostly in the Opposition. The votes they vainly sought to win were not available to persuasion, for they had been bought. What persuasion could do, they did. It was by their efforts that the issues were clarified. It was by their leadership that a spirit of independence and an assertive demand for natural rights was aroused and supported. It was the goal they set around which the underlying forces of social change could converge. This, rather than the winning of immediate victories, was their contribution. It is for this that history is in their debt. They protected the vital and expanding realm of what was discussable, and they greatly enlarged it. And it is this that democracy ultimately requires.

Notes

1. M. Duckitt and H. Wragg, *Selected English Letters (XV–XIX Centuries)* (London: Oxford University Press, 1913), p. 224. Such letters provide valuable insight into the nature of the audience.
2. From his *Second Letter to a Noble Lord*, reinforcing the sentiments he had published in 1790, in his *Reflections on the Revolution in France*.
3. A. J. F. Taylor, introduction to *Pitt the Younger*, by Jarrett, p. 10.
4. John Lockhart, *Memoirs of the Life of Sir Walter Scott, Bart*. 10 vols. (Edinburgh, 1837–38), with Scott's *Journals* and *Familiar Letters*, edited by David Douglas (1890, 1894), 10:32.
5. Lord Roseberry, *Pitt* (London: Macmillan, 1915), p. 95.
6. P. W. Wilson, *Pitt the Younger* (Garden City, N.Y.: Doubleday, Doran, 1932), p. 243.
7. These citations are from Reid, *Fox*, pp. 278–79.
8. Roseberry, *Pitt*, p. 109 and chap. 6, passim.
9. This summation is from Goodrich, *Select British Eloquence*, p. 456.
10. *Reflections on the French Revolution* in *Works*, 4:243.

13
The Problems of Ireland—A Rhetorical Battleground

Irish feelings run high. Their memories are stained with a deep sense of wrongs: of massacres in the time of Elizabeth I and of Cromwell; of pitiless exploitation by landlords; of mercantile policies that strangled their trade; of the denial of religious, civil, and economic justice to the vast Catholic majority; of contemptuous treatment by a ruling class that denied them opportunity to be educated and then sneered at their ignorance. Such conditions condemned Ireland to being for many centuries in Lecky's words, "the most degraded land in Europe." But this is only a part of their story.

The Irishman has become stereotyped. He is sometimes viewed as an awkward rustic with an intense Celtic emotionalism, equally hot in enmity and friendship; with an imagination that sees leprechauns in glens; fiercely proud and quarrelsome; with a temperament inclined both to rollicking good humor and to surly resentment; instantly ready to fight, whether with a shillelagh or with hot words. Such a portrayal, like all stereotypes, conceals more than it reveals. The Irish are far more complex than the cliché suggests.

In many respects the Irish are like other minority peoples who have been exploited, impoverished, belittled, and on occasion aroused to resistance. If they have been combative, it is on such terms as Walter Hussy Burgh declared, to be greeted with a storm of applause, in the Irish Parliament in 1783: "Talk not to me of peace. Ireland is not at peace. It is smothered war. England has sown her laws as dragon's teeth, and they have sprung up armed men."[1] Their resistance consisted in part in organized terrorism, since they were unable to organize armies; and in part it has been a rhetorical campaign of eloquence and argument. Both methods had significant effects, but it was their words that most truly won.

Militarism often has the disadvantage of being largely self-defeating. Winning a war does not insure winning the peace. As the English learned to their own cost, a nation conquered is not likely to become willing or obedient subjects. Police power to counter armed resistance does not suffice. And as the Irish learned, force countered by greater force does not of itself often prevail.

While rhetoric differs from militarism in avoidance of bloodshed, it resembles it in crucial ways. Rhetoric has available the chance of converting enmity into friendship, or at least of surmounting exploitation by enlarging understanding and by demonstrating advantages derived from new relationships that are based on mutual consideration. Discussion may lead to compromises that foster cooperation. The weaponry of persuasion may alter attitudes, revise convictions, and induce feelings that result in a change of policies and of actions. Such verbal weaponry may consist of ridicule, sarcasm, and wit with which to snipe at vulnerable positions. Or conciliatory ambushes of good humor and of concessions may persuade opponents to abandon entrenched positions of superior power. Still other persuasive endeavors may group facts, logic, and emotional appeals in direct frontal attacks. Such verbal strategies as invective, denunciation, and personal abuse may render opposition ineffective. Speech of this sort aims to demolish prestige, to weaken the status, and to undermine the credibility of opponents. Inspirational appeals serve to rally and to unite a following. All such means were freely employed in the verbal warfare waged by eloquent Irish leaders.

"Like the Coldness of Death"

The relationship of Ireland and England as the eighteenth century drew to a close was far from favorable to rational discussion. J. A. Froude piled up evidence to support the claim that the Irish were ungovernable except by force.[2] W. E. H. Lecky wrote six passionate volumes to demonstrate that it was English tyranny that made them intractable.[3] Such a revisionist historian as Edith Johnston shows that English intemperance was matched by stubborn Irish irrationalism.[4] No history is complete, and none can be written except by selecting and arranging facts that accord with the writer's theme. Lecky pointed this out while borrowing an image from Froude in replying to him.

> There is a method of dealing with historical facts which has been happily compared to that of a child with his box of letters, who picks out and arranges those letters, and those only, which will spell the words on which he has previously determined, leaving all others untouched. In Irish history this method has been abundantly practiced.[5]

A rhetorical examination of the Irish question must deal with the "creative stress" which is "at once the expression and the chronicle"[6] that culminated in a burst of passionate speaking by Irish patriots. What these speeches represent is not so much an organized crusade or campaign as they are a series of anguished protests that gradually merged into a set of attainable demands. The evolution was disorderly, for unity among the Irish was difficult to attain. Circumstances rendered it all but impossible.

The injustice entrenched in Ireland was not only policed by absentee English landlords and London politicians but was fully supported by a small minority of self-interested and powerful Irish Anglican aristocrats. Native landlords were far closer to the English rulers in their interests and sympathies than to their Catholic tenants. The established system brought them rental income even in excess of what the farm plots could produce. The fifty-to-one who were Catholics were held under harsh bondage. They were forbidden either to attend local schools or to go abroad for study. They were prohibited from holding office and from voting. They were required to pay tithes to support the Church of England in addition to maintaining their own priests. They were despised and condemned for their faith. Their impoverishment and the resentments that resulted combined to make them unmanageable subjects. Crimes, rioting, and terrorism became widespread. Tenants and workmen, denied the opportunity to support their families, slumped into apathy, laziness, and disorderliness. Hatred, equally venomous on both sides, divided the people from their oppressors. And the fierce competition for the means of survival separated the people from one another.

The spirit of resistance among them was reawakened by the American Revolution. Henry Flood, in a speech in the Irish Parliament in 1783, stated it rightly when he said, "A voice from America shouted to liberty, the echo of it caught your people as it passed the Atlantic, and they renewed the voice till it reverberated here." But the same event also confused further the sentiments of the leading Irish spokesmen. Very few among them had any intention of breaking the union of Ireland with England. What the great majority desired was autonomy within the union. What they sought was not independence but fair treatment as English citizens. This was the sentiment that led Flood to warn the ministry in Westminster that, unless such rights were granted, "destruction will come upon the British Empire like the coldness of death. It will creep upon it from the extreme parts."

The French Revolution had a much more divisive effect. Such youthful radicals as Napper Tandy, Wolfe Tone, and Robert Emmet went to France, met with Napoleon, and pledged to use their Society of United Irishmen to help him to defeat England. The great bulk of the people, however, were horrified by French atheism and remained loyal to their church in its efforts to unite Europe against France. When the French threatened to invade Ireland to use it as a base from which to attack England, Irish spokesmen asked the English for protection. The most able of the Protestant leaders, Henry Grattan, was a friend and disciple of Edmund Burke and fully shared his mentor's dread of Jacobinism and dislike for democracy. The majority in the Irish Parliament opposed emancipation of the Catholics as stoutly as did the majority in England. The Irish aristocrats, like the English exploiters, profited so greatly from the existing system that their primary aim was to maintain it.

The control over the Irish Parliament by the Crown was cemented by corrupt controls that were even more extensive than those that built for the ministry a dependable majority in Westminster. As early as 13 October 1761, Charles Lucas, a pioneer among the rebels, aptly described the typical member as one "who had nothing either to hope or to fear from his constituents, but from a minister his expectations may be reasonably great; he will be tempted to oppose the measures of a good minister, merely that he may be bought into his service, and sell himself to the service of a bad minister for the same advantage; the minister may afford to bid high, when he buys for life." The Earl of Charlemont, another pioneer among the rebels, in making notes of this speech, declared of it that it "raised a spirit in the people without which all our labours would have been fruitless."[7] It should be noted that the speech had public effect only because freedom of the press, allowed in Ireland almost as fully as in England, permitted its publication.

A few other independents in the Irish Parliament also joined in the efforts to undermine the bought majority. Most notable among them was Edmund Malone, a wealthy and prominent judge and father of the noted Shakespeare editor, who was described by Grattan as "a man of the finest intellect that any country ever produced," and who won acclaim even from the English administrators in Dublin as being even more eloquent than Lord Mansfield or the Elder William Pitt. None of Malone's speeches was preserved, but he made his influence felt as one of the first leaders to speak boldly on behalf of Catholic emancipation.[8] Another was Hely Hutchinson, also a member of the privileged class, who became provost of Trinity College, and who made stormy and insistent speeches demanding educational opportunities for Catholics and for Protestant Dissidents.[9] The Earl of Charlemont, a friend of Burke and of David Hume, was too diffident to speak in Parliament, but he used his social status to support those who were rebels against existing laws.

"No Longer a Wretched Colony"

The first of the truly great leaders to speak out for Irish rights was Henry Flood, a man of great wealth, of high intellect, and of established prestige as a son of the chief justice of the Irish bench. Lecky describes him as "one of the greatest of parliamentary reasoners . . . of grave sarcasm, of invective, of weighty judicial statement, and of . . . a keen and prescient, though somewhat skeptical judgment."[10] Through his speeches, in the course of a very checkered career, Flood organized the first effective Opposition in the Irish Parliament and also helped to arouse and to unify public opinion.

Flood's career illustrates clearly the rhetorical problems that beset Irish patriots in that time of transition. They did not have a national constituency to represent, for there was no such thing. The wealthy, educated, and socially dominant families were strongly attached to England both by sentiments and by self-interest. The impoverished, uneducated, and generally despised mass of the people were impelled by their religion to oppose the atheistic French revolutionists, which meant in effect rallying to the support of the English government, even while their religion kept them disenfranchised and deprived of many civil rights.

A leader who felt the grievances suffered by his countrymen was confounded by the disunity resulting from such contradictory factors. Since leadership could come only from the class that was dominant, it was inevitably characterized by prejudices that had come to be accepted as rational convictions. As deeply as Flood wanted to improve the lot of his exploited countrymen, it was difficult for him to know what should be done or how. He never doubted that Ireland was and should be a part of Great Britain. His loyalty to the monarchy never wavered. Moreover, he shared the antagonism felt by his class toward the "popish" Catholics. And he dreaded the prospect that French Jacobinism might result in the destruction of the aristocratic system, to replace it with rule by the many instead of by the best. In these views he was simply taking for granted the values and beliefs of the time. Despite such prejudices, Flood clearly perceived and deeply resented the fact that the Irish people were being brutally exploited. And he determined to exert his best efforts to bring into effect such remedies as he could.

His father's influence brought him into the tightly controlled Irish Parliament in 1759. For sixteen years he spoke often, boldly, and eloquently for the right of the "people" (by which he meant only Protestant landowners) to vote for members of the Irish Parliament; for the establishment of an Irish army that would be under the control of the Irish Parliament; and for "cultivation of the public mind" by broadening educational opportunities. During this period he formed a close friendship with another rising orator, Henry Grattan, who became his chief aide in organizing the parliamentary Opposition. Then in 1775, as the outbreak of the American Revolution led the British ministry to strengthen its parliamentary majority, Flood was offered a huge pension (which he did not need but accepted) and was appointed vice-treasurer and a member of the privy council that served as a pseudocabinet for the lord lieutenant who administered Ireland for the Crown. Flood's followers were astounded by this "apostasy." During his latter years, Flood usually voted with the majority and came to be bitterly denounced by the following he had deserted.

In his own view, Flood remained consistent to his principles and felt that he could battle for them better from inside the government than from within a weak minority. The means by which he sought to do so are indicated in a typical speech he made, in 1783.

> If there is a pride of England, there is a pride of Ireland too. Now I ask which ought to give way, for one must, and I answer impartially, that which has the worst foundation. Now which is that? The pride of England in this case is a pride of wrong, and the pride of usurpation. The pride of Ireland is the pride of right, the pride of justice, the pride of constitution. I will not ask after that, which ought to give way; but it is wrong to put this question principally upon pride.[11]

Irish patriots could applaud such sentiments, and the English rulers could tolerate them. But it is impossible to serve two masters. The choice between them that Flood had to make was forced by the agitation of radicals who demanded self-rule for Ireland and who organized bands of terrorists to cause such disorder that the English might decide to withdraw from the island. More soberly, Wolfe Tone and Robert Emmet, with others, organized the United Irishmen to conduct meetings and build a following pledged to Irish rights. One measure they undertook was to develop a Volunteer army and a Volunteer Assembly that would control it. Since the purported function of these bodies was to enforce order, the English did not forbid them, but the ministry did demand that the army be reduced and that it be under the direction of the lord lieutenant. On this issue Flood supported the government; Henry Grattan supported the Volunteers. In a bitter speech Flood denounced his old friend and aide, using terms that might more truly have been applied to himself—calling Grattan "that mendicant patriot who was bought by his country, and sold that country for prompt payment." Grattan replied by denouncing Flood and then by stating his own case.

> I found Ireland on her knees. I watched over her with paternal solicitude; I have traced her progress from injuries to arms, and from arms to liberty. . . . Ireland is now a nation. In this new character I hail her, and bowing to her august presence, I say, *Esto perpetua!*

The year was 1782, and Ireland was far indeed from being an independent country. But the sentiment for independence had been planted and was being nourished by the radicals, with Grattan as their most effective spokesman. In this same speech he went on to describe the best that could then be said for the small beginnings that had been made.

> She is no longer a wretched colony, returning thanks to her governor for his rapine, and to her king for his oppression; nor is she now a squabbling, fretful sectary, perplexing her little wits, and firing her furious

statutes with bigotry, sophistry, disabilities, and death, to transmit to posterity insignificance and war.[12]

Such sentiments, uttered in the Irish Parliament with such rashness, indicate how far the Irish patriots had proceeded along the way to open rebellion. The fact that they were tolerated, and that Grattan was neither imprisoned nor silenced, also indicates that the English were making a serious endeavor to satisfy the Irish sufficiently to keep them controllable. Various reforms were instituted—mostly refraining from enforcing harsh laws rather than by changing them.

Flood sought to regain the leadership of the patriots, which he had surrendered, by introducing a reform bill that would grant autonomy to the Irish Parliament and provide for election of its membership by Protestant freeholders. He defended his bill with a speech in which he implored King George to recognize "that their humble wish to have certain manifest perversions of the parliamentary representation of this kingdom remedied by the Legislature in some reasonable degree might not be imputed to any spirit of innovation in them, but by a sober and laudable desire to uphold the Constitution . . . and to perpetuate the cordial union of the kingdom."[13] What he proposed was reform that would go far enough to prevent rebellion but that would not weaken the dominance of the Irish landlords by granting Catholic emancipation. The compromise he advocated was unacceptable to both the English government and the increasingly restive Irish populace. Rioting broke out and a mob actually invaded the Irish Parliament. The bill Flood introduced was denied in London. As Lecky summed up Flood's position, "it could not be said that in either country Flood's later years added to his reputation."

Three years later, in 1785, Flood bought a seat in the English Parliament so that he could carry his campaign to Westminster. But his effective influence both inside the government and among the Irish people had come to an end. In a final effort to reestablish his leadership, Flood introduced a bill in the English Commons asking for an additional one hundred members, all Protestants, to be added to the Irish Parliament. Burke, Fox, and Pitt all praised and supported him; Flood ended his speech supporting his bill with a plea for exoneration from the charges his enemies were making against him:

> I appeal to you whether my conduct has been that of an advocate or an agitator; whether I have often trespassed upon your attention; whether ever except upon a question of importance, and whether I then wearied you with ostentation or prolixity. . . . I have no fear except that of doing wrong, nor have I a hope on the subject but that of doing some service before I die. The accident of my position has not made me a partisan; and I never lamented that situation till now that I find myself as unprotected as I fear the people of England be on this occasion.[14]

His bill did not carry, nor did he mollify his critics. His memory is tarnished by his having left the rebels to join the government, and his personality was too pompous to win friendship. What should be noted to his credit is that he stepped forth from his safe and luxurious position to identify himself with the inconsequential group who continued in the movement for Irish rights. And if he did not remain with them to the end, he at least gave them some respectability with which to counter the accusation that they were no more than noisy radicals. Perhaps, as Lecky believed, he sacrificed his fervor to his ambitions. In any event, after the failure of his last effort, he resigned the seats he held in both the Irish and the English Parliaments and retired to his country house in Kilkenny to live out his few remaining years in morose isolation. In December 1791, in his fifty-ninth year, he died—unappreciated by the English and condemned by the Irish. The way of moderation to which he pointed proved to be a futile path.

The radicalism that undermined Flood's compromise efforts was largely instigated by two fiery young men who came from the comfortable Protestant middle class.

Theobald Wolfe Tone, son of a Dublin carriage maker, was educated for the law and admitted to the Irish bar but devoted himself to the writing of pamphlets attacking English rule of Ireland. In 1791 he joined in organizing the Society of United Irishmen, which undertook to unite the Catholics and Protestants to secure parliamentary reform. When this proved to be unavailing, Wolfe flung himself into a violent movement to set up an Irish Republic through armed rebellion. Scorning the moderate appeals of Flood and of Grattan, Tone sought the support of the revolutionaries Danton and Thomas Paine. He went first to America, then to France, where he was named as adjutant-general in the French army. In December 1796, he led a French force of 15,000 men to invade Ireland, and called for an armed rising of the populace. Tone was captured and tried by a court-martial, to which he spoke boldly of his determination "by fair and open war to procure the separation of the two countries." He added, "From my earliest youth I have regarded the connection between Great Britain and Ireland as the curse of the Irish nation." As a soldier captured in war, he asked that he be shot rather than hanged; when this was refused, he managed to die in his cell by cutting his throat with a penknife.

Robert Emmet was the son of the physician to the lord-lieutenant of Ireland. He was educated at the University of Dublin, where he won attention as a fiery orator, while achieving a distinguished academic record in mathematics and chemistry. After a few months of political intrigue with the United Irishmen, he went to France to work on plans for an invasion of Ireland. In October 1802, he returned to Dublin to work in secrecy to organize a rising. When his plans failed and his associates became disillusioned, Emmet donned a green and white uniform, put himself at the head of eighty men and engaged in street brawls until soldiers dispersed his followers. Emmet was captured while trying to escape to America, was tried, and was convicted of treason. Before being hanged on 20 September 1803, he made a speech from the dock that remains an eloquent statement of Irish resistance. "The man dies," he told his judges defiantly, "but his memory lives. . . I wish that my memory and my name may animate those who survive me. . . . When my country takes her place among the nations of the earth, *then* and *not till then*, let my epitaph be written."[15]

"Against Rank Majorities"

In contrast with the ineffectual moderation of Flood and the self-defeating violence of the radicals, the effective leadership of the Irish resistance belonged to Henry Grattan. He was born in 1746 in Dublin, the son of a wealthy Protestant father who served in the Irish Parliament and who was deeply grieved to find his offspring developing liberal tendencies. In Dublin University Grattan distinguished himself as a student of the classics and made a special study of eloquence and rhetoric. He memorized long passages from the Greek and Roman orators and by reciting them aloud he so disturbed his landlady that she had him evicted. While studying law in the Middle Temple in London he went often to the Parliament and was entranced by the speeches of Lord Chatham.

From study of such examples, he developed an oratorical style that was marked by metaphors and sententiously epigrammatic sentences. The speeches that he made then and later throughout his life were marked by such grotesque gestures that he reminded his auditors of a gorilla. Lecky, nevertheless, described him as the finest speaker produced in either island after the time of Chatham.

> Considered simply as a debater, he was certainly inferior to both Fox and Pitt, and perhaps to Sheridan; but he combined two of the very highest qualities of a great orator to a degree that was almost unexampled. . . . No British orator except Burke had an equal power of sowing his speeches with profound aphorisms and associating transient questions with eternal truths. His thoughts naturally crystallized into epigrams; his arguments were condensed with such admirable force and clearness that they assumed almost the force of axioms; and they were often interspersed with sentences of poetic beauty, which flashed upon the audience with all the force of sudden inspiration, and which were long remembered and repeated.[16]

What is most notable about this judgment by Lecky is that it makes no claim whatsoever that Grattan's speaking was persuasively influential. The whole emphasis is upon his literary qualities rather than upon his political effectiveness. This is worthy of note particularly as a reminder that oratory was, at least in that time, considered to be an important part of literature. Orations were designed to appeal to good taste as well as to have practical effects. Speakers were admired for their artistry, and their speeches were heard and were read for pleasure, as were poems and novels. It should not be forgotten that one of Burke's proudest productions was his *Essay on the Sublime and the Beautiful,* which deals with standards of artistic taste rather than with political strategy or with the psychology of motivation, and it is by standards of artistry rather than pragmatic effectiveness that many of the most admired orators—Sheridan, for example—were primarily considered. This did not detract from the importance also attached to the quality of thought presented in the speech. Just as novels were and are esteemed in part because of their insightful depiction of personality, character, and problems, and just as poems gain part of their power by their revelation of significant truths, so too were the speeches estimated in terms of their philosophical soundness. As Burke took pains to explain to a meeting of Sam Johnson's circle, speeches that fail to win votes might nevertheless greatly enhance the reputation of the speaker and win for him genuine admiration for his qualities. The winning of immediate decisions is more often the primary function of speech than of writing, but it is not the only function and may not be always the most significant.

The speaking by Grattan did indeed have practical results—in shaping policies, in forming attitudes, in building a unity of sentiment, and in rallying and leading a political following. It also constituted a body of oral literature in which the Irish people took lasting pride, and which helped to instill within them a sense of their own worth. This may have been its greatest effect of all, for as a people the Irish had been so long and so deeply scorned, and were so far degraded by imposed poverty and constrained ignorance that what they most required was leadership that induced them to rise in their own estimation and to demand acceptance as an estimable part of the human race.

The political career of Grattan commenced in 1775 when he was just twenty-six, when Lord Charlemont brought him into the Irish Parliament as the representative of one of his family-owned boroughs. Grattan quickly became prominent precisely because of his excellence as a speaker. The policies for which he spoke included freedom of Irish trade from imposed restrictions, the maintenance of a separate Irish army, and the autonomous right of the Irish Parliament to make the laws for the Irish people. When that right appeared to have been granted, Grattan celebrated the occasion with a great speech in the Parliament, on 16 April 1782: "I am now to address a free people. Ages have passed away, and this is the first moment in which you could be distinguished by that appelation. I have spoken on the subject of your liberty so often that I have nothing to add, and have only to admire by what heaven-directed steps you have proceeded until the whole faculty of the nation is braced up to the act of her deliverance." Here, in Grattan's phrase, was the crucial achievement: The Irish people had become a nation.

It was not, however, an independent country—nor did Grattan want it to be. As a nation it was, like England and Scotland, an integral part of Great Britain. This was the goal toward which his efforts aimed. In an earlier speech, on 19 April 1780, he had spelled it out precisely. First had come an assertion of his loyalty to the throne: "I am desirous above all things, next to the liberty of the country, not to accustom the Irish mind to an alien or suspicious habit with regard to Great Britain." But if this view was to prevail, England had heavy responsibilities to correct grievous errors that had long persisted. "The British minister mistakes the Irish character; had he intended to make Ireland a slave, he should have kept her a beggar; there is no middle policy; win her heart by the restoration of her right, or cut off the nation's right hand; greatly emancipate, or fundamentally destroy."

No more than Flood, however, did Grattan see clearly into the future. His basic opinions illustrate how definitely the eighteenth century was tied to the past. Neither democracy nor equality—not even equality of justice—was his ideal. It was not improper, in his view, for Catholics to be required to pay their share in supporting the Church of England. As for political control, he was convinced that it should continue to be vested in the aristocracy, the landowners, and the prosperous merchants. He blamed the Volunteers for appealing to "the lowest classes of the populace." The "mass of talent," he believed, was to be found within the "mass of property." He fully believed, with Burke, that the egalitarian principles of Jacobinism must be held at bay.

The greatest advance by Grattan beyond the doctrines of Flood was that he became the outstanding advocate for Catholic emancipation. "Civil and religious liberty," he insisted, "depends on political power; the community that has no share directly or indirectly in political power has no security for its political liberty." In 1808, when further restrictions were advocated against the Catholics, he spoke against them on 25 May: "If you go back, so will the Catholics; if you make out a law against them, they will make out a case against you; we shall have historian against historian, man of blood against man of blood. The parties will remain unreconciled and irreconcilable; each the victim of their own prejudices; and the result will convince you that the victory remains only for the enemies of both." In 1812, while the feelings animated by the French war threatened to reimpose restrictions that had been relaxed, in a speech on 23 April Grattan exclaimed: "You cannot do it; I say you cannot finally do it. The interest of your country would not support you; the feelings of your country would not support you; it is a proceeding that cannot long be persisted in. . . . A majority cannot overlay a great principle. God will guard his own cause against rank majorities. In vain will men appeal to a church-cry, or to a mock thunder; the proprietor of the bolt is on the side of the people."

In his persuasive strategy on behalf of the Catholics, Grattan tactfully appealed to common ground. He avoided making it a party question. He emphasized that the strongest opposition to the French radicalism came from the European Catholics. He warned against the danger of an outbreak of a religious war. And his moderation was successful; he won support where it was needed most. Pitt's agent in Dublin reported to him that "much credit is due to Mr. Grattan . . . My best opinion is that Mr. Grattan is the most important character in Ireland, and that attaching him to Mr. Pitt's government would be essential. This is difficult. He is high-minded, and resentful, and suspicious. He is, however, very steady and honourable, and will act up to his professions. He has great sway over the public mind, and he must play such a part as not to lose his authority. . . . In the uncertainty of events, his conduct here might be decisive."[17]

All through his career, Grattan held steadily to his main aims: free trade and prosperity for Ireland; autonomy for the Irish Parliament, with its electoral base broadened but with the propertied class maintaining firm control; and justice for the Catholics, who consituted the vast majority of the people. He also remained steady in his loyalty to the English connection. His warning to his own countrymen was consistent: Seek necessary reforms but do so with moderation and with loyalty to the constitution.

"If England is a tyrant," he said in his speech on 19 April 1780, and he repeated the same qualifying sentiment again and again throughout his life, "it is you who have made her so; it is the slave that makes the tyrant, and then murmurs at the master he himself has constituted." He drove home his point with unmistakable clarity: "And as anything less than liberty is inadequate to Ireland, so is it dangerous to Great Britain. We are too near the British nation, we are too conversant with her history, we are too much fired by her example, to be anything less than her equal; anything less, we should be her bitterest enemies—an enemy to that power which smote us with her mace, and to that Constitution from whose blessings we were excluded; to be ground as we have been by the British nation, bound by her Parliament, plundered by her crown, threatened by her enemies, insulted with her protection, while we returned thanks for her condescension, is a system of meanness and misery which has expired in our determination, as I hope it has in her magnanimity."

But amid his loyalty to Great Britain, his spirit was Irish to the core. In the conclusion of that speech, he spoke what the great mass of his fellows felt: "I wish for nothing but to breathe, in this our island, in common with my fellow subjects, the air of liberty. I have no ambition, unless it be the ambition to break your chain, and contemplate your glory. I never will be satisfied as long as the meanest cottager in Ireland has a link of the British chain clanking to his rags; he may be naked, he shall not be in irons; and I do see the time is at hand, the spirit has gone forth, the declaration is planted; and though great men should apostasize, yet the cause will live; and though the public speaker should die, yet the immortal fire shall outlast the organ which conveyed it, and the breath of liberty, like the word of the holy man, will not die with the prophet, but survive him."

Grattan's sentences may not always parse. His choice of words and his phrasing may at times have been better suited to lulling thought than to guiding it. Grammar and precision were not decisive factors, any more than his awkward gestures proved to be a diversion. What came through to his listeners and to the Irish people was his pride in being an Irishman. Like a brawler in a pub, standing erect with a shillelagh in his hand, Grattan used words as weapons with which to repel insults and to renounce tyranny. His speeches were neither crammed with facts nor buttressed with argument. Instead, they were animated with manly emotion and spirited independence. In the opinion of one of his liberal associates, William C. Plunket, whose own eloquence "dazzled and astonished the House,"[18] Grattan's speeches "gave results rather than processes of reasoning. Every sentences was a treasure."[19] The kind of treasure they were was best stated by Grattan himself, in words that may well stand as his epitaph: "I found Ireland on her knees. . . . Ireland is now a nation."

"To Be a State Comes Direct from Heaven"

William Plunket, a highly successful lawyer, won Grattan's admiration both for his persuasive eloquence and for his fervent defense of Irish autonomy during the debates in 1800 on Pitt's proposal to dissolve the Parliament in Dublin and to bring Ireland directly under the lawmaking powers of the English Parliament. The British plan to take away this symbol of Irish identity, said Plunket, was a blunder that will put "an end to our dissensions—through the black cloud which they have collected over us, I see the light breaking in upon this unfortunate country. . . . They have united every rank and description of men by the pressure of this grand and momentous subject; and I tell them that they will see every honest and independent man in Ireland rally round her Constitution."[20] It was a brave speech, with Plunket concluding, "I will resist it to the last drop of my blood . . . and swear eternal hostility against the invaders of their country's freedom." The trouble is that he only partly meant it.

As a Presbyterian, Plunket had small sympathy for the Catholics and opposed their political emancipation. As an ambitious lawyer, he found it expedient to work with the British instead of against them. When Robert Emmet was brought to trial, Plunket accepted appointment as one of the prosecutors. In 1812 he won election to the Westminster Parliament and quickly won recognition as one of its most eloquent speakers. In 1822 he was rewarded with appointment as Ireland's attorney-general, in which post he vigorously combated the Catholic Association and other efforts to enlarge the rights of the Catholic masses, with searing speeches against them, especially in 1825. He lived to the age of ninety, highly honored by England, with a peerage, with appointments as chief justice of the Irish Court of Pleas, and finally as lord chancellor of Ireland. By Irish patriots, however, he was still honored for his bold youthful opposition to the "atrocious conspiracy against the liberties of Ireland"; and his checkered career illustrates the dilemma of those who renounced English misgovernment but not English rule.

Within the structure of the existing laws, the ablest defender of the Irish rebels was John Philpot Curran, who came out from an impoverished background to win public acclaim for his patriotism. Though the government sought to entice him with opportunities to gain wealth and position, he refused to curry favor from government officials. His assertive and even arrogant personality impelled him into two duels—one with that radical patriot Wolfe Tone. But he had in equal degree a generosity of spirit and a warmth of heart that made him a champion of the oppressed. He was accounted "a poet of no mean promise—a wit of almost the highest order—and an orator who might compare with the greatest of his countrymen." His speeches were often weak in reasoning and inaccurate in style, but they exhibited "powers of pathos, imagination, and humour that scarcely met with an equal degree in any of his contemporaries."[21] When he won membership in the English Parliament he favored Flood's Reform Bill, argued for Catholic emancipation, sought to reduce the corruptive influence of grants and pensions, and worked to eliminate provisions in the criminal code that bore inequitably against the Irish. In a speech in the Commons on 13 March 1786, Curran ridiculed the system of buying support for the ministry by grants of pensions, which "teaches the idle and dissolute to look up for that support which they are too proud to stoop and earn."

Curran is best remembered, however, for his defense of Hamilton Rowan, secretary of the United Irishmen, who was charged with having signed an appeal on 3 December 1793 for the Irish Volunteers to rise against English rule. The appeal was in fact incentive to armed rebellion: "Citizen soldiers, to arms! Take up the shield of freedom. . . . The nation is neither insolent nor rebellious, nor seditious; while it knows its rights, it is unwilling to manifest its powers; it would rather supplicate administration to anticipate revolution by well-timed reform, and to save the country in mercy to themselves." Despite this gesture of moderation, the appeal concluded: "Let parochial meetings be held as soon as possible; let each parish send delegates; let the sense of Ulster be again declared from

Dungannon on a day auspicious to union, peace, and freedom; and the spirit of the north will again become the spirit of the nation." The tone was deliberately ambiguous, but the call to arms was unmistakable.

In the trial in which Rowan faced execution for treason, Curran defended him with what Lord Brougham called "the greatest speech of an advocate in ancient and modern times." Curran's argument was not that Rowan was innocent of the act charged, but that what he had called for was not treason but the height of patriotic devotion. The case had been called with the speed more typical of martial law than of normal judicial practice, so that Curran had little time in which to prepare the defense. He would conduct the defense, he assured the jury, "in the honest simplicity of my heart . . . promising . . . to avail myself of no technical artifice or subtlety."

The date was 29 January 1794, just a few days after Rowan had been arrested; and because of this unseemly haste, the first question the jury should decide was "whether Mr. Rowan is pursued as a criminal, or hunted down as a victim." The real aim of the prosecutors, Curran said, was to get the trial over with before the public had time to react to it—in short, "to sacrifice whatever little public spirit may remain amongst us." Actually, he told the jury with an assumption of great reluctance, it was not Mr. Rowan but the government that ought to be on trial. The "fundamental principles" of justice "are pillars, the depth of whose foundation you cannot explore without endangering their strength; but let it be recollected that the discussion of such subjects should not be condemned in me, nor visited upon my client: the blame, if any there be, should rest only with those who have forced them into discussion." The freedom of the press "is the right of the people to keep an eternal watch upon the conduct of their rulers"; for which reason, it "has been cherished by the law of England." Thus swiftly he transformed the trial into an examination of the English rule over Ireland:

> What is the fruit of a good government? the virtue and happiness of the people. Do four millions of people in this country gather those fruits from that government? . . . To you, gentlemen of the jury, who are bound by the most sacred obligation to your country and your God, to speak nothing but the truth, I put the question—do the people of this country gather those fruits?—are they orderly, industrious, religious, and contented?—do you find them free from bigotry and ignorance, those inseparable concomitants of systematic oppression?

He reminded the jury of the time ten years earlier when the Volunteers were organized:

> You saw a band of armed men come forth at the call of nature, of honour, and their country. . . . That illustrious, and adored, and abused body of men stood forward and assumed the title, which I trust the ingratitude of

their country will never blot from its history—"THE VOLUNTEERS OF IRELAND."

"The representation of our people is the vital principle of their political existence," he declared. On this basis,

> I call you, therefore, to a plain question of fact. . . . I put it boldly and fairly to you, do you think that the people of Ireland are represented as they ought to be? Do you hesitate for an answer? . . . Do you find that comfort and competency among your people which are always found where a government is mild and moderate, where taxes are imposed by a body who have an interest in treating the poorer orders with compassion, and preventing the weight of taxation from pressing sore upon them?

It was the government that was the oppressor; it was Rowan who had sought to relieve the people from the manifest grievances that bore upon them. It was the people of Ireland who were most in need of defense, and it was the defense of their rights that had brought Rowan to trial. Thus his reasoning ran. "Do you think it wise or humane at this moment to insult them, by sticking up in a pillory the man who dared to stand forth as their advocate?" When this challenge brought forth a burst of applause from the spectators in the courtroom, Curran denied that he had sought to arouse it. The applause, rather, was a spontaneous expression of the yearning for freedom. "It is the mighty theme, and not the inconsiderable advocate, that can excite the interest in the hearer." He proceeded in a spirit of calm reasonableness to deny that either he or his client was rebellious. Their purpose, like that of the Irish people, was to sustain the constitution that guaranteed the rights of Ireland and England as one united nation:

> But to accomplish that union, let me tell you, you must learn to become like the English people. It is vain to say you will protect their freedom, if you abandon your own. . . . Let us follow this a little further—I know you will interpret what I say with the candour in which it is spoken—England is marked by an avarice of freedom, which she is studious to engross and accumulate, but most unwilling to impart. . . .
> If it required additional confirmation, I should state the case of invaded America, and the subjugated Indian, to prove that the policy of England has ever been, to govern her connections more as colonies than as allies; and it must be owing to the great spirit indeed of Ireland if she shall continue to be free.

The constitutional right of the people to speak up on their own behalf was what had come under challenge, for "if any aggregate assembly shall meet, they are censured; if a printer publishes their resolutions, he is punished. . . . If the people say, let us not create tumult, but meet in delegation, they cannot do it." To find Rowan guilty would be to renounce the most precious rights of the whole Irish people. "Upon this subject, therefore, credit me when I say that I am still more anxious for you than I possibly can be for him."

However sound this persuasive strategy may have been, Curran's defensive plea was not successful. The verdict had been decided in advance. After only a ten-minute recess, the jury found Rowan guilty as charged. In an appeal, which was heard only a week later, on 4 February, Curran based his case largely on the speed with which the jury had reached its decision: "I am not arguing that the charge of the court cannot by any possibility be reconciled to the principles of law; I am agitating a more important question; I am putting it to the conscience of the court whether a jury may not have properly collected the same meaning from it which I affixed to it; and whether there ought not to have been a volume of explanation." He concluded with a warning of the consequences of such a court-martial way of conducting the trial. "You are standing on the scanty isthmus that divides the great ocean of duration, on one side of the past, on the other of the future; a ground that, while you yet hear me, is washed from beneath our feet."[22]

There were other voices that sounded calls much more revolutionary—that gave support for armed rebellion by radical members of the United Irishmen, in their demand for a complete breaking away from Great Britain. Two of them were brothers of the Seares family, who in 1798 were tried for treason and were quickly condemned to death. After the sentencing, John, the elder, spoke to the judges not on his own behalf, but for his brother: "I only ask that disposing of me, with what swiftness either the public mind or justice requires, a respite may be given to my brother, that the family may acquire strength to bear it all." His request was brusquely refused. In the following year, a brilliant Cork barrister, Thomas Goold, denounced the Union Bill in a rousing speech that ended with a call for unending rebellion. "Our patent to be a state, not a shire," he said, "comes direct from heaven. The Almighty has in majestic characters signed the charter of our independence. The great Creator of this world has given our beloved country the gigantic outlines of a kingdom. The God of nature never intended that Ireland should be a province, and by God she never shall."[23]

It cannot be doubted that these speeches—by Flood and Grattan, by Plunket and Curran, by the radicals Emmet and Goold—had significant effects. The reactions to them were partly in Ireland—in clarifying the need for independence and in uniting the deeply divided peoples, at least on this central theme—and partly in England, where the public was brought to realize (as it had been regarding India) that its government was guilty of serious wrongs and that some remedy must be accepted. As so often happens, however, when great social changes have to be made, the proposed remedies were too little and too late. Speakers who came to understand the needs did their best to point the way, but government, encumbered as always by the clashing of divergent interests, gave heed in only partial steps.

The Irish Reform Bill, which Pitt managed to secure in 1793, did indeed extend the protection of the laws more broadly to the Irish people, but it continued to exclude Catholics from the right to hold office. The result was to heighten the spirit of resistance that the reform aimed to reduce. In Lecky's estimation: "Few greater mistakes of policy could be made than to give political equality to the great mass of ignorant Catholics, who were for the most part below political interests, and at the same time to refuse it [the right to hold office] to the Catholic gentry. The continued disability was certain to produce renewed agitation, and it was equally certain that this agitation would be ultimately successful. The disability fell on the very class which would feel it most keenly and which deserved it least. Whatever controversy there might be about the sentiments of the mass of the Irish peasantry or of the Catholic priesthood, there was at least no question that the few Catholic gentry of Ireland had shown themselves for generations uniformly and almost effusively loyal."[24] By this unwise restriction, the final step of unifying Ireland was taken. Henceforth, the aristocrats and the people had a common cause. The only ones who remained loyal were in the Protestant minority that clung to England as its only protection. It was on this ground that the future struggle was waged.

The culmination of the Irish epic came in the following generations, but the foundation of the demand for total independence was built through the progression of rhetorical efforts of leaders who developed the case that the wrongs of Ireland were too grievous to be borne and that they could only be rectified by the Irish people themselves. Military revolt, such as that of the American colonies, was not available to Ireland. It lay too close to England, and it was too weak. Rhetorical protests, accompanied as they were and handicapped as they were by bursts of violence, accomplished the effects of arousing the populace and of forging a unity that surmounted their deep divisiveness. The demand for freedom expanded until it no longer could be denied. And accompanying it there was developed a love of country that proved to be an irresistible force. It brought the landed aristocracy and the peasantry into one common bond. And it stretched on across the ocean to the multiple thousands who emigrated as their last desperate means of finding a livelihood. Even from abroad, whether in England or in America, this patriotic sentiment animated such eloquent spokesmen yet to come as Daniel O'Connell, Charles Stewart Parnell, John Edward Redmond, and William Bourke Cockran. And even the humbler emigrants, who had no political podium, found effective expression, less through speaking than in their songs, such as the plaintive urgency in such verses as:

Some day I'll to home again to Ireland,
Though if only at the closing of my day,
To see the men and women digging praties [potatoes],
And to watch the sun go down in Galway Bay.

Notes

1. Cited from T. M. Kettle, *Irish Oratory and Orators* (Dublin: Talbot Press, 1916), p. 110.
2. J. A. Froude, *The English in Ireland in the Eighteenth Century* (London: Macmillan, 1861).
3. W. E. H. Lecky, *A History of Ireland*, 4 vols. (London: Longmans, Green, 1892), abridged by L. P. Curtis, Jr. (Chicago: University of Chicago Press, 1972); idem, *Leaders of Public Opinion*, 2 vols. (London: Longmans, Green, 1891).
4. Edith M. Johnston, *Great Britain and Ireland, 1760–1800* (Edinburgh: St. Andrews University Press, 1963).
5. Lecky, *History of Ireland*, 1:xxvi.
6. Kettle, *Irish Oratory*, intro.
7. Lawrence Henry Gipson, *The Triumphant Empire* (New York: Knopf, 1967), p. 15, quoting from the Charlemont MSS.
8. Lecky, *Leaders of Public Opinion*, 1:36–37.
9. Ibid., 1:37–40.
10. Ibid., 1:40.
11. Kettle, *Irish Oratory*, in which the full speech is included, pp. 96–107.
12. Ibid., p. 132. Other quotations from Grattan's speeches are from ibid., pp. 112–44.
13. Lecky, *Leaders of Public Opinion*, 1:79.
14. Ibid., 1:90.
15. The speeches by Tone and by Emmet are cited from Kettle, *Irish Oratory*, pp. 280, 322–40.
16. Ibid., pp. 98–99.
17. Ibid., p. 161.
18. Lecky, *History of Ireland*, 1:439.
19. Lecky, *Leaders of Public Opinion*, 1:220.
20. Kettle, *Irish Oratory*, pp. 288–89.
21. Ibid., pp. 278, 290.
22. These two speeches are from ibid., pp. 147–75.
23. Ibid., pp. 278, 290.
24. Lecky, *History of Ireland*, 1:253–54.

14
Scotland—A Rhetorical Highland

The highlands of Scotland have long sheltered a sturdy people who are notably self-reliant and independent-minded. *Montani semper liberi* was a Roman saying, and the Roman conquest of Great Britain never extended north of Hadrian's wall. The English secured an Act of Union with Scotland in 1707 but were never able to dominate their Scottish neighbors. The long history of Scotland reflects hardship and struggle but not submission. Then, in the eighteenth century, Scotland experienced its own Renaissance.

Particularly in the second half of the century Scotland displayed such intellectual brilliance that some historians called it the Second Periclean Age.[1] It proved to be a rhetorical highland. During this period the Scots enjoyed the new experience of being the teachers rather than the taught. Both London and Paris acknowledged the guidance of the intellectual centers of Edinburgh, Glasgow, and Aberdeen. Nothing like this happened before, nor has it been equalled since. The transformation not only changed the Scots' view of themselves but also won for them a new image below the border and on the Continent. Self-pride was always one of their characteristics. Psychologically as well as physically their homeland was inviolable. They were Britons, closer racially to the Irish than to the English, but with a difference. Then, in this period, their influence began to flow outward.

"Demands and Feeds upon Communication"

As a historian in love with their culture pointed out, it was four hundred years of bitter warfare with England that "hammered them into being a nation."[2] No more than the Irish were they sentimentally attached to either the people or the government of England. The factors that induced in both countries resentment and dislike toward their stronger neighbor were somewhat similar. Yet the relations of the Scots and the Irish with England in this period took very different forms. While the Irish were drawing apart from England, the Scots moved toward a more cordial understanding. Both Ireland and Scotland in this time developed an unusually eloquent and persuasive body of spokesmen, but the nature of their speaking was markedly different. Irish eloquence dwelt upon their grievances. The Scots had different feelings and delivered a different kind of message. Many of them sought their fortunes south of the border—like William Murray, the first Lord Mansfield, who was cited by Boswell as "the greatest man in England," and of whom Dr. Johnson observed that "much may be made of a Scotchman if he be caught young."[3]

Many of the circumstances that shaped their relations with England were the same in Scotland and Ireland. In both countries the people were plagued by internal disunity resulting from bitter rivalry among their clans. Both had long histories of conflicts with the English. In their customs, their speech, and their cultures, both differed more from the English than from one another. In both, the dominant religion was in conflict with Anglicanism. In both areas the people were impoverished and both, with reason, blamed the English for it. Both peoples were weakened by internal divisions, and in both their search for unity focused on resistance to and conflicts with the English. Yet the sentiment that came to prevail was anti-English in Ireland and pro-English in Scotland. The Scottish-Irish differences proved to be more significant than their similarities.

Part of the reason is racial. The Scots were more like the Irish, in their Celtic and Gaelic origins, but in Scotland there was a considerable admixture of Anglians, Normans, and Scandinavians. There is some truth in the stereotype that portrays the Irish as romantically imaginative and emotional, the Scots as being hardheaded in their practicality. Political factors were more important. In 1603 England and Scotland came to have a common monarch. When the Scot James VI became James I of England, he commented wistfully that "God made us all in one island, encompassed by the sea and of its nature indivisible." His hope for a union was long delayed, but by the Act of Union England and Scotland were joined as one nation in 1707. The reason for the delay was that strong barriers existed that never have been wholly overcome. "They differed in religion, in law, government, economic development, and social structure. It was only up to a point that they shared the same language. Between the two peoples, at most levels, there was a cordial dislike and occasionally open hostility. To each the other kingdom was the ancient enemy."[4] Hadrian's Wall was in many respects as much a dividing line as was the Irish Sea.

Yet while the Irish were developing a bilious spirit of rebellion, the Scots were manifesting an urbane cosmopolitanism that drew them toward Paris and then gradually, and in a different way, toward London. Scottish intellectuals became the influential and respected shapers of European thought. The mere catalog of them is impressive. Among them were Henry

Home (better known as Lord Kames) and David Hume, in philosophy, and Adam Smith in economic theory. Both Hume and William Robertson matched Edward Gibbon's reputation as historians. Lord Monboddo caught the startled attention of the time with his observation of the biological resemblance between men and monkeys. Joseph Black was acknowledged as the leader in medicine. James Hutton made a revolutionary contribution to geology with his *Theory of the Earth*. James Watt nudged the industrial revolution into gear with his invention of the steam engine. George Campbell, Thomas Reid, and Hugh Blair (along with Bishop Whately in Ireland) made important contributions to rhetorical theory. Moreover, the new status of Scotland drew some Englishmen to the north to make their most notable achievements—among them William Hunter, the great chemist, and Sydney Smith, who went to Edinburgh reluctantly but found it the suitable place in which to establish the outstanding literary periodical, the *Edinburgh Review*.

Contrary to Dr. Johnson's scornful observation that education was as scarce in Scotland as bread in a besieged town, and while "English education was a joke in poor taste," it was "the austere, turbulent, democratic universities of Calvinist Scotland which sent a stream of brilliant, hardworking, career-seeking and rationalist young men into the south."[5] Seldom elsewhere has there been such a profusion of innovative minds.

The reasons are difficult to identify. One of them surely is the state of mind that led Scots to become the leaders in the study of rhetoric. Intellectualism demands and feeds upon communication—as is well instanced in the Athens of Pericles and Socrates, the Rome of Cicero, and the Concord of Emerson. Ideas interact, and minds both deepen and expand as they interrelate. In Scotland, various influences joined to produce a profusion of stimulative communication.

The traditional infighting among the clans was diminished by the new discipline imposed following the Act of Union. The young sons of clansmen turned from fighting to studying, so that the universities greatly expanded. Social clubs developed, centering largely in Edinburgh, to make it "a much more professional society than that of London or Paris."[6] "Clubbiness" (to use one of Dr. Johnson's favorite terms) was characteristic of the intellectual circles. Typical of their mode of influencing one another is the small circle that planned and then edited the *Edinburgh Review*, and the somewhat larger discussion group that assembled to hear George Campbell read the manuscript drafts of his chapters on rhetoric and then to discuss what they implied and what further clarification or amplification they needed. As thoughts were shared and criticized, thereby improving them, the same process intensified the spirit of emulation and of rivalry, which led to still further intellectual expansion and depth. As a result, Scottish philosophy and economic theory and scientific innovations swept across Europe. Scottish literature, too—especially the poetry and novels of Sir

Walter Scott and the poems of Robert Burns—won a great following in England.

Such success, however, did not greatly change the long-held feeling of the English that Scots were largely uncouth semibarbarians. South of the border, Scots as individuals were not well received. Superiority does not win friends easily. Samuel Johnson was far from being exceptional in his belittlement of the people and the society of Scotland. In the cities of England, "Scots were so much disliked at that time that it was almost unsafe for one to appear on the streets or in a tavern."[7] Amid all this prejudice, and despite the suspicion and the envy directed against them, Scots made their way successfully in English public life. They made it chiefly by saying much that mattered, and by saying it in ways that led to their ideas being welcomed and accepted.

Among other things, they had much to say about the nature of discourse, and its value. John Campbell wrote distinguished biographies of English jurists. David Hume and Adam Smith wrote about eloquence and how to make it effective. So did the "philosopher of common sense," Thomas Reid. So did such preachers and teachers as Hugh Blair and George Campbell. What they stressed was that discourse should be not so emphatically *expressive* (stressing what it means to the speaker) but more definitely *communicative* (aimed to influence the responses of the hearers). They varied significantly among themselves in their philosophical standards; but what chiefly interested them was how minds influence one another and how behavioral changes are brought about. Ideas and sentiments that are most influential, they pointed out, are those which speakers and listeners hold in common. It was in this spirit that Sir Walter Scott directed attention away from Scottish-English differences to the Saxon-Gaelic struggle to resist Norman-French injustice; and it was from this point of view that Robert Burns wrote of sentiments and experiences that were drawn from daily life, general observations, and shared beliefs.

The society in which they lived was invigorating and innovative. The union with England opened wider opportunities to Scot traders. In 1723 a Society of Improvers in the Knowledge of Agriculture was organized in Edinburgh and initiated improvements that spread rapidly through England and Europe. "Better living conditions led to marked improvement in health and vigor."[8] Roads and canals were developed to speed transportation. When London became their political capital, Scots came to consider their internal politics more a "boisterous game" than a serious struggle over issues.[9] Religion was less a cause of dissension in Scotland than in Ireland, or even than in England, for the Presbyterian majority was guaranteed freedom for their beliefs by the Act of Union, and was at least moderately tolerant. What was occurring in Scotland "was revolutionary change, not a mere shift of emphasis within the same system." What was coming to pass was the emergence of "new ideas and new values."[10] There can be no simple explanation of how it happened, but surely major reasons were the curbing of the traditional armed conflicts among the rival clans, the nurturing influence of improved material welfare, and the stimulation of a new sense of community among the intellectuals.

The problems that were of greatest concern to the Scotsmen of the time were those which could best be solved through discussion and debate. They were not the kinds of problems that induce rioting and terrorism, such as those which plagued Ireland. There was great dissatisfaction in Scotland with the Continental wars—and especially with the resultant taxation—that England waged. There was considerable sentiment for reestablishing the Stuart dynasty or, if that could not be done, for annulling the Act of Union. What these feelings led to, however, was not (as in Ireland) a unifying national association, but rather a division of the people into three contending groups. The Jacobites wistfully and futilely longed for restoration of the Stuarts. The Court party, whose members were rewarded with places and pensions for their loyalty to the ministry, worked to strengthen the connection with England. And a third group consisted of country gentry, whose aim was to regain the powers and the privileges that traditionally belonged to the clans. Such aims (except the last) could not be attained by armed force; they did stimulate argumentative talk.

The union with England satisfied some and aggrieved others. Edinburgh lost its status as the capital, but Scots were determined that it not sink into being merely a provincial center. The Scottish language was threatened by the extensive use of English. The control of politics by bribery led to bitter rivalry concerning who would get the grants, and to resentment against those who were bought to serve English interests. Further resentment arose from the diversion of local taxes to expenditure by the English. The establishment of free trade helped some Scots, but the heightened competition from English industry hindered others. Scottish laws had to be reconciled with English laws. Religious controversies grew sharper, partly because the gentry tended toward episcopalianism, the masses of the people to presbyterianism, and partly because the new skepticism fathered by Hume brought religious faith itself into dispute. Catholics, Baptists, Quakers, Jews, and Congregationalists (who were heirs of Puritanism) were not numerous in Scotland, but the intensity of their feelings, along with the basic episcopal-presbyterian split, added fuel to "the national predilection for ecclesiastical controversy."[11] Differences of opinion on all such questions, as well as the burgeoning of new ideas, required "talking out."

"For a generation or more the benefits of the Union seemed to hang fire." But after the 1745–46 revolutionary effort fizzled in failure, "Scotland sprang forward along the path toward happier days. . . . Released from the prison of poverty where she had languished for ages, Scotland burst into sudden splendour."[12] Conditions favored internal unity, for (again in sharp contrast to Ireland) the lairds and the populace not only shared the same religion but also felt strong bonds of comradeship. For one thing, the children of the lairds and the commoners went to the same schools. The landlords were not absentee Englishmen but local clan chiefs. As the laird rode daily through his lands, he had to listen to the sharp tongues of an outspokenly independent race. Yet the dissensions that accompany democracy were lacking since the people were content with the tradition that only members of the nobility could sit in their Parliament or govern their local affairs. Aristocrats and commoners attended the same kirks and, whether Anglican or Presbyterian, their religious services were quite similar. Public order was enforced even more by preachers than by the police; robbery and disorder were infrequent. Even the substitution of English for their old Gaelic speech encountered little opposition, since it opened their minds to a vastly enlarged world. As Trevelyan observed, "The enjoyment of toleration, better education, English influence, and the indefinable 'spirit of the age' broadened their vision as the years went by."[13] Better living conditions discouraged emigration, and the population grew from about 1,000,000 at the opening of the century to 1,625,000 at its close. While the Irish were seething with a spirit of revolt, the Scots were generally content.

Their political concerns were dealt with largely in London, and it was there that the leading Scots made their reputations. They were a varied lot, five of whom became especially notable. Among them were Lord Bute, the friend and confidant of George III, and Henry Dundas, "that clever but unprincipled adventurer,"[14] who became the principal dispenser of patronage for William Pitt, thereby gaining influence and also arousing strong resentments among those whom he overlooked or rejected. The speakers who best represented the Scots to the outside world were a trio of remarkable ability: William Murray, the first earl of Mansfield; a Whig lawyer and parliamentarian, James Mackintosh; and Thomas Erskine, the outstanding lawyer of his time and (fully as much as Fox and Sheridan) a prime defender of English liberties during the period of reaction against French Jacobinism. All of them had their great success in London and are remembered not as Scots but as Englishmen. Together they demonstrated that the union was a success and that Great Britain benefited enormously from the flow of Scottish influence into the south.

"No Prosecution for Mere Opinions"

William Murray, Lord Mansfield, born near Perth, was sent to England at the age of eleven for study at Westminster School of Christ Church in Oxford, and then to Lincoln's Inn, where he prepared for his profession as a lawyer. He devoted himself to study of the great classical orators, particularly Cicero, whose speeches he studied with great care and translated first from Latin into English and then back again into Latin. To gain facility in extemporaneous speaking, he joined the debating society in Lincoln's Inn. In the words of a contemporary, Lord John Campbell, by the time of his admission to the bar in 1730, "he had made himself not only acquainted with international law, but with the codes of all the most civilized nations . . . he was thoroughly imbued with the literature of his own country . . . he had a sincere desire to be of service to his country; and he was animated by a noble aspiration after honourable fame."[15] After a few years of practice, his abilities brought him both great wealth and wide public acclaim.

In 1742 he entered Parliament, where, as a Tory, he came under severe attacks by the Elder William Pitt. As Goodrich estimates, "Never were two men more completely the antipodes of each other. . . . Pitt was ardent, open, and impetuous; Murray was cool, reserved, and circumspect. The intellect of Pitt was bold and commanding; that of Murray was subtle, penetrating, and refined. Pitt sought power; Murray, office and emolument. . . . 'In closeness of argument, in happiness of illustration, in copiousness and grace of diction, the oratory of Murray was unsurpassed. . . . When measures were attacked, no one was better capable of defending them; when reasoning was the weapon employed, none handled it with such effect; but against declamatory invective, his very temperament incapacitated him for contending with much advantage.' . . . Pitt could only attack, Murray only defend."[16]

The distinction Goodrich and Campbell made between the two as to their manner of speaking was sound, but Goodrich's summation of their basic motivation is highly questionable. Pitt surely sought more than power. He wanted power not for its own sake but to use it to extend the empire. Neither did he, by any means, scorn wealth and status. No fairer was the judgment that Mansfield selfishly sought material rewards. In the long run, the service he rendered in clarifying both law and judicial process was a service to the country comparable to that of Pitt. Pitt stormed his way through public life, utilizing his charisma as a club with which to beat down opposition. Mansfield, more soberly, dealt with facts and with well-reasoned distinctions to rescue equity from the accumulation of technicalities that gave the great advantage in the courts to the side able to engage the most skilled advocates. Pitt's career was impeded largely by the king's dislike of him (and the dislike of him by the Court party). Mansfield's career was hindered by his being a Scot and by the reputation he acquired of being a defender of privilege. As for the former, his biographer put it bluntly: "The only objection that can be made to him is what he can't help, which is that he is a Scotchman"; and he cited the prejudicial observation by Lord Shelburne that, "like the generality of Scots, Lord Mansfield has no regard to truth whatever."[17]

While Pitt was winning more popularity than he deserved as the Great Commoner (for he never believed in democracy), Mansfield's political career was frankly devoted to the defense of the privileged classes and of the party in power. In that sense, at least, it may be said of him what a twentieth-century politician said of one of his own opponents: "He's a real opportunist—he never throws his bread upon the waters until he makes sure that the tide is coming in." But when viewed in the context of the times, this charge, too, was unfair. Only a few radicals among Mansfield's associates were venturing to defend popular rights against entrenched aristocratic advantages. Basically, it might be said of him that his career was curiously bifurcated: as a political champion of privilege and as a judicial supporter of the full legal rights of every citizen, however poor and helpless he might be.

Mansfield's personal appearance was attractive and his voice was so clear and delicate that it was likened to the trilling of a nightingale. His social conduct and geniality in conversation made him an agreeable companion— in the words of Dr. Johnson: "not a mere lawyer; he drank champagne with the wits." As George Campbell noted of him, his pronunciation was always marked by Scotticisms. But his intellectual abilities won for him recognition as one of the greatest men of his time.

Despite his efforts to rescue legal processes from their maze of technicalities, it was Mansfield's skill in advocacy that made him most effective. As Lord Ashburton noted, "It was extremely difficult to answer him when he was wrong, and impossible when he was right." Both his political views and his methods in persuasion are well represented in a speech he made in the Lords, on 3 February 1766, in which he undertook to prove that the American colonials were rightly subject to taxation by the Parliament because they were "virtually" represented in it:

> There can be no doubt, my Lords, but that the inhabitants of the colonies are as much represented in Parliament, as the greatest part of the people of England are represented; among nine millions of whom there are eight which have no votes in electing members of Parliament. . . . A member of Parliament, chosen for any borough, represents not only the constituents and inhabitants of that place. . . . He represents the city of London, and all other commons of this land, and the inhabitants of all the colonies and dominions of Great Britain; and is, in duty and conscience, bound to take care of their interests.[18]

This claim of "virtual representation" was scornfully brushed aside by the Elder Pitt as being inapplicable to the colonies; but it was not questioned— either by him or by Mansfield—as being both true and proper for the people of England. Neither was Mansfield effectively answered when he denounced the public clamor for the seating of John Wilkes, saying of it, "Audacious addresses in print dictate to us, from those they call the *people*, the judgment to be given. . . . God forbid it should! We must not regard political consequences, how formidable soever they might be." The idea of democracy had not yet taken root.

In 1756 Mansfield took his place as chief justice of the King's Bench, and it was as a lawyer and as a judge, rather than in his political speaking, first in the Commons and afterward in the Lords, that he made his greatest contribution. Despite his early and impressive mastery of legal history, what he accomplished in reshaping judicial processes resulted from his impatience with, rather than citations of, established practices. He disdained consultation with his colleagues on the bench and impatiently cut off such arguments by attorneys as he considered to be prolix, or abstruse, or intended to delay. Even the great Lord Erskine was forced to confess that "he treated me, not with contempt indeed, for of that his nature was incapable, but he put me aside with indulgence, as you do a child when it is lisping its prattle out of season." In the opinion of Pitt, "he was a very bad judge, proud, haughty to the bar and hasty in his determinations." When he considered that a legal plea was being presented pretentiously, he would show his distaste by ostentatiously reading a newspaper. When Blackstone's *Commentaries* appeared, he compared it unfavorably to his own *Fragment on Government*. In short, his temperament scarcely seemed to be judicial. Yet to young and inexperienced lawyers he was courteous and helpful. And most significantly, of the thousands of cases that he decided over a period of thirty-two years, for only twenty of them was a dissenting opinion recorded, and only six were reversed on appeal.[19] This despite the fact that he insisted on such haste in clearing the calendar of the court that he heard as many as twenty-six cases in a single day.

Perhaps his most influential presentation, however, was made not as a judge but as an advocate. This was a defense he made of a Dissenter, Allen Evans, whose case was being heard on appeal in the House of Lords. To "roast the Dissenters," a curious law was in effect to impose a fine on any citizen who refused to serve in any office to which he was elected, while concurrently Dissenters were prohibited from holding any public office. The City of London, needing money to pay for a new mayoralty mansion, elected Evans as sheriff and then, since he was disqualified from accepting the office, fined him six hundred pounds for neglect of his public duty. The reasoning by the prosecutors was that he could hold the office if only he would forgo his dissent and become an Anglican. Far from being a unique case, this mode of raising revenue was commonly practiced throughout England. Mansfield's sense of outraged justice led him to support Evans in a speech on 4 February 1769 that came to be widely discussed and was estimated by Lord Campbell as "one of the finest specimens of forensic eloquence to be found in our books." What Mansfield argued, in effect, was that a municipality could not have it both ways: It could not restrain Dissenters from holding public office and concurrently fine them for not doing so. The prosecutorial argument—that Evans should solve the dilemma by renouncing his religion—Mansfield held to be intolerable. "Conscience is not controllable by human laws, or amenable to human tribunals," he said. "Persecution, or attempts to force conscience, will never produce convictions, and are only calculated to make hypocrites or martyrs." So far as liberalism extended in that day, Mansfield stated it as the basis for his defense.

> The common law of England, which is only common reason or usage, knows of no prosecution for mere opinions. For atheism, blasphemy, and reviling the Christian religion, there have been many persons prosecuted and punished upon the common law. But bare non-conformity is no sin by the common law; and all positive laws inflicting any pains or penalties for non-conformity to the established rites and modes, are repealed by the Act of Toleration, and Dissenters are thereby exempted from all ecclesiastical censures.

The argument prevailed. Not only was Evans found not guilty, but the City of London was adjudged the guilty party. The law was repealed.

In another debate in the Lords, on 8 May 1770, Mansfield's bifurcated views—defending privilege as a general principle while insisting on justice in specific cases—came to the test. It was his devotion to justice that proved to be the stronger. The Commons had passed a bill depriving members of Parliament of their traditional right to freedom from arrest in cases where they refused to pay their debts. The Lords were expected to veto the bill. Mansfield defended the justice of the bill so effectively that he won enough votes to sustain it. His tone was conciliatory, and his reasoning was too sound to be resisted.

> When I consider the importance of this bill to your Lordships, I am not surprised that it has taken so much of your consideration. It is a bill indeed of no common magnitude. It is no less than to take away from two thirds of the Legislative body of this kingdom certain privileges and immunities of which they have been long possessed. Perhaps there is no situation the human mind can be placed in that is so difficult, and so trying, as where it is made a judge in its own cause.

Then, gently, he posed the issue: "Shall it be said that you, my Lords, the grand council of the nation, the highest judicial and legislative body of the realm, endeavor to evade by *privilege* those very laws which you enforce on your fellow subjects? Forbid it, justice." He concluded his speech by denying the charge that he was trying, by his stand, to win public popularity.

> I now come to speak upon what, indeed, I would gladly have avoided, had I not been particularly *pointed* at for the part I have taken in this bill. It has been said by a noble Lord on my left hand that I likewise am running

the race of popularity. If the noble lord means by popularity that applause bestowed by after ages on good and virtuous actions, I have long been struggling in that race, to what purpose only long-trying time can alone determine. But if the noble lord means that mushroom popularity which is raised without merit, and lost without a crime, he is much mistaken in his opinion. I defy the noble lord to point out a single action in my life where the popularity of the times has ever had the smallest influence on my determinations. I thank God I have a more permanent and steady rule for my conduct—the dictates of my own breast. Those that have foregone that pleasing adviser, and given up their minds to be the slave of every popular impulse, I sincerely pity. I pity them still more if their vanity leads them to mistake the shouts of a mob for the trumpet of their fame.

His speech succeeded in winning the votes needed to secure the approval of the Lords for the bill. The victory was particularly notable in that the members had to vote against their own personal interest in order to support the measure. Moreover, the advantage the bill rejected was deeply rooted in tradition. In fact, so strongly did precedent favor the special privileges that the bill renounced that even after both Houses of Parliament concurred in surrendering them, the judiciary reinstituted them on the ground that to deny them was unconstitutional. Considering such circumstances, the success of this speech is a tremendous proof of Mansfield's persuasive powers and of the high respect accorded him by his peers. It also emphasizes the sense of justice that was the lodestar of his long career.

Nevertheless, the hope he expressed for lasting fame has not been well realized. The legal profession continues to honor him, but such historians as mention his public speaking tend to cite his cringing under the sarcastic attacks made upon him by the Elder William Pitt in the House of Commons. Anthologists have neglected him, since his speeches are models of decorum and sound reasoning rather than being marked with scintillating passages.

He deserves to be remembered better than he is. He served as chief justice on the King's Bench for more than three decades. He proved that a Scotchman could rise to the highest levels of influence in the fiercely competitive public forum south of the border. When he died at the age of eighty-nine, after a ten-day illness, his mind still remained uncommonly clear. It is the clarity of his vision of the meaning and of the importance of justice for which he merits being still honored today.

"Where Man Can Freely Exercise His Reason"

A Scot who succeeded Mansfield as one of the most eloquent and influential spokesmen from his homeland, was Sir James Mackintosh. Like

Mansfield, he held firmly to "the conviction that justice is the permanent interest of all men, and all commonwealths." Unlike Mansfield, however, he did not believe that law itself is a concept that must never be subservient to "mere opinions." His view instead was the pragmatic belief that "a real philosopher ought to regard truth itself chiefly on account of its subserviency to the happiness of mankind."[20] What animated him was to discover and to develop means by which human welfare might be improved. He joined the Whig Party, and his votes in the Commons generally supported the emerging trend toward liberal reforms. In sum, what Mansfield sought to preserve, Mackintosh sought to improve. His speeches were soundly intellectual but were also warmed with sympathy. As one of his contemporaries observed, his speaking in Parliament "wins its way into the heart, while it at once enlightens and satisfies the understanding." Like his contemporary, William Wilberforce, he displayed a goodness of heart that won the affection and admiration of even his opponents. When he died in 1832, at the age of sixty-seven, his departure from the public scene was "more regretted" and he himself was "less envied than any public man of his age."[21]

Mackintosh was born in a small town near Inverness on 24 October 1765, when the Second Periclean Age was at its zenith. The American Revolution, the Irish resistance, and the French Revolution were all in the making as he was growing up. It was a time of swift change marked by innovative ideas. His own development represents the practicality with which his fellow Scots were bringing philosophy to bear on the decision-making processes in politics and in law. Even in his childhood he combined in remarkable degree a profundity of mind with a winning personality. Throughout his career he won friends even among those with whom he habitually disagreed. Even as he shifted sides in midstream on the great issue of the effects of the French Revolution, he remained among those esteemed to be pointing the way toward a future that shook off the clinging impediments of established hierarchal inequities. In the transitional period in which he lived, he offered enlightening insight that helped toward the improvement of society.

Born the son of a captain in the British army, with neither wealth nor social position to assist him, and with his youth spent in rural seclusion, his mastery of books was such that "the name of *Jamie Mackintosh* was synonymous, all over the countryside, with a prodigy of learning." At the age of thirteen, he devoted himself to politics and extemporaneous speaking. He won the adherence of his sports-minded school fellows in organizing a schoolroom House of Commons, in which he brilliantly paraphrased the speeches of Pitt and Fox, and when none was able to answer him, he would shift sides to demonstrate the contrary strength of the views of Lord North. Two years later, at King's College in Aberdeen, he entered upon the study of philosophy so effectively and he became known as the New Plato. His next move was to Edinburgh, where he earned his degree in medicine. Like many other ambitious young Scots he went to London, only to find that the prejudice against Scots prevented him from gaining a medical practice. For this reason, he enrolled in Lincoln's Inn, to prepare for a career in law. By this time he was married, and in order to earn a living he became a journalist, with such effectiveness that he soon earned an adequate income and came into favorable public notice.

He joined several Whig clubs and in their meetings proved himself so capable in debate that few, even of the leading men, cared to contest with him. At the age of twenty-six in 1792 he leaped suddenly into fame through publication of a book, *Vindiciae Gallicae: Defence of the French Revolution against the Accusations of the Right Honourable Edmund Burke*. Despite the urgency of Burke's feelings and his sensitivity to criticism, he nevertheless expressed his admiration for Mackintosh's presentation. So did Fox and also George Canning—who read the book with "as much admiration as he had ever felt." The book was so well received that three successive printings were quickly called for. Shortly, thereafter, the excesses of the Terror in Paris induced Mackintosh to change his mind. As he wrote to Burke, "Since that time a melancholy experience has undeceived me on many subjects in which I was the dupe of my own enthusiasm." He was still a student in Lincoln's Inn, and he stood unveiled in a very public way as having been basically and ostentatiously wrong on the most urgent issue of the day. Yet instead of sinking under the weight of failure, he soon rose to new acclaim.

In 1799, four years after he commenced the practice of law, he undertook to give a series of lectures, "The Law of Nature and of Nations." He persuaded the reluctant benchers of Lincoln's Inn to allow him the use of their hall, which they granted after making clear their disapproval of his book on France. The lecture hall was crowded with a more distinguished group of public men than ever had met for such an occasion. Lawyers, members of Parliament, and country gentry contended to get seats. Even the lord chancellor, whose press of public business prevented his attendance, asked for copies of the lectures. They were widely reported and ardently discussed.

At this juncture, Mackintosh felt impelled to undertake the defense of a French émigré, Jean Peltier, who was publishing a French-language newspaper in London, devoted to attacks upon Napoleon, and whom, by the insistence of Napoleon, the English government charged with libel. Under the law, Peltier was undoubtedly guilty. Nevertheless, Mackintosh prepared to defend him on the theme of freedom of the press. The law prohibiting the libel of governments was not only clear but was stringently enforced. Napoleon was adamant that his critic must be condemned and silenced, and he sent two of his high officials to sit directly beside the jury box. England and France were so near to war that there was strong inducement for the court to divert or delay it by finding Peltier guilty, and under the law there was no just basis for his defense.

Mackintosh opened the defense on 21 February 1803, before the King's Bench, with a mild assurance to the jury that "I am incapable of lending myself to the passions of any client, and I will not make the proceedings of this court subservient to any political purpose." Nevertheless, he quickly stated the issue in political terms: "Gentlemen, the real prosecutor is the master of the greatest empire the civilized world ever saw. The defendant is a defenceless, proscribed exile.... You will not think unfavorably of a man who stands before you as the voluntary victim of his loyalty and honor. If a revolution (which God avert) were to drive us into exile, and to cast us on a foreign shore, we should expect, at least, to be pardoned by generous men for stubborn loyalty and unseasonable fidelity to the laws and government of our fathers." Peltier, he reminded the jury, had been a distinguished man of letters, and in his exile he was reduced to earn a bare living by editing a journal that was unread in England, since it was in a foreign language, and was unread in France, to which its import was prohibited. His only distinction was that he was the sole public advocate of a once admired French royalty. And why was the journal published in England? It was because there alone in all Europe was freedom of the press protected:

> One asylum of free discussion is still inviolate. There is still one spot in Europe where man can still freely exercise his reason on the most important concerns of society—where he can boldly publish his judgment on the acts of the proudest and most powerful tyrants. The press of England is still free. It is guarded by the free Constitution of our forefathers; it is guarded by the hearts and arms of Englishmen; and I trust I may venture to say, that if it be to fall, it will fall only under the ruins of the English empire. It is an awful consideration, gentlemen: every other monument of European liberty has perished; that ancient fabric, which has been gradually reared by the wisdom and virtue of our fathers, still stands. It stands (thanks be to God!) solid and entire; but it stands alone, and it stands amid ruins.

The speech did not—could not—prevent a verdict of guilt. Lord Erskine, who listened to it, before going to bed wrote to Mackintosh: "I can not shake off from my nerves the effect of your powerful and most wonderful speech ... I perfectly approve the verdict, but the manner in which you opposed it I shall always consider as one of the most spendid monuments of genius, literature, and eloquence."[22] It proved to be the last of Mackintosh's great speeches. He went off to India; eight years later he returned to a professorship in little-known Haillybury College. Even throughout this long twilight of his career he remained well liked and respected. His personality and abilities helped to dispel the English prejudice against the Scots.

"The Most Masterly Review"

Another Scottish lawyer, greater than Mackintosh, whose fame came to dominate the legal profession in London, was Thomas Erskine. Like Mackintosh, Erskine proved to be relatively ineffective in Parliament, but through a course of twenty-eight years he had no rival and no challenger as a trial lawyer. But this is an understatement of the extent of his fame. "It is even doubtful that Erskine has ever had a peer among all English-speaking advocates," is the judgment of a rhetorician who made a special study of his career.[23] A specialist in English law advises that students of law "could engage in no better employment than a careful study of Erskine's defences."[24] His success derived from the rhetorical cast of his mind, which resulted in "his astute identification of the most advantageous point for adjudication . . . and his unequalled powers of extemporaneous composition."[25] His greatest contribution was the conversion of specific cases into general principles, transforming "the concerns of private individuals into monuments of national freedom."[26] Historians applaud his defense of liberties against the "sadistic terrorism" of the repressive laws that were hurriedly passed to stem the influence of Jacobinism.[27] Fellow attorneys admire him as "the incomparable forensic orator of England."[28] His achievements are impressive, and he won them by the sheer power of his eloquence.

Erskine was the third son of an impoverished Scottish nobleman. Luckily, he inherited a brilliant mind and an indomitable spirit from his mother. His start in life was not impressive. After an early education in the small town of Saint Andrews, he was taken with his family to Bath, to be close to the philanthropic Lady Huntingdon, an enthusiastic follower of the evangelist George Whitefield. Against his will, he was enlisted in the navy by his father. Then, at the age of twenty, he fell in love with a country lass and, ignoring the protests of his family, married her. He shifted into the army and was sent off for a two-year stint on the island of Minorca. There commenced his real education, consisting of inspired study of English literature. Upon returning to London, he was induced by his admiration for Lord Mansfield to become an attorney. He studied law privately, while matriculated at Trinity College, Cambridge. During these years he was so impoverished that he lived, as he said, on "cow heel and tripe." He never became a profound legal scholar, but by taking part in debates in various London societies he developed the power of persuasive speech.

His career thereafter burst into brilliance. By the happy accident of a casual conversation, he was selected as a junior counsel to help in the defense of Thomas Baillie, administrator of Greenwich Hospital, who was charged with having misappropriated hospital funds. The senior counsels for Baillie all urged a compromise settlement. Then Erskine rose, after the judges thought the case was completed. He threw the court into a "trance of amazement," by showing that the real culprit was the Earl of Sandwich, who had made Baillie his scapegoat. Baillie was acquitted. Erskine put his one-guinea fee into a small box that he carried about with him the rest of his life as a reminder of the start of his career.

A few months later Erskine was selected as a defense counsel by Admiral Lord Keppel, who was brought to trial for alleged misconduct in a naval battle against the French. Erskine won his acquittal and was rewarded with the enormous fee of one thousand pounds. In quick succession he won further impressive victories on behalf of victims of the libel laws. Then came up a notable case, the trial of Lord George Gordon, in which case Erskine again was a junior counsel. His address to the jury stands not only as a prime example of forensic eloquence but in the judgment of Lord Brougham, "among the finest efforts of genius in our language." From this case he went on to others—the defense of the dean of Saint Asaphs, of a London printer John Stockdale, of a fellow attorney John Frost, of a shoemaker named Thomas Hardy, of a discharged soldier named William Hadfield who tried to assassinate George III, and of many more (ranging from treason to adultery), in which his pleas were acclaimed as "the most perfect exhibitions of power over the minds of a jury."[29]

While he became "the best-paid barrister in Britain,"[30] he also came to be known as the "Advocate of the People," for "his talents were not less at the service of indigent but deserving clients."[31] His success went far beyond pecuniary gain. His arguments extended the boundaries of civic freedom and of natural rights. During his brief service in Parliament, and on merely ceremonial public occasions, his speaking tended to be dull. But in the courtroom, in defense of human dignity, he proved what rhetoric can accomplish.

> As an advocate no language can exaggerate his merits. Cautious, wary, astute, clear in his discernment, and almost infallible in his judgment, no point that could really serve his client went unobserved. . . .
> He was the favorite of every jury, and I might add of every Judge before whom he was in the habit of practicing. . . . He was the only orator within my knowledge who possessed the real power of pathos, who could excite the passions, and make the sympathies of his audience subservient to his purpose.[32]

What Erskine was able to accomplish may be sufficiently illustrated from his defense of Lord Gordon, which presented him with as great difficulties as a defense attorney may experience.

The time was the beginning of June 1780. The general affairs of Great Britain were in sad disarray. The war with America was going badly. The beginnings of the industrial revolution were creating mass unemployment. Dissatisfaction and a lack of esteem for government were rife. Religion was a central problem. Protestants united to focus their general discontent against what they feared was a popish conspiracy to restore long-suspended civil rights to Catholics. A minor and generally ineffectual spokesman for this reactionary zeal was Lord Gordon, a feckless young Scotch nobleman whose anti-Catholic speeches in Parliament were as dull as they were frequent. Out of doors, however, he appeared as a unifying symbol. He was named president of the Protestant Association and his denunciations of popery had wide public appeal. To a session of the Commons on 2 June Lord Gordon presented a petition against Catholic emancipation that had been signed by 120,000 citizens; a crowd of 60,000 of them gathered outside Westminster Hall to demonstrate their support for it. Gordon warned the crowd to be "quiet and peaceful." Then he stridently denounced the government, while calling out to the crowd the names of members of Parliament who spoke against the petition.

Throughout the day the crowd milled aimlessly through the streets, but in the evening violence erupted. Houses were burned and Catholic chapels destroyed. The disturbance spread. On 5 June the celebration of King George's forty-second birthday was broken up by the mob. The next forty-eight hours were riotous. Newgate Prison was attacked and 300 prisoners were released. Lord Mansfield's mansion was demolished. The mob surged toward the Inns of Court—where Lord Erskine confronted them at Temple Gate with a loaded canon and turned them away. The army was called out and several hundreds of the rioters were killed. By nightfall of 7 June, this "Gordon Riot" was brought under control. Two days later Lord Gordon was arrested for high treason. For eight months he was held in the Tower of London, awaiting trial. The court appointed a leading barrister, Lloyd Kenyon, to defend him; Gordon's friends asked Thomas Erskine to serve as junior counsel.

Erskine was relatively inexperienced—never yet had he addressed a jury. The presiding judge was Lord Mansfield, whose house had been destroyed. The substantial sentiment of the country demanded the expected verdict of guilt. The nation had been narrowly saved from bloody revolution and the culprit well merited the execution that was his due. Witnesses were heard, and Kenyon presented a dull and ineffective plea on Gordon's behalf. Erskine was scheduled to speak next, but he asked to be allowed to wait until the prosecution finished its presentation. Under the rules governing cases of treason, the trial had to be completed in one single sitting. By the time Erskine rose, the time was past midnight; everyone was weary; there was no doubt what the verdict should be. Erskine pushed aside a mass of papers on his desk and expressed regret that time was not available for him to call more witnesses. His animated voice and manner revived the flagging interest of the jury. He invited their attention to himself.

> Gentlemen, I feel myself entitled to expect from you and the court the greatest indulgence and attention. I am indeed a greater object of your compassion than even my noble friend whom I am defending. He rests secure in conscious innocence, and in the well-placed assurance that it can suffer no stain at your hands. Not so with me. I stand up before you a troubled, I am afraid a guilty man, in having presumed to accept the awful trust which I am now called upon to perform. . . . Alas! Gentlemen, who am I? A young man of little experience, unused to the bar of criminal courts, and sinking under the dreadful consciousness of my defects. I have, however, this consolation, that no ignorance nor inattention on my part can possibly prevent you from seeing . . . that the Crown has established no case of treason.

He reminded the jury of the attorney general's description of the crime as "the very highest and most atrocious that a member of civil life can possibly commit . . . not merely an injury to society . . . but an attempt to dissolve and destroy society altogether." This overstatement, Erskine perceived, provided the opportunity he sought. He stressed his own crucial point: that Lord Gordon never had had any intention of stirring up a revolution. Gordon's sole responsibility was in having assembled a crowd to support a lawful petition. What followed was far from his intent and therefore was outside his responsibility. He emphasized his crucial defense: "that it is the *intention* of assembling them which forms the guilt of treason. . . . The hostile *mind* is the crime." Unless "the prisoner is a determined traitor *in his heart*, he is not guilty."

The prosecution had charged that "he ought to have foreseen that so great a multitude could not be collected without mischief." But the real guilt lay upon the government itself. Troops had not been called out during a delay of two days. And why not? The "unanswerable defense" of the government for such a delay was that "it neither did nor could possibly enter into the head of any man in authority to prophesy . . . the disgraceful acts which followed." Erskine turned to the jury with a confident gesture. The prosecution had destroyed its own case. "Do they wish you, while you are listening to the evidence, to connect it with unforeseen consequences, in spite of reason and truth?" He ended, then, with another reference to himself, similar to that with which he had begun:

> I shall now, therefore, relieve you from the pain of hearing me any longer. . . . I shall make no address to your passions. I will not remind you of the long and rigorous imprisonment he has suffered; I will not speak to you of his great youth, of his illustrious birth, and of his uniformly animated and generous zeal in Parliament for the Constitution of his country. Such topics might be useful in a dubious case; yet even

then, I might have trusted to the honest hearts of Englishmen to have felt them without excitation. At present, the plain and rigorous rules of justice and truth are sufficient to entitle me to your verdict.

The hour was 4:00 A.M. Erskine had spoken for more than three hours. And he won the verdict he sought. But he had much more than merely won this case. He also established in English jurisprudence the cardinal principle that crime depends on intention. Accidental or incidental results of an action cannot be held to be evidence of guilt; there must be motivation; there must be intent. And yet one more thing he also accomplished—to show that a Scot could stand in the center of English power and represent the best impulses that underlay the united society.

Erskine went on to many more courtroom triumphs, but upon this case his reputation was built. As Lord Campbell noted of this trial, "Here I find not only great acuteness, powerful reasoning, enthusiastic zeal, and burning eloquence, but the most masterly review ever given of the English law of high treason—the foundation of all our liberties."[33]

While Erskine's reputation rose to the heights in England, the Scots were piqued because of his neglect of them. Not once had he visited his native land since he left it in the uniform of a midshipman. Citizens of Edinburgh invited him as guest of honor at a great public dinner in 1820. He sought to excuse his seeming neglect of his birthplace, telling them that "however we may be driven to seek our fortunes in the most distant countries, we are still eager to return to our own." And return he finally did, the following year. Despite all his great successes, his fortune was dissipated through careless speculations. He came back to the home of his sister-in-law where in 1823, at the age of seventy-three, he died. His death was quietly observed.

"There is no marble monument erected to Erskine's memory"—as Campbell reports—"nor any mural inscription to celebrate his genius and public services; but the collection of his speeches will preserve his name as long as the English language endures."[34]

In his latter years, his service as lord chancellor was undistinguished, for his knowledge of the law was far from profound. But as an advocate, his power of concentrating the thoughts of the jury upon crucial points, and his ability to arouse their feelings on behalf of his clients, has not been surpassed. In the annals of the law, he remains an inspiration and an exemplar of how to plead a cause.

Notes

1. This is the theme of Wallace Notestein, *The Scot in History*, (New Haven: Yale University Press, 1946).
2. Ibid., p. xii.

3. *Boswell's Life of Johnson*, I: 469 and 576.

4. P. W. J. Riley, *The Union of England and Scotland: A Study of Anglo-Scottish Politics in the Eighteenth Century* (Manchester: Manchester University Press, 1978), P. xiv.

5. Hobsbawn, *Age of Revolution*, p. 30.

6. Notestein, *Scot in History*, p. 259 and chap. 23, "Society and Talk."

7. Ibid., p. 334.

8. William Ferguson, *Scotland, 1689 to the Present*, (New York: Praeger, 1968), p. 174.

9. Ibid., p. 212.

10. Ibid., p. 233.

11. Ibid., p. 130.

12. G. M. Trevelyan, *English Social History* (London: Longmans, 1944), pp. 418–19.

13. Trevelyan, *English Social History*, illustrates this theme, pp. 416–62.

14. Wingfield-Stratford, *British Civilization*, p. 815. In 1806 Erskine, as chancellor, presided over the impeachment trial of Dundas before the House of Lords, in which Dundas was found innocent of the charge of "high crimes and misdemeanors." See Lloyd Paul Stryker, *For the Defense: Thomas Erskine, The Most Enlightened Liberal of His Times, 1750–1823* (Garden City, N.Y.: Doubleday, 1947), 4.5.405–24.

15. Quoted by Goodrich, *Select British Eloquence*, p. 144.

16. Ibid., p. 145, still quoting John Campbell.

17. C. H. S. Fifoot, *Lord Mansfield* (Oxford: Oxford University Press, 1936), pp. 34, 33.

18. This and Mansfield's other principal speeches are found in Goodrich, *Select British Eloquence*, pp. 148–62.

19. Fifoot, *Lord Mansfield*, pp. 46–49.

20. He stated these convictions in his introductory lecture in a series entitled "The Law of Nature and of Nations," presented at Lincoln's Inn, 1799.

21. Goodrich, *Select British Eloquence* (pp. 821–26, 827–50), presents a well-balanced account of his life and reprints his most influential speeches.

22. Ibid., p. 825.

23. Carroll C. Arnold, "Lord Thomas Erskine: Modern Advocate," *Quarterly Journal of Speech*, 44 (February, 1958): 17–30.

24. J. A. Lovatt-Fraser, *Erskine* (Cambridge: Cambridge University Press, 1932), p. xi.

25. Bryant et al, *Select British Speeches*, p. 295.

26. Lovatt-Fraser, *Erskine*, p. x.

27. Wingfield-Stratford, *British Civilization*, p. 818.

28. Stryker, *For the Defense:* p. vii.

29. Cited by Goodrich, *Select British Eloquence* (pp. 635, 708), who published Erskine's most memorable jury pleas (pp. 637–784).

30. Stryker, *For the Defense*, p. 98.

31. John Campbell, *The Lives of the Lord Chancellors . . . of England* 7 vols. (Philadelphia: Lea and Blanchard, 1848), 6:320.

32. Comment by Sir James Scarlett, cited by Lovatt-Fraser, *Erskine*, pp. 145–47.

33. Campbell, *Lives of the Lord Chancellors*, 6:327–28.

34. Ibid., 6:510.

Epilogue

With the deaths of Lord Chatham, Edmund Burke, the Younger William Pitt, Charles James Fox, and Richard Brinsley Sheridan, an epoch ended and a new one was about to commence. The historic scene resembled a vast drama, with the curtain dropping on a cast of magnificent characters. The plot had extended over a period of some two thousand years, with a tremendous variety of events and persons but with a central theme that gave meaning and continuity to them all. However gradually and uncertainly, and with however many handicapping hesitations and temporary reversals, the countervailing movements had been from diversity of languages, customs, and interests to the growth of a commonality of culture, and, concurrently, from hierarchal privilege and authority toward acknowledgment and accommodation of the needs and wants of the many.

By no means had Great Britain become democratic, either in its structure or in its sentiments. That transformation remained to be accomplished in the next era, when there would be a new cast of characters, with such names as Canning and Russell, Macaulay and Palmerston, Bright and O'Connell, Spurgeon and Drummond, Disraeli and Gladstone, Lloyd George and Churchill, along with many, many more. Nevertheless, by the closing decades of the eighteenth century, the way was clearly pointed toward the changes that were to come.

The time span from the landing of Julius Caesar to the Napoleonic Wars is a stretch of more than eighteen centuries. During the time, at least fifty generations lived through an enormous variety of events and conditions. From the time of Caractacus and Cerealis and Boudicca on to Augustine, and Bede, and Alfred, and Wilfrid, the barbaric and warring tribes gradually and at least partially became a nation. The spirit of independence and self-will that marked those primitive tribesmen persisted into more settled times, to shape moot courts and shire assemblies in which community problems were talked about and acceptable solutions were devised.

With the Norman Conquest, the people had to adjust themselves to a new foreign rule in a language that was not their own and with a social system more rigid than they had known. The incredible hardships of the Black Death shook up the society and led to a chorus of new voices, speaking not from the strata above but in their own midst. A new kind of influence, the vividly personalized preaching of the Lollards, the Franciscan and Dominican monks, and other itinerants, speaking to the people of their earthly as well as spiritual concerns, and in their own language, their own way of talk, stirred the society with a ferment of new ideas and aspirations.

In the time of the Tudors, religious and political revolutionism led some to martyrdom and many to self-assertion, with an emergent leadership that spoke out for the good of the realm as contrasted with privileges for the few. In the time of the Stuarts the debates burst out of gentility into violence, with a new kind of politics and with new forms and a new spirit in religion. When the Hanoverians came to the throne, elitism made a last stand, to be overwhelmed by a rising clamor for reform.

The history of public speaking in Great Britain is an account of individual influence. It portrays the persuasive leadership of men, and some few times of women, who used their exceptional skill in speech to point the way for their fellow countrymen through times of uncertainty and morasses of difficulties. It is a narrative of the drawing together of dissimilar peoples into one nation that developed a core of strength sufficient to extend outward into a global empire. It depicts the growth of ideas, and ideals, and institutions that characterize the people and the society of the British Isles.

As the nation developed, there were strains and resentments that sometimes checked and partly reversed the general trends. There was a peculiarly British folk experience in the creating of a system of common law, in devising means for settling problems through discussion, and in developing an unwritten constitution strong enough to asssure stability and flexible enough to permit adjustments to the constant barrage of change. There was also a severe struggle of conscience, recurrent in different ways in successive centuries, as Catholics, Anglicans, Puritans, Baptists, Quakers, Presbyterians, and Methodists pursued their particular visions of reality.

During all this expanse of time, there was, as there had to be, a continuing search for new social agreements suitable for changing conditions. In part such agreements were hammered together by force, through bursts of violence that imposed temporary solutions. However, in order for new ways to become deeply rooted and decisive, they had to be explained, and justified, and made appealing and meaningful. Even the problems that were fought out had also to be talked out to render them socially effective. This was the role of public speaking in shaping the character of the nation.

Essentially, this history is an examination of how individuals exerted leadership through persuasion—for good ends and sometimes for bad; whether in wisdom or in folly; seeking in either circumstance to guide the course the society would take. Seldom were the controversies clear-cut contests between some who were good and others who were bad. Historical progress, however dubious such a concept may be, does not consist of a series of verbal jousts between forward-looking liberals and backward-looking conservatives. Whether John Ball and Lilburne, Eliot, Cromwell, and Pym, Tillotson and Andrewes, Halifax and Bolingbroke, Fox and Wesley, were statesmanlike or demagogic, wise men or visionaries, they did speak up as social guides and as inciters to social action.

What clearly appears in surveying history is that again and again, in many areas of life, important issues have to be resolved. Crucial choices have to be made. Available solutions for urgent problems have to be found. And a workable consensus has to be forged. For such purposes in Great Britain arguments pro and con were presented, buttressed generally with impassioned appeals. Whether particular speakers were right or wrong, patriotic or self-serving, principled or opportunistic, is seldom self-evident. Another question on which judgments must vary is the degree and the kinds of influence upon the flow of events that has been exercised by debates and discussions. Motivations are generally obscure; both causes and effects, especially considered in terms of broad social conditions, are multiform and ambiguous or inscrutable. It would be naive to assert that a speech or a debate *settles* an issue; but then, neither does a war. Each in its own way has its own contribution to make.

In this history, the outstanding public speakers, in generation after generation, are discussed, with accounts of what they talked about and why; of how they composed and presented their speeches; of what qualities of style, and methods, and personalities made them effective; of what kinds of audiences they addressed, and what kinds of responses they secured. Major speeches at critical junctures in the nation's history are summarized, with their styles illustrated in brief quotations, and with their persuasive patterns analyzed. More important, however, than individual speakers and particular speeches is the cardinal, overriding fact that *discussion* was utilized as a means for solving problems, and that freedom in and provisions for discussion evolved as a fundamental cultural characteristic of the British personality and of the British society. This is the central theme that this history examines.

Abbreviations

CM	*Communication Monographs*
CQ	*Communication Quarterly*
CSSJ	*Central States Speech Journal*
JC	*Journal of Communication*
P and R	*Philosophy and Rhetoric*
QJS	*Quarterly Journal of Speech*
SM	*Speech Monographs*
SSCJ	*Southern Speech Communication Journal*
TS	*Today's Speech*
WJSC	*Western Journal of Speech Communication*

Selected Readings

General References

A one-volume work that interprets the ideational developments through the course of British history is that by Esme Wingfield-Stratford, *The History of British Civilization* (London: Routledge Kegan Paul, 1928 and many succesive printings). Also helpful in tracing the changing value systems of the English people are Emile Legouis and Louis Cazamian, *A History of English Literature*, rev. ed. (New York: Macmillan, 1929); and David Daiches, *A Critical History of English Literature*, 2 vols. (New York: Ronald Press, 1970). More detailed discussions are found in the *Oxford History of England* and the *Cambridge History of English Literature*. Their bibliographies list standard histories, special studies, and bibliographies.

The texts (often only approximate) of speeches in Parliament during the period are in William Cobbett, *The Parliamentary History of England . . . to the Year 1803*, 36 vols. (London: T. C. Hansard, 1806–20). This Hansard edition draws from the two major earlier sources: Simonds D'Ewes, *Journal of All the Parliaments during the Reign of Queen Elizabeth*, rev. ed. (London, 1682); and John Almon, *The Debates and Proceedings in the British House of Commons, 1745–74*, 11 vols. (London, 1766–75).

Convenient Anthologies

Adams, Charles Kendall. *Representative British Orations*. 12 vol. New York: Putnam, 1892.

British Orations from Ethelbert to Churchill. Rev. ed. London: Everyman, 1960.

Bryan, William Jennings, and Frances W. Halsey. *The World's Famous Orations*. 10 vol. New York: Funk and Wagnalls, 1906.

Bryant, Donald C., et al. *An Historical Anthology of Select British Speeches*. New York: Ronald Press, 1967.

George-Brown, Lord. *The Voices of History: Moments from the Great Speeches of the English Language*. New York: Stein and Day, 1980.

Goodrich, Chauncey A. *Select British Eloquence*. Introduction by Bower Aly. Indianapolis: Bobbs-Merrill, 1963. See Carroll C. Arnold, "Goodrich Revisited," *QJS* (February 1962): 13–14; and John P. Hosher, "Lectures on Public Speaking by Chauncey Allen Goodrich," *SM* (1947): 1–37.

Hazeltine, Mayo W., et al. *Masterpieces of Eloquence.* 25 vol. New York: P. F. Collier and Sons, 1905.

Platz, Mabel. *Anthology of Public Speeches.* New York: H. W. Wilson, 1940.

Pollard, Arthur. *English Sermons.* London: British Book Center, 1963.

Strother, David B. *Modern British Eloquence.* New York: Funk and Wagnalls, 1969. (Includes portraits of speakers.)

Guides for Rhetorical Criticism: Books

Andrews, James R. *The Practice of Rhetorical Criticism.* New York: Macmillan, 1983.

Arnold, Carroll C. *Criticism of Oral Rhetoric.* University Park: Pennsylvania State University Press, 1974.

Arnold, C. and John Waite Bowers, eds. *Handbook of Rhetorical and Communication Theory.* Boston: Allyn and Bacon, 1984.

Bailey, F. G. *The Tactical Uses of Passion: An Essay on Power, Reason, and Reality.* Ithaca, N. Y.: Cornell University Press, 1983.

Bitzer, Lloyd F., ed. *The Prospect of Rhetoric.* Englewood Cliffs, N. J.: Prentice-Hall, 1971.

·Black, Edwin. *Rhetorical Criticism: A Study in Method.* New York: Macmillan, 1965.

Brook, Bernard L., and Robert L. Scott. *Methods of Rhetorical Criticism: A Twentieth Century Perspective.* Detroit: Wayne University Press, 1980.

Bryant, Donald C. *Rhetorical Dimensions in Criticism.* Baton Rouge: Louisiana University Press, 1973.

Carr, E. H. *What is History?* London: Penguin Books, 1964, 1984.

Douglas, Donald G., ed. *Philosophers on Rhetoric: Traditional and Emerging Views.* Skokie, Ill.: National Textbook Publishing Co., 1973.

Folger, Joseph P., and Marshall Scott Poole. *Working through Conflict: A Communication Perspective.* Glenview, Ill.: Scott, Foresman, 1984.

Geyl, Pieter. *Debates with Historians.* New York: Meridian Books, 1958.

Golden, James L., Goodwin Berquist, and William. E. Coleman, eds. *The Rhetoric of Western Thought.* Dubuque, Iowa: Kendall/Hunt, 1976.

Hill, B. W. *British Parliamentary Parties: 1742–1832.* London: George Allen & Unwin, 1985.

Hill, Christopher. *Intellectual Origins of the English Revolution.* Oxford: Clarendon Press, 1965.

———. *The World Turned Upside Down: Radical Ideas during the English Revolution.* London: Temple, Smith, 1972.

Howell, Wilbur S. *Eighteenth Century English Logic and Rhetoric.* Princeton, N.J.: Princeton University Press, 1971.

Jennings, Sir Ivor. *The Queen's Government.* London: Penguin Books, 1934.

Johannesen, Richard L., ed. *Contemporary Theories of Rhetoric.* New York: Harper and Row, 1971.

———. *Ethics in Human Communication.* Prospect Heights, Ill.: Waveland, 1981.

Klapp, Orin E. *Symbolic Leaders: Public Drama and Public Men.* Chicago: Aldine Publishing Co., 1964.

Knapp, Mark L., and Gerald R. Miller. *Handbook of Interpersonal Communication.* Beverly Hills, Calif.: Sage Publications, 1985.

Nichols, Marie Hochmuth. *Rhetoric and Criticism.* Baton Rouge: Louisiana State University Press, 1963.

Nilsen, Thomas R. *Essays on Rhetorical Criticism.* New York: Random House, 1968.

———. *Ethics of Speech Communication.* New York: Bobbs-Merrill, 1966.

Oliver, Robert T. *Becoming an Informed Citizen.* New York: Holt, Rinehart and Winston, 1964.

———. *Four Who Spoke Out: Burke, Fox, Sheridan and Pitt.* Syracuse, N.Y.: Syracuse University Press, 1946. Reprint. Freeport, N.Y.: Books for Libraries, 1969.

———. *The Healthy Mind in Communion and Communication* (with Dominick A. Barbara). Springfield, Ill.: Charles C. Thomas, 1962.

———. *Making Your Meaning Effective.* Boston: Holbrook Press, 1971.

———. *The Psychology of Persuasive Speech.* New York: Longmans Green, 1942, rev. 1957. Reprint. New York: David McKay, 1968.

Smith, Mary John. *Persuasion and Human Action: A Review and Critique of Social Influence Theories.* Belmont, Calif.: Wadsworth Publishing Co., 1982.

Stewart, Charles J., Craig Allen Smith, and Robert E. Denton. *Persuasion and Social Movements.* Prospect Heights, Ill.: Waveland Press, 1984.

White, Eugene E., ed. *Rhetoric in Transition: Studies in the Nature and Uses of Rhetoric.* University Park: Pennsyvlania State University Press, 1980.

Guides for Rhetorical Criticism: Periodical Essays

Andrews, James R. "The Rhetoric of a Lobbyist: Benjamin Franklin in England, 1763–1775." *CSSJ* 18 (November 1967): 261–67.

Arnold, Carroll C. "The Nature of Speaking-Listening Man and His Works." *CM* 8 (September 1960): 23–25.

———. "Oral Rhetoric, Rhetoric, and Literature." *P and R* 1 (Fall 1968): 191–210.

———. "Rhetorical and Communication Studies: Two Worlds or One?" *WJSC* 36 (Spring 1972): 75–81.

———. "What's Reasonable?" *CQ* 19 (Summer 1971): 19–23.

Baskerville, Barnett. "Must We All Be 'Rhetorical Critics'?" *QJS* 43 (April 1977): 107–16.

Bass, Jeff D. "The Rhetorical Opposition to Controversial Wars: Rhetorical Timing as a Generic Consideration." *WJSC* 43 (Summer 1979): 180–91.

Bauman, Richard. "Aspects of Seventeenth Century Quaker Rhetoric." *QJS* 56 (February 1970): 67–74.

Benson, Thomas W. "The Senses of Rhetoric: A Topical System for Critics." *CSSJ* 29 (Winter 1978): 237–50.

Berguist, Goodwin F., Jr. "Revolution through Persuasion: John Pym's Appeal to the

Moderates in 1640." *QJS* 49 (February 1963): 23–30.

Bevilqua, Vincent M. "Rhetoric and the Circle of Human Studies: An Historiographic View." *QJS* 55 (December 1969): 343–57.

Bitzer, Lloyd F. "A Re-Evaluation of Campbell's Doctrine of Evidence." *QJS* 46 (April 1960): 135–40.

———."The Rhetorical Situation." *P and R* 1 (January 1968): 1–14. (All the essays in this initial issue offer valuable guidance.)

Bormann, Dennis R. "Some 'Common Sense' about Campbell, Hume and Reid; Extrinsic Evidence." *QJS* 71 (November 1985): 395–421.

Bormann, Ernest G. "Fantasy and Rhetorical Vision: The Rhetorical Criticism of Social Reality," *QJS* 48 (December 1972): 396–407.

———. "Fetching Good out of Evil: A Rhetorical Use of Calamity." *QJS* 63 (April 1977): 130–39.

Brockreide, Wayne. "Rhetorical Criticism as Argument." *QJS* 40 (April 1974): 165–74.

Bryant, Donald C. "Arguing about Human Understanding." *CM* 49 (September 1982): 137–47.

———. "Edmund Burke: New Evidence—Broader View." *QJS* 38 (December, 1952): 435–45.

———. "Rhetoric: Its Function and Its Scope." *QJS* 39 (December, 1953): 401–24.

Chenowith, Eugene C., Michael T. Dues, and Uvieja Z. Good. "The Significance of Humanistic Rhetoric in British Public Address." *CSSJ* 42 (Summer 1969): 115–21.

Chesebro, James. "Definition as Rhetorical Strategy." *Pennsylvania Speech Communication Annual* 41 (1985): 5–15.

Cohen, Herman. "Hugh Blair on Speech Education." *SSCJ* 29 (Fall 1963): 1–11.

Consigny, Scott. "Rhetoric and Its Situations." *P and R* (Summer 1974): 175–86.

Crable, Richard E. "Ethical Code, Accountability, and Argumentation." *QJS* 64 (February 1978): 23–32.

Croft, Albert J. "The Functions of Rhetorical Criticism." *QJS* 42 (October 1956): 283–91.

Crowell, Laura. "The Speaking of John Pym, English Parliamentarian." *SM* 33 (June 1966): 77–101.

———. "Three Plain Speakers in Stuart England." *QJS* 53 (October 1967): 272–78.

Czubaroff, Jeanine. "Intellectual Respectability: A Rhetorical Problem." *QJS* 60 (April 1974): 155–64.

Dance, Frank E. X. "The 'Concept' of Communication." *JC* 20 (Spring 1977): 201–10.

———. "The Rhetorical Primate." *JC* 27 (Spring 1977): 12–16.

Dieter, Otto A. *"Arbor Picta:* The Medieval Tree of Preaching." *QJS* 51 (April 1965): 123–44.

Douglass, Rodney B., and Carroll C. Arnold. "On Analysis of *Logos:* A Methodological Inquiry." *QJS* 56 (February 1970): 22–32.

Eakins, Barbara. "The Evolution of Rhetoric: A Cosmic Analogy." *SSCJ* 39 (Spring 1970): 193–203.

Edney, Clarence W. "Campbell's Lectures on Pulpit Eloquence." *SM* 19 (March 1952): 1–10.

Ehninger, Douglas. "Argument as Method: Its Nature, Its Limitations, Its Use." *CM* 37 (June 1970): 101–10.

———. "Dominant Trends in English Rhetorical Thought, 1750–1800." *SSCJ* 18 (September 1952): 3–12.

Erdman, David V. "Coleridge in Lilliput: The Quality of Parliamentary Reporting in 1800." *SM* 27 (March 1960): 33–62.

Farrell, Thomas B. "Knowledge, Consensus, and Rhetorical Theory." *QJS* 42 ((February 1976): 1–14.

Feezel, Jerry D. "A Qualified Certainty: Verbal Probability in Arguments." *SM* 41 (November 1974): 348–56.

Fisher, Walter R. "The Importance of Style in Systems of Rhetoric." *SSCJ* 27 (Spring 1962): 173–82.

———. "Method in Rhetorical Criticism." *SSCJ* 42 (Winter 1969): 101–9.

———. "Toward a Logic of Good Reasons." *QJS* 44 (December 1978): 376–84.

Frandsen, Kenneth D. "The Eloquence of Opposition: William Windham against the Peace of Amiens." *SSCJ* 19 (Summer 1964): 316–25.

Golden, James L. "James Boswell on Rhetoric and Belles-Lettres." *QJS* 50 (October 1961): 266–76.

———. "John Wesley on Rhetoric and Belles-Lettres." *SM* 28 (November 1961): 250–61.

———. "The Rhetorical Theory of Adam Smith." *SSCJ* 33 Spring 1968): 200–215.

Goulding, Daniel J. "Parliamentary Reporting in Great Britain during the 17th and 18th Centuries." *16 (November 1965): 275–78.*

Graves, Michael P. "Functions of Key Metaphors in Early Quaker Sermons, 1761–1800." *QJS* 69 (November 1983): 364–78.

Gregg, Richard B. "A Phenomenologically Oriented Approach to Rhetorical Criticism." *CSSJ* 17 (May 1966): 83–90.

———. "The Rhetoric of Evidence." *WJSC* 31 (Summer 1967): 180–89.

———. "Some Psychological Aspects of Argument." *WJSC* 28 (Fall 1964): 222–30.

Gronbeck, Bruce E. "Government's Stance in a Crisis: A Case Study of Pitt the Younger." *WJSC* 34 (Fall 1970): 250–61.

Hance, Kenneth C. "Historical and Critical Research." *CQ* 19 (Winter 1971): 59–63.

Hauser, Gerard A. "Rhetoric as a Way of Knowing." *CQ* 19 (Winter 1971): 43–48.

Heisy, Ray. "The Scottish Tradition in Pulpit Rhetoric." *SSCJ* 36 (Spring 1971): 255–66.

Hill, L. Brooks. "The Lockeian Influence in the Evolution of Rhetorical Theory." *CSSJ* 26 (Summer 1975): 107–14.

Holtzman, Paul D. "Confirmation of Ethos as a Confounding Element in Communication Research," *SM* 33 (November, 1966):464–66.

Howell, Wilbur Samuel. "Adam Smith's Lectures on Rhetoric: An Historical Assessment." *SM* 36 (November 1969): 393–418.

Jensen, J. Vernon. "British Voices on the Eve of the American Revolution: Trapped by the Family Metaphor." *QJS* 63 (February 1977): 43–50.

Jones, W. R. " 'Actions for Slander'—Defamation in English Law, Language, and History." *QJS* 57 (October 1971): 274–83.

Karstetter, Allan B. "Toward a Theory of Rhetorical Irony." *CM* 31 (June 1964): 162–78.

Keefe, Daniel J. "Logical Empiricism and the Study of Human Communication." *CM* 42 (August 1975): 169–83.

Kelley, William G., Jr. "Rhetoric as Seduction." *P and R* 6 (Spring 1973): 69–80.

———. "Thomas Reid on Common Sense: Meta-Rational Approach to Truth." *SSCJ* 39 (Fall 1973): 40–54.

Kennedy, George. "Antony's Speech at Caesar's Funeral." *QJS* 54 (April 1968): 99–106.

King, Andrew A. "The Rhetoric of Power Maintenance: Elites at the Precipice." *QJS* 62 (April 1976): 127–34.

Kline, John A. "Dogmatism of the Speaker and Selection of Evidence." *CM* 38 (November 1971): 101–10.

Landfield, Jerome B. "Sheridan's Maiden Speech: Indictment by Anecdote." *QJS* 43 (April 1957): 137–42.

Lantz, William Carson. "Rhetoric and Theology: Incompatible?" *WJSC* 19 (March 1955): 77–82.

Lewis, W. David. "Public Speaking—Source and Force in History." *TS* 3 (November 1955): 22–25.

Lomas, Charles W. "Resources for the History and Criticism of Public Address." *CQ* 19 (Winter 1971): 37–42.

McGee, Michael Calvin, and Martha Anne Martin. "Public Knowledge and Ideological Argumentation." *CM* 50 (March 1983): 47–65.

McGuire, Michael. "The Ethics of Rhetoric: The Morality of Knowledge." *SSCJ* 45 (Fall 1979): 133–48.

McKerrow, Ray E. "Campbell and Whately on the Utility of Syllogistic Logic." *WJSC* 40 (Winter 1976): 3–13.

———. "Probable Argument and Proof in Whately's Theory of Rhetoric." *CSSJ* 26 (Winter 1975): 259–66.

McNally, James R. "Toward a Definition of Rhetoric." *P and R* 3 (Spring 1970): 71–81.

Martin, Albert T. "Paper Geniuses of the Anglican Pulpit." *QJS* 51 (October 1965): 286–93.

Measall, James S. "William Pitt and the Suspension of Habeas Corpus." *QJS* 60 (December 1974): 468–76.

Miller, Carolyn R. "Genre as Social Action." *QJS* 70 (May 1984): 151–67.

Mohrmann, G. P. *"The Civile Conversation:* Communications in the Renaissance." *CM* 39 (August 1972): 193–204.

Munshaw, Joe A. "The Structure of History: Dividing Phenomena for Rhetorical Understanding." *CSSJ* 25 (Fall 1974): 225–32.

Murphy, Richard. "The Earliest Teaching of Rhetoric at Oxford." *SM* 27 (November 1960): 345–47.

———. "The Medieval Arts of Discourse: An Introductory Bibliography." *SM* 29 (June 1962): 71–72.

———. "Rhetoric in the Earliest Years of Printing, 1465–1500." *QJS* 70 (February 1984): 1–11.

Nadeau, Ray "Oratorical Formulas in Seventeenth Century England." *QJS* 38 (April 1952): 149–54.

Nelson, Paul E. "The Fugal Form of Charles James Fox's 'Rejection of Buonaparte's Overtures,'" *WJSC* 36 (Winter 1972): 9–14.

North, Helen F. "Rhetoric and Historiography." *QJS* 42 (October 1956): 234–42.

Oliver, Robert T. "Culture and Communication." *Vital Speeches of the Day* 29 (15 September 1963): 721–24.

———. "A Rhetorician's Criticism of Historiography." In *Eastern Public Speaking Conference: 1940, pp. 161–72.* New York: H. W. Wilson, 1940.

———. "Speech and the Community: Social Diseases of Irresponsible and Ineffective Speech." *Vital Speeches of the Day* 29 (15 May 1963): 459–62.

———. "The Varied Rhetorics of International Relations." *WJSC* 25 (Fall 1961): 213–21.

Parker, Douglas H. "Rhetoric, Ethics, and Manipulation." 5 (Spring 1972): 69–87.

Post, Robert M. "Pathos in Robert Emmet's Speech from the Dock." *WJSC* 30 (Winter 1966): 19–25.

Railsback, Celeste Condit. "Beyond Rhetorical Relativism: A Structural-Material Model of Truth and Objective Reality." *QJS* 69 (November 1983): 351–63.

Ray, John W. "The Place of Oratory in the Political Philosophy of Thomas Hobbes." *WJSC* 37 (Summer 1973): 166–74.

Rea, Robert R. "The Earl of Chatham and the London Press, 1775." *Journalism Quarterly* 31 (Spring 1954): 186–92.

Reed, Robert Michael. "Missionary Smith: A Crucial Incident of the British Anti-Slavery Movement." *CSSJ* 29 (Spring 1978): 61–71.

Reid, Loren D. "Charles Fox and the London Press." *QJS* 47 (December 1961): 390–97.

———. "Did Charles Fox Prepare His Speeches?" *QJS* 24 (February 1938): 17–26.

———. "The Last Speech of William Pitt." *QJS* 49 (April 1963): 133–37.)

———. "Speaking in the Eighteenth Century House of Commons." *CM* 16 August 1949): 135–43.

———. "The Westminster Election and Scrutiny." *QJS* 52 (February 1966): 1–9.

Ryan, Halford Ross. "*Kategoria and Apologia:* On Their Rhetorical Criticism as a Speech Set." *QJS* 68 (August 1982): 254–61.

Sanders, Robert E. "Style, Meaning, and Message Effects." *CM* 51 (June 1984): 154–67.

Simons, Herbert W. "Persuasion in Social Conflicts: A Critique of Prevailing Conceptions and a Framework for Future Research." *SM* 29 (November 1972): 227–47.

———. "Requirements, Problems, and Strategies: A Theory for Social Movements," *QJS* 56 (February 1970): 1–11.

Skopec, Eric William. "Thomas Reid's Fundamental Rules of Eloquence." *QJS* 64 (December 1978): 400–408.

Smith, Charles Daniel. "Lord North, a Reluctant Debater: The Making of a Cabinet Minister, 1754–1767," *QJS* 53 (February 1967): 17–27.

Snow, Vernon F. "Robert C. Johnson's Appraisal of Edmund Burke's Eloquence." *QJS* 42 (October 1956): 243–49.

Space, Patricia R. "Sympathy and Propriety in Adam Smith's Rhetoric." *QJS* 60 (February 1974): 92–99.

Sproule, J. Michael. "The Psychological Burden of Proof: On the Evolutionary Development of Richard Whately's Theory of Presumption." *SM* 43 (June 1976): 115–29

Strother, David B. "John Bright: The Devil's Advocate." *SSCJ* 24 (Summer 1959): 201–9.

Thomas, Gordon L. "Hugh Latimer: Preacher *Ad Populum.*" *QJS* 51 (February 1965): 28–34.

Timmis, John H., III. "Christian Rhetoric and the Western Church Fathers." *CSSJ* 27 (Winter 1976): 28–84.

Wallace, Karl R. "Discussion in Parliament and Francis Bacon." *QJS* 43 (February 1957): 12–21.

———. "The English Renaissance Mind and English Rhetorical Theory." *WJSC* 28 (Spring 1964): 70–83.

———. "Francis Bacon and Method: Theory and Practice." *CM* 40 (November 1973): 243–72.

———. "Rhetorical Exercises in Tudor Education." *QJS* 22 (February 1936): 28–51.

———. "The Substance of Rhetoric: Good Reasons." *QJS* 49 (February 1963): 239–49.

———. "Tudor-Stuart Speakers." *QJS* 47 (December 1961): 2–5.

Walter, Otis M. "Thinking and Speaking about Causes." Parts 1, 2. *TS* 9 (September 1961): 12–14; (November 1961): 20–21.

Wasby, Stephen L. "Rhetoricians and Political Scientists: Some Lines of Interest." *SSCJ* 36 (Spring 1961): 231–42.

Weedon, Jerry. "Locke on Rhetoric and Western Man." *QJS* 56 (December 1979): 378–87.

Wichelns, Herbert. "The Literary Criticism of Oratory." In *The Rhetorical Idiom,* edited by Donald C. Bryant, (Ithaca, N.Y.: Cornell University Press, 1958), pp. 5–42.

Wieman, William E. "Guns or Butter: The American Revolution as a Parliamentary Ploy." *CSSJ* 26 (Winter 1975): 244–52.

Wilkerson, K. E. "On Evaluation Theories of Rhetoric." *P and R* 3 (Spring 1970): 82–96.

Wilson, John F. "Six Rhetorics for Perennial Study." *CQ* 19 (Winter 1971): 49–54.

Wood, Julia T. "Alternative Portraits of Leaders: A Contingency Approach to Perceptions of Leadership." *WJSC* 43 (Fall 1979): 260–70.

Woodward, Gary C. "Mystifications in the Rhetoric of Cultural Dominance and Colonial Control." *CSSJ* 26 (Winter 1975): 298–303.

Zarefsky, David. "The Great Society as a Rhetorical Proposition." *QJS* 65 (December 1979): 346–78.

Index

> . . . index learning turns no student pale,
> Yet holds the eel of science by the tail.
> —Alexander Pope

Absolutism defended, 106, 111
Act of Settlement, 147, 151, 152
Act of Toleration, 146, 292
Act of Union, 107, 283, 284, 286, 287
Adams, John, 19
Addington, Henry, 261
Addison, Joseph, 132, 148
Adolphous, John, 216
Agenda, effects of, 226–27
Alcuin, 39
Aldhelm, 35–36
Alfred (Anglo-Saxon king), 37, 39–40, 42, 43, 45, 237
Allegory, 147
Ambiguity, uses of, 226
American Revolution, 19, 179, 212–14, 266, 268, 299
Anabaptists, 113
Andrewes, Launcelot (bishop), 116–17
Anglicans, 109, 115, 116–18, 138, 140–42, 189–90, 195–96, 254
Anglo-Saxon Chronicle, 29, 39
Anne (queen of England), 132, 156
Aristotle, 14, 84, 180
Arminians, 109, 114, 115
Army, fear of, 161
Arnold, Carroll C., 28, 52
Ashburton, John Dunning, 290
Ashley, Maurice, 139
Atterbury, Francis (bishop), 157
Attlee, Clement, 51
Audience: adaptation to, 57, 68–69, 159, 164, 158–60, 178; nature of, 68, 150–51, 163, 164, 178, 210–11, 244–45, 258

Augustine (archbishop of Canterbury), 33–34, 48
Austen, Jane, 51

Bacon, Francis, 15, 68, 84–85, 100–101, 108, 109, 134–36
Baillee, Thomas, 298
Ball, John, 59–61, 78
Baptists, 132, 143–44, 187
Baxter, Richard, 126, 142–43
Bede (Baeda), the Venerable, 30, 33, 34, 37–39, 45
Begums of Oudh, 239, 242–46
Bennett, John, 101
Berkeley, George (bishop), 147
Berners, John Bouchier, 60
Bertha (queen), 33
Bible: authority of, 56, 57, 77, 259; nature of, 56, 72–74, 113, 117; translations of, 57, 88, 117
Bismark, Prince Otto E. L. von, 188
Black, Joseph, 285
Black Death, 18, 58, 59, 303
Blair, Hugh, 285, 286
Boethius, Anicius, 39
Boleyn, Anne, 87
Bolingbroke, Henry St John, 18, 152–60, 169, 174, 179
Boniface, 36, 39
Boswell, James, 163, 284
Boudicca (Boadicea), Queen, 31
Brailsford, H. N., 113
Brigance, William Norwood, 19
Brooke, Rupert, 51

315

Brougham, Henry, Lord, 20, 156, 203, 205, 217, 229, 278
Bryson, Lyman, 12
Buckingham, George Villiers, Duke of, 111
Bunyan, John, 130, 143–44, 147
Burgh, Walter Hussy, 264
Burke, Edmund, 20, 167, 201, 202, 205, 208, 211, 214–21, 223, 229, 232, 234, 239–40, 251–53, 256–58, 266, 267, 270, 273, 295, 303
Burnet, Richard (bishop), 142
Burney, Francis (Fanny), 216
Burns, Robert, 51, 286
Bute, John Stuart, Earl of, 174, 179, 185, 199, 209, 288
Byron, George Gordon, Lord, 245

Cabinet, development of, 158
Cade, Jack, 78
Caesar, Julius, 29–30, 49, 94–97, 162
Campbell, George, 285, 286, 290, 301
Campbell, John, Lord, 286, 289, 291
Canning, George, 295
Canute (king of England), 43, 50, 53
Caractacus, 30
Carlyle, Thomas, 17–18
Cartwright brothers, 250
Catherine of Aragon (queen), 86
Catholics, 35, 56–69, 86–88, 93, 105, 107, 108, 109, 142, 157, 277; disabilities of, 205, 207, 261, 266; English, 36, 86–88, 91, 106, 111, 132, 138, 142, 146–47; Irish, 35–37, 266, 277, 281
Caxton, William, 71
Cecil, William, Lord Burghley, 100
Cerealis, Petillius, 30–31
Cervantes, Miquel de, 80–81
Charisma, 31, 170–75, 221
Charles I (king of England), 110–12
Charles II (king of England), 133
Chatham, Earl of (William Pitt the Elder), 18, 20, 152–53, 156, 168, 169, 171–85, 187, 203, 204, 208, 209, 211–15, 221, 224, 229, 267, 272, 289, 290, 291, 303
Chrimes, S. B., 75
Church: Established, 37, 69, 71, 86–87, 93, 106, 109, 111, 112, 116–18, 132, 138, 140–42, 144, 251, 254, 266; power of, 56, 70; status of, 67, 91
Churchill, John, 147, 154
Churchill, Sir Winston, 12, 20, 51, 130, 154, 167, 171, 224
Church-State relations, 34, 37, 151

Cicero, Marcus Tullius, 29–30, 84, 163, 176, 182, 285
Civil War, 104, 126, 130, 137, 189
Clement VII (pope), 87
Clergy: itinerant, 37, 57, 69; settled, 37–38, 69–72; status of, 69
Clive, Robert, 239
Closet dialogues, 147
Clubs, 176, 191, 199, 208, 211, 285. *See also* Societies
Cockran, William Bourke, 281
Coifi, 35
Coke, Sir Edward, 118
Cole, Henry, 91
Colet, John, 67, 72–73, 77
Colman (bishop of Lindisfarne), 36–37
Columba (abbot of Iona), 35
Common law, 42–43, 250, 292, 304
Community spokesmen, 42
Consensus, 80, 104, 106
Conversation, 42–43, 58, 64, 82–83, 84, 104–05, 133–34, 195, 248–49, 290
Copernicus, Nicolaus, 80
Cornwal, John, 52–53
Corruption, effects of, 150–51, 201, 209, 235–36, 267, 277, 287
Cotton, John, 116
Courtesy, books of, 84
Covenanters, 109, 113
Cowper, William, 249
Cranmer, Thomas, 87, 91–92
Croke, John, 100
Cromwell, Oliver, 125–28
Cromwell, Richard, 138
Cromwell, Thomas, 87
Cunningham, G. G., 216, 246
Curran, John Philpot, 277–80

Dante, Alighieri, 80–81
Danton, Georges Jacques, 271
Debate-Discussion dichotomy, 110
Defoe, Daniel, 28, 132, 147, 189
Delivery, 142–43, 173–74, 189, 194–95, 197–98, 290
Demagoguery, 190, 199, 201
Democracy: inclinations toward, 54–55, 59–61, 66, 67, 78, 81, 83–84, 104–28, 175, 224, 229, 237–38, 247; retreat from, 126–27, 130, 139, 150–51, 178, 224, 248–63, 274–75, 290
Demosthenes, 163, 176, 182
Denunciation, 176–77, 190

Newcastle, William Cavendish, Duke of, 168, 174, 179, 181, 183
Newman, John Henry (cardinal), 131
Newton, Sir Isaac, 132
Niles, Hezekiah, 19
Normanization of England, 43–44, 47–49, 303
North, Frederick, Earl of Guilford, 174, 179, 203, 209, 218, 220, 221, 223, 237, 239
Notestein, Wallace, 105
Nouveau riche, 104

Oaths, importance of, 42, 44
O'Connell, Daniel, 167, 281
Official position, effects of, 55, 226–27
Oglethorpe, James Edward, 192–93
Oliver, F. S., 16–17, 156
Opposition: advantages of, 223, 160–61; functions of, 208, 211, 263, 268
Oratory as literature, 272–73
Organizational communication, 34, 36, 40–42, 45, 47–49, 57
Ormonde, James Butler, Duke of, 157
Oswald, King, 35
Oxford humanists, 82

Paine, Thomas, 271
Palmerston, Henry John Temple, Viscount, 20
Parliament, evolution of, 66, 85–86, 97–103, 105–7, 111, 118–28, 139, 158, 175
Parliamentary reports, 75, 99, 153
Parliamentary speaking, 75; courage in, 97–99, 118–20, 239, 248–63; effects of, 150–52, 176–77, 211, 240, 244, 248–50, 262
Parnell, Charles Stewart, 281
Patrick, Saint, 35
Pecock, Reginald, 67, 73, 77
Pelham, Henry, Earl of Granville, 174, 179, 180, 181, 246
Peltier, Jean, 295–96
Penn, William, 134, 146
Pepys, Samuel, 51, 133–34
Persuasion: costs of, 11, 88–92, 235, 239, 249, 257; patterns of, 17, 31–32, 60–61, 93–97, 98–102, 122, 236, 241, 253–54, 262, 275
Pierce, Charles, 5
Pitt, William, the Elder. *See* Chatham, Earl of
Pitt, William, the Younger, 205, 208, 214, 224–28, 229, 231, 238, 239–46, 251–53, 270, 272, 275, 281, 288, 303
Plato, 16
Plunket, William C., 276–77
Pole, Reginald, 87, 88

Pompadour, Jeanne Antoinette, 199
Pope, Alexander, 51, 154, 156
Popish plot, 139
Preachers, types of, 57, 68–71, 114–18, 140–46
Preaching, 57, 93; influence of, 33–35, 53–54, 57, 112, 143, 189–90; setting for, 69, 88, 194, 196
Presbyterians, 105, 112, 124, 132, 288
Preston, John, 23, 113–14
Pretender, the Old, 151, 156, 158
Pretender, the Young, 158
Price, Dr. Richard, 238
Pride, Colonel Thomas, 125
Primary sources, 22
Propositions of Newcastle, 125
Public opinion: development of, 59–61, 66, 75, 202, 239, 250; influence of, 78, 147, 183, 201, 208, 211–12; rejection of, 110, 160, 237, 290–91
Public speaking: historiographic guides to, 20; importance of, 11–15, 18–20, 23, 27, 68, 70, 94, 97, 99, 150–53, 172, 175, 234–35, 237, 248–49, 256, 280–81, 304–5; limitations of, 185, 230, 244, 246–47, 254, 256; misconceptions about, 17; neglect of, 5
Pulteney, William, 152, 162, 169, 174
Puritans, 97, 106, 111, 112–13, 123, 124, 125, 132
Pym, John, 118–20, 121, 124

Quakers, 113, 132, 143–46, 187
Quintilian, Marcus Fabius, 84

Raleigh, Sir Walter, 108
Rationalistic deism, 132, 151, 187
Reason, authority of, 74, 187
Redmond, John, 281
Reid, Loren D., 221, 285
Reid, Thomas, 285, 286
Religion: bases of, 56, 143–45, 191; changes in, 56, 86–93, 140–46, 188, 196; discussable realm of, 54–55, 56, 91, 93, 132, 188, 254, 287, 304; effects of, 54–55, 83, 85, 250, 292
Rhetoric, 14; influence of, 38–40, 132; nature of, 18–20, 35, 40, 65, 135–36, 265; systems of, 14, 134–36, 286
Rhetorical circumstances, 14, 33, 56, 59, 64–65, 67, 80–81, 88, 89, 108–10, 118–19, 121, 131, 137, 138, 148, 151, 208, 248, 286–88, 293, 295, 299
Rhetorical criticism, 16–17, 20–23, 164, 197
Rhetorical occasions, 21–22, 94, 125, 132, 241
Rhetorical questions, 20–23
Rhetoric in being, 50

Rhetoric of silence, 144–45
Richard II (king of England), 61–62
Richardson, Sir Thomas, 134
Ridicule, 217–18, 222–23, 239, 260
Ridley, Nicholas, 83
Robertson, Charles, 225
Robertson, William, 285
Robespierre, Maximilien, 208
Robinson, Jack, 231
Rochester, John Wilmot, Earl of, 133
Rogers, John, 88
Roman conquest of Britain, 29–33
Romanticism, 249
Rousseau, Jean Jacques, 248–49
Rowan, Hamilton, 277–80
Rowse, A. L., 82
Russell, Conrad, 105
Russell, John (bishop), 75
Russell, Lord John, 139, 147, 221
Rye House plot, 139

Sacheverell, Henry, 188–90
St. John, Oliver, 121
Sanders, Lloyd C., 246
Sarcasm, 158–60, 166, 180, 203, 215, 217–18, 222, 231, 258–60, 262, 267
Scotland, 29, 105, 107, 120, 123, 126, 283–301
Scots: antagonism toward, 28, 105, 286, 289, 295; education of, 285; leadership by, 283–86; rhetorical systems of, 286
Scott, Sir Walter, 48, 252, 286
Seares brothers, 280
Selden, John, 116
Sermons, 133; Anglican, 114, 115–16, 117–18, 141–42, 189–90; audiences for, 70, 194; Dissenting, 60–61, 116, 142–43; early evangelical, 33–34, 35; effects of, 70, 132–33, 189–90; Methodist, 193, 197–98; model forms of, 71–72; Presbyterian, 194–95; in the vernacular, 53–54
Shaftesbury, Anthony Ashley Cooper, Earl of, 139, 147
Shakespeare, William: as a rhetorician, 77, 93–97, 108
Sheridan, Richard Brinsley, 20, 167, 208, 211, 228–32, 242–46, 251, 261–63, 272, 303
Shippen, William, 161
Shire courts, 42
Sidney, Algernon, 139
Slave trade, debates on, 203–5, 227–28
Smith, Adam, 285, 286
Smith, Sydney, 285
Smith, V. A., 234

Societies, 204, 205, 208, 230–31, 250, 266, 285, 286
Society of Friends. *See* Quakers
South Seas Bubble, 157–58
Speaker-Spokesman dichotomy, 17, 42, 131
Speaking-Writing dichotomy, 15–16, 135, 147, 256–57
Speech days, 67–68
Spenser, Edmund, 114
Stephen, Leslie, 203, 214–15
Stigand (archbishop of Canterbury), 44
Stockdale, John, 298
Strabo, 29
Strafford, Earl of, 104, 112, 120–23. *See also* Wentworth, Thomas
Style: adapted to audience, 120; architectonic, 35; exclamatory, 178, 215, 276; imagery in, 34–35, 43, 117–18, 240; intricate and ornate, 36, 116; obscure, 226; persuasiveness of, 120; simple and direct, 197; urban mode, 120
Suckling, Sir John, 133
Sunderland, Earl of, 139
Sun Yat-sen, 12
Swift, Jonathan, 51, 132, 147, 154–55

Tacitus, 27, 30–31, 68
Tandy, Napper, 266
Taylor, A. P. J., 22
Taylor, Jeremy (bishop), 117–18
Temple, Richard Grenville, Earl of, 212
Tennyson, Alfred Lord, 51
Textual authenticity, 21
Theodore (archbishop of Canterbury), 37, 48
Tillotson, John (bishop), 140–42, 148
Tone, Theobald Wolfe, 266, 271
Tories, 131, 139, 140, 151–52, 229, 245, 289
Toynbee, Arnold, 18, 137
Trevelyan, George Macaulay, 22, 48, 288
Trivium, 68
Twain, Mark, 229
Tyler, Watt, 59, 61, 62

Unification of England, 27–33, 37, 47–52
Union of Ireland and England, 225, 266, 268, 271, 274–75, 276, 279
United Irishmen, 266, 269, 277
Utopia, 83–84

Vaihinger, Hans, 13
Voice, qualities of, 47, 78, 194–95, 215, 232
Voltaire, François Marie Arouet de, 154, 253

Walpole, Horace, 182, 183, 201
Walpole, Robert, 151–52, 162, 169, 171, 174, 177, 178, 180, 190, 224, 246
War, futility of, 75, 137, 178, 259–60, 264, 281
Wars of the Roses, 82
Warton, Thomas, 207
Watson, J. Steven, 212, 246
Watt, James, 285
Wavell, Sir Archibald, 15
Wentworth, Peter, 97–99
Wentworth, Thomas, 104, 111–12, 118. *See also* Strafford, Earl of
Wesley, Charles, 188, 191, 192, 193, 196
Wesley, John, 188, 191–98
Wesley, Samuel (father), 190–91
Wesley, Samuel (brother), 191
Wesley, Susanna, 191
Whately, Richard (bishop), 285
Whigs, 30, 131, 139, 140, 151–52, 161, 165, 176, 181, 189, 204, 217, 225, 237, 238, 241, 245, 251–52, 257, 294
Whitby, Convocation of, 36
White, Eugene, 194
Whitefield, George, 188, 191, 194–95, 297
Whitelocke, Bulstrode, 121–22
Wichelns, Herbert A., 13
Wilberforce, William, 198, 202–5, 227, 294
Wilde, Oscar, 51
Wilfrid (archbishop), 36–37, 45
Wilkes, John, 198–202, 203, 290
William III (king of England), 130, 140, 147
William the Conqueror, 44–45, 47–48, 52
Wingfield-Stratford, Sir Esme, 48, 150, 234, 246
Wit, 133, 160, 182, 202, 231
Witan (Witenagemot), 27–28, 30, 41–42
Wolsey, Thomas (cardinal), 86
Woodward, G. W. O., 102
Wordsworth, William, 216
Wrawe, John, 59
Wraxall, Nathaniel William, 208, 226, 229, 239
Wulfstan (archbishop of York), 44–45
Wycliffe, John, 54, 56–57, 158–59, 169
Wyndham, William, 152, 157, 158–59, 169

Zyskind, Harold, 18